# Revitalizing Victimization Theory

*Revitalizing Victimization Theory: Revisions, Applications, and New Directions* revises some of the major perspectives in victimization theory, applies theoretical perspectives to the victimization of vulnerable populations, and carves out new theoretical territory that is clearly needed but has yet to be developed. With the exception of a handful of isolated works in the mid-twentieth century, theory and research on victimization did not come into its own until the late 1970s with the articulation of lifestyle and routine activity theories. Research conducted within this tradition continues to be an important part of the overall criminological enterprise, and a large body of empirical knowledge has been generated. Nevertheless, *theoretical* advances in the study of victimization have largely stalled within the field of criminology. Indeed, little in the way of new theoretical headway has been made in well over a decade. This is an ideal time to revitalize victimization theory, and this volume does just that. It is an ambitious project that will hopefully reignite the kinds of theoretical discussions that once held the attention of the field.

The work included here will shape the future of victimization theory and research in years to come. This volume should be of interest to a wide range of criminologists and have the potential to be used in graduate seminars and upper-level undergraduate courses.

**Travis C. Pratt** is Research Director of the Harris County Community Supervision and Corrections Department and Fellow of the University of Cincinnati Corrections Institute. He conducts research in the areas of correctional policy, the sources of criminal behavior, and the nature of victimization.

**Jillian J. Turanovic** is an Associate Professor and Director of the Crime Victim Research and Policy Institute in the College of Criminology and Criminal Justice at Florida State University. Her research is aimed at examining various issues in criminological theory and correctional policy, with a special focus on victimization, violence, and the life course.

***SERIES EDITORS***

Advances in Criminological Theory

# Revitalizing Victimization Theory

## Revisions, Applications, and New Directions

Advances in Criminological Theory
Volume 27

**Travis C. Pratt**
**Jillian J. Turanovic**
**editors**

Routledge
Taylor & Francis Group
NEW YORK AND LONDON

First published 2021
by Routledge
52 Vanderbilt Avenue, New York, NY 10017

and by Routledge
2 Park Square, Milton Park, Abingdon, Oxon OX14 4RN

*Routledge is an imprint of the Taylor & Francis Group, an informa business*



*Library of Congress Cataloging-in-Publication Data*
Names: Pratt, Travis C., editor. | Turanovic, Jillian J., 1985– editor.
Title: Revitalizing victimization theory: revisions, applications, and new directions/edited by Travis C. Pratt, Jillian J. Turanovic.
Description: New York, NY: Routledge, 2021. |
Includes bibliographical references and index.
Identifiers: LCCN 2020046338 (print) | LCCN 2020046339 (ebook) |
ISBN 9780367747992 (hardback) | ISBN 9781003159629 (ebook)
Subjects: LCSH: Victims of crimes.
Classification: LCC HV6250.25 .R48 2021 (print) |
LCC HV6250.25 (ebook) | DDC 362.8801–dc23
LC record available at https://lccn.loc.gov/2020046338
LC ebook record available at https://lccn.loc.gov/2020046339

ISBN: 978-0-367-74799-2 (hbk)
ISBN: 978-0-367-74803-6 (pbk)
ISBN: 978-1-003-15962-9 (ebk)

Typeset in Times New Roman
by Newgen Publishing UK

# Contents

**Part III. New Theoretical Applications**

# List of Illustrations

### Figures



### Tables

# Contributors

*Martin A. Andresen* is a Professor in the School of Criminology at Simon Fraser University, British Columbia, Canada and an Associate Professor in the School of Criminology and Criminal Justice at Griffith University, Queensland, Australia.

*Kevin M. Beaver* is Judith Rich Harris Professor of Criminology in the College of Criminology and Criminal Justice at Florida State University, USA.

*Mark T. Berg* is an Associate Professor in the Department of Sociology and Criminology at the University of Iowa, USA.

*Francis T. Cullen* is Distinguished Research Professor Emeritus and Senior Research Associate in the School of Criminal Justice at the University of Cincinnati, Ohio, USA.

*Laura C. Frizzell* is a Doctoral Student in the Department of Sociology at The Ohio State University, USA.

*Michael R. Gottfredson* is Chancellor's Professor of Criminology, Law and Society, Law and Sociology, at the University of California, Irvine, USA.

*Tarah Hodgkinson* is a Lecturer in the School of Criminology and Criminal Justice at Griffith University, Queensland, Australia.

*Bridget Joyner* is a Doctoral Student in the College of Criminology and Criminal Justice at Florida State University, USA.

*Timothy Kang* is an Assistant Professor in the Department of Sociology at the University of Saskatchewan, Canada.

*Candace Kruttschnitt* is Professor Emerita of Sociology at the University of Toronto, Ontario, Canada and Fellow of the Royal Society of Canada.

*Charis E. Kubrin* is a Professor of Criminology, Law and Society at the University of California, Irvine, USA.

*Teresa C. Kulig* is an Assistant Professor in the School of Criminology and Criminal Justice at the University of Nebraska at Omaha, USA.

*Adrienne L. McCarthy* is a Doctoral Student of Sociology in the Department of Sociology, Anthropology and Social Work at Kansas State University, USA.

*Daniel P. Mears* is Mark C. Stafford Professor of Criminology in the College of Criminology and Criminal Justice at Florida State University, USA.

*Hollie Nyseth Brehm* is an Associate Professor of Sociology at The Ohio State University, USA.

*Graham C. Ousey* is a Professor of Sociology at the College of William and Mary, Virginia, USA.

*Callie Marie Rennison* is a Professor in the University of Colorado Denver School of Public Affairs, USA.

*Christopher J. Schreck* is a Professor of Criminal Justice at the Rochester Institute of Technology, New York, USA.

*Kevin F. Steinmetz* is an Associate Professor of Sociology in the Department of Sociology, Anthropology and Social Work at Kansas State University, USA.

*Heather Zaykowski* is an Associate Professor of Sociology at the University of Massachusetts Boston, USA.

# Introduction: Revitalizing Victimization Theory

*Travis C. Pratt and Jillian J. Turanovic*

Criminology—a field that has dedicated itself to understanding the nature of crime—has always focused the bulk of its attention on offenders. Victims of crime, on the other hand, have traditionally gotten a lot less scholarly attention. To be sure, entire schools of thought regarding what causes people to engage in offending were seemingly in mass production for much of the early to mid-20th century, ranging from positivist and revived classical traditions (Becker, 1968), to social disorganization (Shaw & McKay, 1942), to strain/anomie and its offshoots (Merton, 1938; see also Cloward & Ohlin, 1960; Cohen, 1955), to differential association/social learning (Burgess & Akers, 1966; Sutherland, 1947) and control theories (Hirschi, 1969; Matza, 1964). Yet when it came to theoretical development about the sources of victimization, only a few scattered perspectives popped up during this same time period (Luckenbill, 1977; Mendelsohn, 1963; Schafer, 1968; von Hentig, 1948; Wolfgang, 1958), and thinking about victimization never really "caught on" in any significant way.

That all changed, however, in the late 1970s. It started on the heels of a "crime spike" in the United States in the 1960s, where rates of nearly all forms of crime were on the rise (Cullen & Gilbert, 1982). This development presented a puzzling paradox: The United States was an economically prosperous nation that seemed to be experiencing both exceptional affluence and elevated crime rates (Blau & Blau, 1982). These were two things that criminologists did not think were supposed to coexist, because the prevailing professional wisdom at the time was that social problems like crime were intimately tied to economic conditions (Pratt & Cullen, 2005). So when things improved economically—like they did in post-World War II America—crime was supposed to go down (McDonald, 1976; Quinney, 1974; Turner, 1978). That it did not begged the question of what, then, was going on?

In response, two primary explanations emerged that quickly took hold. First, Hindelang, Gottfredson, and Garofalo (1978) analyzed data from the recently created National Crime Survey (NCS)—a national survey effort that began in 1972 that reflected growing concern over the consequences of an increasingly mobile (both geographically and socio-economically) and ideologically shifting American population (Hindelang, 1976; see also Turanovic & Pratt, 2019). Hindelang et al. (1978) found that the risk of victimization was tied to certain sociodemographic characteristics, where those who were young, male, and members of racial/ethnic minority groups were most likely to be the victims of crimes. These differences in victimization risk were viewed as a function of the lifestyles that different demographic groups engaged in. Individuals who engaged in lifestyles that were *risky*—those that routinely exposed them to "high risk times, places, and people"—were more likely to experience victimization (Hindelang et al., 1978, p. 245). These lifestyle patterns were primarily viewed as being shaped by "structural constraints," or social forces stemming from inequalities in the social structure, such as economic deprivation and racial segregation, that disproportionately affected racial minority groups. In short, Hindelang et al. (1978) highlighted the link between doing risky things in risky settings and becoming the victim of crime.

But at around this same time, Cohen and Felson (1979) made an important observation: people do not have to be doing "risky" things to be victimized. In their development of routine activity theory, they noted that broader structural changes—like a stronger economy—meant that more people would be leaving the safety of their homes to go to work and entertain themselves (Hawley, 1950; Reiss, 1976). This increased dispersion of activities away from the home meant that houses would be more likely to be left unguarded (increasing rates of burglary and theft victimization; Reppetto, 1974; Sutherland, 1937) and people would be more likely to be out in public spaces, physically mingling with potentially motivated offenders (increasing rates of personal victimization; Cohen, Kluegel, & Land, 1981; Short & Strodtbeck, 1965). Put simply, according to the routine activity perspective, it is not the "risky" behaviors that elevate one's chances of being victimized, but rather it is the normal patterns of going about our daily lives that put us at a greater risk of victimization (Felson & Cohen, 1980; Felson & Eckert, 2019).

The presentation of routine activity theory to the world resulted in a flurry of empirical work testing its core propositions at both the macro- and micro-levels (Pratt & Cullen, 2005; Pratt & Turanovic, 2016; Schreck, 2017). Research conducted within this tradition continues to be an important part of the overall criminological enterprise (Natarajan, 2011; Pratt, Holtfreter, & Reisig, 2010; Wilcox & Cullen, 2018), as does its close cousin the risky lifestyles perspective (Turanovic & Pratt, 2014; Turanovic, Reisig, & Pratt, 2015; Wolfe & McLean, 2017). And just as important, these ideas have proven to be incredibly influential in crime control policy circles (Clarke, 1995; Cook, Reynald, Leclerc, & Wortley, 2019; Guerette & Bowers, 2009). But there is a problem here: *theoretical* advances in the study of victimization have largely stalled.[1] While the production of new theories of offending has once again dominated the contemporary criminological landscape (see, e.g., Agnew, 2014; Pratt, 2016; Sampson, 2012), little in the way of new theoretical headway has been made with respect to victimization in over two decades (see, e.g., the discussion by Pratt, Turanovic, Fox, & Wright, 2014). The absence of contemporary theoretical development is rendered even more conspicuous given the virtual explosion of empirical work on the causes and consequences of victimization over the last few decades (Lauritsen & Rezey, 2018; Macmillan, 2001; Sharkey, 2018; Turanovic, 2018; Turanovic & Pratt, 2019).

We therefore see this as an ideal time to revitalize victimization theory in important ways. Specifically, we see the need for theoretical perspectives on victimization to undertake three critically important tasks—none of which are small jobs. The first one entails revising the key ideas that arguably represent the "core" of theories of victimization (see, e.g., the approach taken by Cullen, Wright, & Blevins, 2006). Doing so would involve carefully examining issues like the wide range of individual and contextual factors that recent research has revealed to be linked to victimization, and the growing body of empirical literature that attempts to more fully account for what has been called the "victim-offender overlap" (Beckley et al., 2018; Lauritsen & Laub 2007; van Gelder, Averdijk, Eisner, & Ribaud, 2015). And after considering this new information, the next step would be to take another look at theoretical perspectives ranging from routine activity to control theories, and from cultural theories to environmental criminology.

Second, we need to push theories of victimization into new contexts, to identify new theoretical mechanisms that might be at work, and to develop new theoretical perspectives that address emerging problems in victimization theory. We should, for example, develop more fully theoretical explanations of victimization in contexts where peoples' autonomy is restricted (e.g., for those housed in prisons and jails, for those involved in intimate partner relationships, and for children at school; Mendez, Ruiz-Esteban, & Lopez-Garcia, 2017; Muftic, Finn, & Marsh, 2015; Wooldredge & Steiner, 2012). We could also explore more thoroughly the potential causal processes underlying forms of victimization that are often overlooked by the criminological community, like cybervictimization and human trafficking (Anderson, Kulig, & Sullivan, 2019; Jose, Kljakovic, Scheib, & Notter, 2012; Pratt, 2018), as well as state-based forms of violence and victimization like genocide and other atrocity crimes (Nyseth Brehm, 2017). Doing so would provide the field with new lines of inquiry and new ways of thinking about the potential "generality" (or perhaps lack thereof) of theoretical explanations of victimization.

And third, we need to expand our theoretical lens so that we take a much more unapologetically interdisciplinary approach to thinking about victimization. Crime and victimization have always been studied by scholars from multiple fields—from sociology and psychology to myriad others in between (Laub, 2004; Walsh & Ellis, 2007; West & Farrington, 1973)—all of which have something of potential importance to say about why criminal events occur. The same holds true for victimization, where scholars from education, developmental psychology, and public health often see things differently than criminologists do (Turanovic, Pratt, Kulig, & Cullen, 2021). For instance, the theoretical perspectives that guide the work in these fields tend to see victimization as the product of "vulnerability"—whether social, cognitive, or physical—that can peg someone as a "misfit" who deviates from group norms in some identifiable way (Christensen, Fraynt, Neece, & Baker, 2012; Olweus, 2013; Wright, Giammarino, & Parad, 1986). Others from these fields see victimization in the context of the extent to which it can be used to navigate social hierarchies—that is, when victimization is used as a weapon to secure one's social rank (Faris & Felmlee, 2014; Griffiths, Yule, & Gartner, 2011). Either way, the broader point here is that criminology does not "own" the study of victimization, and if we are going to take the study of victimization seriously, then we are going to have to embrace a broader outlook with respect to how to think theoretically about the victim side of the criminological equation.

This book is intended to accomplish just that. And in doing so, the chapters presented here are organized into three sections. Part I is

*Revisiting Major Perspectives in Victimization Theory*. Much of what serves as theoretical guidance in the study of victimization are ideas that were developed and established many decades ago (Turanovic & Pratt, 2019). These ideas were innovative and have sparked a large body of empirical literature (Forde & Kennedy, 1997; Schreck, Wright, & Miller, 2002; Rountree, Land, & Miethe, 1994). The four chapters in this section update these major perspectives in victimization theory in light of the empirical developments that have occurred. These contributions not only "take stock" of the empirical status of these theories, but they do so in ways that accommodate the empirical literature and will generate renewed interest in them.

First up, Christopher J. Schreck and Mark T. Berg explore the implications of the ideas of victimization and vulnerability for criminological theory. They begin by noting that criminological theories often overlook the victim—something that positivist theories of crime are particularly guilty of. Given this critique, they ultimately argue that choice theories provide the most fruitful context for organizing the known "facts" about victimization. Next, Michael R. Gottfredson revisits victimization through the lens of control theory. He argues that the accumulated evidence is unequivocal in that various kinds of control mechanisms—including strong social bonds and self-control—are consistently related to a wide array of risky behaviors that, in turn, influence the likelihood of victimization. Moving forward, he emphasizes the importance of thinking about victimization within the context of choice theories of crime. Charis E. Kubrin and Graham C. Ousey then revisit victimization and vulnerability in cultural theories of crime. They detail how cultural theories of crime represent an unexplored avenue for future victimization scholarship, and then go on to identify new ways that the culture-victimization nexus can push victimization research to ask new questions and to reexamine existing theoretical debates. Rounding out this section is an essay by Martin A. Andresen and Tarah Hodgkinson, where the authors reassess perspectives on environmental design and victimization. They outline the various ways that environmental criminology—and spatial-temporal criminology more generally—have contributed to the understanding of victimization. They then make a compelling case for examining important questions concerning the unintended consequences—including the further victimization of poor and marginalized groups—of certain crime prevention strategies.

Part II is *Victimization and Vulnerable Populations*. Victimization is often tightly connected with power differentials between people (Daly,

1997; Juvonen & Graham, 2014; Simon, 1975). And as stated above, those who experience victimization are often members of socially vulnerable populations (Chakraborti & Garland, 2012; Kulig, Pratt, Cullen, Chouhy, & Unnever, 2017; Myers, Turanovic, Lloyd, & Pratt, 2020). The chapters in this section bring a much-needed theoretical understanding of victimization among such vulnerable populations and apply a theoretical lens to victimization in these contexts in a way that will shape and direct future empirical research.

Leading this section off, Holly Nyseth Brehm and Laura C. Frizzell examine the relationship between victimization and the state by focusing on victims of atrocity crimes. Honing in on the victimology of genocide, crimes against humanity, and war crimes, they call for an integrated theoretical approach for understanding atrocity crime victimization at the individual, group, community, and national levels. Next, Candace Kruttschnitt and Timothy Kang revisit and revise theoretical perspectives on the victimization of women. They identify the types and contexts of victimization most commonly experienced by women (including intimate partner violence and sexual assault) and call for a "context-congruent" theoretical approach that can account for the unique characteristics of women's victimization, their agency in both precipitating and disrupting violence, and the ways that structural and social contexts shape the causes and consequences of women's victimization over the life course. Daniel P. Mears then takes up the task of addressing theories of victimization in the correctional setting. Noting that prisons and jails represent unique contexts that serve unique populations, he argues that theoretical advances in the understanding of victimization among incarcerated persons can be critical not only for informing policy and practice within correctional systems, but that it can also help to inform the study of victimization in society more generally. In the final chapter in this section, Heather Zaykowski and Callie Marie Rennison examine theories aimed at explaining victimization at school. Specifically, they use data from the National Crime Victimization Survey (NCVS) to reveal that students' rates of violent victimization away from school are higher than they are while they are at school. In essence, schools are relatively safe places, so it is important that future research be directed toward understanding *why* the school context operates the way that it does.

Finally, Part III is *New Theoretical Applications*. There is no doubt that victimization research has become more interdisciplinary in recent years (Evans & Smokowski, 2016; Tan & Haining, 2016; Troop-Gordon,

2017). But what is lagging behind are theoretical statements about different dimensions and forms of victimization. In short, there are substantive areas of victimization research that need theoretical guidance but do not yet have it. The chapters in this section therefore are intended to carve out new theoretical territory in the study of victimization.

First up, Kevin M. Beaver and Bridget Joyner discuss biosocial perspectives on victimization. Noting the important contributions made in the last several years by biosocial criminology to our understanding of human behavior, they apply this lens to the potential genetic architecture of victimization. They discuss the implications of biosocial criminology for the extent to which genetic influences might be related to the odds of being victimized, and then ultimately call for integrating behavior genetic studies into certain mainstream theories of victimization. Kevin F. Steinmetz and Adrienne L. McCarthy follow that up with an essay on theoretical perspectives on cyberspace victimization. They note that common technological solutions to cybercrime and victimization (e.g., credit-monitory, anti-virus, and firewall protection) often result in the growth and centralization of state and corporate power, while at the same time ignoring the conditions that draw people to engage in cybercrime in the first place. They call for the application of a "realist criminology" of the internet, which they argue would lead to solutions to internet-facilitated crime and victimization that would avoid unnecessary expansions of state and corporate surveillance systems and related harms. And in the final chapter in the volume, Teresa C. Kulig and Francis T. Cullen offer up a theory of sex trafficking victimization. They begin by detailing how commercial sex has been reclassified from an offense punishable by criminal sanctions to one where the sex actor is portrayed as a victim in need of assistance. They then lay out a systematic, descriptive theory of how sex trafficking is an ongoing enterprise that develops in multiple stages from initial recruitment to eventual closure.

Overall, we are excited for what this book has to offer to readers who are interested in thinking more critically about the nature of victimization. In the chapters that have been assembled here, a solid roster of some of the top scholars in the field have revisited many of the "classic" ideas about the sources and consequences of victimization, and new theoretical territory has been carved out. These new ways of thinking will inevitably bring about new avenues for research that will encourage researchers to push the boundaries of this substantive area both theoretically and empirically. And just as important, we are optimistic that the work collected here will help to influence the development of policies aimed at reducing victimization and will help to minimize the suffering experienced by victims of crime. In the end, there was a time when theorizing about victimization was a core part of the criminological enterprise; we hope that this volume represents an important step toward returning victimization theory to that coveted seat at the intellectual table.

## Note

1 We recognize that there has been considerable theoretical development with respect to specific forms of victimization, like intimate partner violence (Bell & Naugle, 2008; Johnson, 1995; Kelly, 2011) and sexual assault (Culatta, Clay-Warner, Boyle, & Oshri, 2020; Schwartz & DeKeseredy, 1997; Schwartz & Pitts, 1995). Our point here, however, is that efforts to specify new criminological ideas about victimization more generally—or to otherwise revise existing ones—have been largely absent since self-control was integrated into the study of victimization by Schreck (1999).

## References

Agnew, R. (2014). Social concern and crime: Moving beyond the assumption of simple self-interest, 2013 Presidential Address to the American Society of Criminology. *Criminology, 52,* 1–32.

Anderson, V. R., Kulig, T. C., & Sullivan, C. J. (2019). Estimating the prevalence of human trafficking in Ohio, 2014–2016. *American Journal of Public Health, 109,* 1396–1399.

Becker, G. S. (1968). Crime and punishment: An economic approach. *The Journal of Political Economy, 76,* 169–217.

Beckley, A. L., Caspi, A., Arseneault, L., Barnes, J. C., Fisher, H. L., Harrington, H., … Moffitt, T. E. (2018). The developmental nature of the victim-offender overlap. *Journal of Developmental and Life-Course Criminology, 4,* 24–49.

Bell, K. M., & Naugle, A. E. (2008). Intimate partner violence theoretical considerations: Moving towards a contextual framework. *Clinical Psychology Review, 28,* 1096–1107.

Blau, J. R., & Blau, P. M. (1982). The cost of inequality: Metropolitan structure and violent crime. *American Sociological Review, 47,* 114–129.

Burgess, R. L., & Akers, R. L. (1966). A differential association-reinforcement theory of criminal behavior. *Social Problems, 14,* 118–147.

Chakraborti, N., & Garland, J. (2012). Reconceptualizing hate crime victimization through the lens of vulnerability and 'difference'. *Theoretical criminology, 16*(4), 499–514.

Christensen, L. L., Fraynt, R. J., Neece, C. L., & Baker, B. L. (2012). Bullying adolescents with intellectual disability. *Journal of Mental Health Research in Intellectual Disabilities, 5,* 49–65.

Clarke, R. V. (1995). Situational crime prevention. *Crime and Justice: A Review of Research, 19,* 91–150.

Cloward, R. A., & Ohlin, L. E. (1960). *Delinquency and opportunity: A theory of delinquent gangs*. New York: The Free Press.

Cohen, A. K. (1955). *Delinquent boys: The culture of the gang*. New York: The Free Press.

Cohen, L. E., & Felson, M. (1979). Social change and crime rate trends: A routine activity approach. *American Sociological Review, 44,* 588–608.

Cohen, L. E., Kluegel, J. R., & Land, K. C. (1981). Social inequality and predatory criminal victimization: An exposition and test of a formal theory. *American Sociological Review, 46,* 505–524.

Cook, A., Reynald, D. M., Leclerc, B., & Wortley, R. (2019). Learning about situational crime prevention from offenders: Using a script framework to compare the commission of completed and disrupted sexual offenses. *Criminal Justice Review, 44,* 431–451.

Culatta, E., Clay-Warner, J., Boyle, K. M., & Oshri, A. (2020). Sexual revictimization: A routine activity theory explanation. *Journal of Interpersonal Violence, 35,* 2800–2824.

Cullen, F. T., & Gilbert, K. E. (1982). *Reaffirming rehabilitation.* Cincinnati, OH: Anderson.

Cullen, F. T., Wright, J. P., & Blevins, K. R. (2006). *Taking stock: The status of criminological theory, Advances in criminological theory.* Vol. 15. New York: Routledge, Taylor and Francis.

Daly, K. (1997). Different ways of conceptualizing sex/gender in feminist theory and their implications for criminology. *Theoretical Criminology, 1,* 25–51.

Evans, C. B. R., & Smokowski, P. R. (2016). Theoretical explanations for bullying in school: How ecological processes propagate perpetration and victimization. *Child and Adolescent Social Work Journal, 33,* 365–375.

Faris, R., & Felmlee, D. (2014). Casualties of social combat: School networks of peer victimization and their consequences. *American Sociological Review, 79*(2), 228–257.

Felson, M., & Cohen, L. E. (1980). Human ecology and crime: A routine activity approach. *Human Ecology, 8,* 389–406.

Felson, M., & Eckert, M. A. (2019). *Crime and everyday life*. 6th edition. Thousand Oaks, CA: Sage.

Forde, D. R., & Kennedy, L. W. (1997). Risky lifestyles, routine activities, and the general theory of crime. *Justice Quarterly, 14,* 265–294.

Griffiths, E., Yule, C., & Gartner, R. (2011). Fighting over trivial things: Explaining the issue of contention in violent altercations. *Criminology, 49,* 61–94.

Guerette, R. T., & Bowers, K. J. (2009). Assessing the extent of crime displacement and diffusion of benefits: A review of situational crime prevention evaluations. *Criminology, 47,* 1331–1368.

Hawley, A. (1950). *Human ecology: A theory of community structure*. New York: Ronald.

Hindelang, M. J. (1976). *Criminal victimization in eight American cities: A descriptive analysis of common theft and assault*. Cambridge, MA: Ballinger.

Hindelang, M. J., Gottfredson, M. R., & Garofalo, J. (1978). *Victims of personal crime: An empirical foundation for a theory of personal victimization.* Cambridge, MA: Ballinger.

Hirschi, T. (1969). *Causes of delinquency*. Berkeley, CA: University of California Press.

Johnson, M. P. (1995). Patriarchal terrorism and common couple violence: Two forms of violence against women. *Journal of Marriage and Family, 57,* 283–294.

Jose, P. E., Kljakovic, M., Scheib, E., & Notter, O. (2012). The joint development of traditional bullying and victimization with cyber bullying and victimization in adolescence. *Journal of Adolescence, 22,* 301–309.

Juvonen, J., & Graham, S. (2014). Bullying in schools: The power of bullies and the plight of victims. *Annual Review of Psychology, 65,* 159–185.

Kelly, U. A. (2011). Theories of intimate partner violence: From blaming the victim to acting against injustice: Intersectionality as an analytic framework. *Advances in Nursing Science, 34,* E29–E51.

Kulig, T. C., Pratt, T. C., Cullen, F. T., Chouhy, C., & Unnever, J. D. (2017). Explaining bullying victimization: Assessing the generality of the low self-control/risky lifestyle model. *Victims and Offenders, 12,* 891–912.

Laub, J. H. (2004). The life course of criminology in the United States: The American Society of Criminology 2003 Presidential Address. *Criminology, 42,* 1–26.

Lauritsen, J. L., & Laub, J. H. (2007). Understanding the link between victimization and offending: New reflections on an old idea. *Crime Prevention Studies, 22,* 55–75.

Lauritsen, J. L., & Rezey, M. L. (2018). Victimization trends and correlates: Macro- and microinfluences and new directions for research. *Annual Review of Criminology, 1,* 103–121.

Luckenbill, D. F. (1977). Criminal homicide as a situated transaction. *Social Problems, 25,* 176–186.

Macmillan, R. (2001). Violence and the life course: The consequences of victimization for personal and social development. *Annual Review of Sociology, 27*(1), 1–22.

Matza, D. (1964). *Delinquency and drift.* New York: John Wiley and Sons.

McDonald, L. (1976). *The sociology of law and order.* Boulder, CO: Westview.

Mendelsohn, B. (1963). The origin of the doctrine of victimology. *Exerpta Criminologica, 3,* 239–245.

Mendez, I., Ruiz-Esteban, C., & Lopez-Garcia, J. J. (2017). Risk and protective factors associate to peer school victimization. *Frontiers in Psychology, 8,* 441(1–8).

Merton, R. K. (1938). Social structure and anomie. *American Sociological Review, 3,* 672–682.

Muftic, L. R., Finn, M. A., & Marsh, E. A. (2015). The victim-offender overlap, intimate partner violence, and sex: Assessing differences among victims, offenders, and victim-offenders. *Crime and Delinquency, 61,* 899–926.

Myers, W., Turanovic, J. J., Lloyd, K. M., & Pratt, T. C. (2020). The victimization of LGBTQ students at school: A meta-analysis. *Journal of School Violence,* in press.

Natarajan, M. (ed). (2011). *Crime opportunity theories: Routine activity, rational choice and their variants.* London, UK: Routledg/Taylor & Francis.

Nyseth Brehm, H. N. (2017). Subnational determinants of killing in Rwanda. *Criminology, 55,* 5–31.

Olweus, D. (2013). School bullying: Development and some important challenges. *Annual Review of Clinical Psychology, 9,* 751–780.

Pratt, T. C. (2016). A self-control/life-course theory of criminal behavior. *European Journal of Criminology, 13,* 129–146.

Pratt, T. C. (2018). The myth of the tech-savvy teen and the clueless senior citizen: Revisiting technology-based victimization over the life course. *Criminal Justice Review, 43,* 360–369.

Pratt, T. C., & Cullen, F. T. (2005). Assessing macro-level predictors and theories of crime: A meta-analysis. *Crime and Justice: A Review of Research, 32,* 373–450.

Pratt, T. C., Holtfreter, K., & Reisig, M. D. (2010). Routine online activity and internet fraud targeting: Extending the generality of routine activity theory. *Journal of Research in Crime and Delinquency, 47,* 267–296.

Pratt, T. C., & Turanovic, J. J. (2016). Lifestyle and routine activity theories revisited: The importance of "risk" to the study of victimization. *Victims and Offenders, 11,* 335–354.

Pratt, T. C., Turanovic, J. J., Fox, K. A., & Wright, K. A. (2014). Self-control and victimization: A meta-analysis. *Criminology, 52,* 87–116.

Quinney, R. (1974). *Critique of the legal order: Crime control in a capitalist society.* Boston, MA: Little, Brown.

Reiss, A. J. (1976). Settling the frontiers of a pioneer in American criminology: Henry McKay. Pp. 64–88 in Short, J. F. (Ed.), *Delinquency, crime, and society.* Chicago: University of Chicago Press.

Reppetto, T. J. (1974). *Residential crime.* Cambridge, MA: Ballinger.

Rountree, P. W., Land, K. C., & Miethe, T. D. (1994). Macro-micro integration in the study of victimization: A hierarchical logistic model analysis across Seattle neighborhoods. *Criminology, 32,* 387–414.

Sampson, R. J. (2012). *Great American city: Chicago and the enduring neighborhood effect.* Chicago: University of Chicago Press.

Schreck, C. J. (2017). Routine activity theory. Pp. 67–72 in Teasdale, B., & Bradley, M. (Eds.), *Preventing crime and violence: Advances in prevention science.* Switzerland: Springer International Publishing.

Schreck, C. J., Wright, R. A., & Miller, J. M. (2002). A study of the individual and situational antecedents of violent victimization. *Justice Quarterly, 19,* 159–180.

Schwartz, M. D., & DeKeseredy, W. (1997). *Sexual assault on the college campus: The role of male peer support.* Thousand Oaks, CA: Sage.

Schwartz, M. D., & Pitts, V. L. (1995). Exploring a feminist routine activities approach to explaining sexual assault. *Justice Quarterly, 12,* 9–31.

Shafer, S. (1968). *The victim and his criminal: A study in functional responsibility.* New York: Random House.

Sharkey, P. (2018). The long reach of violence: A broader perspective on data, theory, and evidence on the prevalence and consequences of exposure to violence. *Annual Review of Criminology, 1,* 85–102.

Shaw, C. R., & McKay, H. D. (1942). *Juvenile delinquency and urban areas.* Chicago: University of Chicago Press.

Short, J. F., & Strodtbeck, F. (1965). *Group process and gang delinquency.* Chicago: University of Chicago Press.

Simon, R. J. (1975). *Women and crime.* Lexington, MA: Lexington Books.

Sutherland, E. H. (1937). *The professional thief.* Chicago: University of Chicago Press.

Sutherland, E. H. (1947). *Principles of criminology.* 4th Edition. Philadelphia, PA: J.B. Lippincott.

Tan, S. Y., & Haining, R. (2016). Crime victimization and the implications for individual health and wellbeing: A Sheffield case study. *Social Science and Medicine, 167,* 128–139.

Troop-Gordon, W. (2017). Peer victimization in adolescence: The nature, progression, and consequences of being bullied within a developmental context. *Journal of Adolescence, 55,* 116–128.

Turanovic, J. J. (2018). Toward a life course theory of victimization. In S. H. Decker & K. A. Wright (Eds.), *Criminology and public policy* (2nd ed., pp. 85–103). Philadelphia, PA: Temple University Press.

Turanovic, J. J., & Pratt, T. C. (2014). "Can't stop, won't stop": Self-control, risky lifestyles, and repeat victimization. *Journal of Quantitative Criminology, 30,* 29–56.

Turanovic, J. J., & Pratt, T. C. (2019). *Thinking about victimization: Context and consequences*. London, UK: Routledge/Taylor and Francis.

Turanovic, J. J., Pratt, T. C., Kulig, T. C., & Cullen, F. T. (2021). *Confronting school violence: A synthesis of six decades of research*. Cambridge, UK: Cambridge University Press.

Turanovic, J. J., Reisig, M. D., & Pratt, T. C. (2015). Risky lifestyles, low self-control, and violent victimization across gendered pathways to crime. *Journal of Quantitative Criminology, 31,* 183–206.

Turner, J. H. (1978). *The structure of sociological theory*. Homewood, IL: Dorsey.

van Gelder, J. L., Averdijk, M., Eisner, M., & Ribaud, D. (2015). Unpacking the victim-offender overlap: On role differentiation and socio-psychological characteristics. *Journal of Quantitative Criminology, 31,* 653–675.

von Hentig, H. (1948). *The criminal and his victim: Studies in the sociobiology of crime*. New Haven, CT: Yale University Press.

Walsh, A., & Ellis, L. (2007). *Criminology: An interdisciplinary approach.* Thousand Oaks, CA: Sage.

West, D. J., & Farrington, D. P. (1973). *Who becomes delinquent? Second report of the Cambridge Study in Delinquent Development*. London, UK: Heinmann.

Wilcox, P., & Cullen, F. T. (2018). Situational opportunity theories of crime. *Annual Review of Criminology, 1,* 123–148.

Wolfe, S. E., & McLean, K. (2017). Procedural injustice, risky lifestyles, and violent victimization. *Crime and Delinquency, 63,* 1383–1409.

Wolfgang, M. E. (1958). *Patterns of criminal homicide*. Oxford, UK: Oxford University Press.

Wooldredge, J., & Steiner, B. (2012). Race group differences in prison victimization experiences. *Journal of Criminal Justice, 40,* 358–369.

Wright, J. C., Giammarino, M., & Parad, H. W. (1986). Social status in small groups: Individual-group similarity and the social "misfit." *Journal of Personality and Social Psychology, 50,* 523–536.

# Part I

## Revisiting Major Perspectives in Victimization Theory

# 1

# What Ideas of Victimization and Vulnerability Mean for Criminological Theory: A Logical Appraisal[1]

*Christopher J. Schreck and Mark T. Berg*

No criminologist disputes that the victim is a central actor in a criminal incident, yet theories about crime causation rarely permit this actor any role. In this chapter, we show that theories about offenders in fact contain an implicit internal logic that requires a theory of victimization. We will show how attention to this logic can reward theorists with a range of hypotheses about the nature and distribution of victimization, the interplay of offenders with their targets, and target behavior. We will *not* show that any given theory's logic can be made to produce hypotheses that are supported by the findings of good science. Where this proves to be the case, it follows that criminology benefits by having a new tool for falsifying its theories of crime. We believe that efforts to derive theories of victimization in this fashion can revitalize interest in criminological theory, and encourage crime researchers to value and promote original research in topic areas that are scientifically important but that have been long neglected thanks to widespread uncritical acceptance that the target adds little to the understanding of crime's causes.

To guide this task, we develop two distinct ideas that all criminological theories tacitly accept in one form or another. The *idea of victimization* defines whether a theory of crime endorses the view that victimization is an event with inherent qualities, and thus whether it is possible to have an a priori expectation that humans will be responsive to the threat and experience of victimization. This idea also determines whether the target has the ability to influence the decisions of the offender, and thus answers the question about whether the target merits any attention in a theory of crime. Theories about offenders also implicitly specify an *idea of vulnerability* to explain and predict differential risks of victimization across the population. We conduct a logical analysis to derive ideas of victimization and vulnerability from two examples of substantive positivist crime theory (cultural deviance and integrated theories) and contrast their claims against similar ideas generated from choice theory. Although our results favor choice theories, this chapter has a constructive goal that should appeal to theorists of all stripes: a demonstration of a process anyone can use on their own with their preferred theory.

## Criminological Theory, the Victim, and Intellectual Orthodoxy

For decades, criminology seemed poised to incorporate the victim into its theories of crime. In 1958, Marvin Wolfgang published a landmark study showing that many victims of homicide had arrest records. Killers and their victims often were people of the same sort. Wolfgang's timing seemed ideal, as the criminologists of the late 1950s worked amidst the greatest flowering of theory ever seen. Conceptual schemes destined to become classics had been coming in quick succession (Cloward & Ohlin, 1960; Cohen, 1955; Merton, 1938; Shaw & McKay, 1942; Sutherland, 1947), with more on the way (Hirschi, 1969; Wolfgang & Ferracuti, 1967). Moreover, Wolfgang's contemporaries were not embarrassed to speak of the victim's role in crime causation. Donald Cressey (1954), protégé and heir of Edwin Sutherland, conceded that "antagonistic or irritating behavior on the part of the victim" often preceded a homicide incident. Edwin Schur (1957) remarked that conmen exploited the dishonesty of their marks (see, also, Sutherland, 1937; von Hentig, 1948), and he made another interesting and prescient observation: "a probable influence on victim behavior is risk-taking." Schur goes on: "businessmen are particularly likely marks," and their victimization may owe to "certain values of the business community which seem to underlie the trend to what [C. Wright] Mills (1956) terms a 'structural immorality.' " Crime scholars in the mid-20th century thus appeared to be neither prone to a romanticized view of victims nor, it seemed, noticeably prejudiced against the topic itself.

At the same time, however, the consensus also appeared to be that victims and their offenders, more often than not, were unlike one another. Sykes and Matza (1957, p. 665) are but one example: "There is much evidence that juveniles often draw a sharp line between those who can be victimized and those who cannot. Certain social groups are not to be viewed as 'fair game'...in general, the potential for victimization would seem to be a function of the social distance between the juvenile delinquent and others...'don't steal from friends' or 'don't vandalize a church of your own faith.'" The leading theories of victims of that time took a similar line, with their categories often describing victims who did not resemble offenders (Schafer, 1968; von Hentig, 1948). Wolfgang's work cast doubt on such ideas, suggesting that crime theories could profit from revisiting the matter. By the 1970s, large-scale data supplying the basic facts about victimization were becoming widely available. The first waves of the National Crime Survey—later the National Crime Victimization Survey (NCVS)—confirmed that victims and offenders resembled one another socially and demographically (Hindelang, Gottfredson, & Garofalo, 1978). Forty years ago, Wolfgang and Singer (1978, p. 379) would regard the future with cautious optimism: "theory building will probably come shortly."

Criminology, for reasons that will become clear later, had other plans. Until the 1990s, one would have looked in vain for any meaningful mention of the victim in any of the leading theories of crime (Akers, Krohn, Lanza-Kaduce, & Radosevich, 1979; Braithwaite, 1990; Moffitt, 1992; Sampson & Laub, 1993; Thornberry, 1987).[2] The few theories of victims to have lasting importance developed independently (Cohen & Felson, 1979; Hindelang et al., 1978). Moreover, by the 1970s, political advocacy had seized control of scientific discourse and promoted an idealized image of the victim, often attacking anything contrary to this image as "victim-blaming" (Best, 1997; Felson, 1991; Meier & Miethe, 1993; Straus, 1999). Realizing the vast opportunities for knowledge being lost, Meier and Miethe (1993) would urge the integration of theories of victimization and offending. Their efforts to inspire criminology, like Wolfgang's, were futile. The victim continues to play no obvious role in recent published work on theories of crime causation (e.g., Agnew, 2014; Wikstrom, Oberwittler, Treiber, & Hardie, 2012) and only relatively lately have any of the important crime theorists made the effort to explain why victims and offenders are often the same people (e.g., Agnew, 2002). Crime theory textbooks barely mention victimization outside of their descriptions of routine activity theory (e.g., Akers, Sellers, & Jennings, 2016; Bernard, Snipes, Gerould, & Vold, 2015). Even a decade ago, the leading criminological journals attached low priority to work with any focus on victimization (Addington, 2008). If it turns out that one can logically derive all manner of testable claims from any given theory of crime concerning ideas of victimization and vulnerability, it becomes evident that criminology's priorities are not simply mistaken but in fact obstruct the ability of the field to assess the validity of the theories it has created. That is to say, however convincing a theory seems to be at explaining the offender, its inability to produce a believable explanation about victimization constitutes falsification of that theory.

## Positivism, Substantive Positivism, and Choice

Theories of crime are more than simply lists of variables and causal arrows; they are logical systems. The advantage of treating theory as a logical system is that by working from its ideas or assumptions the scientist has a foundation for making sense of emerging facts, sorting which of these facts matter and which do not, and then developing meaningful original research questions. Since the late 1960s, with the advent of social control theory (Hirschi, 1969), the most pronounced theoretical fault line in criminology arguably has been between two logical systems: substantive positivism and choice (Akers, 1996; Hirschi, 1996; Kornhauser, 1978; Roshier, 1989). In this paper, we limit our focus to a contrast of these systems. In so doing, we acknowledge working within the definitions of these as presented in Hirschi and Gottfredson (1990). We further acknowledge that each logical system allows the theorist the creative freedom to explore many alternative points of emphasis, far more than we can develop here. Substantive positivism encompasses the theories of the social science disciplines, such as sociology, psychology, and biology, and we include integrated frameworks. Choice theory, for its part, includes deterrence theory, social disorganization theory, social control theory, routine activity theory, and self-control theory. For all this variety in the direction theorists can elect to go, logical systems nevertheless impose general rules for how one may approach the question of the victim. Put differently, as we will show, any assumptions a theorist makes about the offender immediately constrains what that theorist might say about anything relating to the target and even the very nature of victimization.

Before describing the important assumptions of these systems, we first should distinguish positivism from substantive positivism. Positivism is a philosophy that advocates the techniques of natural science when conducting observation (Bryant, 1985). This perspective requires all who make factual claims to submit high quality positive observational proof. Positivism thus refers to the method of inquiry and, over the last half-century, scientific research would show that Wolfgang's findings were no accident of bad data. Offenders and victims clearly resembled each other everywhere one looked (Berg, 2012; Gottfredson, 1984; Hindelang et al., 1978). Those who self-reported much offending also tended to say they experienced a lot of victimization (Jensen & Brownfield, 1986; Lauritsen, Sampson, & Laub, 1991), and no reputable study has ever found anything other than a strong and positive relationship between an individual's offending and victimization (Lauritsen & Laub, 2007). Indeed, both phenomena appear to have identical correlates (Lauritsen, Laub, & Sampson, 1992). Positivism thus is responsible for the basic facts of victimization that, we will argue, valid theories of crime causation must also account for.

Positivism is supposed to give scientists the tools to adjudicate between rival theories, but, in criminology, it *became* a theory whose basic principles would dominate criminological thought thereafter (Laub & Sampson, 1991). *Substantive positivism*, as Hirschi and Gottfredson (1990) called it, was the extension of positivism to matters of theory creation and had originally developed as a reaction against defects in early versions of classical thought (Durkheim, 1982 [1895]; Roshier, 1989). Social scientists rejected the classical idea of hedonistic utility maximization as "unproven" and pre-scientific; properly conceived theory would instead begin with the assumption that people had no nature at all. Acceptance of this assumption forces the theorist to look for the causes of human action in phenomena that are outside the individual's control. Different behaviors implied different causes, thus urging criminologists to prefer separate theories for each discrete behavior—that is to say, substantive positivist criminology tended toward typological theories. While some of the more ambitious theories might focus on general causes of crime, more usually one will see theories of crime subtypes: violence among disadvantaged African Americans (Anderson, 1999), international differences in serious violence (Messner & Rosenfeld, 1994), white-collar crime (Sutherland,

Geis, & Goff, 1983), child abuse (Azar, 1991), intimate partner violence (Jewkes, 2002), simply to name a few. This assumption of differential causes also predisposes the criminological theorist to perceive victims as a separate group from their offenders (e.g., Schur, 1957; Sykes & Matza, 1957).

It is beyond our remit to summarize the criticisms against substantive positivism; however, we should note that in Hirschi and Gottfredson's (1990) view, thanks to its having appropriated the external features and jargon of science, the perspective benefits in that it appears attractive and reasonable. On the other hand, theories of offenders that conform to its assumptions pay a steep price in parsimony, accuracy, and overall usefulness (see, also, Kornhauser, 1978; Matza, 1964; Pfohl, 1994; Taylor, Walton, & Young, 1973). As we will show, these problems reappear with any attempt to employ the core assumptions of substantive positivism to understand ideas of victimization and the vulnerability. These assumptions, it turns out, make very clear why the victim has for so long been of so little scientific interest to the "positivist" crime theorist—as well as why only the offender, or the offender's motivation, can matter in the explanation of crime. We concede that such a position appears superficially attractive and reasonable, but this comes at the price of creating a logical trap that results in predictions about patterns of victimization and victim behavior that data generally do not confirm. This has serious consequences for the credibility of any such theories of crime, and exposes the speciousness of the sometimes vast evidence purportedly supporting them. We also found that theoretical integration, essentially a modern revival of substantive positivism, solves none of these problems.

Choice theories, by contrast, began as general theories of behavior that were applicable to any crime and, indeed, any action at all (Gottfredson, 2011). Choice theories perceive humans, whether they become victims or offenders, as active decision makers who are pursuing their own interests. That is, their actions are at all times understood as guided by the pursuit of advantage and avoidance of pain. The question the choice theorist attempts to answer is why something as seemingly advantageous as crime yet happens so infrequently, and so choice theories of crime therefore attempt to locate the most important restraints upon criminal action (Bentham, 1970 [1789]; Hirschi, 1969). We will show that it follows from the same assumptions that people are capable of independently reasoning what victimization means as well as its probable consequences. This awareness, in turn, incentivizes them to act from time to time, very often successfully, to make the passing offender do something else. Choice theory also recognizes that the ability to manage exposure to victimization is nevertheless variable, and thus endorses an *idea of vulnerability* to account for when people must reconcile a desire for security with competing desires to engage in other advantageous action. That is to say, unlike in substantive positivist theories, victims are just as scientifically interesting to the choice theorist as offenders, and a choice theory of crime has little difficulty accounting for basic facts about victimization. In the following sections, we develop the connections between the theoretical assumptions of substantive positivism and choice, and show how these lead to distinct and testable ideas of victimization and vulnerability.

## The Idea of Victimization

### *The Substantive Positivist View*

An *idea of victimization* is implicit in all theories of crime. Building from the source assumptions of the theory in question, one can construct the essential qualities of victimization and whether or not humans have an instinctive desire and capacity to respond to victimization or its possibility—namely potential targets, offenders, or as a society. If the crime theorist can accept that humans will try to influence a potential offender's decision to act, and permit them to be successful, there would be convincing reason to include propositions about the target's role in crime causation alongside those that created the offender. There would also be a clear incentive for theorists to advocate research studying not just offenders but also the underlying reasons for target behavior.

We noted earlier that substantive positivist crime theories in fact are silent about victims, and have persistently ignored theory and research on victimization. The passage of more than six decades since Wolfgang's (1958) book is ample evidence that substantive positivist criminology lacks the internal motivation to include target and victim behaviors within its theories, or even to comprehend and value research on these topics. This lack of concern becomes less of a mystery after developing the assumptions behind substantive positivism. Recall that the perspective rejects human nature. A specific configuration of positive causes outside of the individual's control determines all behavior, including crime. It follows that the absence or an insufficiency of these causes would preclude the behavior in question. For instance, if socialization is required to make one steal, its absence makes theft impossible. If we allow that targets and victims are also human, the theorist must assume that these lack a basic nature as well—otherwise, whatever nature they grant to the victim or a target must apply equally to the offender. One thus cannot admit that nature bestows upon people any particular attitude toward their own victimization, such as valuing their own lives (see, for instance, Sutherland, 1956, p. 20), because to do so instantly forces the same rules back upon the offender and thus fundamentally alters the theory. In a deterministic framework, such as one typically finds with substantive positivism, people cannot *independently* perceive relationships between phenomena, discern meaning or ideas from them, consult their own interests, and then act accordingly. The theorist has no choice but to rely on prior antecedents to explain how potential targets and victims think, act, and react. If a person's conception of victimization is thus caused, the meaning of "victimization" becomes dependent on exposure to these causes and becomes variable across individuals and groups.[3] Victimization, like crime, becomes a matter of normative conflict. "Victimization," like "crime," becomes an arbitrary concept containing no inherent properties or meaning. Absent prior causes, people cannot define what is happening to them as victimization. Even when they can, absent a different combination of prior causes, targets would lack the capacity to undertake even the simplest and most accessible precautionary actions, like avoiding dangerous areas or people or hiding valuables. Put another way, the moment one accepts determinism as the basis for a theory of crime then one also accepts the view that the offender's targets have no natural defenses and victimization has no automatic consequences.

This understanding of victimization is not trivial, because it shapes the characterization of crime victims and ultimately the decision of the crime theorist to assign independent causal value to target behavior. Consistent with the notion that victimization varies in meaning across individuals and groups, substantive positivists were predisposed to look for (and find) crime victims who were indifferent to their own victimization. This is evident from some of the terminology encountered: e.g., "learned helplessness" and "false consciousness" (Gondolf & Fisher, 1988; Jost, 1995; Peterson & Seligman, 1983). The rare crime scholars who mention victims do not use such terms, but they appear to draw roughly similar inferences. Baumer, Horney, Felson, and Lauritsen (2003, p. 43), for instance, summarized Elijah Anderson's (1999) description of the robbery process in the inner city thus: "[the code of the street] may *provide the victim with the background knowledge of 'how to get robbed'*; it may even allow him or her the presence of mind to *assist the assailant in this task*" (emphasis ours). That is to say, earlier socialization causes targets to conform to a script in which they are deferential to the robber's acquired need to display power. When substantive positivists mention target behavior, as here, there is often little sign that targets have any fundamental or consistent desire to oppose the offender. Theorists are thus free to simply disregard the target and proceed straight into the causes that produce the offender. As a result, as Gottfredson and Hirschi (2003) observed, substantive positivist theories assume that no explanation for criminal opportunity was needed because offenders made their own.

We believe that there are hidden dangers for substantive positivist theories of crime in embracing hard determinism (see Matza, 1964)[4], fixating upon the offender, and leaving no explanatory room at all for the victim. The outsized importance given to motivational factors is what is responsible for the "embarrassment of riches" problem that David Matza (1964) had famously described, where the theorized social causes of crime affect so many people and yet fail to deliver much crime (see, also, Kornhauser, 1978). In this light, integrating a more developed *idea of victimization*—for instance, one in which the theorist accepts that everyone opposes their own victimization and that the resulting protective behavior limits the offender—would seem to be an attractive solution, since it suggests a constraint that might plausibly let the theory retreat into "soft determinism." Unfortunately, there are unintended but catastrophic logical problems. If one assumes that humans actually want to avoid harm to themselves, the theorist has introduced an aspect of human nature that he or she must now apply to the offender as well. This one modification ultimately forces the theorist to concede that both victims and offenders are reasoning and acting according to their self-interest rather than under the compulsion of some external prior antecedent. And accepting this position means prioritizing restraints over positive antecedent causes. If a crime theory allows that a potential victim's precautionary or defensive behavior can thwart an offender, it implies that something as simple and instantaneous as locking a door overcomes motivations acquired across years of socialization. It also suggests the possibility that, acting in the moment, offenders are more concerned with ease and convenience than social frustration or adherence to grand, if deviant, ideals. It also implies that the victim's decisions are deserving of attention, thus exposing theories that are too preoccupied with offenders as misleading and likely to produce bad policy. Substantive positivism thus leaves the crime theorist with every reason to want to ignore the victim, leaving little reason to wonder why calls for integrating theories of crime and victimization have gone unheeded.

Substantive positivism also relieves the state from having any particular interest in the matter of the victimization of its members. By precluding victimization from any automatic harmful consequences except those brought about by exposure to prior antecedents, substantive positivism offers no compelling reason for policy makers to believe that the care of victims ought to be as much a priority as the punishment or treatment of offenders. Instead, as Kornhauser (1978, p. 45) sourly observed in her description of the cultural deviance perspective, "Each subgroup does not define as victims members of other groups… All are busy stealing everyone else blind. In violent crimes, each man's hand is raised against his brother. Thus modern man avoids Hobbesian chaos: he joins the war of all against all; his culture endorses it. All are socialized to preserve the society to which they are bound by their common complicity in crime. *Thus disorder caused by culture is order, war is peace*" (emphasis ours). Victimization in substantive positivism is simply a feature of social organization, even evidence of cohesion, not a contributing factor to a defective or failing society.

### *The Choice Theory View*

Choice theories, on the other hand, begin with the criminal act and, as we will show, are able to specify that victimization is an idea with inherent qualities and natural consequences. Thanks to the assumption of a hedonistic and calculating human nature, people can independently anticipate these consequences—whether they are the offender or a potential target—and act accordingly. Further, victimization becomes an idea with effects felt throughout society. Crime, to the choice theorist, has definite meaning, being an act of force or fraud committed by someone in the pursuit of self-interest (Gottfredson & Hirschi, 1990). This definition makes clear that the inducement to crime exists only for the offender. Implied in this definition is that crime is an interaction so one-sided that no human will voluntarily consent to being someone else's victim, which is why offenders find it necessary to employ force or fraud to achieve their ends. One can develop from this the idea that victimization has distinctive and universal qualities, materially shaping the actions of potential targets, would-be offenders, and broader society.

Whereas victimization has no meaning in substantive positivism, in choice theory its essential quality is that it is all pain, administered at the hands of someone else. This pain is instantly recognized by the recipient as illegitimate because it was not voluntary, had no valid cause, and because it produces no redeeming or foreseeable benefit. This pain, moreover, violates the right to one's own body and property, and so produces feelings of fear, danger, or uncertainty. Given that aversion to pain is natural among humans, we can infer that the dislike of being or becoming someone's victim is found everywhere. Adapting the sanctioning systems of Bentham (1970 [1789]), the perspective allows that the pains of victimization can be variable in type (physical, emotional, financial, social), degree (from trivial to lethal), and duration, but the fact that the offender had to resort to force or fraud exposes any claim that humans are inherently indifferent to their own victimization. Whether one acknowledges an incident using the word "victimization" is also irrelevant to this fundamental dislike, and neither does it matter to the victim whether such acts are officially legal or illegal, whether the person inflicting it is a loved one or not, and irrespective of culture or time period. Neither does acceptance of the fact of victimization, or later rationalization of an incident, imply that victims wanted it or would appreciate experiencing it again. Consistent with Feinberg (1984), the *idea of victimization* excludes voluntary acts of self-harm, or pretending or seeking injury for the sake of personal, economic, or political advantage. Also excluded are incidents of "passing unpleasantnesses" that only provoke hurt feelings, disgust, and anger but no tangible injury or feelings of fear, danger, or threat. Trivial affronts, while having validity as an interpersonal grievance, are soon forgotten among reasonable people.

Victimization is more than simply disliked. The hedonistic aspect of human nature suggests that people everywhere will act autonomously to try to avoid it just as they would any other painful thing, unless otherwise prevented. The inducements of safety-mindedness certainly seem to be compelling. Gottfredson and Hirschi's (1990) analysis of the nature of crime makes it clear that the pain of being a victim is far greater than the pleasure of being an offender. A murderer removes a pest, which is of trivial and ephemeral benefit, but the outcome for the victim is rather more serious and permanent. A burglar pawns goods for pennies on the dollar; however, the victim bears the cost of lost peace of mind, repair of doors and furniture, and the cost of replacement of stolen property. This asymmetry suggests that there is strong natural incentive for humans to avoid becoming a victim. Indeed, one may go as far as to call this "self-preservation," and infer that this tendency is not only present but also more powerful or consistent than the motivation to commit crime. This suggests why people leave lights on, put their valuables away, avoid dangerous areas, or lock doors far more often than they steal or hit others. Self-preservation means that, when a threat is detected or anticipated, *decision makers will, without the necessity of prior antecedents, see the value of trying to prevent, resist, or mitigate the possibility or impact of their own victimization. And they will do so up to the point they are constrained by the courses of action available or by competing notions of self-interest.*

The *idea of victimization* in choice theory also implies what effects being targeted will have on the victim and society. We noted above that feelings of fear, threat, and danger automatically follow from victimization. Evident in early classical theories (Beccaria, 1963 [1764]) is the notion that a natural byproduct of the threat and experience of victimization is diminished investment and participation in society, as interests suffer and people retreat to safety (e.g., Ferraro, 1995; Krulichová & Podana, 2018), in turn promoting Hobbesian chaos. Just as a rational and humane system of criminal laws is in the interest of society, *so too is the protection of its members and mitigating the effects of their victimization.*[5] In recognition of this, choice theories are friendly to the idea that awareness of someone's victimization causes other members of society to be concerned for the victim's well-being. They will also worry about themselves, and desire to punish offenders and make them unwelcome. Applying this idea to individuals and their relationships, one thus arrives at social control theory (Hirschi, 1969; Sampson & Laub, 1993). On a larger scale, communities see victimization as a threat to prosperity and smoothly functioning interdependence and thus organize in part to facilitate keeping crime out (Sampson, Raudenbush, & Earls, 1997; Shaw & McKay, 1942). At the societal level, the state creates legislation and relevant institutions to protect its members (Beccaria, 1963 [1764]). The theorists explicating these conceptual schemes were concerned foremost with identifying the salient restraints upon the offender, so consideration of how these function to support the victim and preserve social trust naturally alters one's view of these theories substantially. For instance, where there is debatable evidence that attempts to modify the criminal code can produce measurable deterrent effects, widespread awareness of the enactment or execution of just criminal laws may nevertheless help reassure society that it is safe to continue collectively beneficial activity. Academic criminologists dispute the degree social bonds restrain crime (Hirschi, 1969; Hirschi & Gottfredson, 1995; Sampson & Laub, 1993), but the presence of reciprocal bonds of loyalty, trust, and affection—augmented by effective neighborhood organizations (Sampson et al., 1997)—may not only inspire mutually protective behavior (Schreck & Fisher, 2004; Schreck, Wright, & Miller, 2002) but help people manage fear and injuries from victimization. The supportive responsiveness of others to victimization preserves social relationships and feelings of collective efficacy. Conversely, society's failure to act effectively to restore confidence after victimization fosters political disaffection, fear, distrust of others, reduced economic output, poorer physical and mental health, greater expenditure of time and resources on protective behavior, and broken personal relationships. Unlike in substantive positivism, choice theory takes the position that victimization does not promote or represent an alternative expression of society; on the contrary, victimization is the destroyer of society.

The *idea of victimization*, in choice theory, has obvious implications for shaping the actions of the offender. Offenders also value self-preservation. For the offender, crime is only attractive when it brings clear and definite advantage or relief from pain at little risk or effort. Unlike in substantive positivist theory, where the offender boldly acts with cool assurance and indifference to danger and victims are barely a challenge, choice theory conceives that the would-be offender is often anxiously mindful of the intended victim and the perils of the immediate situation. Almost all of the time, a cursory assessment of the situation reveals that a crime committed now would probably be a terrible choice. Thanks to the target's actions and local circumstances, a successful crime would take far more effort and at far greater immediate risk for physical and legal danger than the offender finds worthwhile. The *idea of victimization* is useful because, since an amoral human nature implies that crime ought to be out of control, it helps solve Matza's (1964) embarrassment of riches problem without violating internal logical consistency. People want advantage, but, at the same time, self-preservation is advantageous. If opportunities for crime are too plentiful to quantify with accuracy (Gottfredson, 2011), so too are casual decisions people are inclined to make that substantially increase its difficulty, danger, and inconvenience. Crime instead happens in a moment of human weakness for shortsighted judgment with temptation nearby, and with the unpleasant consequences seeming far off and unlikely. The actions of the victim in providing an opportunity for another person to give in to weakness are therefore obvious and of great theoretical interest to the choice theorist, and thus the *idea of victimization* seamlessly feeds into the *idea of vulnerability*.

## The Idea of Vulnerability

### *The Substantive Positivist View*

The *idea of vulnerability* is a theory's answer to the question about what inspires offenders to prefer some targets and not others, and is usually implicit rather than explicit. This idea speaks to what we might predict about the broader pattern of victimization, including whether victims and offenders are often the same people, and, if so, why. Although substantive positivism never openly acknowledges an *idea of vulnerability*, its theories nevertheless take a clear position on the meaning of vulnerability and the determination of who falls victim. Vulnerability to crime is commonly understood in academic criminology to mean the proximity of a desirable target to someone who is inclined to commit crime, who perceives that the tempting reward is within easy reach, and who then reasons that the crime is only minimally risky and getting away with it is likely. Substantive positivism, as we suggested above, must *reject* this definition with prejudice, as well as all related theories (e.g., Cohen & Felson, 1979; Hindelang et al., 1978; Miethe & Meier, 1990; Wilcox, Land, & Hunt, 2003). To endorse this definition suggests not only that the true cause of crime is more likely to be found in the immediate situation than distant motivational antecedents, it also implies a reasoning offender who must respond to such things as risk and difficulty. It also implies victims act in their own interest and offenders fear what potential targets are doing—an *idea of victimization* antithetical to that found in substantive positivism.

Substantive positivism's assumptions, as we will demonstrate, force us to simplify vulnerability down to the "motivated offender." *Whatever the theory says is the offender's motivation, there the victim will be.* That is, the very nature of motivation means that offenders are particular about whom they target, as required in the assumption of causal determinism. If wealth acquisition motivates the offender, only those with money are vulnerable and victimization data would reflect this.

Motivation, presumably, is sufficient to ensure the offender can find a way to get within striking distance of the target; substantive positivist theories usually gloss over this issue, so one cannot be sure. In some cases, theorists solve this problem by making the required victims offer themselves up for predation. For instance, Schur (1957) never quite gives an explanation as to why businesspersons and their swindlers combine to interact in the first place; however, he implies that victims of con men are socialized to *seek out* their victimizers. Amir (1971) similarly posits in statement of obvious absurdity that some women seek their rapists out of a spirit of "rebellion." Further, because the assumption of determinism makes anything like victim avoidance or defensive behavior theoretically uncertain, "guardianship" is never an issue for the offender, at least not for long. Redefining vulnerability to offender motivation means that if one can eliminate the causes that motivate the offender to commit crime, then the theorist can all but guarantee complete safety for potential victims. This is how targets become invulnerable in substantive positivism, not through their own defensive action.

Simplifying vulnerability in this manner, to where only the offender's specific motivation is needed to give meaning to vulnerability, is not necessarily problematic for a crime theory, provided the offender's motivations produce victims such as those shown in victimization data. Unfortunately, this does not appear to be the case. Recall that we know that victims and offenders are often the same people (Lauritsen & Laub, 2007; Wolfgang, 1958). Offenders and victims share all the same correlates, for instance divorce, job loss, accidents, educational failure, and substance use. We present two case studies below as illustrations for how substantive positivism addresses the *idea of vulnerability*, and explain how their internal logic results in predictions inconsistent with the results of good research.

*A Case Study: Cultural Deviance Theory.* Sellin (1938) and Sutherland (1947) developed widely influential cultural accounts of rule breaking and for them the "justifications and rationale" for all acts of crime were products of group socialization. Any explanation of crime, in their view, must attend to differential exposure to norms in favor or against rule breaking. Part of the long-recognized appeal of the cultural deviance perspective lies in its description of society as coercively enforcing the values of the powerful upon the politically and socially marginal, which resonates with those friendly to social justice within criminology and sociology (e.g., Kornhauser, 1978; Taylor et al., 1973). Many victimologists also appear to endorse this perspective (Karmen,

2016). Cultural deviance theory begins with the assumption that there is no human nature. Whatever people do, even how they perceive reality, is wholly the product of their socialization. Cultural variability (in particular, notions of right and wrong) is infinite. Crime is thus a function of normative conflict, where the powerful formally define notions of right and wrong; however, informally, each subculture struggles to hold onto its identity. It is difficult to overstate the influence of these tenets on classic and contemporary criminological theory (Anderson, 1999; Haynie, 2001; Matsueda & Anderson, 1998; Steffensmeier & Allan, 1996; Sutherland, 1947; Wolfgang & Ferracuti, 1967).

The implications of cultural deviance for the offender are well understood. Offenders must positively learn to commit crime, thus committing crime in response to their socialization and the value the group assigns to certain actions. One can infer from this that a victim's precautions only matter to the degree that the offender has learned to define "precautionary behavior" as meaningful; offenders operate in their own reality, and accordingly are under no requirement to respond to victim actions in the expected way. We will return to this point in a moment. When we turn to the victim, it follows that the population of likely victims too will conform to their socialization. As Sutherland (1956) pointed out, some subcultures value life while others do not; self-preservation, fundamental to choice theories and the basis for precautionary behavior, is treated in cultural deviance theory as an "ethnocentric value" (Kornhauser, 1978, p. 36). Weis and Borges (1973, p. 81) echo this sentiment: "Rooted in the social structure which is characterized by male domination, the socialization processes of the male and the female act to mold women into victims and provide the procedure for legitimizing them in this role." Anderson (1999, p. 125), more recently, wrote "Assailant and victim must both know their roles… [the robber] wants to wield his power undisputed…nothing conveys this recognition better than the clear act of total deference." In these examples, people can be socialized through their culture to tamely accept criminal damage to their material interests and physical well-being.

In normal understanding, the ability to engage in precautionary behavior speaks to the *idea of vulnerability*. The internal logic of cultural deviance does not leave this impression; in fact, there is a much stronger impression that *whatever the target does, it does not matter*. Since offenders define reality as their culture does, not as the target intends, precautions have no meaning unless the offender was socialized in the first place to fear or respect them. Precautions, properly understood in cultural deviance theory, are—like any symbol—infinite in their variety and all arbitrary as far as the criminal act is concerned. All victim action is therefore as meaningful or meaningless as the placement of a religious decal on a car in the belief that it will stop a thief from stealing it. That is to say, no one will see the point of locking the door unless the culture provides the appropriate socialization; however, none of it matters unless the offender was raised in a culture that taught its members to respect locks or decals more than automobile theft. Precautions and difficulties (guns, doors, savage dogs, concealment and avoidance, prayer) thus are all symbolic—the offender can and does simply disregard them. For example, Anderson (1999) is clear that the attacker who is motivated to engage in assault will proceed anyway, in spite of the victimization script requiring immediate resistance from the target and possibly lethal reprisal.[6] "People often feel constrained not only to stand up and at least attempt to resist during an assault but also to 'pay back'—to seek revenge—after a successful assault on their person…their very identity, their self-respect, and their honor are [at stake]" (Anderson 1999, p. 76). In this way, cultural deviance theory nullifies Cohen and Felson's (1979) concept of guardianship beyond any hope of reconciliation. "Precautionary behavior" as such, in cultural deviance theory, is "culturally inappropriate" for stopping the offender. In order for precautionary behavior to have any possibility of achieving the intended effect, cultural deviance theory must presuppose so many normative coincidences that the attempt inevitably brings into stark relief Dennis Wrong's (1961) criticism of its "oversocialized" human nature. Victim precautions or defensive behavior therefore cannot figure in the *idea of vulnerability*.

In cultural deviance theory, the offender is required to be the cause of crime and the offender's motivation is what defines the *idea of vulnerability*.[7] Offenders learn, from the subculture, to regard certain people or actions as necessitating a sequence of behaviors that the broader society calls "criminal." Given the infinite variability of culture, specifically notions of right and wrong, across the world (Kornhauser, 1978), "vulnerability"—which really would be anything about a person that triggers the offender to act—thus can mean literally anything and may or may not have anything to do with the objective qualities of what a victim does or says. For instance, "Theoretically, victim precipitation of forcible rape means that in a particular situation *the behavior of the victim is interpreted by the offender as a direct invitation for sexual relations* or as a sign that she will be available … if he will persist in demanding it" (Amir, 1967, p. 493; emphasis ours). Menachem Amir, a student of Marvin Wolfgang who was applying his subcultural perspective to female rape victims, specifically means that rapists learn to react "in a particular situation" to certain traits of women, such as their gender, dress, reputation, or alcohol usage, with forcible rape.[8] That is, the offender selects victims based on some arbitrary criterion: gender, race, religion, membership in some outgroup, or a particular behavior defined as warranting a criminal response. Cultural deviance theory implies no consensus in laws or values, neither can there be consensus across the world or within complex societies about who offenders prefer to target and what aspects of a person's actions constitutes "vulnerability."

When we turn to the evidence, cultural deviance theory suggests patterns of victimization and victim behavior that the data do not support. Precautionary behavior, at least those that do not entail painful expense or inconvenience, is actually widespread (Meier & Miethe, 1993). Rates of victimization even among college students—whose age places them among those with the highest risk of victimization—suggest they are far more effective at avoiding victimization than not (Fisher, Sloan, Cullen, & Lu, 1998). When we turn to the victim–offender correlation, cultural deviance allows for this as a possibility, but not as a basic fact. Some cultural deviance theories postulate that offenders and victims can be the same people (at least in areas where reprisal is a norm; see Singer, 1981, 1986), but more usual is the assertion that offenders target members of out-groups (e.g., Anderson, 1999; Kornhauser, 1978; Sykes & Matza, 1957; Weis & Borges, 1973). Data in fact show that the correlation between victimization and offending persists everywhere around the world where there is sound information on victims and offenders (e.g., Lauritsen & Laub, 2007; Posick, 2013). Offenders and victims everywhere also appear to share the same correlates (e.g., Gottfredson, 1984; Lauritsen et al., 1992; Straus, 1999). While cultural diversity across the world is self-evident, basic patterns of victimization are more noteworthy for their consistency than their differences—indicating that differences of culture are not behind them.

*A Case Study: Integrated Criminological Theory.* Integrated theories were developed with the intention of moving criminology beyond what Hirschi (1989) had termed the "oppositional theoretical tradition," where crime theories (usually strain, cultural deviance, and control theories) fought unproductively over logical assumptions—in fact, the very complaint that led to the creation of substantive positivism in the first place. Integrationists would instead revive what they believed were the best aspects of substantive positivist open-mindedness by pitting the leading variables from each theory head to head, creating a new theory only from what survived. The theoretical integrationist would be more concerned about empirical adequacy and less bothered about logical controversies and disciplinary allegiance, in this way giving the appearance of fairness; however, in practice disciplinary allegiances and logical controversies stubbornly persisted (e.g., Elliott, Huizinga, & Ageton, 1985; see Hirschi, 1987). Critics alleged that "fairness," to an integrationist, only meant impartiality toward the theories and ideas that substantive positivism had created and endorsed. Discredited substantive positivist theories thus received a level of solicitous treatment in integrated models that would not be extended to choice theories (Hirschi, 1979; Hirschi, 1989). That is to say, integration has to be understood as simply a reaffirmation of the longstanding tenets of substantive positivism. Since substantive positivism and theoretical integration share the same precepts, the pioneering integrationists did not consider the victim as something problematic for the offender—or even to consider victimization as an important correlate of crime (e.g., Elliott et al., 1985; Johnson, 1979; Thornberry, 1987). If they addressed the *idea of vulnerability* directly at all, they followed the usual substantive positivist protocol and defined it entirely in terms of the offender's motives (e.g., Agnew, 2014). The offender, as before, is the true cause of crime—leaving integrated theories vulnerable to the same incorrect predictions noted earlier with cultural deviance theories, including being unable to anticipate or account for the correlation between victimization and offending or the existence of shared predictors.

On the other hand, a virtue of integrated theory is its supposed flexibility and open-mindedness. What is to stop someone from retrofitting an integrated theory to account for ideas of victimization and vulnerability? Robert Agnew's (1992) general strain theory is the most important contemporary integrated theory and, to his great credit, he published a paper theorizing that victimization (or vicarious victimization) created negative affect, or strain, which could lead to crime (Agnew, 2002). His theory does not automatically preclude an *idea of victimization*. Although adopting a strain orientation, Agnew deeply infuses his theory with the choice perspective: offenders act when the benefits are high and the costs are low. He also grants people the ability to be responsive to pain, or "negative stimuli" (Agnew, 2007, 2012).[9] All of this suggests that people have some capacity for independent reasoning, although the theory does not directly say this. The experience or threat of victimization that brought on strain might thus lead to crime, but because of Agnew's decision to take the choice perspective seriously the theory seems to allow that victims or those who fear victimization can be inspired to cope with their strain by taking precautionary action instead. Moreover, if offenders attend to costs and benefits, as the theory claims, this would allow them to be deterred by such precautions.

To the degree that general strain theory endorses the precepts of choice theory, it avoids many of the pitfalls that considering victims would normally invoke; however, to the degree it adheres to substantive positivism it creates difficulties for itself. One of Hirschi and Gottfredson's (1990) criticisms of substantive positivism is the inability of its theories to distinguish between what are causes and what are effects. They wrote: "First, throughout the 20th century, evidence has accumulated that people who tend to lie, cheat, and steal also tend to hit other people; that the same people tend to drink, smoke, use drugs, wreck cars, desert their spouses, quit their jobs, and come late to class. Second, evidence has accumulated that differences in such tendencies across people are reasonably stable over the life course" (Hirschi & Gottfredson, 1990, p. 421). They also have a higher risk of becoming victims (Schreck, 1999). Choice theory, thanks to its internal logic, views tendencies for all of these things to happen in the same people as originating from low self-control (Gottfredson & Hirschi, 1990). Their correlations with offending are spurious. The integrationist, in contrast, only perceives variables and statistically significant correlations. Which are causes, which ones are effects? What multivariate coefficients are real and meaningful, and which ones are simply artifacts of differences in measurement (but that conceptually measure the same thing)? Relying on the presuppositions of substantive positivism, Agnew draws the appropriate conclusion that crime is the effect and other conditions correlated with crime must be a cause. Victimization is similarly relegated (Agnew, 2002).

Although this does superficially grant general strain theory the ability to "explain" the victimization–offending correlation, one of the basic facts all crime theory should account for, it introduces an unexpected problem. Namely, general strain theory is not capable of having an *idea of vulnerability*, at least not without producing a causal model of tortuous complexity. Recall that the correlates of crime and victimization are the same. Note, too, that general strain theory has systematically assimilated virtually every known correlate in order to explain crime—at least 80 variables by a recent count (see Felson & Eckert,

2018). While giving the illusion of an intellectually vital and compelling theory of crime, the humble victimologist is unfortunately left with *no* unique variables to explain why individuals became victims in the first place. General strain theory, left unmodified, finds itself predicting that victimization or vulnerability is random—or even *not caused* (recall that all distinct phenomena in substantive positivism have to possess unique causes). At this late date, such a hypothesis would encounter difficulty from the facts. It seems to us that the only recourse for general strain theory to save itself is to specify causal arrows going from every other variable (e.g., crime, divorce) *back* to victimization. This resolution seems to make sense, in light of the basic principles of the theory where the offender commits crime to cope with strain, implying that victims are targeted specifically with this motive in mind. By committing crime, the offender becomes a source of strain to others and thus a victim. If one can allow the inclusion of a causal arrow from offending back to victimization, one cannot stop there. After all, evidence shows that people who perform poorly in social interactions on a variety of dimensions are odious to others and get attacked (Tedeschi & Felson, 1994). And if one can do this, one must include arrows between each source of strain with the other sources. In this way, any attempt to develop the *idea of vulnerability* results in an exaggerated complexity that makes general strain theory indistinguishable from Thornberry's (1987) interactional theory. If one believes that the purpose of theory is to reduce complexity (Hirschi, 1989; Hirschi & Gottfredson, 2008; Lauritsen, 2005), general strain theory loses its value as a theory of crime. General strain theory is not unique in this problem, as it would apply to any integrated theory (e.g., Agnew, 2014; Bernard & Snipes, 1996; Elliott et al., 1985; Wikstrom et al., 2012) where no internal logic exists to allow the theorist to draw a line between causes and effects. Successfully accommodating ideas of victimization and vulnerability would first require that integrated theories become choice theories, making integrated theories redundant.

*The Choice Theory View*

As we did with substantive positivist theories, we begin deriving an *idea of vulnerability* in choice theory by working from its source assumptions and developing the perspective of the person contemplating the crime (Felson, 1994; Gottfredson & Hirschi, 1990). In choice theory, offenders want pleasure and to avoid pain. Crime is one of many tools for achieving advantage, one that is simple and available to anyone, but in fact useful only in limited circumstances (Gottfredson & Hirschi, 1990). Simply put, offenders want to escape the scene of the crime and enjoy their rewards, and so are naturally responsive to the *idea of victimization* outlined earlier. Self-preservation is rarely far from the thoughts of would-be offenders, in that they try to anticipate how their actions might prompt resistance from targets, bystanders, and police. The common offender is not a martyr. Even if the opportunity for robbery presents itself, the prospect of not dying at the hands of the intended target or police does have its compensations. In this way, the offender is not forced to commit crime (Gottfredson, 2011), and indeed crime data show that offenders rarely do. Those persons who prioritize short-term advantage over long-term and uncertain negative consequences, which is to say those with low self-control, will tend to be the ones most susceptible when a superficial look reveals that the situation appears promising (Gottfredson & Hirschi, 1990). This means that offenders everywhere understand and respond to vulnerability intuitively, if not always accurately—it is *anything* about the victim and the setting that, from a quick glance, makes the task of committing crime seem easy enough and sufficiently rewarding, and that would make an attempt attractively risk-free.

Drawing from the *idea of victimization* presented earlier, one can reason that offenders are so rarely successful because the target—no less than the offender—wants pleasure and to avoid pain, and so does not want victimization. Nevertheless, evidence shows that people (1) have a variable and imperfect ability or willingness to anticipate offenders and take precautions reliably (e.g., Schreck, 1999), and (2) have to navigate settings, over which they have incomplete control, settings that sometimes will permit the offender to act with impunity (Clarke, 1995; Felson, 1994). Both elements comprise the *idea of vulnerability* in choice theory and are consistent with its assumptions. As they pursue their agendas, people can act upon their immediate settings in ways that influence their vulnerability; however, the setting also acts upon them. Turning to the choices of individual victims, pioneering work on victimization sometimes pushed in this direction. Hindelang and his colleagues (1978) acknowledged that some victims might provoke their offender or else cause their own vulnerability. Gottfredson (1984), reporting results from London data, would argue that both victimization and offending appeared to be consequences of weak social control (see, also, Lauritsen et al., 1992). Evidence from a Finnish study of adolescents found that after accounting for selection, conceivably a proxy for decision-making, the association between routine activities and victimization was spurious (Felson, Savolainen, Berg, & Ellonen, 2013). These findings suggest a person's own internal decision calculus very much shapes the structure of their immediate environment.

*Choice and Vulnerability*

While there is much research on offender decision-making, some of which are classic (e.g. Cornish & Clarke, 1986; Felson, 1994), scholarship on the decisions potential *targets* make that result in some of them becoming victims is harder to find. The choice perspective, upon inspection, appears able to suggest a potentially rich theory that is consistent with current knowledge, while also making inferences future research could profitably examine and develop. As a start to this process, we here derive a basic picture of how such a theory might look.

In the choice perspective, safety from victimization is its own incentive. The question turns to why humans would fail to do their utmost to procure that safety. Choice theories in criminology are restraint theories, which suggests the answer to this question—namely, that some circumstance reduces the desire and ability of the individual to act with effectiveness or at all. Some, but not all, of these barriers reflect the necessity of having to triage limited personal resources. Others fall within the realm of individual choice, specifically the necessity of having to manage multiple competing interests and obligations. If we return to the idea that humans are governed by pain and pleasure, it would seem to follow that many actions that a dispassionate commentator believes could *optimally promote* safety may in fact not be all that pleasurable to the person actually facing the choice, and may contain their fair share of pain, inherent danger, or unacceptable sacrifice. Or, put differently, competing desires in the moment (having fun, doing things that feel good, not spending too much money) may seem more advantageous, especially if someone imperfectly grasps the consequences an action may set in motion. Choice theory thus suggests that why people do things that assist, alert, or provoke the offender rests in the fact that:

(1) Such actions, in the moment, seem advantageous to the potential victim (they are gratifying or avoid pain); they represent otherwise rewarding activities (Lyng, 1990);

(2) The risk of falling victim because of the action is not immediately obvious at the time, meaning it is not considered as a serious possibility until it is too late; some targets are ignorant of their danger or fail to adequately anticipate the risks; and
(3) Even when the prospect of victimization is a recognized possibility, some people possess a self-serving faith that they have a uniquely excellent ability to manage the immediate situation and thus escape the costs (i.e., faith that the offender is less competent than they are). Therefore, they do not alter their current action as long as continuing it is gratifying; and
(4) Many forms of precautionary behavior require sacrifice and offer little inherent gratification beyond peace of mind about an event that might but usually does not occur at some unknowable point in the future. Thus, the decision-maker will be less reliable at using those precautions when they become inconvenient, take effort, and that instill no other sense of enjoyment.

We can expand any of the four points above by adapting the general principles of certainty, swiftness, and severity, famously explicated by other choice theorists to understand crime (Beccaria, 1963 [1764]; Gottfredson & Hirschi, 1990). First—before, during, and after the crime—actions that produce immediate and obvious advantage for the target will be considered more pleasurable than those where the benefits are deferred into the future, are uncertain, or unseen. For instance, a person who feels safe in the moment will be less willing to sacrifice much in order to take precautions than one who feels that victimization is *certain*. A feeling of certainty of victimization tends to appear when people are uncomfortably aware of incivilities, disorder, or who have recently become victims (Ferraro, 1995; Rountree, 1998). Fear and experiences with victimization do correspond with extensive safety-minded behavior (Schreck, Berg, Fisher, & Wilcox, 2018). Certainty of victimization also may be at the heart of why someone in a bar may be more belligerent in a confrontation whenever friends are nearby. Disputatiousness is known to increase the chances of provoking attack (Felson, Berg, Rogers, & Krajewski, 2018), but the presence of protectors might make the antagonist believe that the certainty is less—and therefore continuing what appears to be a gratifying course of action. After the crime, there is rarely any certainty that contacting the police will result in the restoration of, for example, stolen property, thus explaining why most crimes go unreported. But, even if the police are ineffective, people may report anyway simply to enjoy the *certain* benefits accruing from filing an insurance claim.

Second, the target is more likely to perceive the quickest (or *swiftest*), that is to say easiest, precautionary behaviors as more pleasurable than any requiring greater investment of time, resources, and effort. Doing nothing is the easiest choice of all; many people make this choice when they feel safe. This is why, from the standpoint of crime prevention policy, precautions that do not require the active cooperation of the target are to be preferred over those that do. For instance, over those that do, like automatically locking doors, automatic updates of computer security software.[10] Otherwise, the more that precautionary or defensive behavior entails effort, risk, inconvenience, cost, or thought, the less inclined the target will be to see them as realistic or worthwhile. For example, moving to another neighborhood to avoid victimization is often a costly ordeal, and thus targets tend not to resort to it as often as they would to locking a door or altering routines. Even when altering a routine, choice theory suggests that people will tend to do so in a way that is least intrusive to their other interests.

Third, targets are inclined to make decisions that produce results that are *gratifying* in themselves. While locking a door is easy, the action is not inherently rewarding apart from a feeling of security. Contrast the door lock with defensive firearms, which can be repurposed for recreational use, offer social benefits (feelings of community with other owners), besides also producing feelings of power (Kleck, 1988). Gratification even plays a role during an incident. For instance, in an armed robbery where the offender has the initiative, the choice of compliance—if it offers the possibility of life and health—might appear more gratifying than fight or flight. In this way, the choice theorist does not see compliance as a role one is *socialized* to adopt for specific crime types (e.g., Anderson, 1999; Weis & Borges, 1973), but rather as a rational response to any situation where the target believes that attempted resistance or escape would be hopeless and dangerous. We have described here the roles of certainty, swiftness, and severity (gratification) in isolation; however, as should be evident from the examples, they very likely interact in ways that are complex—offering considerable scope for empirical research and theoretical development. For instance, firearms may be gratifying to own and carry for some, but choice theory suggests that others would be deterred to the degree they find them to be expensive, difficult to maintain or store safely, and dangerous. While weapons and firearms may be gratifying, they are not easy to own; however, the more certain that violent victimization appears to be, the more willing people may be to incur such costs anyway (Schreck et al., 2018).

The classical ideas of certainty, swiftness, and severity imply that the failure to undertake precautionary behavior is as rational as the decision to be safety conscious. However, these considerations are influenced by human variability in the tendency to make judgment errors, especially the sort of errors in which a person *habitually* is unresponsive to reasonably foreseeable long-term consequences of immediate actions. For instance, theft of one's car is an obvious risk of leaving its doors unlocked and engine running while quickly stepping into a store. While the decision to leave one's car in such a state may reflect an accurate awareness of the area's safety, more often the overriding consideration is the desire to minimize hassle—and then hoping for the best. This tendency to make choices that consistently favor immediate and tangible gratifying action while ignoring long-term consequences is called low self-control (Gottfredson & Hirschi, 1990), and theory and research has linked low self-control to victimization as well as crime (Schreck, 1999; Turanovic & Pratt, 2019). Low self-control thus not only frees people to commit crime, but it makes criminal attempts upon them easier, less risky, and more rewarding for other offenders. Before an incident, low self-control makes immediately gratifying behavior more attractive, and makes the prospect of victimization appear less certain than it actually is (thus safety less important a consideration). Being less willing to take precautions does not mean that those with low self-control want victimization, but that they will defer defensive action as far as they can into the future—quite possibly, the moment they realize they are in fact the intended target. That is, people with low self-control feel safer because they overestimate their ability to manage a potential offender in the immediate situation, while discounting the offender's opportunism and tendency only to act when the odds of success and escape appear favorable. As a result, precautionary behavior seems harder, more tedious, and pointless. Only precautions that are immediately gratifying, like carrying a weapon, have any attraction. During an incident, low self-control makes the target more likely to be injured; it fosters the delusion that fight or flight is realistic when it is not. Afterward, low self-control makes the target less likely to learn from the incident and make appropriate safety-minded changes.

Low self-control is not the only cause of vulnerability, but the concept offers a parsimonious account for the victim–offender correlation. Since low self-control tends to result in decisions that are ultimately dangerous to physical health and future prospects and that are disruptive of relationships with others (e.g., Moffitt et al., 2011), besides being illegal, choice theory thus has no problem predicting that offenders and victims will share the same correlates. Both victims and offenders are more likely to feel no particular closeness to their parents (Hirschi, 1969; Lauritsen et al., 1992; Schreck et al., 2002). Like high rate offenders, repeat victims are more likely to catch communicable diseases and die prematurely (Pridemore & Berg, 2017). Victims and offenders are both more likely to have criminal friends (Haynie, 2001; Schreck, Fisher, & Miller, 2004). Both victims and offenders tend to spend time engaged in activity with peers away from adult supervision (Lauritsen et al., 1991; Osgood, Wilson, O'Malley, Bachman, & Johnston, 1996). Frequent victims and offenders also do not appear to learn from their previous mistakes, going on to further offending and victimization (Lauritsen & Quinet, 1995; Schreck, Stewart, & Fisher, 2006). Further, since vulnerability and criminality both emerge from low self-control, choice theory views offending and victimization as *spuriously* correlated. Victimization does not improve or worsen an offender's judgment (e.g., Schreck, Berg, Ousey, Stewart, & Miller, 2017; Schreck et al., 2006) any more than offending makes one better or worse at avoiding criminal predation. From the perspective of choice theory, placing victimization among the list of explanatory variables of crime is illegitimate.

### *The Setting and Vulnerability*

The question now turns to those who nevertheless take all the precautions that their circumstances allow and yet become victims. Thanks to human nature, there is never perfect safety. Innocuous acts, as well as those essential for survival and prosperity, are calculated risks. All decision makers have to prioritize competing interests and otherwise uncontroversial choices—like leaving the house to go to work—can create windows of opportunity for offenders. For instance, burglars prefer empty homes (Cohen & Felson, 1979; Mayhew, 1987). The *idea of vulnerability* thus must acknowledge the innocent victim (e.g., Schreck, Stewart, & Osgood, 2008), people who commit no crimes and yet become victims. The choice perspective is therefore friendly to situational crime theories (e.g., Felson, 1994), as they share the same assumptions but with the setting as the unit of analysis rather than the individual. Each setting has characteristics that influence the base-rate of risk. For instance, Poyner and Webb (1991) found that homes that faced each other directly from across the street, thus improving natural surveillance, had less burglary than those that were staggered. Non-criminals who live in a severely disadvantaged, high-crime area will tend to experience more victimization irrespective of their choices—a higher concentration of offenders makes the detection and exploitation of even momentary defects in precautions more likely—although offenders will experience still more (Stewart, Schreck, & Simons, 2006). Nevertheless, evidence shows that non-criminal residents will still try to minimize their exposure (Skogan & Maxfield, 1981; Teitelman et al., 2010). In neighborhoods with a smaller preponderance of people who endorse a code of honor organized around violent behavior, which would arguably have a higher preponderance of those with low self-control, victims are more likely to be non-offender victims (Berg, Stewart, Schreck, & Simons, 2012). In this way, the situation acts upon the individual just as the individual acts upon the situation (Gottfredson, 2011).

## Conclusion

There can be little question that criminological theories have seldom treated victim action as a problem for the offender. The historical record is clear that empirical findings about the similarity of offenders and victims (Wolfgang, 1958) and their correlates (Hindelang et al., 1978; Lauritsen et al., 1992) made little impression on theorists. To explain crime, the reasoning goes, one simply needs to understand the antecedents responsible for producing the offender; by implication, the offender's target is scientifically uninteresting. Only belatedly has victimization begun to attract the attention of any of the leading crime theorists (e.g., Agnew, 2002), and here victimization was only of interest insofar as research repeatedly proved it to be powerfully correlated with crime (see Lauritsen & Laub, 2007). What produced this intellectual orthodoxy? There is little question that substantive positivism has had far-reaching influence on criminological theory and its development (Hirschi & Gottfredson, 1990; Laub & Sampson, 1991). The rejection of a human nature, and the consequent assumption of determinism, naturally favors the creation of theories that differentiate offenders and victims. Pioneering substantive positivists were not shy about saying so (Schur, 1957; Sykes & Matza, 1957). The emergence of victimology as a field, and its concern with victim-blaming (Karmen, 2016), further reified this distinction.

Our view is that the intellectual orthodoxy that substantive positivism has fostered within criminology is mistaken, and that the victim and victimization represent topics of vital importance to the crime theorist. As it happens, every theory about offenders implies a corresponding theory of victimization. However much a crime theorist might insistently deny the victim, integrity to internal logic exposes such a position as false. A theory of crime specifies the meaning and consequences of victimization for humans and society (the *idea of victimization*). Any assertion a theory makes about the processes that produce an offender also defines the reasons offenders select some targets and take no action upon others (the *idea of vulnerability*). Both ideas flow logically from a theory's underlying assumptions about human nature. It follows from this that not only should crime theorists develop these ideas from their own theories going forward, but also that researchers should evaluate these theories according to their ability to accurately predict crucial facts concerning victimization. If a theory fails to make such predictions, or cannot even be made to do so (see, as one possible example, Blumstein, 1986), we believe that criminologists should treat that theory as falsified.

Substantive positivist theories, thanks to determinism, seem to us to take a clear position on victims: victims are not a problem for the offender. The choice perspective, which assumes that humans are rational and self-seeking, takes the opposite side: the offender will not act unless the target's behavior creates the incentive and offers confidence of success (which rarely happens). Indeed, the odds are usually so stacked against the offender that often, when they do act, they run away leaving their plans incomplete (see Perkins, Klaus, Bastian, & Cohen, 1996). The assumption of determinism, in substantive positivism, makes victims passive and defenseless by default. Choice theory, in contrast, thanks to its assumption of a hedonistic human nature, perceives people as active decision makers who in some fashion understand victimization well enough to want nothing to do with it. (The theory does not argue that their actions guarantee safety, only that they will take such action as seems best to them.) Substantive positivism, having enfeebled the victim, emphasizes only the offender and distant motivational causes. Choice theories, seeing both offenders and victims as active decision makers, considers both to be important and prioritizes the concrete realities of the immediate situation. In substantive positivism, victimization has no inherently damaging effects on society, and instead it is simply an aspect of some forms of social organization. As far as victims go, those who rule society are free to take them or leave them. Choice theory takes the position that victimization is injurious to society, and that any society valuing its credibility will try to protect its members.

With respect to the *idea of vulnerability*, substantive positivism and choice theory again take contrary positions. In substantive positivist theories, understanding the offender's motivation is all that is necessary to ascertain who is vulnerable. Cultural deviance models provide the clearest contrast to choice theory, and here one can only conclude that precautions on the part of the victim are irrelevant to vulnerability unless, by chance, the offender defines some arbitrary symbol as an invitation to stop. Vulnerability becomes a function of offender motivation—in some cases, cultural norms require a person to attack someone of a higher social class, in other cases it can be some other trait. Cultural deviance models give the theorist no a priori expectation that victims and offenders will be the same people, and suggest that identification in each group requires different correlates; predictions victim data in fact refute. In choice theory, however, offenders everywhere want easy, certain, and immediate benefits and they are not especially choosey. Anyone in the moment who can supply these will be vulnerable. Vulnerability arises partly from the fact that routine decisions necessary simply to exist involve risks and sacrifices in security; sometimes, these are calculated. In this respect, choice theory allows for innocent victims—people who do not commit crime, who generally make minimally risky decisions, but become victims. Choice theory has no essential quarrel with situational crime theories where each setting presents a base level of victimization risk affecting everyone (Felson, 1994). Vulnerability also arises because people act upon their setting just as the setting acts upon them, and on occasion pursue gratifying behavior to the point they alert would-be offenders to their presence and simplify the risks and difficulty of a crime to manageable levels. Having low self-control does not mean that people want victimization, but it does mean that they are more likely to express such tendencies consistently and thereby become victims (Schreck, 1999). Since low self-control is of obvious relevance to crime (Gottfredson & Hirschi, 1990), choice theory thus accounts for the correlation between the two. Low self-control, in predicting all manner of injurious outcomes arising from bad judgment, also accounts for the shared substantive correlates of offending and victimization.

In light of the consistency between theoretical claims and what data show, we believe that choice theory represents the most promising direction forward. We, of course, did not examine the perspective of every major crime theory, such as those from biological or psychological positivism, the life course and developmental conceptual schemes, or theories with alternative conceptions of human nature from those we consider here (Agnew, 2014; Sampson & Laub, 2005; Tittle, 1995). If any perspective aligns with substantive positivism, we are skeptical that it can meaningfully contribute to new ideas of victimization and vulnerability.[11] Agnew's (2014) idea of altruistic social concern as an aspect of human nature, for instance, is intriguing in that it—on paper—moves his theory beyond substantive positivism or choice and into a different realm altogether. In our admittedly cursory estimation, however, the theory remains a straightforward integrated model. Social concern is cast in the causal diagram as an aspect of human nature that is acted upon by biological factors as well as traditional criminological concepts—effectively making human nature simply another variable. This notion of malleable human nature has also appeared elsewhere (e.g., Sampson & Laub, 2005). Like Cullen (2017), in his criticism of agency, we are not opposed to efforts to develop these lines and are interested in seeing where they lead; however, we are not sure that these perspectives would incorporate ideas of victimization and vulnerability more efficiently than other integrated crime theories, let alone choice theory. We also do not assert that our conception of victimization and vulnerability represent the final, definitive version even for the choice perspective. We do believe that useful progress will come from critics and researchers who are prepared to develop these ideas with the assumptions of choice theory in mind, rather than from those insisting choice theory make concessions to substantive positivism (Hirschi & Gottfredson, 2008).

Our object was to develop the implications of substantive positivism for ideas of victimization and vulnerability, and contrast these with those suggested by choice theory. In developing these ideas, we would remind readers of Kornhauser (1963), who wrote in her critique of criminological theory "it is not claimed that any particular theorist in either camp is necessarily aware of these assumptions; on the contrary, the views just outlined are almost entirely implicit rather than explicit" (quoted in Hirschi, 1996, pp. 251–252). Because intellectual orthodoxy is by definition pervasive, scholars simply accept its strictures without realizing it and so fail to reflect on the wisdom behind their reasons for doing so. The fact that assumptions pass unnoticed does not mean they are not there and cannot be brought into the light. Hirschi (1996) went on:

> [Kornhauser] thought it unnecessary to ask permission before listing the "logical presuppositions" of theories, and she said so… [Substantive positivist theorists], in contrast, would require that analysts restrict their attention to assumptions stated as such by the theorist as constituent, explicit elements of the theory. Which of these views is more likely to advance theoretical understanding of crime? On the evidence, it seems to me, Kornhauser's perspective is decidedly superior. Armed with their ideas and assumptions, she can predict what…theorists will say before they say it.

This was our inspiration. Substantive positivists may see things differently from us, but now they will have to commit themselves to a clear position in print and give their reasons, exposing formerly unstated ideas and assumptions to scrutiny and, in so doing, advancing theoretical understanding and debate.[12]

## Notes

1 The authors are grateful for the constructive comments from Frank Cullen, Marcus Felson, Michael Gottfredson, Steven Messner, Pamela Wilcox, and Lieven Pauwels. Please direct correspondence to Christopher J. Schreck (cjsgcj@rit.edu).

2 Wolfgang's results on the similarity of victims and offenders only influenced the development of his own theory (see Amir, 1971; Singer, 1981, 1986). A rare exception to this pattern is the chapter on the nature of crime in Gottfredson and Hirschi's (1990) *A General Theory of Crime*. Victims were not the central focus, but it is obvious that they saw victim actions as materially influencing the calculations of the offender.

3 That is to say, if victimization has no fixed or automatic meaning, it follows that a person or group conceivably might aspire to become, say, a murder or robbery victim (see, for instance, Amir, 1971). As further evidence, the substantive positivist definition of crime is logically consistent with what determinism implies about victimization. As one put it, "It is vain to seek the causes of crime, as such, anywhere and everywhere. Crime is a legal category. The only thing that is alike in all crimes is that they are alike violations of the law … It has no inherent quality or property attaching to it" (MacIver, 1942, p. 88). Substantive positivists therefore built their theories of crime causation around explanatory variables (like culture, anomie, and strain) as they relate to the offender, antecedents that critics have noted to be far distant from the criminal act itself (Hirschi & Gottfredson, 1990; Matza, 1964). We noted at the beginning that the victim is a central participant in the events surrounding this very act. By thus

assuming crime possesses only arbitrary qualities, victimization becomes theoretically unimportant.

4 From Hirschi (1996): "Sutherland was so wedded to logical determinism that he reaffirmed his allegiance in the first sentence introducing his famous theory. 'A scientific explanation consists of a description of the conditions which are always present when the phenomenon occurs and which are never present when the phenomenon does not occur." Enrico Ferri (1905), one of the founders of substantive positivism, saw the phenomenon of crime as akin to fixed physical laws: "The level of crime each year is determined by different conditions of the physical and social environment … in accordance with a law, which, in analogy to the law of chemistry, I have called the law of criminal saturation. As a given volume of water at a definite temperature will dissolve a fixed quantity of chemical substance and not an atom more or less; so in a given social environment … a fixed number of delicts, no more and no less, can be committed." Arthur Schopenhauer (2012) could not have been more succinct: "Accordingly, the whole course of a man's life, in all its incidents great and small, is as necessarily predetermined as the course of a clock." If a criminological theory does not speak to the actions of the victim, and almost none do, it is because the theorist has no reason to think that the victim matters.

5 This does not mean that society will offer equal protection to all members, as political leaders will enact and enforce criminal laws as their understanding of personal and organizational advantage dictate. Politically and economically marginal groups thus may see political authorities prepared to tolerate criminal acts against them, such as historically with wife-beatings or lynchings; the further alienation from society of already marginal groups produces little cost for the politician. This is how choice theory might account for the well-known social construction of victimization phenomenon, where formerly tolerated actions become acknowledged as a societal concern and made illegal (Brownstein, 1994).

6 Note the contrast with the robbery script, noted earlier, in which targets behave very differently. Cultural deviance perspectives assume no consistency in responses to criminally injurious actions, which agrees with our point that the meaning of "victimization" to the victim in Anderson's account is a product of exposure to socialization rather than any inherent quality common to all acts of victimization.

7 This is a somewhat more confusing point in cultural deviance theory. *Theoretically*, the offender (or the offender's imagination) is always the cause. See, for instance, Weis and Borges' (1973, p. 80) response to Amir's (1971) claim that "In a way, the victim is always the cause." But Amir is correct, too. From the perspective of the offender, in cultural deviance theory, something about the *victim* is always the cause.

8 One can see fundamentally similar ideas repeated under various guises even into the present—where offenders respond to perceptions (or, more accurately, delusions) brought on by prior socialization or happenstance exposure to social structures rather than objective realities (Grasmick, Tittle, Bursik, & Arneklev, 1993; Matsueda, Kreager, & Huizinga, 2006).

9 We here remind readers of our earlier comment how this seemingly innocuous concession to choice theory creates a logical problem that obviates the value of the remaining tenets of general strain theory—in particular, the assertion that offenders act when the source of strain is important to them. Assertions

such as these preclude an *idea of victimization*; the offender, once they have formed the intention to commit a crime thanks to this motivation, is no longer constrained by any defense or difficulty. Offenders create their own opportunities (Gottfredson & Hirschi, 2003; Gottfredson & Hirschi, 2019). Put differently, as we will show, one can conceive of general strain theory as what a choice theory would look like after being burdened with unnecessary and misleading concepts.

10 The theory also would suggest that people who find precautions (automatic or otherwise) to be a source of delay, with respect to addressing what they understand to be more immediate concerns, might even go as far as to deactivate or circumvent them if they can. For instance, the idea of swiftness implies that someone who is using a smartphone can grow frustrated with lags from frequent automatic security subroutines or demands from the operating system to install updates.

11 For reasons of space, we also omitted macro-level explanations of crime, namely classic strain and social disorganization. Recent applications of strain models continue to fail to acknowledge an *idea of victimization* (e.g., Rosenfeld, 2017); in these accounts, social structure does not appear to affect or even inspire victim resistance. Ideas of victimization do have interesting implications. For instance, precautionary behavior might be considered a very compelling part of the cultural expression of legitimate means, or even a satisfying reason why most anomic persons choose conformity over crime. But, as Kornhauser (1978) wrote, the strain theorist likely cannot do so because shifting the focus of the offender from the benefits of crime to include the costs and difficulty would makes strain models into control theories. Disorganization models, by contrast, imply that social structures exist, at least in part, to resist the activity of offenders. The question of ideas of victimization and vulnerability is worth exploring, since strain theories continue to retain currency (Agnew, Cullen, Burton Jr., Evans, & Dunaway, 1996; Burton Jr., Cullen, Evans, & Dunaway, 1994; Cullen & Messner, 1997; Messner & Rosenfeld, 1994).

12 The passage of time makes it difficult to fully appreciate Kornhauser's (1978) importance and the impact of her work on making theorists reconsider (or "clarify") the structure and assumptions of their theories. See, for instance, reactions her work has provoked (e.g., Akers, 1996; Bernard, 1984, 1987; Cullen, Wilcox, Sampson, & Dooley, 2015; Matsueda, 1988).

## References

Addington, L. A. (2008). *Current issues in victimization research and the NCVS's ability to study them*. Prepared for presentation at the Bureau of Justice Statistics Data User's Workshop, February 12, Washington, DC. Retrieved from https://bjs.gov/content/pub/pdf/Addington.pdf

Agnew, R. (1992). Foundation for a general strain theory of crime and delinquency. *Criminology*, *30*, 47–88.

Agnew, R. (2002). Experienced, vicarious, and anticipated strain: An exploratory study on physical victimization and delinquency. *Justice Quarterly*, *19*, 603–632.

Agnew, R. (2007). *Pressured into crime: An overview of general strain theory*. New York: Oxford University Press.

Agnew, R. (2012). Reflection on "A revised strain theory of delinquency." *Social Forces*, *91*, 33–38.
Agnew, R. (2014). Social concern and crime: Moving beyond the assumption of simple self-interest. *Criminology*, *52*, 1–32.
Agnew, R., Cullen, F. T., Burton Jr., V. S., Evans, T. D., & Dunaway, R. G. (1996). A new test of classic strain theory. *Justice Quarterly*, *13*, 681–704.
Akers, R. L. (1996). Is differential association theory/social learning cultural deviance theory? *Criminology*, *34*, 229–247.
Akers, R. L., Sellers, C. S., & Jennings, W. G. (2016). *Criminological theories: Introduction, evaluation, and application.* New York: Oxford University.
Akers, R. L., Krohn, M. D., Lanza-Kaduce, L., & Radosevich, M. (1979). Social learning and deviant behavior. *American Sociological Review*, *44*, 636–655.
Amir, M. (1967). Victim precipitated forcible rape. *Journal of Criminal Law, Criminology, and Police Science*, *58*, 493–502.
Amir, M. (1971). *Patterns of forcible rape.* Chicago: University of Chicago.
Anderson, E. (1999). *Code of the street.* New York: Norton.
Azar, S. T. (1991). Models of child abuse: A metatheoretical analysis. *Criminal Justice and Behavior*, *18*, 30–46.
Baumer, E., Horney, J., Felson, R. B., & Lauritsen, J. L. (2003). Neighborhood disadvantage and the nature of violence. *Criminology*, *41*, 39–72.
Beccaria, C. (1963 [1764]). *On crimes and punishments.* Indianapolis: Bobbs-Merrill.
Bentham, J. (1970 [1789]). *An introduction to the principles of morals and legislation.* London: Athlone.
Berg, M. T. (2012). The overlap of violent offending and violent victimization: Assessing the evidence and explanations. In M. Delisi & P. Conis (Eds.), *Violent offenders: Theory, research, policy, and practice* (pp. 17–38). Burlington, MA: Jones and Bartlett.
Berg, M., Stewart, E., Schreck, C., & Simons, R. (2012). The victim-offender overlap in context: Examining the role of neighborhood street culture. *Criminology*, *50*, 359–290.
Bernard, T. J. (1984). Control criticisms of strain theories: An assessment of theoretical and empirical adequacy. *Journal of Research in Crime and Delinquency*, *21*, 353–372.
Bernard, T. J. (1987). Testing structural strain theories. *Journal of Research in Crime and Delinquency*, *24*, 262–280.
Bernard, T. J., & Snipes, J. B. (1996). Theoretical integration in criminology. *Crime and Justice*, *20*, 301–348.
Bernard, T. J., Snipes, J. B., Gerould, A. L., & Vold, G. B. (2015). *Vold's theoretical criminology.* New York: Oxford University.
Best, J. (1997). Victimization and the victim industry. *Society*, *34*, 9–17.
Blumstein, A. (1986). *Criminal careers and career criminals.* Washington DC: National Academy Press.
Braithwaite, J. (1990). *Crime, shame, and reintegration.* New York: Cambridge University Press.
Brownstein, H. H. (1994). *The social reality of violence and violent crime.* Needham Heights, MA: Allyn and Bacon.
Bryant, C. (1985). *Positivism in social theory and research.* New York: St. Martin's Press.

Burton Jr., V. S., Cullen, F. T., Evans, T. D., & Dunaway, R. G. (1994). Reconsidering strain theory: Operationalization, rival theories, and adult criminality. *Journal of Quantitative Criminology*, *10*, 213–239.

Clarke, R. (1995). Situational crime prevention. In M. Tonry & D. Farrington (Eds.), *Crime & justice* (pp. 91–150). Chicago: University of Chicago Press.

Cloward, R., & Ohlin, L. (1960). *Delinquency and opportunity: A theory of delinquent gangs.* New York: Free Press.

Cohen, A. K. (1955). *Delinquent boys.* Glencoe, IL: Free Press.

Cohen, L., & Felson, M. (1979). Social change and crime rate trends: A routine activity approach. *American Journal of Sociology*, *86*, 90–118.

Cornish, D., & Clarke, R. (1986). *The reasoning criminal: Rational choice perspectives on offending.* New York: Springer-Verlag.

Cressey, D. R. (1954). The differential association theory and compulsive crimes. *Journal of Criminal Law, Criminology and Police Science*, *45*, 29–40.

Cullen, F. T. (2017). Choosing our criminological future: Reservations about human agency as an organizing concept. *Journal of Developmental and Life Course Criminology*, *3*, 373–379.

Cullen, F. T., & Messner, S. F. (1997). The making of criminology revisited: An oral history of Merton's anomie paradigm. *Theoretical Criminology*, *11*, 5–37.

Cullen, F. T., Wilcox, P., Sampson, R., & Dooley, B. (2015). *Challenging criminological theory: The legacy of Ruth Rosner Kornhauser.* New Brunswick, NJ: Transaction.

Durkheim, E. (1982 [1895]). *The rules of sociological method.* New York: The Free Press.

Elliott, D. S., Huizinga, D., & Ageton, S. S. (1985). *Explaining delinquency and drug use.* Beverly Hills, CA: Sage.

Feinberg, J. (1984). *Harm to others: The moral limits of the criminal law.* New York: Oxford University Press.

Felson, M. K. (1994). *Crime and everyday life: Insights and implications for society.* Thousand Oaks, CA: Sage.

Felson, M. K., & Eckert, M. (2018). *Introductory criminology: The study of risky situations.* New York: Routledge.

Felson, R. B. (1991). Blame analysis: Accounting for the behavior of protected groups. *The American Sociologist*, *22*, 5–23.

Felson, R. B., Berg, M. T., Rogers, E. M., & Krajewski, A. (2018). Disputatiousness and the offender-victim overlap. *Journal of Research in Crime and Delinquency*, *55*, 351–389.

Felson, R. B., Savolainen, J., Berg, M. T., & Ellonen, N. (2013). Does spending time in public settings contribute to the adolescent risk of violent victimization. *Journal of Quantitative Criminology*, *29*, 273–293.

Ferraro, K. (1995). *Fear of crime: Interpreting victimization risk.* Albany, NY: State University of New York Press.

Ferri, E. (1905). *Criminal sociology.* Boston: Little, Brown, and Company.

Fisher, B. S., Sloan, J. J., Cullen, F. T., & Lu, C. (1998). Crime in the ivory tower: The level and sources of student victimization. *Criminology*, *36*, 671–710.

Gondolf, E., & Fisher, E. (1988). *Battered women as survivors: An alternative to treating learned helplessness.* Lexington, MA: D.C. Health and Co.

Gottfredson, M. R. (1984). *Victims of crime: The dimensions of risk.* London: Home Office.

Gottfredson, M. R. (2011). Sanctions, situations, and agency in control theories of crime. *European Journal of Criminology*, *8*, 128–143.

Gottfredson, M. R., & Hirschi, T. (1990). *A general theory of crime.* Palo Alto, CA: Stanford University.

Gottfredson, M., & Hirschi, T. (2003). Self-control and opportunity. In C. Britt & M. Gottfredson (Eds.), *Advances in criminological theory* (pp. 5–19). New Brunswick, NJ: Transaction.

Gottfredson, M., & Hirschi, T. (2019). *Modern control theory and the limits of criminal justice.* New York: Oxford.

Grasmick, H., Tittle, C., Bursik Jr., R., & Arneklev, B. (1993). Testing the core empirical implications of Gottfredson and Hirschi's general theory of crime. *Journal of Research in Crime and Delinquency*, *30*, 5–29.

Haynie, D. L. (2001). Delinquent peers revisited: Does network structure matter? *American Journal of Sociology*, *106*, 1013–1057.

Hindelang, M., Gottfredson, M., & Garofalo, J. (1978). *Victims of personal crime.* Cambridge, MA: Ballinger.

Hirschi, T. (1969). *Causes of delinquency.* Berkeley CA: University of California.

Hirschi, T. (1979). Separate and unequal is better. *Journal of Research in Crime and Delinquency*, *16*, 34–38.

Hirschi, T. (1987). Review of Explaining Delinquency and Drug Use by Delbert S. Elliott, David Huizinga, and Suzanne S. Ageton. *Criminology*, *25*, 193–202.

Hirschi, T. (1989). Exploring alternatives to integrated theory. In S. Messner, M. Krohn, & A. Liska (Eds.), *Theoretical integration in the study of crime and deviance* (pp. 37–49). Albany, NY: State University of New York Press.

Hirschi, T. (1996). Theory without ideas: Reply to Akers. *Criminology*, *34*, 249–256.

Hirschi, T., & Gottfredson, M. (1990). Substantive positivism and the idea of crime. *Rationality and Society*, *2*, 412–428.

Hirschi, T., & Gottfredson, M. R. (1995). Control theory and the life-course perspective. *Studies on Crime & Crime Prevention*, *4*, 131–142.

Hirschi, T., & Gottfredson, M. R. (2008). Critiquing the critics. In E. Goode (Ed.), *Out of control: Assessing the general theory of crime* (pp. 217–232). Palo Alto, CA: Stanford University.

Jensen, G. F., & Brownfield, D. (1986). Gender, lifestyles, and victimization: Beyond routine activity theory. *Violence and Victims*, *1*, 85–99.

Jewkes, R. (2002). Intimate Partner Violence: Causes and Prevention. *The Lancet*, *359*, 1423–1429.

Johnson, R. E. (1979). *Juvenile delinquency and its origins.* Cambridge, UK: Cambridge University.

Jost, J. T. (1995). Negative illusions: Conceptual clarification and psychological evidence concerning false consciousness. *Political Psychology*, *16*, 397–424.

Karmen, A. (2016). *Crime victims: An introduction to victimology, 9th Edition.* Boston, MA: Cengage.

Kleck, G. (1988). Crime control through the private use of armed force. *Social Problems*, *35*, 1–21.

Kornhauser, R. R. (1978). *Social sources of delinquency: An appraisal of analytic models.* Chicago: University of Chicago.

Krulichová, E., & Podana, Z. (2018). Adolescent fear of crime: Testing Ferraro's risk interpretation model. *European Journal of Criminology*, *16*, 746–766.

Laub, J. H., & Sampson, R. J. (1991). The Sutherland-Glueck debate: On the sociology of criminological knowledge. *American Journal of Sociology*, *96*, 1402–1440.

Lauritsen, J. (2005). Explaining patterns of offending across the life course: Comments on interactional theory and recent tests based on the RYDS-RIS data. *Annals of the American Academy of Political and Social Science*, *602*, 212–228.

Lauritsen, J. L., & Davis-Quinet, K. (1995). Repeat victimization among adolescents and young adults. *Journal of Quantitative Criminology*, *11*, 143–166.

Lauritsen, J. L., & Laub, J. H. (2007). Understanding the link between victimization and offending: New reflections on an old idea. *Crime Prevention Studies*, *22*, 55–76.

Lauritsen, J. L., Laub, J. H., & Sampson, R. J. (1992). Conventional and delinquent activites: Implications for the prevention of violent victimization among adolescents. *Violence and Victims*, *7*, 91–108.

Lauritsen, J. L., Sampson, R. J., & Laub, J. H. (1991). The link between offending and victimization among adolescents. *Criminology*, *29*, 265–292.

Lyng, S. (1990). Edgework: A social psychological analysis of voluntary risk taking. *American Journal of Sociology*, *95*, 851–886.

Matsueda, R. L. (1988). The current state of differential association theory. *Crime & Delinquency*, *34*, 277–306.

Matsueda, R., & Anderson, K. (1998). The dynamics of delinquent peers and delinquent behavior. *Criminology*, *36*, 269–308.

Matsueda, R., Kreager, D., & Huizinga, D. (2006). Deterring delinquents: A rational choice model of theft and violence. *American Sociological Review*, *71*, 95–122.

Matza, D. (1964). *Delinquency and drift.* New York: John Wiley & Sons.

Mayhew, P. (1987). *Residential burglary: A comparison of the United States, Canada, and England and Wales.* Washington DC: National Institute of Justice.

McIver, R. M. (1942). *Social causation.* Boston: Ginn and Co.

Meier, R. F., & Miethe, T. D. (1993). Understanding theories of criminal victimization. *Crime and Justice*, *17*, 459–499.

Merton, R. K. (1938). Social structure and anomie. *American Sociological Review*, *3*, 672–682.

Messner, S., & Rosenfeld, R. (1994). *Crime and the American Dream.* Belmont, CA: Thomson.

Miethe, T., & Meier, R. (1990). Opportunity, choice, and criminal victimization: A test of a theoretical model. *Journal of Research in Crime and Delinquency*, *27*, 243–266.

Mills, C. W. (1956). *The power elite.* New York: Oxford.

Moffitt, T. E. (1992). Adolescence-limited and life-course-persistent antisocial behavior: A developmental taxonomy. *Psychological Review*, *100*, 674–701.

Moffitt, T. E., Arsenault, L., Belsky, D., Dickson, N., Hancox, R., Harrington, H., … Sears, M. (2011). A gradient of childhood self-control predicts health, wealth, and public safety. *Proceedings of the National Academy of Sciences*, *108*, 2693–2698.

Osgood, D. W., Wilson, J. K., O'Malley, P. M., Bachman, J. G., & Johnston, L. D. (1996). Routine activities and individual deviant behavior. *American Sociological Review*, *61*, 635–655.

Perkins, C., Klaus, P., Bastian, L., & Cohen, R. (1996). *Criminal victimization in the United States, 1993.* Washington DC: US Department of Justice.

Peterson, C., & Seligman, M. E. (1983). Learned helplessness and victimization. *Journal of Social Issues*, *39*, 103–116.

Pfohl, S. J. (1994). *Images of deviance and social control: A sociological history.* New York: McGraw-Hill.

Posick, C. (2013). The overlap between offending and victimization among adolescents: Results from the second International Self-Report Delinquency Study. *Journal of Contemporary Criminal Justice*, *29*, 106–124.

Poyner, B., & Webb, B. (1991). *Crime free housing.* Oxford, UK: Butterworth.

Pridemore, W. A., & Berg, M. T. (2017). What is past is prologue: A population-based case-control study of repeat victimization, premature mortality, and homicide. *Aggressive Behavior*, *43*, 176–189.

Rosenfeld, R. (2017). *Studying crime trends: Normal science and exogenous shocks*. Sutherland Award Address to the American Society of Criminology, Philadelphia, PA.

Roshier, B. (1989). *Controlling crime: The classical perspective in criminology.* Chicago: Lyceum Books.

Rountree, P. W. (1998). A reexamination of the crime-fear linkage. *Journal of Research in Crime and Delinquency*, *35*, 341–372.

Sampson, R. J., & Laub, J. H. (1993). *Crime in the making: Pathways and turning points through life.* Cambridge, MA: Harvard University.

Sampson, R. J., & Laub, J. H. (2005). A general age-graded theory of crime: Lessons learned and the future of life-course criminology. In D. F. Farrington (Ed.), *Integrated developmental & life-course theories of offending: Advances in criminological theory, volume 14* (pp. 165–182). New York: Routledge.

Sampson, R., Raudenbush, S., & Earls, F. (1997). Neighborhoods and violent crime: A multilevel study of collective efficacy. *Science*, *277*, 918–924.

Schafer, S. (1968). *The victim and his criminal.* New York: Random House.

Schopenhauer, A. (2012). *On human nature: Essays in ethics and politics* (T. B. Saunders, Trans.). Mineola, NY: Dover Publications.

Schreck, C. J. (1999). Criminal victimization and low self-control: An extension and test of a general theory of crime. *Justice Quarterly*, *16*, 633–654.

Schreck, C. J., & Fisher, B. (2004). Specifying the influence of family and peers on violent victimization: Extending routine activity and lifestyles theories. *Journal of Interpersonal Violence*, *19*, 1021–1041.

Schreck, C. J., Berg, M. T., Fisher, B. S., & Wilcox, P. (2018). That door you just kicked in was locked for your protection, not mine: Developing and testing competing theoretical models of crime prevention behavior. *Journal of Research in Crime and Delinquency*, *55*, 316–345.

Schreck, C. J., Berg, M. T., Ousey, G. C., Stewart, E. A., & Miller, J. M. (2017). Does the nature of the victim-offending association fluctuate over the life course? An examination of adolescence and early adulthood. *Crime and Delinquency*, *63*, 786–813.

Schreck, C. J., Fisher, B., & Miller, J. (2004). The social context of violent victimization: A study of the delinquent peer effect. *Justice Quarterly*, *21*, 23–47.

Schreck, C. J., Stewart, E. A., & Fisher, B. S. (2006). Self-control, victimization, and their influence on risky lifestyles: A longitudinal analysis using panel data. *Journal of Quantitative Criminology*, *22*, 319–340.

Schreck, C. J., Stewart, E. A., & Osgood, D. W. (2008). A reappraisal of the overlap of violent offenders and victims. *Criminology*, *46*, 871–906.

Schreck, C. J., Wright, R. A., & Miller, J. M. (2002). A study of individual and situational antecedents of violent victimization. *Justice Quarterly*, *19*, 159–180.

Schur, E. M. (1957). Sociological analysis of confidence swindling. *Journal of Criminal Law, Criminology, and Police Science*, *48*, 296–304.

Sellin, T. (1938). Culture conflict and crime. *American Journal of Sociology*, *44*, 97–103.

Shaw, C., & McKay, H. (1942). *Juvenile delinquency in urban areas.* Chicago: University of Chicago.

Singer, S. I. (1981). Homogeneous victim-offender populations: A review and some research implications. *Journal of Criminal Law and Criminology*, *72*, 779–788.

Singer, S. I. (1986). Victims of serious violence and their criminal behavior: Subcultural theory and beyond. *Violence and Victims*, *1*, 61–70.

Skogan, W. G., & Maxfield, M. G. (1981). *Coping with crime: Individual and neighborhood reactions.* Thousand Oaks, CA: Sage.

Steffensmeier, D., & Allan, E. (1996). Gender and crime: Toward a gendered theory of female offending. *Annual Review of Sociology*, *22*, 459–487.

Stewart, E. A., Schreck, C. J., & Simons, R. L. (2006). I ain't gonna let no one disrespect me: Does the code of the street reduce or increase violent victimization among African-American adolescents. *Journal of Research in Crime and Delinquency*, *43*, 427–458.

Straus, M. (1999). The controversy over domestic violence by women: A methodological, theoretical, and sociology of science analysis. In X. Arriaga & S. Oskamp (Eds.), *Violence in intimate relationships* (pp. 17–44). Thousand Oaks, CA: Sage.

Sutherland, E. (1937). *The professional thief.* Chicago: University of Chicago.

Sutherland, E. (1947). *Principles of criminology.* Philadelphia: Lippencott.

Sutherland, E. H. (1956). *The sutherland papers.* A. K. Cohen, A. R. Lindesmith, & K. Schuessler (Eds). Bloomington, IN: Indiana University Press.

Sutherland, E. H., Geis, G., & Goff, C. (1983). *White collar crime: The uncut version.* New Haven, CT: Yale.

Sykes, G. M., & Matza, D. (1957). Techniques of neutralization: A theory of delinquency. *American Sociological Review*, *22*, 664–670.

Taylor, I., Walton, P., & Young, J. (1973). *The new criminology: For a social theory of deviance.* London: Routledge and Kegan Paul.

Tedeschi, J. T., & Felson, R. B. (1994). *Violence, aggression, and coercive actions.* Washington DC: American Psychological Association.

Teitelman, A., McDonald, C. C., Wiebe, D. J., Thomas, N., Guerra, T., Kassam-Adams, N., & Richmond, T. S. (2010). Youth's strategies for staying safe and coping. *Journal of Community Psychology*, *38*, 874–885.

Thornberry, T. P. (1987). Toward an interactional theory of delinquency. *Criminology*, *25*, 863–892.

Tittle, C. (1995). *Control balance: Toward a general theory of deviance.* Boulder, CO: Westview.

Turanovic, J., & Pratt, T. (2019). *Thinking about victimization.* London: Routledge.

von Hentig, H. (1948). *The criminal & his victim.* New Haven, CT: Yale University.

Weis, K., & Borges, S. S. (1973). Victimology and rape: The case of the legitimate victim. *Issues in Criminology*, *8*, 71–115.

Wikstrom, P. O., Oberwittler, D., Treiber, K., & Hardie, B. (2012). *Breaking rules: The social and situational dynamics of young people's urban crime.* London: Oxford University.

Wilcox, P., Land, K. C., & Hunt, S. A. (2003). *Criminal circumstance: A dynamic, multi-contextual criminal opportunity theory*. New York: Aldine de Gruyter.

Wolfgang, M. (1958). *Patterns in criminal homicide*. London: University of Oxford.

Wolfgang, M., & Ferracuti, F. (1967). *Subculture of violence: Towards an integrated theory in criminology*. London: Travistock.

Wolfgang, M., & Singer, S. I. (1978). Victim categories of crime. *The Journal of Criminal Law and Criminology*, *69*, 379–394.

Wrong, D. (1961). The oversocialized conception of man in modern sociology. *American Sociological Review*, *26*, 183–193.

# 2

# Modern Control Theory, Lifestyle, and Criminal Victimization

*Michael R. Gottfredson*

Research on criminal victimization has made enormous strides in recent decades. The range of these contributions spans criminology and, at a minimum, includes basic measurement studies, offense-specific analyses of crime incidents and prevention methods, research on connections between early life-events and subsequent victimization experiences, studies of theories of crime and victimization, studies of victimization accomplished through social media and the internet, research about the consequences of victimization and social policies, and comparative or global studies of victimization. As a consequence, there is an increasingly rich source of findings from victimization scholars critical for evaluating basic explanations of crime (see, Turanovic & Pratt, 2019 for a comprehensive review and analysis). Given the centrality of these findings, criminology has an obligation to consider how they pertain to the scope and validity of putatively general theories of crime.

Although a thorough consideration of victimization work is well beyond what may be undertaken in a chapter, victimization research and theory have been integral to the development of modern control theory (e.g., Gottfredson & Hirschi, 1990, chapter 2; Gottfredson & Hirschi, 2019, chapter 6). Recent theoretical advances in victimization theory (Schreck,1999; Turanovic & Pratt, 2014; Turanovic & Pratt, 2019; Turanovic, Pratt, & Piquero, 2018) and in the application of control theory concepts to criminal victimization (Berg, 2012; Berg & Mulford, 2020; Nofziger, 2009; Schreck, 1999; Schreck, Berg, & Rogers, 2020;

Schreck & Berg, 2021; Turanovic & Pratt, 2019) demonstrate that considerable advances in crime theory can occur with ever-greater integration of victimization research with a broad range of theoretical issues in criminology.

Understanding crime from the perspective of victimization has had formative effects for some general theories. As Schreck (1999) and Schreck and Berg (2021) have effectively argued, victimization is an important perspective from which to judge the scope and validity of *all* general theoretical perspectives. Thus, it is timely to consider how modern control theory is situated with respect to some of the major trends in victimization scholarship. The purposes of this essay will be to consider briefly the connections between victimization and modern control theory, to discuss the importance of the victimization perspective for all etiological perspectives that aspire to generality, and to reinforce suggestions about the pursuit of further advances via this methodology (see, Schreck & Berg, 2021; Turanovic & Pratt, 2019).

From the impressive body of recent empirical victimization work, several conceptual advances and key research threads stand out for their impact and can serve as a platform for this discussion. These include the persistent finding of a correlation between offending and victimization (the so called "victim–offender overlap"); the relationship between causal theories of individual differences in propensity and those, including some victimization perspectives, that are said to ignore offender characteristics and instead focus exclusively on places, situations, or opportunities; the role of early childhood experiences and environments on subsequent victimization and offending; and finally, advances in considering the role of self- and informal controls when considering victimization. Each of these areas is the subject of important contemporary theoretical work, fundamental to advances in crime theory, and that justify the idea of the centrality of victimization research for basic theory in criminology. At the very least, these developments in victimization research and theory greatly enrich modern control theory in many ways, a topic we can develop subsequent to a brief description of our own general theory of crime (Gottfredson and Hirschi, 2019).[1]

## The Framework of Modern Control Theory

Figure 2.1 presents a simple schematic of important elements of modern control theory (Gottfredson & Hirschi, 2019) useful for thinking about how contemporary victimization work relates to the

**Figure 2.1**
**Schematic Depiction of Critical Elements of Modern Control Theory**

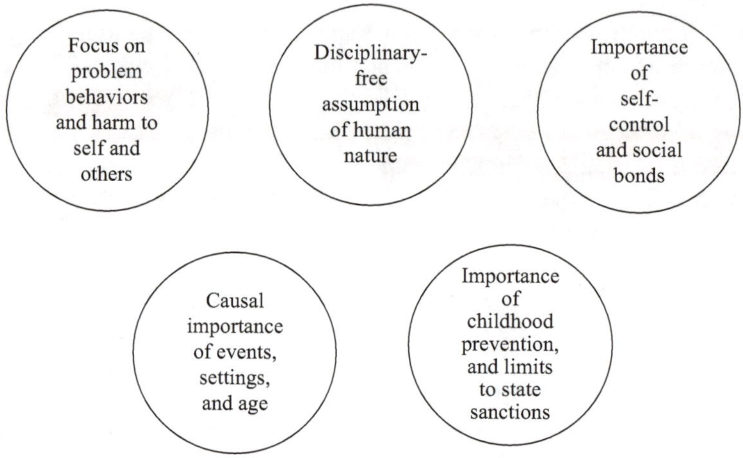


theory.[2] These key elements collectively differentiate our perspective from other theories of crime. They include how the dependent variable is conceptualized, the animating assumption of human nature providing for a cross-disciplinary focus on problem behaviors, a developmental focus beginning with early childhood, the accumulated evidence about the importance of self-control and informal social controls for understanding personal victimization, the importance of characteristics of events or settings as causes of crime, the importance of including a direct age effect in theories of crime, and the accumulating evidence from policy-related research about the comparative benefits of prevention early in life in contrast to policies focused on the criminal justice system. Taken together, these elements of our control theory of crime provide a logically consistent, empirically grounded general theory, one that, arguably, must be able to accommodate the principal contemporary victimization findings in order to be valid and have useful scope.

As with many perspectives originating in several disciplines, our control theory relies on the assumptions of choice and rationality. It is a theory of action, positing individual differences in a general disposition to pursue or delay immediate pleasures and to avoid personally painful acts as a significant cause of crime and delinquency, a tendency we refer to as self-control.[3] The assumption employed by control theory is not that people are naturally bad or immoral, but rather that they act rationally in their self-interest; it derives from the general theory of behavior suggesting that people will, absent restraints to the contrary, act in accordance with their view of self-interest. Self-control and social bonds (Hirschi, 1969) provide restraints to crime; yet, since these vary among people, people vary in the extent to which these restraints limit their acts that are harmful to others (and, ultimately, to self). A central feature of our control theory is that it incorporates a general, disciplinary-free definition of the dependent variable, one that is not synonymous with crimes as that term is often used in criminology or strictly with legal definitions for crime and delinquency. Rather, our focus is on *acts* that provide near-term benefits to the actor, but which can carry subsequent negative consequences. Such a definition permits inclusion of most behaviors that are violations of delinquency statutes and criminal laws (but not all), as well as many behaviors that cause harm, but which are not violations of criminal laws.

Using the concept of problem behaviors as the general focus for control theory, rather than restricting the focus of the theory to violations of the law ("crime"), enables the theory to logically incorporate a substantial body of empirical research from education, public health, psychology and economics that focus on other problem behaviors, including victimization, directly into criminology. Our theory also fosters the study of the causes of crime, delinquency, and victimization early in life, thus enabling thinking about behaviors or acts as the focus of attention, not on their age-dependent legal labels.

The development of strong social bonds and strong self-control create many life-long advantages for individuals and reduce the harms caused by victimization, both to the actor and to the victim. As there is a fundamental, substantial relationship between age and the frequency of creating these harms, generally preventing adolescent offenses is an especially important focus for both research and policy. (The general age distribution of crime can be summarized as rising rapidly through preadolescence, peaking in late adolescence or early adulthood, and then declining rapidly and then continuously throughout life.)

Preventing risky health behaviors and substance abuse and promoting educational success are key advantages of higher levels of self-control emerging from childhood, advantages that accrue across the life-course. The theory requires no special motivation for crime and delinquency other than the general pursuit of personal gains and avoidance of pains that are built into the acts themselves. All of the motives for human action thus can be and are, from time to time, motives for delinquency and crime, as is the desire to avoid experiences seen as unpleasant. This desire to avoid unpleasant consequences of acts includes sanctions by the state, as well as informal controls, or the restrictions or unpleasant experiences in everyday environments (such as schools and the disapproval of valued parents, family, teachers, and friends). It includes as well the immediate potential harms attendant on crime, including from the potential victim or "target" of the offense. For modern control theories, including our own, the concept of rationality is essentially the same as that employed by modern theories of opportunity in criminology (see, e.g., Clarke, 2018).

The concepts of self-control and the related idea in psychology of self-regulation are now among the most widely researched perspectives in several fields, from psychology and public health to education and criminology. Several systematic meta-analyses and general reviews of the role of self-control in predicting delinquency, crime, and victimization have found very substantial support for our perspective in the empirical literature (e.g., Nofziger, 2009; Pratt, 2016; Pratt & Cullen, 2000; Pratt, Turanovic, Fox, & Wright, 2014; Schreck, 1999; Vazsonyi, Mikuška, & Kelley, 2017; for general reviews, see Gottfredson & Hirschi, 2019, chapter 1).

Finally, modern control theory begins with the observation that crimes and delinquencies are events; they require for their occurrence an individual disposed to behave in ways that facilitates delinquent or criminal acts and also "targets" and "opportunities." For our own general theory, both individual dispositions and suitable situations are proximate causes of crime:

> In our theory, crimes have minimal elements over and above their benefits to the individual: for example, they require goods, services, victims, and opportunity, elements that do vary from time to time and place to place … crimes require more than individual tendencies for their performance. They also require goods, victims, physical abilities, and the absence of threats of immediate punishment. (Gottfredson & Hirschi, 1990, pp. 177–179)

The research on situational factors helping to explain crime has grown significantly. In addition to surveys of the activities of adolescents, it includes factors that range from making criminal events more difficult, to enhancing supervision, and making targets less attractive.

Of course, differences in self-control and in social bonds are themselves predictive of individual differences in opportunities as they are associated with daily activities and settings in which people interact. The very substantial self-selection (and selection by others) due to self-control differences into settings, peer or friendship groups, institutions (e.g., schools, marriages, jobs), leisure activities and the like, is highly pertinent to both victimization and offending. Untangling selection from the direct effects of settings and opportunities themselves is a challenging enterprise (as Wikström, Mann, and Hardie (2018) and Wikström, Oberwittler, Treiber, and Hardie (2012) have demonstrated). But situational crime explanations are not well specified when they neglect individual dispositions of potential offenders, as is sometimes advocated (e.g., Clarke, 2018; Felson & Clarke, 1998; Weisburd, Groff, & Yang, 2012). Theories that stipulate both types of these important proximate causes (propensities and events) provide stronger general theories for explanations of crime and victimization.

With these elements of modern control theory in mind, we can turn to the contemporary research and commentary on the several key issues in victimization theory identified above (and in Figure 2.1) to illustrate how they are important considerations for the theory.

## Control Theory, the Criminal Event, and the "Logical Requisite" Movement

Much has been accomplished in criminology due to the foundational insights of Cohen and Felson (1979) in their routine activity theory, Mayhew, Clarke, and Hough (1976) in developing opportunity theory, and Brantingham and Brantingham (1978, 1995) in presenting situational/ environmental theory. Each of these perspectives argue for the benefits of beginning criminological analysis with a conception of crime as an event, an event with the logical requisites of an intersection in time and space of an actor (or actors) possessing a propensity to offend, a target of interest, and a lack of restraints or impediments to the act. Our own basic theories have employed a similar idea, both with respect to victimization (Gottfredson, 1981, 1986; Hindelang, Gottfredson, & Garofalo, 1978) and to offending (Gottfredson & Hirschi, 1990, 2019).

As one illustration of this "criminal event" perspective, Gottfredson and Hirschi used research about the nature of crime and victimization to infer tendencies of those most likely to offend, an approach fundamental to development of our conception of self-control and, hence, the development of our general theory of crime (see, Gottfredson & Hirschi, 1990, chapter 2). Integral to the logic of this theory is the attempt to infer the nature of "criminality" from the nature of crime (1990: 14), creating an image of the propensity of those most likely to be involved, a propensity we described as self-control. Hindelang et al. (1978) used a similar method of studying the elements of personal victimization to infer characteristics of those most at risk for victimization (see also Gottfredson, 1981).

Victimization research enabled both the lifestyle and the self-control perspectives. Part of the early motivation to focus attention on logical requisites in the development of crime theory was the enhanced ability to examine the risk of crime from victim survey data rather than strict reliance on data only available from official crime sources. In early victim surveys, information useful for the construction of both numerators and denominators for risk rates was simultaneously collected from representative population samples, data that could be manipulated flexibly to show with greater clarity the way risks of crime varied systematically with characteristics of place, time, setting, and people. Another source of the motivation came from an interest in social indicator modeling, based on macro trends for social and demographic variables (Cohen & Felson, 1979), which used the logical structure of crime to provide substantial clues about sources for change in patterns and trends in crime. A third important source for this "logical requisite" approach was the observation that an offender focus in criminology seemed to many to have borne little fruit with respect to crime policy. From this perspective, the focus on elements of crime apart from a focus on offenders, such as the time and place of occurrence, the target of the offense, and types of available restraints to crime, might offer better public policy ideas helpful in reducing crime and delinquency. This latter motivation remains central today, in the theory of situational crime prevention, focused policing efforts, some "rational choice" perspectives, and the singular focus of some place-based theories of crime causation.

This focus on criminal events, and what such a focus could portend, was advanced clearly by Brantingham and Brantingham:

> (Our) model assumes motivation and addresses the complementary issue of why particular crimes occur where and when they do … [suggesting that] … spatial and temporal patterns of crime can be identified at many levels of environmental aggregation, from the level of individual rooms within buildings to the city-wide level and beyond. … these observed

patterns are the empirical trace of a multi-level decision process. (1978, pp. 108–115)

There is really little question as to how substantial the logical requisite movement has been in enriching empirical criminology. The result of these ideas has been the creation of a large, empirical literature demonstrating effects of studying crime opportunities. These include routine activity theories, those choice models that have been linked to situational crime theory (for examples, see Brantingham & Brantingham, 1995; Clarke, 2018; Wilcox & Cullen, 2018), and place-based criminology (Weisburd et al., 2012). Each of these in significant respects can be associated with this "logical requisite" movement in criminology. So, too, can both modern control theory and the lifestyle theory of personal victimization (Gottfredson, 1981, 1986; Gottfredson & Hirschi, 2019; Hindelang et al., 1978).

*Bringing the Offender Back into Victimization Theory*

A problematic issue emergent in the "logical requisites" literature, however, has been differences among theorists about whether work in criminology that includes a focus on explaining individual and group differences in offending should be integrated with explanations that begin with a focus on victims or in some cases "targets," "places," or "situations." As contemporary victimization scholars have pointed out (Pratt & Turanovic, 2016; Turanovic & Pratt, 2019) there are substantial differences among theories using the logical requisite method in the extent to which individual or group differences in propensity are either implicitly or explicitly included as causal elements along with the situational and event causes of crime. There are (at least) two strong views about this question: briefly stated, one view suggests that it is neither possible nor advisable for a general theory of crime to absent explanations of offending based on individual and group differences from a theory of crime or victimization; the other view is that a theory of victimization is both possible and better if it ignores ideas about differences among people in the tendency to engage in crime and delinquency.

The first perspective can be represented by work in the control theory tradition (Schreck, 1999; Schreck & Berg, 2021; Schreck et al., 2020), by situational action theory (Wikström & Treiber, 2016; Wikström et al., 2018), and recent advances in the lifestyle perspective on causes of victimization (Pratt & Turanovic, 2016; Turanovic &

Pratt, 2019). Arguably, this position is, at least implicitly, also a necessary one for a wide range of theoretical perspectives stipulating individual and group differences in propensities from labeling, cultural, and strain theories to social disorganization, and dual systems models. The second view can be represented by situational crime prevention perspectives, some versions of opportunity theory, contemporary policing theories focusing on "hot spots" and place-based models, and some general place-based theories that explicitly argue against consideration of differences in propensities (*cf.*, Clarke, 2018; Felson & Clarke, 1998; Weisburd et al., 2012). In our view, whatever the initial stance of a theory may be (many offender-based perspectives, of course, did not focus on this matter too much), it is entirely appropriate, even essential, to examine each theory that aspires to the status of a general theory against the major findings of contemporary victimization research precisely on this question (see, Schreck & Berg, 2021, for a compelling exposition of this perspective).

For control theory, the idea that theories of offending and theories of criminal victimization can be conceptualized as distinct branches of criminology seems curious. After all, the idea of crime, as it is ordinarily used in criminology, presupposes harm to others, or, in most cases, a victim or victims (although not in every case harm to a specific victim). For ordinary crimes, victims are a logical requisite for a criminal event and so, at least at the logical, or abstract level, must be part of the explanation. As a result, it is clear that a valid general theory of crime must at minimum be consistent with a valid general theory of victimization (and vice versa). Thus, modern control theory appears to us to clearly fall squarely on the integrationist side of this matter, both as a logical and an empirical matter (see Gottfredson & Hirschi, 2019).[4]

Similar issues have been effectively raised by Wikström and Treiber (see also, Wikström, et al., 2018) in discussion of situational action theory in juxtaposition with routine activity perspectives:

> Arguing that if someone is motivated to commit a crime and faces a suitable target lacking adequate guardianship, he or she will commit an act of crime does not take us very far towards understanding what causes that crime, or the role of the environment. For example, it does not explain why some people, but not others, commit an act of crime in response to (particular) suitable targets lacking guardianship; why some targets are suitable to some people, but not others; or why some forms

> of guardianship, but not others, influence some people's, but not others', crime involvement. (2016, p. 420)

Wikström and Treiber put the matter succinctly: Felson and Clarke's "opportunity makes the thief" is better stated as "thieves take opportunity."

The argument that a complete theory of victimization must consider differences among people in their tendency to be in situations conducive to victimization and that this consideration provides clear differentiation among theories (in this case, between lifestyle theory and routine activity theory) has been most effectively and clearly advanced by Turanovic & Pratt in a series of foundational papers on lifestyle theory (2014; 2019; Pratt & Turanovic, 2016; see also, Berg & Mulford, 2020). They note that a major difference between these perspectives is the role that individual and group differences play (among other causes) in lifestyle theory, a role that is absent in the routine activity perspective. Routine activity theory as proposed is essentially a theory about the environmental influences of targets and guardians that simply stipulates offenders, whereas lifestyle theory

> … emphasizes the role of being exposed to "high risk times, places, and people" when it comes to victimization. In this conception, both risk and victimization are viewed in *probabilistic* terms, as variables that exist along a continuum. For example, they contend that participating in risky behaviors—such as robbing people, taking drugs, and stealing things—does not necessarily guarantee that one will be victimized, but that engaging in such behavior elevates the odds of it happening. (Pratt & Turanovic, 2016, p. 336)

We will return to these contributions to lifestyle and self-control perspectives below, but clearly, such conceptual demonstrations of the role individual and group differences can play in otherwise event-based theories provides a foundation for integrating a large body of research and theory into the victimization literature and helps establish fruitful directions for research (many of which are outlined in Berg & Mulford, 2020; Schreck, 1999; Schreck & Berg, 2021; and Turanovic & Pratt, 2019). For present purposes, suffice it to say that modern control theory finds the idea of integrating people with places a compelling one, one entirely consistent with the principal elements of the logical requisite movement *and* with the causal role of settings and situations in our own general theory of crime (see, Figure 2.1).

*A Brief Note About Age as a Cause of Victimization*

Modern control theory includes age as a direct cause of delinquency and crime (Figure 2.1), unlike many other perspectives. The reasons for this are numerous, but treating age as a cause has numerous benefits for crime theories (in addition to the fact that such a stance is consistent with the best available empirical evidence). It is also well established (at least since systematic findings from victimization research were reported (e.g., Gottfredson, 1981, 1984, 1986; Hindelang et al., 1978) that many types of interpersonal victimization also follow an age pattern similar to the pattern for offending. In fact, the age-victimization curve and the age-offending curve are remarkably similar (see Turanovic & Prat, 2019, p. 30).

The age-crime curve is, of course, along with the clustering of crime events in time and space, perhaps the oldest empirical finding in criminology. Having created an empirical distribution of age-standardized crime rates, the Belgian demographer/mathematician Quetelet smoothed the empirical distribution he found in his data, fit the curve, and concluded:

> Of all the causes which influence the development of the propensity to crime, or which diminish that propensity, age is unquestionably the most energetic. Indeed, it is through age that the physical power and passions of man are developed, and their energy afterwards decreases with age. Reason is developed with age, and continues to acquire power even when strength and passion have passed their greatest vigor. (Quetelet, 1842, p. 92 *et seq*. and Plate 4)

Arguably, modern criminology has not advanced beyond Quetelet's observation or his "explanation" (see the analysis of contemporary "explanations" for the age effect in Gottfredson & Hirschi, 2019, chapter 3). In any event, this "age propensity" shows itself not just in rates of offending, but for much of personal victimization as well.

*Offending, Victimization, and Modern Control Theory*

The considerable empirical work on the correlation between offending and victimization is clearly relevant for all causal theories of crime and delinquency. The relationship became central to criminology as an empirical matter with Wolfgang's studies of homicides in offense and arrest records in police files in Philadelphia and with his depiction of "victim-precipitation" (or better put, perhaps, as active involvement) in homicide cases (1957; 1958).[5] The relation was subsequently identified much more generally in early self-reported victimization studies when schedules for self-reported offending were included along with self-reported victimization in general population samples, initially in Britain (Gottfredson, 1984, 1986; Hough & Mayhew, 1983; Sparks, Genn, & Dodd, 1977).

In the initial British Crime survey, for example, the relationship between self-reported violence offenses and personal victimization during the reference period was relatively large and the general relationship between a scale of self-reported delinquencies and personal victimization was also notable (Gottfredson, 1984, p. 16). The data also revealed a correlation between self-reported arrests and victimization (1984, p. 45). Also shown in this survey was the link to potential environmental causes (1984, p. 43) and importantly to several of the limited indicators of lifestyle in the data (such as heavy drinking). Several forms of accidents were also studied, and each demonstrated a correlation with victimization. Age, in particular, seemed highly related to personal victimization, net the limited lifestyle variables available to study.

Important subsequent research and commentary has substantiated the connection using a variety of methods and data and has explored its meaning (major examples include, Berg, 2012; Berg & Loeber, 2011; Berg & Mulford, 2020; Chen, 2009; Gruszczyaska, Lucia, & Killias, 2012; Ousey, Wilcox, & Fisher, 2011; Pauwels & Svensson, 2011, 2013; Posick, 2013; Pridemore & Berg, 2017; Schreck, 1999; Schreck & Berg, 2021; Schreck, Stewart, & Osgood, 2008; Sullivan, Ousey, & Wilcox, 2016; van Gelder, Averdijk, Eisner, & Ribaud, 2015; Wittebrood & Nieuwbeerta, 1999).

Prior to widespread use of victimization surveys with the inclusion of self-reported offending items, many of the patterns depicted in survey data were, of course, suggestive of strong etiological links between offending and victimization. These initial victimization surveys did not contain much data on offenders (only victim reports of some basic demographic data and whether or not the victim knew the offender), but the patterns in the data were at least suggestive of important causal links. This link was important to our own lifestyle theory and to its connection to control theory:

> One of the central building blocks of the lifestyle concept has been the discovery that the factors most closely associated with victimization are factors which have also been found to be associated with offending … [These data] at least suggest that similar mechanisms may operate to produce both. In control theory terms, the processes that reduce the restraints to offend are similar to the processes in lifestyle terms that affect the probability that persons will be in places at times and around people where the risk of victimization is high. … The argument is not that these processes produce offenders and victims who are one and the same, though often this is the case; rather it is that they produce the likely pools of victims and the likely pools of offenders and the circumstances that they are likely to come into contact with one another. (Gottfredson, 1981, p. 726)

In contemporary victimization research, this connection is raised, in part, by the literature demonstrating the role of self-control and informal controls as fundamental causes of crime, delinquency, and victimization (Nofziger, 2009; Pratt, & Turanovic, 2016; Pratt et al., 2014; Schreck, 1999; Schreck & Berg, 2021; Schreck et al., 2020; Turanovic & Pratt, 2014; Turanovic et al., 2018). As Berg and Mulford have recently noted (2020, p. 49): "Overall, the effects of self-control are among the most consistent individual-level predictors of the victim–offender overlap."

The overlap also raises the control theory concepts of choice and versatility (and the importance of the a general focus on problem behaviors) with respect to both offenders and to victims (see Figure 2.1 and Gottfredson, 2018; Gottfredson & Hirschi, 2019; Pratt, 2016; Pratt et al., 2014; Schreck & Berg, 2021; Turanovic & Pratt, 2019). And, as Turanovic and Pratt have shown, the overlap fundamentally raises the issues of how personal characteristics, risk-taking, and similar behavioral differences interact to play a role in how the places and settings associated with crime should be understood in explanations of victimization (Pratt & Turanovic, 2016; Turanovic & Pratt, 2014, 2019).

A series of recent papers fundamentally develops both empirical and conceptual connections between victimization research and these elements included in modern control theory (Berg, 2012; Berg & Mulford, 2020; Nofziger, 2009; Pratt et al., 2014; Schreck, 1999; Schreck & Berg, 2021; Schreck et al., 2020). In a formative paper, Schreck (1999) presents both empirical data and strong conceptual arguments linking control theory to criminal victimization. Schreck convincingly links elements of self-control to the concept of risk of victimization and to the concept of lifestyle, and underscores the problem behavior concept integral to modern control theory (see, Figure 2.1; see also the discussion in Berg & Mulford, 2020). Further, in describing the implications of work integrating victimization into control theory, Schreck and Berg (2021) show the centrality of the concepts of victim and victimization to *all* crime theories:

> however convincing a theory seems to be at explaining the offender, its inability to produce a believable explanation about victimization constitutes falsification of that theory (p. 18).

The sweep of Schreck and Berg's arguments is impressive. They are backed both by logic and data, and include the strong implications of the choice perspective fundamental to control theory. They show how the *nature of victimization itself* has consequences for all theories of offending. Consider just one example of their ability to deduce qualities of actors from the nature of the acts:

> choice theory conceives that the would-be offender is often anxiously mindful of the intended victim and the perils of the immediate situation. Almost all of the time, a cursory assessment of the situation reveals that a crime committed now would probably be a terrible choice. Thanks to the target's actions and local circumstances, a successful crime would take far more effort and at far greater immediate risk for physical and legal danger than the offender finds worthwhile (Schreck & Berg, 2021, p. 27).

The integration of the concept of self-control fundamentally into victimization theory via the lifestyle perspective is provided by Pratt and Turanovic (2016; Turanovic & Pratt, 2019). Their innovative conceptualization and analysis put "risk" back into event/opportunity theory in a compelling way, a necessary conflation of people and places in order to understand the victim–offender overlap, as well as why a propensity such as self-control could help explain lifestyle differences. Schreck and Berg (2021) very effectively do so as well, making the case that: "Low self-control … not only frees people to commit crime, but it makes criminal attempts upon them easier, less risky, and more rewarding for other offenders" (p. 40–41) and that as a result "the concept [self-control] offers a parsimonious account for the victim-offender correlation."

*Victimization in a Choice Theory of Crime*

Early proponents of the logical requisite movement urged a choice perspective be adopted, in part as a corrective to the then dominance of offender theories that overpredicted the amount of offending actually engaged in even by the most active offenders (see, discussion in Brantingham & Brantingham, 1978, p. 113). For example, in proposing a focus on opportunities in his classic paper illustrating benefits of victimization survey data, Hough (1987) also recommended deployment of the choice concept for crime theory and illustrates its utility in contemplating the meaning of victimization correlates. Contemporary victimization theorists make the idea central to revitalized lifestyle theory and to the meaning of the self-control/victimization link. As indicated above, Schreck and Berg describe the importance of choice as an integral element of the role of self-control; in their further conceptual extension and development of the importance of victimization for control theory, Schreck, Berg, and Rogers (2020) provide insights into the concept of vulnerability and extend the implications of the ideas of choice to situational causes of crime. One inescapable conclusion from their work:

> although offenders have freedom to choose to commit crime, per the claims of self-control theory, ample exposure to easy inducements to violence make crime more likely even for those with more self-control. This implies that the target is a matter of scientific importance in self-control theory (2020, p. 20).

Central to their arguments for a revitalized lifestyle theory, Turanovic and Pratt (2019, p. 50) state the issue of choice directly by asking: "where did the offender and decisions that they make go in the victimization equation?" In their review of the nature of offending, they argue the need for a choice model, because it is the case that most offenders are not "relentless in their pursuit to victimize others." Instead, offenders are rather opportunistic or adventitious:

> when it comes to the criminal event, much of it on the part of the offender is simply impulsive and unplanned, where the opportunity to victimize someone—whether it be the person themselves or their property—presents itself unexpectedly … And even when an offense is actually planned, offenders tend to drift toward easy opportunities (2019, p. 49).

Their concept of "risky lifestyles," and their connection of these to the concept of self-control, and to how individuals select in and out of activities and settings in which victimization is more or less likely, enhances greatly our ability to explain victimization and provides an agenda for ever-better studies of both self-control and victimization.[6] At a minimum, their focus on combining characteristics of crimes as events (such as place, time, method, and victims) with study of individual differences in offending yields a stronger, more complete theory for criminology (see, also, the general discussions in Nofziger & Kurtz, 2005; Turanovic et al., 2018).

*Early Childhood Environments, Victimization, and Offending*

One last major trend in victimization research meriting consideration, if only briefly, in this chapter is the meaning of the considerable evidence about the long-term consequences of differences in early childhood environments, including victimization and trauma early in life, for subsequent problem behaviors. The life-course consequences of childhood traumas and harms are critical to include as a test for *any* general theory of crime and victimization, including modern control theory (Gottfredson & Hirschi, 2019; Meyers, Lloyd, Turanovic, & Pratt, 2018; Pratt, 2016; Turanovic, 2019; Turanovic & Pratt, 2019). Research on harmful parenting or caretaker practices, including abuse and neglect, has long established a relationship between childhood environments, elements of socialization, and a variety of subsequent problem behaviors. As Figure 2.1 depicts, these causes serve as part of the foundational set of facts for modern control theory (Gottfredson & Hirschi, 1990, 2019, esp. pp. 98–102) and have been shown to have crucial consequences for many problem behaviors that occur throughout life (for Gottfredson & Hirschi, 2019, chapters 1, 11). Some contemporary theories of crime seriously downplay the influence of the early environments or argue erroneously that they have minimal impact in late adolescent or adult behavior. While childhood causes are important, they are, of course, certainly not dispositive of subsequent problem behaviors or in every case even consequential, but theories that do not recognize their critical influence are misspecified and sacrifice explanatory power. More importantly, they jeopardize attention to important public policy implications of a considerable body of research suggesting strong attention to the quality of early childhood experiences (see, Gottfredson & Hirschi, 2019 for a discussion of this problem). In the context of victimization research, childhood victimization and trauma and abuse and neglect have been shown to have very significant, serious, and continuing consequences for a wide variety of life-outcomes (see also the excellent analysis and theoretical discussion in Meyers et al., 2018 and Turanovic & Pratt, 2019, chapter 6).

## Modern Victimization Theory

It must be true that crime theory is victimization theory (and vice versa). An opportunity theory absent an image of the offender is incomplete and risks being inaccurate. Most situational crime theories actually imply an image of offending, an implication that should be made explicit, both in the interests of a more complete explanation and for critical public policy issues. Inspection of many situational crime prevention methods said to be effective show that they presume an opportunistic or adventitious actor, presence of other problem behavior (excessive alcohol use) or age (targeted to adolescents), all of which, of course, are indicators of individual differences in propensities. After all, a theory of "place" that depends for its validity on records of law enforcement, such as calls for police services or arrests, is based fundamentally both on the behavior of the law enforcement agencies and on differences among people in the area or the population generating the police response data. Given the fundamentally disproportionate distributions of crime and victimization, by place, time, demographic and social characteristics, and settings, theories of victimization need to be fully general theories to be useful. (This includes being attentive to the theory's view of the role of the criminal justice system and its collateral consequences.) In this respect among others, the contemporary work on lifestyles, self-control, choice and risk (Schreck & Berg, this volume; Turanovic & Pratt, 2019) appear, as a matter of evidenced-based criminology, to lead us in the right direction.

## Notes

1 Although these topics can be highlighted, they are not distinct issues. Rather, they interact to form a set of ideas and findings critical for all theories. Taken together, research and conceptualization in these areas are solidifying our base of fundamental knowledge that both challenges many existing perspectives and enables theoretical development toward empirically grounded, general theories of crime and victimization.

2 This section draws upon Gottfredson, 2018 and Gottfredson & Hirschi, 2019, chapter 11, which provide justification for these elements and some of their implications for global criminology.

3 We use the term self-control to refer to the general tendency to favor near-term self-interest over subsequent harms. In our use of the term, self-control is not a "propensity for crime" (a concept explicitly at odds with control theory) but rather a general tendency, shaping human action, which allows reconciliation of seemingly disparate findings about behavior from a wide range of disciplines, and one consistent with the longstanding versatility effect found in criminology (Gottfredson and Hirschi, 2019, esp. chapter 11). We have not argued that self-control is the "sole" cause of crime, contrary to some curious mischaracterizations of the theory (see Gottfredson and Hirschi, 2019 for a critique of such views) and we differentiate our use of the term from other uses.

4 A related line of theoretical development demonstrates how key theoretical concepts embedded in other explanations for crime fare when tested as explanations for victimization (e.g., Berg, 2012; Kubrin & Weitzer, 2003; Ousey, Wilcox, & Fisher, 2011; Pauwels & Svensson, 2011; Wikström & Treiber, 2016).

5 Perhaps as a consequence of a singular focus on homicide, but also as a result of the influence of the cultural theories of Sellin (1938), Wolfgang's work depicted all homicide as aggression and used the idea of victim-precipitation (the first person to use or threaten force in an encounter that culminated in homicide) to illustrate a model in which such interactions were said to illustrate "values" in the "subculture of violence." However, even his data suggested considerable versatility in offending and victimization, versatility difficult to reconcile with the elements of the cultural perspective. Such a crime-specific focus has, arguably, led criminology into more than one theoretical problem, as offenders and victims stubbornly refuse to be so narrowly labeled.

6 A research agenda focused on indicator development of key theoretical concepts is vital to advancing both modern control theory concepts such as self-control and social bonds, (see, Gottfredson & Hirschi, 2019) and for lifestyle theory (Turanovic & Pratt, 2019). There also continues to be pressing need to evaluate the correlates of self-reported victimization with measurement issues in mind—that is, the reliability and validity of both the self-reported victimization and offending measures, both of which have known limitations and response biases. Just as one example: the correlation between self- reported offending and victimization likely is to some degree also produced by correlation of these biases rather than only by the correlation of "true" variance. The overlap may be partially attributable, for example, to the precipitation notion of Wolfgang, in which "offenders" may report themselves as "victims' although in fact they may have been the cause of the "assault" by another, as an independent observer might conclude. On the other hand, the "event" nature of measuring victimization also might be implicated in the correlation, given that a continuous period victimization (both actually assaults and extended periods of fear of assault) is seriously undercounted in an event methodology.

## References

Berg, M. (2012). The overlap of violent offending and violent victimization: Assessing the evidence and explanations. In M. Delisi & P. Conis (Eds.), *Violent offenders: Theory, research, policy, and Practice* (pp. 17–38). Burlington, MA: Jones and Bartlett.

Berg, M., & Mulford, C. (2020). Reappraising and redirecting research on the victim– offender overlap. *Trauma, Violence, & Abuse*, *21*, 16–30.

Berg, M. T., & Loeber, R. (2011). Examining the neighborhood context of the violent offending-victimization relationship: A prospective investigation. *Journal of Quantitative Criminology*, *27*, 427–451.

Brantingham, P., & Brantingham, P. (1978). A theoretical model of crime site selection. In M. Krohn and R. Akers (Eds.), *Crime, law and sanctions: Theoretical perspectives. Sage research progress series in criminology, volume 6* (pp. 105–118). Beverley Hills: Sage.

Brantingham, P., & Brantingham, P. (1995). Criminality of place: Crime generators and crime attractors. *European Journal on Criminal Policy and Research*, *3*, 5–26.

Chen, X. (2009). The link between juvenile offending and victimization: The influence of risky lifestyles, social bonding, and individual characteristics. *Youth Violence and Juvenile Justice*, 7, 119–135.

Clarke, R. (2018). Situational crime prevention. *Oxford research encyclopedia of criminology and criminal justice*. N.Y. Oxford University Press.

Cohen, L. E., & Felson, M. (1979). Social change and crime rate trends: A routine activity approach. *American Sociological Review*, *44*, 588–608.

Felson, M., & Clarke, R. (1998). Opportunity makes the thief. *Police Research Paper 98*. London: Home Office.

Gottfredson, M. (1981). On the etiology of criminal victimization. *The Journal of Criminal Law and Criminology*, *72*, 714–726.

Gottfredson, M. (1984). *Victims of crime: Dimensions of risk.* Home office research study No. 81. London, England: Her Majesty's Stationary Office.

Gottfredson, M. (1986). Substantive contributions of victimization surveys. *Crime and Justice*, *7*, 251–287.

Gottfredson, M. (2018). General theory and global criminology: Childhood environments, problem behaviors, and a focus on prevention. *Asian Journal of Criminology*, *13***,** 347–365.

Gottfredson, M., & Hirschi, T. (1990). *A general theory of crime*. Stanford, CA: Stanford University Press.

Gottfredson, M., & Hirschi, T. (2019). *Modern control theory and the limits of criminal justice*. N.Y.: Oxford University Press.

Gruszczyaska, B., Lucia, S., & Killias, M. (2012). Juvenile victimization from an international perspective. In J. Junger-Tas, I. Marshall, D. Enzmann, M. Killias, & M. Gruszczyaska (Eds.), *The many faces of youth crime: Contrasting theoretical perspectives on juvenile delinquency across countries and cultures* (pp. 95–116). New York: Springer.

Hindelang, M., Gottfredson, M., & Garofalo, J. (1978). *Victims of personal crime: An empirical foundation for a theory of personal victimization.* Cambridge, MA: Ballinger.

Hirschi, T. (1969). *Causes of delinquency*. Berkeley: University of California Press.

Hough, M. (1987). Offenders' choice of target: Findings from victim surveys. *Journal of Quantitative Criminology*, 3, 355–369.

Hough, M., & Mayhew, P. (1983). *The British crime survey: First report. Home office research study, no. 76.* London: H.M. Stationery Office.

Kubrin, C., & Weitzer, R. (2003). Retaliatory homicide: Concentrated disadvantage and neighborhood culture. *Social Problems*, *50*, 157–180.

Mayhew, P., Clarke, R., & Hough, M. (1976). *Crime as opportunity.* Home Office Research Study, no. 34. London: H.M. Stationery Office

Meyers, W., Lloyd, K., Turanovic, J., & Pratt, T. (2018). Revisiting a criminological classic: The cycle of violence. *Journal of Contemporary Criminal Justice*, *34*, 266–286.

Nofziger, S. (2009). Victimization and the general theory of crime. *Violence and Victims*, *24*, 337–350.

Nofziger, S., & Kurtz, D. (2005). Violent lives: A lifestyle model linking exposure to violence to juvenile violent offending. *Journal of Research in Crime and Delinquency*,*42*, 3–26.

Ousey, G., Wilcox, P., & Fisher, B. (2011). Something old, something new: Revisiting competing hypotheses of the victimization-offending relationship among adolescents. *Journal of Quantitative Criminology*, *27*, 53–84.

Pauwels, L., & Svensson, R. (2011). Exploring the relationship between offending and victimization: What is the role of risky lifestyles and low self-control? A test in two urban samples. *European Journal of Criminal Policy and Research*, *17*, 163–177.

Pauwels, L., & Svensson, R. (2013). Violent youth group involvement, self-reported offending and victimization. *European Journal of Criminal Policy and Research*, *19*, 369–386.

Posick, C. (2013). The overlap between offending and victimization among adolescents: Results from the second international self-report delinquency study. *Journal of Contemporary Criminal Justice*, *29*, 106–124.

Pratt, T. (2016). A self-control/life-course theory of criminal behavior. *European Journal of Criminology*, *13*, 129–146.

Pratt, T., & Cullen, F. T. (2000). The empirical status of Gottfredson and Hirschi's general theory of crime: A meta-analysis. Criminology, 38, 931–964.

Pratt, T., Turanovic, J. (2016). Lifestyle and routine activity theories revisited: The importance of 'risk' to the study of victimization. *Victims and Offenders*, *11*, 335–354.

Pratt, T., Turanovic, J., Fox, K., & Wright, K. (2014). Self-control and victimization: A meta-analysis. *Criminology*, 52, 87–116.

Pridemore, W., & Berg, M. (2017). What is past is prologue: A population-based case- control study of repeat victimization, premature mortality, and homicide. *Aggressive Behavior*, *43*, 176–189.

Quetelet, L.(A). (1842; 1969). *A treatise on man and the development of his faculties* (Solomon Diamond, Trans.). Gainesville, Fl.: Scholars' Facsimiles & Reprints.

Schreck, C. (1999). Criminal victimization and low self-control: An extension and test of a general theory of crime. *Justice Quarterly*, *16*, 633–654.

Schreck, C., & Berg, M. (2021). What ideas of victimization and vulnerability mean for criminological theory: A logical appraisal. In T. Pratt & J. Turanovic (Eds.), *Revitalizing victimization theory: Revisions, applications, and new directions.* Advances in criminological theory. New York: Routledge.

Schreck, C., Berg, M., & Rogers, E. (2020). The victim's low self-control and verbal provocation tendencies as inducements to violence: A dyadic analysis of offenders and their targets. Draft MS, Rochester Institute of Technology, Rochester, NY.

Schreck, C., Stewart, E., & Osgood, D. (2008). A reappraisal of the overlap of violent offenders and victims. *Criminology*, *46*, 871–906.
Sellin, T. (1938). Culture conflict and crime. *American Journal of Sociology*, *44*, 97–103.
Sparks, R., Genn, H., & Dodd, D. (1977). *Surveying victims: A study of the measurement of criminal victimization.* New York: Wiley.
Sullivan, C. J., Ousey, G. C., & Wilcox, P. (2016). Similar mechanisms? A comparative longitudinal study of adolescent violence and victimization. Journal of Interpersonal Violence, 31, 1367–1392.
Turanovic, J. J. (2019). Heterogeneous effects of adolescent violent victimization on problematic outcomes in early adulthood. Criminology, 57, 105–135.
Turanovic, J., & Pratt, T. (2014). Can't stop, won't stop: Self-Control, risky lifestyles, and repeat victimization. *Journal of Quantitative Criminology*, *30*, 29–56.
Turanovic, J., & Pratt, T. (2019). *Thinking about victimization: Context and consequences.* London: Routledge.
Turanovic, J., Pratt, T., & Piquero, A. (2018). Structural constraints, risky lifestyles, and repeat victimization. *Journal of Quantitative Criminology*, *34*, 251–274.
van Gelder, J. L., Averdijk, M., Eisner, M., & Ribaud, D. (2015). Unpacking the victim- offender overlap: On role differentiation and socio-psychological characteristics. *Journal of Quantitative Criminology*, *31*, 653–675.
Vazsonyi, A. T., Mikuška, J., & Kelley, E. L. (2017). It's time: A meta-analysis on the self-control-deviance link. *Journal of Criminal Justice*, *48*, 48–63.
Weisburd, D., Groff, E., & Yang, S. (2012). *The criminology of place.* N.Y.: Oxford University Press.
Wikström, P., & Treiber, K. (2016). Situational theory: The importance of interactions and action mechanisms in the explanation of crime. *Oxford handbook of criminology.* Oxford: Oxford University Press.
Wikström, P., Mann, R., & Hardie, B. (2018). Young people's differential vulnerability to criminogenic exposure: Bridging the gap between people- and place-oriented approaches in the study of crime causation. *European Journal of Criminology*, *15*, 10–31.
Wikström, P., Oberwittler, D., Treiber, K., & Hardie, B. (2012). *Breaking rules: The social and situational dynamics of young people's urban crime.* Oxford: Oxford University Press.
Wilcox, P., & Cullen, F. (2018). Situational opportunity theories of crime. *Annual Review of Criminology*, *1*, 123–148.
Wittebrood, K., & Nieuwbeerta, P. (1999). Wages of sin? The link between offending, lifestyle and violent victimization. *European Journal of Criminal Policy and Research*, *7*, 63–80.
Wolfgang, M. (1957). Victim precipitated homicide. *Journal of Criminal Law, Criminology and Police Science*, *48*, 1–11.
Wolfgang, M. (1958). *Patterns in criminal homicide*. Philadelphia: University of Pennsylvania Press.

# 3

# Understanding Victimization: The Role of Cultural Theories

*Charis E. Kubrin and Graham C. Ousey*

With few exceptions (e.g., von Hentig 1948; Wolfgang 1958), victimization theory and research began in earnest in the late 1970s. The introduction of Hindelang, Gottfredson, and Garofalo's (1978) lifestyle theory and Cohen and Felson's (1979) routine activities theory were notable launching points. Since that time, the study of victimization has become a vibrant part of the criminological enterprise, with substantial empirical research generated. Nevertheless, some argue that *theoretical* advances in the study of victimization have stalled (Schreck & Berg, this volume; Turanovic & Pratt, 2019). Indeed, although some scholars have elaborated beyond basic concepts of lifestyle and routine activities perspectives (Finkelhor & Asdigian 1996; Wilcox, Land, & Hunt, 2003), little in the way of new theoretical ground outside these frameworks has been developed and tested.

The current chapter is an effort at reinvigoration of victimization theory, carving out new theoretical territory by introducing the role of cultural resources in understanding criminal victimization. We begin by reviewing victimization theory and scholarship, highlighting its contributions to criminology. Next, we discuss critiques of this body of work, focusing on the limitations hindering theoretical development beyond existing frameworks. We then introduce cultural theories, explaining why these popular explanations of offending may be fruitful for theoretical advancements in victimization scholarship. After reviewing the small but important literature proposing cultural frameworks as explanative of victimization, we offer ways that victimization scholarship can move forward, incorporating cultural theories into new theoretical lines of investigation. Our hope is that this chapter will stimulate theoretical debate and encourage empirical investigation.

## Victimization Research

The 1970s marked a period of tremendous growth of theory and research on victimization. The introduction of the National Crime Victimization Survey (NCVS) in 1973 was certainly a key contributor. The NCVS provides crucial information on aggregate trends in victimization, crimes not reported to U.S. law enforcement agencies (Lauritsen 2001), and detailed information on non-fatal personal victimization experiences such as rape and sexual assault, robbery, aggravated and simple assault, and personal larceny. It also covers household property victimization including burglary, motor vehicle, and other theft. NCVS data also reveal characteristics of crime events including time and place of occurrence, weapon use, and nature of injury/consequences. Finally, the NCVS yields essential information about the demographic characteristics of offenders and victims and about the nature of the offender–victim relationship (Turanovic & Pratt, 2019, pp. 14–15).

Based on the valuable data contained in the NCVS, researchers have identified important correlates of victimization including age, gender, and race, among others. Evidence indicates victimization rates are highest among those between 12 and 17 years of age (Turanovic & Pratt 2019, pp. 30–32) and are higher for males than females (Lauritsen, 2001, p. 13). Moreover, victimization rates—especially for violence—are higher for African-Americans than for their white counterparts (Berg, 2014, p. 631). In sum, being young, male, and African-American is associated with an elevated risk of victimization. Why might this be the case? For answers, we turn to theories of victimization.

## Theories of Victimization

Not long after the arrival of NCVS data, two theories emerged as leading frameworks in the study of criminal victimization. Lifestyle theory (Hindelang et al., 1978) and routine activities theory (Cohen & Felson, 1979) have been at the center of victimization research (Turanovic & Pratt, 2019, p. 10) since their emergence in the late 1970s. These perspectives explain victimization risk in terms of differential criminal opportunity, which varies with behavioral routines (McNeeley

& Wilcox, 2015b, p. 923). Although formulated as distinct theories, their compatibility led some scholars to integrate their ideas into a combined lifestyles-routine activities (L-RAT) perspective (Cohen, Klugel, & Land, 1981; McNeeley, 2015). The integrated L-RAT theory revolves around several concepts including exposure and proximity to motivated offenders, target attractiveness, and guardianship. Researchers have pushed for further expansion of concepts in this framework. Target congruence theory, for example, proposes target antagonism, target vulnerability, and target gratifiability to address L-RAT's inability to explain the victimization of young children by family members or to explain why some motivated offenders are more enticed by some potential victims than others (Finkelhor & Asdigian, 1996).

Despite efforts integrating the lifestyle and routine activities frameworks, some scholars continue to emphasize their key differences. Turanovic and Pratt (2019, p. 36), for example, highlight that the theories feature a major difference with respect to what constitutes "risky" behavior. They argue that lifestyle theory emphasizes how victimization varies according to demographic characteristics associated with risky behavior. The group most victimized, young minority males, is theorized to spend more time participating in risky activities (e.g., deviant behavior), in high-risk situations (e.g., unsupervised), at high-risk times (e.g., night hours), and with high-risk individuals (e.g., others inclined to offend). Thus, lifestyle theory argues participation differences in *risky* activities drive differences in victimization likelihood. According to Turanovic and Pratt (2019), routine activities theory, in contrast, downplays the emphasis on risky behavior, arguing instead that victimization varies simply as a function of an individual's *routine* activities (e.g., how often they go to the store, to work, or to school).

## Critique of Victimization Theories

Although theoretical and empirical advancements in opportunity theories are valuable, there is concern that victimization theory has taken a wrong turn and gone off course (Pratt & Turanovic, 2016; Turanovic & Pratt, 2019). One reason for this concern is victimization researchers have virtually ignored offenders in explaining victimization. Thus, while the offender's perspective is a fundamental part of mainstream criminological theory, "it is curiously absent from much of the victimization literature" (Turanovic & Pratt, 2019, p. 51), leaving some wondering: What happened to offender motivation?

Ignoring offender motivation is a problem because research on offender decision-making reveals "social facts" critical for understanding patterns of victimization. First, typical offenders "are not masterminds" (Turanovic & Pratt, 2019, p. 49) but rather drift toward easy opportunities and targets (Wright & Decker, 1997), even when they have planned an offense (St. Jean, 2007). Second, less than 10 percent of individuals in the population account for more than half of all crimes committed (Piquero, Farrington, & Blumstein, 2003). And third, there is strong evidence of "victim–offender" overlap, with individuals who commit crimes at a heightened risk of also being crime victims (Berg, 2012; Hindelang et al., 1978; Jennings, Piquero, & Reingle, 2012; McNeeley & Wilcox, 2015a; Sampson & Lauritsen, 1990; Schreck, Stewart, & Osgood, 2008; Wolfgang, 1958). Thus, while in *theory* all individuals can engage in crime under the right circumstances, the *empirical* truth is that only a small handful of the population does so—even when attractive opportunities present themselves (Turanovic & Pratt, 2019, p. 50).

For these reasons, it is a poor strategy to ignore offenders when seeking understanding of victimization risk. Yet, the idea that offender motivation matters because some individuals are more impulsive, aggressive, and prone to offend than others virtually disappeared from discussions of victimization with the introduction of routine activities theory (Turanovic & Pratt, 2019, p. 54). This is because the theory takes as given that offender motivation is present, assuming that if an attractive target appears in a context of weak guardianship, individuals have sufficient motivation to take advantage, resulting in high probability of crime. However, thinking this way about victimization offers no explanation as to why, when faced with the same potential target, only a small subset of individuals choose to become offenders while most others will pass up the opportunity (p. 56).[1]

Given this reality, critics assert there is need to consider offenders in efforts to understand victimization. Figuring out how to do so is the challenge. More pointedly, how can this happen without simply reproducing existing theories of offending? Following the insights of Schreck (1999), Turanovic and Pratt (2019) identify one theory of offending, self-control theory, as potentially fruitful. They argue that individuals who lack self-control are more likely to self-select into risky lifestyles, which in turn can lead to increased victimization (p. 40). The effects of self-control on victimization operate largely through their influence on risky lifestyle choices, such as substance abuse and criminal behavior.

Thus, individuals with low self-control are more likely to offend and to place themselves in the riskiest situations, enhancing the likelihood of becoming victims of crime.

To build on this effort, we assert that cultural theories, long conceptualized as theories of offending, are informative and relevant for understanding victimization. To date, a handful of scholars have considered the possibility that cultural theories offer insights into victimization (Baumer, Horney, Felson, & Lauritsen, 2003; Berg, 2014; McNeeley & Wilcox, 2015a, 2015b; Schreck, Ousey, Fisher, & Wilcox, 2012; Stewart, Schreck, & Simons, 2006) but more theoretical headway is necessary. This chapter builds upon this small but important body of research, identifying new theoretical territory worth pursuing.

## Cultural Theories of Offending

Cultural perspectives have deep roots in theoretical efforts to explain crime (Cloward & Ohlin, 1960; Cohen, 1955; Kornhauser, 1978; Merton, 1938; Miller, 1958; Sellin, 1938; Shaw & McKay, 1942; Sutherland, 1956; Wolfgang & Ferracuti, 1967). For the most part, cultural arguments offer insights about offending, providing explanations about how cultural resources such as values and beliefs motivate individuals to commit crime (Cloward & Ohlin, 1960; Cohen, 1955; Sutherland, 1956; Wolfgang & Ferracuti, 1967) or about how culture builds constraints that limit involvement in crime (Kornhauser, 1978; Warner, 2003). Varied strands of cultural theory appear in the criminological literature and it is beyond the scope of this chapter to review them exhaustively. Rather, as way of background, we provide broad categorization of the major flavors of cultural theory frameworks.[2]

The first framework we label *deviant subculture* theories. These theories of offending suggest that crime is motivated by a coherent set of values and beliefs distinct from those of society's conventional mainstream (Harding & Hepburn, 2014). These theories reject the assumption that individuals have an inherent human nature and assume cultural relativism. This means all cultures are equally valid, with standards of right and wrong depending on the values specific to a given subculture (Kornhauser, 1978; Kubrin, 2015). Thus, individuals commit crime because they have internalized a value system that opposes mainstream culture and defines acts of force and fraud as an acceptable, even preferred, means of achieving culturally prescribed ends (e.g., social status, power, or money). Which theoretical arguments fit within the category of deviant subculture is not precisely clear, but theories emphasizing cultural conflict (Sellin, 1938), cultural transmission (Sutherland, 1956), and the emergence of race-, class- or neighborhood-specific subcultures (Cloward & Ohlin, 1960; Cohen, 1955; Miller, 1958; Wolfgang & Ferracuti, 1967) are the most prominently cited examples (e.g., Kornhauser, 1978; Kubrin, 2015). Consistent with the deviant subculture framework, some empirical research suggests that the likelihood of criminal offending is associated with evidence of "oppositional," "street code," or "violent" subcultural values (Brezina, Agnew, Cullen, & Wright, 2004; Felson, Liska, South, & McNulty, 1994; Stewart & Simons, 2006). However, evidence that these values represent a coherent cultural system distinct from mainstream culture is limited (see Harding & Hepburn, 2014).

A second category of theories invoking culture as an explanation of offending are *cultural heterogeneity* theories (Sellin, 1938). These theories assert that crime is more likely when individuals' exposure is to conflicting cultural value systems, rather than one dominant and unified value system. This condition of conflicting culture is most likely to occur in poor, socially isolated neighborhoods (Berg, Stewart, Brunson, & Simons, 2012; Harding & Hepburn, 2014). An early example of cultural heterogeneity is evident in Shaw and McKay's (1942) work, suggesting that poorer communities of increasing ethnic diversity—e.g., due to immigration—exhibit mixtures of competing values, especially regarding the appropriateness of illicit conduct (Berg et al., 2012). Recent work furthers this line of theorizing, asserting that disadvantaged neighborhoods tend to develop "a mix of competing and conflicting cultural elements, some of which are oppositional…but most of which are conventional" (Harding & Hepburn, 2014, pp. 44–45). A consequence of exposure to greater heterogeneity in cultural orientations is that individuals lack clarity about which potential lines of actions are best for a given situation. Since neither conventional nor deviant orientations dominate areas characterized by cultural heterogeneity, individuals face a wider range of options to choose from when plotting a course of action (Berg et al., 2012; Harding, 2007). Thus, according to Berg et al. (2012, p. 417): "…youth are able to find sufficient normative justification to make an unobstructed transition from involvement in conventional behaviors to unconventional alternatives when conventional behavior becomes personally unfulfilling, ineffective, or encumbered by obstacles." In sum, contrary to subcultural theory's belief that a rigid set of values prescribes a narrow code of acceptable conduct, cultural heterogeneity theory suggests that the development of a broad repertoire of cultural tools results in an array of behavioral outcomes that can land at varying spots along the continuum from "conventional" to "criminal."

Although the idea that cultural heterogeneity may affect crime has been around at least since the work of Shaw and McKay, few studies have directly tested the cultural heterogeneity–crime association. An exception is the study by Berg et al. (2012), which examines several hypotheses regarding the connection between cultural heterogeneity and crime. Most notably, it reports that the odds of violent delinquency are greater in neighborhoods characterized by greater cultural heterogeneity. Moreover, the inhibiting effect of holding a conventional conduct frame on violent delinquency is weaker in neighborhoods with higher cultural heterogeneity than in neighborhoods with lower cultural heterogeneity. Stated alternatively, "…youth committed to pro-social conduct frames are less likely to act in accordance with these frames in neighborhoods defined by cultural heterogeneity" (Berg et al., 2012, p. 428).

A final class of theories are *cultural attenuation* theories. Originating in the work of Ruth Kornhauser (1978), these approaches generally reject the idea that an influential alternative culture challenges or competes with conventional cultural systems, even in poor communities. Rather, these theories posit that a single unified conventional cultural system prevails everywhere in a given society. The moral validity of the value system is unchallenged by alternatives. However, relevance of cultural values to everyday life may weaken because harsh structural conditions inhibit their realization (Kornhauser, 1978; Kubrin, 2015; Warner, 2003). As a result, conventional values become so infrequently used that there is a loss of effectiveness in their ability to reinforce conventional lines of action (Warner, 2003). Thus, in cultural attenuation theories, it is not differences in the exposure to varying cultural orientations (i.e., deviant vs. conventional) that matter for crime and delinquency, it is the strength of the (conventional) culture. When cultural attenuation increases, its ability to provide for the social control of behavior diminishes, and the likelihood of crime rises.

One of the most salient developments in cultural theory has been what some refer to as the "cultural turn" (Harding & Hepburn, 2014). The cultural turn describes a shift in thinking from the *culture as values* perspective to the *culture in action* perspective (Sampson & Bean, 2006). The former is the traditional vision of cultural influence on crime, viewing culture as a defined set of values that members of a given culture learn through socialization. These values prescribe the desired ends and the means of achieving them. From this vantage point, crime results because either: (a) people are exposed to cultural values that define crime as desired action or as an acceptable means to desired ends; or (b) conventional (i.e., crime proscribing) values are weakened by the existence of contradictory value systems or because structural constraints are so limiting that conventional values are disused and not reinforced. In contrast, the culture-in-action framework suggests that "culture is not a unified system that pushes action in a consistent direction" (Swidler, 1986, p. 277) as much as it is fragmented pieces of information—scripts, styles, frames, narratives, meanings—that individuals select from as they formulate behavioral options in response to a given context or situation. Culture is a toolkit that provides resources allowing individuals "to do different kinds of things in different circumstances" (Swidler, 1986, p. 276). In short, culture does not begin and end with values. Although individuals may hold certain values, their behaviors may not adhere to them because they use other cultural resources (e.g., scripts, frames) to actively construct lines of action perceived as situationally appropriate and effective for the tasks at hand. To date, only a handful of studies adopt the culture-in-action framework in empirical studies of crime (Berg et al., 2012; Kubrin & Weitzer, 2003; Lee & Ousey, 2011; Swartz, Wilcox, & Ousey, 2017) but it is gaining traction as scholars continue to identify limitations in the traditional culture as values perspective.

In summary, it is clear that cultural theories occupy a prominent place in criminological theory. They do not present one unified thesis, with at least three major frameworks evident in the literature. Regardless of differences, they all identify ways that cultural resources—values, frames, scripts, etc.—affect crime. Yet, they primarily offer insights on the motivations and constraints that underlie involvement in criminal *offending*. Efforts to apply cultural theories as a means of better understanding criminal *victimization* are far scarcer (cf. Baumer et al., 2003; Berg, 2014; McNeeley & Wilcox, 2015a, 2015b; Schreck et al., 2012; Stewart et al., 2006). In the remainder of this chapter, we address that scarcity, identifying ways that cultural frameworks are useful to the study of victims and victimization.

## Bringing Theories of Offending to Victimization

Criminal victimization varies across communities and across individuals within those communities (e.g., Berg & Loeber, 2011; Kennedy

& Forde, 1990; Lauritsen, 2001; Miethe & McDowall, 1993; Miethe & Meier, 1994; Rountree, Land, & Miethe, 1994; Sampson & Wooldredge, 1987; Smith & Jarjoura, 1989; Van Wilsem, Wittebrood, & De Graaf, 2006; Velez, 2001; Villarreal & Silva, 2006; Wilcox, Madensen, & Tillyer, 2007). To date, researchers primarily explain these variations in terms of two criminological perspectives: routine activities theory and social disorganization theory. As noted earlier, routine activities points to how variations in the routines of individuals may expose them to situations of greater risk. Research shows victimization risks are higher for individuals engaging in crime and hanging out with deviant peers (Berg & Loeber, 2011). Victimization risks are also higher for those who frequent bars and places where teens congregate (Rountree et al., 1994), use alcohol (Berg & Loeber, 2011), take few safety precautions (Miethe & McDowall, 1993; Rountree et al., 1994), spend more time away from home (Lauritsen, 2001), or spend more nights out engaging in leisure activities (Sampson & Wooldredge, 1987). Consistent with social disorganization theory, studies also report that victimization rates are elevated in neighborhoods where structural conditions foster breakdown in collective social control. This includes places with greater economic disadvantage (Lauritsen, 2001; Miethe & McDowall, 1993; Sampson & Wooldredge, 1987; Wilcox et al., 2007), racial and ethnic diversity (Smith & Jarjoura, 1989), population instability (Browning, 2002; Lauritsen, 2001; Smith & Jarjoura, 1989; Velez, 2001), single-parent households (Sampson, 1985; Sampson & Wooldredge, 1987; Smith & Jarjoura, 1989), and incivilities/disorder (Rountree et al., 1994). In short, past research suggests that routine activities and social disorganization theories are critical to understanding victimization patterns.

While accepting the value of routine activities and social disorganization theories, we contend that the criminal victimization literature would benefit from the input of additional criminological theory frameworks. Cultural theories are one example. As we discuss below, these perspectives delineate mechanisms by which the quantity—and nature—of criminal victimization varies both across individuals and places.

### *Cultural Theories of Offending and Victimization: Initial Evidence*

A small but growing literature tackles the challenge of identifying how cultural frameworks elucidate victimization patterns (Baumer et al., 2003; Berg, 2014; McNeeley & Wilcox, 2015a, 2015b; Schreck et al., 2012; Stewart et al., 2006). To date, this literature focuses somewhat narrowly on the cultural arguments advanced in Elijah Anderson's (1999) *Code of the Street*. Anderson contends that in neighborhoods characterized by social isolation and little trust in the police, there exists a "code of the street," or oppositional culture, in which respect, toughness, and self-reliance are highly prized forms of social capital, and a broad set of informal rules govern interpersonal behavior, including crime. Across this handful of studies, researchers have set out to document the role that street values play in victimization, particularly in disadvantaged neighborhoods.

Baumer et al. (2003, pp. 39–40) ask: How does the nature of violence differ across neighborhoods? Anderson (1999) suggests that violence in neighborhoods characterized by the street code differs from that occurring elsewhere. Notably, it differs in the extent to which it involves victim resistance, injury, and offender weapon use. This is because street code culture delineates how individuals should respond when assaulted or robbed. In street code culture, standing up to others when challenged or attacked is critical to preserving one's reputation and maintaining respect. Thus, in neighborhoods where the street code operates, residents will be more likely to stage resistance when facing an assault. Residents in street code neighborhoods, including "decent people" opposed to street code values, are constrained to act in accordance with this cultural code (Baumer et al., 2003, p. 41). Thus, because the street code discourages disputants from backing down from conflict, assaults in disadvantaged neighborhoods should result in injuries more often than in non-disadvantaged communities (Baumer et al., 2003, p. 42). Furthermore, the ever-present threat of violence and lack of faith in formal mechanisms of social control offering adequate protection from violent attacks may lead individuals from disadvantaged neighborhoods to arm themselves for protection, giving rise to an "arms race" (see also Blumstein, 1995; Sheley & Wright, 1995).

In comparison to assaults, robberies represent different interactional situations with unique behavioral expectations, according to Anderson (1999). Rather than the vigorous resistance prescribed in assaults, the street code outlines victim etiquette that grants offenders the respect demanded to maximize the chances of non-injury and survival. A key aspect of this etiquette is compliance—or total deference—by the victim (Baumer et al., 2003, p. 42). In this way, the victim's actions (e.g., eye contact, resistance) during a robbery impact levels of force used by the offender.[3] For Baumer and colleagues, this implies that in disadvantaged neighborhoods, background knowledge of "how to get robbed" means that residents are less likely to resist, resulting in a lower likelihood of injury than would be the case in neighborhoods where this victim script is absent.

In sum, these arguments constitute a theory of the way that neighborhood culture affects victimization risk, which generates specific hypotheses about the culture–victimization link: (1) Victims of assault in disadvantaged neighborhoods (with a street code culture) are more likely to resist during assault and more likely to be injured; (2) Victims of robbery in disadvantaged neighborhoods (with a street code culture) are less likely to resist and less likely to be injured; and (3) Offenders in disadvantaged neighborhoods (with a street code culture) who assault or rob residents should be more likely to use firearms (Baumer et al., 2003, p. 44).

To test these hypotheses, Baumer et al. (2003) use data on assaults and robberies from the NCVS. They find support for Anderson's description of the nature of violence in neighborhoods with varying socio-economic conditions but only mixed support for his claim that the differences are due to neighborhood effects (p. 60–61). For assaults, Baumer et al. (2003) find that victims from disadvantaged neighborhoods are significantly more likely to resist with force than are victims in non-disadvantaged neighborhoods. Moreover, they find that offenders who commit assaults in disadvantaged neighborhoods are more likely to be armed with guns. Baumer et al. (2003) do not find support, however, for the hypothesis that assault victims in disadvantaged neighborhoods are more likely to be injured, after controlling for demographic and situational factors (p. 61). For robberies, they find that victims in disadvantaged neighborhoods are significantly less likely to (nonforcefully) resist when robbed (compared to victims from relatively affluent areas), supporting Anderson (1999). However, offenders in disadvantaged neighborhoods are no more likely to use firearms than in other neighborhoods, contrary to expectations.

Stewart et al. (2006, p. 430) also pose questions about cultural influences on criminal victimization. They suggest that implicit in Anderson's (1999) argument is the notion that street code values are protective and should increase one's safety during a confrontation, especially if the individual resides in a disadvantaged neighborhood (p. 428). The street code, they suggest, entails beliefs that victimization would be worse without adherence to its behavioral expectations, making it necessary for maximizing personal safety in a dangerous environment (p. 432). We see evidence of this when residents adopt defensive and threatening postures and behaviors, including carrying weapons (p. 433). Stewart et al. (2006) emphasize three main points regarding street code implications for victimization:

> ...Anderson's (1999) work suggests that the tough, violent persona called for by the code of the street is required to increase safety in high-crime settings for several reasons. First, a failure to appear tough and ready to fight for one's honor effectively serves as an invitation for those following the street-code script to attack and harass...Second, residents of disadvantaged and violent neighborhoods cannot depend on the authorities to offer protection, and those who do are treated with the contempt reserved for those who violate the code of the streets (i.e., reliance on others suggests cowardice)...Third, Anderson (1999) argued that residing in a disadvantaged and violent neighborhood makes it difficult for residents to look out for one another and develop strong community ties and work effectively to inhibit victimization.... (pp. 433–434)

Stewart et al. (2006) test these ideas using two waves of data from the Family and Community Health Study, a sample of 720 African-American adolescents in 259 neighborhoods. Contrary to expectations derived from Anderson (1999), they find the street code is a risk factor rather than protective factor for victimization. Adolescents who adopted the street code were more likely to have been victimized, even after controlling for neighborhood characteristics, demographic correlates of victimization, and prior victimization. Moreover, their results point to an amplifying effect whereby victimization risk associated with adopting street code values is greater in neighborhoods that are more violent (p. 447).[4] Stewart et al. (2006) interpret these findings as suggesting that the street code encourages individuals to associate, or come into contact, with potential offenders (p. 448).

Whether cultural values contribute to victimization risk also is an issue addressed in Schreck et al. (2012). The authors propose that subculture of violence theories are "typological" explanations of victimization. In other words, those with violent subculture values are more prone to violent crime victimization than nonviolent victimization. If correct, individuals holding values reflective of a violent subculture—or street code—should exhibit a distinctive pattern in which their victimization experiences are more likely to feature violent crime than nonviolent crime when compared to individuals without such values. Schreck et al. (2012)

test this argument with data from a four-wave panel study of adolescents from urban and rural schools in Kentucky. They examine whether individuals expressing greater adherence to violent subculture values are at greater risk for violent than nonviolent victimization relative to those expressing weaker adherence to such values. Evidence supporting the subculture of violence theory was limited. Although adherence to subculture of violence values is associated with a heightened tendency for violent victimization in the first wave of the survey, the association did not replicate in the data from waves 2 through 4. Moreover, adherence to violent values is a consistent predictor of overall victimization levels. In short, the results of Schreck et al. (2012) suggest that subculture of violence more consistently predicts victimization, in general, than it does violent victimization specifically.

Yet another study tests hypotheses about racial variation in the nature of violent victimization (Berg, 2014). Addressing the question, Why are black males at greater risk for serious but not minor forms of violent victimization? (p. 630), Berg (2014) offers two potential explanations, one of which (differential exposure) invokes cultural mechanisms. Social psychological violence theories, he notes, suggest that racial differences in the nature of violent victimization are a function of adversary effects, or an offender's tactical response to threats posed by opponents (p. 632). In this context, group stereotypes provide actors with expectations about the potential actions of others (e.g., blacks are disproportionately violent) or reputational, situational, and dispositional attributes of the victim affect how offenders treat them in violent encounters (e.g., blacks are more likely to communicate an intimidating posture during hostile situations) (p. 633). Alternatively, the differential exposure, or routine activities/lifestyle theory, explanation emphasizes patterns of differential exposure to particularly dangerous situations where firearms are more common. Along these lines, Berg (2014) references Anderson's (1999) street code thesis to explain why "blacks may be more regularly exposed to ecological settings where firearm violence is more prevalent" (p. 634). Berg's (2014) hypothesis with regard to the differential exposure explanation is that black males are more likely to suffer gun victimization than white males because their routine activities/lifestyles differentially expose them to situations where the risk for gun violence is higher, consistent with the street code. If this hypothesis is valid, Berg (2014) argues, routine activities/lifestyle measures will explain a significant portion of the direct effects of victims' race (black) on risk for weapon victimization.

Using data from the Pittsburgh Youth Study, Berg (2014) finds that, first, black victims are more likely than white victims to be confronted by offenders armed with firearms (vs. being unarmed), consistent with previous research. Second, regarding the exposure thesis, he finds that individuals who participate in the illicit economy and who reside in risky neighborhoods are more likely to be victimized with a gun (vs. unarmed). Moreover, the addition of these measures results in a significant reduction of the race effect (although race remains significant). Finally, Berg (2014) reports that 24 percent of the race effect is indirect, with the differential association measures accounting for the bulk of indirect effects (i.e., about 19 percent) (p. 645). He concludes that group differences in exposure to risky social settings—associated with the street code—are partly responsible for racial disparities in the nature of violent victimization and calls on future researchers to isolate additional street code mechanisms that may account for the neighborhood risk differential (p. 646) (see also Piquero et al., 2005, p. 204–205).

Finally, a pair of studies by McNeeley and Wilcox (2015a, 2015b) directly examine the street code values–victimization link. Drawing from previous research showing street culture adoption increases risk of victimization, McNeeley and Wilcox (2015a) incorporate concepts from routine activities theory, particularly Finkelhor and Asdigian's (1996) notion of target congruence, or the extent to which target characteristics of potential crime victims match up with the needs, motive, or reactivities of offenders. Applying target congruence, McNeeley and Wilcox (2015a) suggest that adoption of street values could theoretically increase *or* decrease victimization:

> First, as suggested by Anderson (1999), code-related values could serve as a protective factor against victimization through a reduction in target vulnerability: Members of disadvantaged communities adopt the code of the street to demonstrate their dominance to others, sending a signal that they are not viable targets for victimization. Conversely, street values could increase the risk of victimization through an increase in target antagonism and/or target gratifiability…those who adopt the street code are likely to behave in a manner that is perceived as threatening or insulting, making them likely to be perceived as antagonistic and precipitating victimization. (p. 1052)

McNeeley and Wilcox (2015a) further argue that because of target congruence, street code-related values could influence property crime victimization and again the expected direction of the effect is unclear.

Analyzing Seattle Neighborhoods and Crime Survey data on multiple types of victimization, McNeeley and Wilcox (2015a) find that various individual-level street values measures are positively associated with assault victimization, consistent with prior research, as well as risk of vandalism and burglary, but not theft. They also find that while the street code is associated with property victimization, it provides a stronger and more consistent contribution to violent victimization. Their findings provide additional evidence that individuals holding values in line with the street code are at increased risk of victimization, particularly violent victimization (p. 1061).

In a follow-up study, McNeeley and Wilcox (2015b) examine the complex interplay between adherence to the code, residents' routine activities at micro-level places, and the broader neighborhood context derived from Anderson (1999). While adherence to the street code arguably reduces target vulnerability, McNeeley and Wilcox (2015b) suggest it may not always compensate for increased risks introduced by an individual's setting and activities. For example, public activities increase the risk of victimization for adopters of the street code by increasing their proximity and exposure to motivated offenders and by influencing their behavior during such exposures. For these reasons, McNeeley and Wilcox (2015b) propose that street codes and routine activities interact in affecting victimization, with adherence to the street code enhancing one's risk of victimization among those with more frequent engagement in public activities (p. 925). Results from their analysis of Seattle Neighborhoods and Crime Survey data support this hypothesis. For individuals with more public lifestyles, stronger belief in the street code led to increased incidents of violence. In contrast, for those who less frequently engaged in activities away from home, belief in the street code was not strongly associated with assault (p. 935). McNeeley and Wilcox (2015b) suggest that their finding that public activities moderate the influence of street code adoption on victimization might explain why previous studies show a positive relationship between street codes and victimization (p. 936), contrary to theoretical expectations.

Each study discussed above contributes important findings to the victimization literature as well as offering initial insight into how cultural theories of offending may be useful to the study of victimization. Indeed, these studies offer several key conclusions. First, while Anderson's (1999) theoretical work generates competing hypotheses regarding what impact the adoption of street code values have on victimization, research findings suggest that street code adoption *increases* the risk of victimization, especially violent victimization. Second, research reveals an amplifying effect whereby the victimization risk associated with street code values is greater in more disadvantaged or violent neighborhoods. Finally, group differences in exposure to risky social settings—associated with the street code—are partly responsible for racial disparities in violent victimization. At the same time, there is much room left for theoretical development in this line of research, a topic to which we now turn.

### *Moving Victimization Theory Forward*

The research reviewed above indicates that cultural theories are of increasing value in the study of victimization. Yet, it also highlights limitations that illuminate major fronts on which cultural theories of victimization may advance. First, this literature highlights the fact that the incorporation of cultural theorizing into victimization research is narrowly focused, relying almost exclusively on Anderson's street code thesis for theoretical grounding and hypothesis generation. While this is somewhat understandable given the important position that Anderson's work occupies in efforts to understand the culture–crime nexus, the neglect of other potentially useful cultural frameworks works to the detriment of the field. Indeed, as Lindegaard, Miller, and Reynald (2013) point out, urban scholars have produced "complex theorizing about the sources, components, reproduction and disjunctures of culture….Yet, criminologists have relied disproportionately on Anderson's (1999) *Code of the Street*, limiting a fuller understanding of how culture might relate to victimization risks" (p. 968).

In our view, preoccupation with Anderson's work limits theoretical development by circumscribing the social and geographic contexts to which cultural theory-victimization research is oriented. Because Anderson's theory addresses a particular setting—economically disadvantaged, racial minority-inhabited neighborhoods in a large city—criminologists have a tendency to constrain their theorizing and research activity to similar locations. As a result, we tend to think of cultural codes and their effects on victimization as relevant only among people of color inhabiting low-income, urban communities, and we are slow to explore influences of cultural codes on crime and victimization in other settings. This is an unfortunate development because criminology's "[e]mphasis on the urban underclass belies the importance of codes for all people, including those living outside the inner city" (Copes, Hochstetler, & Forsyth, 2013, p. 762).

In addition, we contend that an overreliance on Anderson's concept of the "street code" has limited criminologists' efforts to theorize freely about how various cultural concepts—beyond street codes—are associated with criminal offending and victimization. The failure to think beyond the concept of street codes is of course limiting in its own right. However, this problem is compounded by the fact that the street code concept is arguably fuzzy in both conceptualization and measurement. Indeed, scholars have previously noted that street codes are depicted in varying ways from "opposition culture" to "value orientation" to "personal identity" to "etiquette" or "script" (Wacquant, 2002, p. 1492). Thus, while criminologists seem to agree that street codes may affect the behaviors of criminal offenders and victims, "investigators have not been in agreement about just what the codes are or how they constrain behavior" (Copes et al., 2013, p. 762).

A second front on which scholars can advance victimization theory involves further integration of cultural theory with key components of other essential victimization perspectives, such as routine activities. Work by McNeeley and Wilcox (2015a, 2015b) offers one leading example, though we believe there are more opportunities to realize. A strength of the routine activities framework is that it pushes scholars to recognize that more than just offender motivation is critical to understanding variations in offending. The values, beliefs, and strategies of actions of potential victims also matter, as do those of potential "third party guardians" who may be present to varying degrees across diverse social and spatial contexts. Cultural theories are useful because they help us understand what those values, beliefs, and strategies of action are and how they operate to influence each component of the "crime-triangle" that is central in routine activities and other criminal opportunity perspectives. Cultural theories help explain why some individuals are more motivated to commit crimes; they explain why some individuals are more vulnerable to victimization while others are competent at avoiding it; and they explain why some places are more effective at limiting the probability that interactions between potentially motivated offenders and potentially suitable targets will yield crime. In other words, cultural theories help us understand why the convergence of motivated offenders, suitable targets, and capable guardianship may—or may not—result in criminal incidents. In the following paragraphs, we briefly discuss ways in which cultural theories may integrate with opportunity theories to better explain criminal victimization.

### *Cultural Theories, Neighborhood Context, and Routine Activities*

Initial work on how cultural frameworks elucidate victimization theory reveals the importance of context for understanding the individual-level street code–victimization link. Consistent with this, victimization researchers remind us that "victimization events do not occur in a social or situational vacuum" (Turanovic & Pratt, 2019, p. 67) and emphasize that "when it comes to victimization, context matters" (p. 75). How so? At least two layers of context are relevant for cultural theories of offending: the broader neighborhood context and the more micro situational context. We argue both contexts operate simultaneously to influence victimization and deserve attention in research moving forward.

At the broader level, structural conditions in communities shape opportunities and social interactions in important ways, with consequences for victimization. Take, for example, concentrated disadvantage. Communities characterized by structural disadvantage often have a greater share of residents who adopt street code values, and thus are willing to victimize others. At the same time, residents of disadvantaged communities face greater pressures to engage in certain lifestyles that are "risky" in that they expose them to crime and violence. Finally, residents in disadvantaged communities have less access to (or at least perceive they have less access to) behavioral alternatives, forcing residents to buy into cultural responses, elevating victimization risk (Turanovic & Pratt, 2019, p. 75).

Combining cultural theories of offending with insights from routine activities theories takes this line of reasoning even further. Routine activities theories argue that certain behavioral routines can increase one's likelihood of victimization. Of course it is often not the mundane behavioral routines that truly elevate victimization risk but instead more "high risk" behaviors (e.g., getting drunk in public, hanging out with deviant peers, committing crimes against others) that are more likely to put individuals in high-risk locations with high-risk offenders. That is, variations in the lifestyles and routine activities in which residents engage carry different levels of risk for whether residents end up putting themselves in particular places at particular times, and of coming into contact with particular individuals.

Combining these insights, structural conditions of communities, such as concentrated disadvantage, can encourage criminal attitudes and beliefs as well as limit the extent to which residents are able to avoid coming into contact with risky people and risky settings. For victims of crime, structural conditions also shape responses to victimization by influencing the degree to which victims are able (or even willing) to adopt protective strategies or behaviors that might reduce their exposure to potential offenders.

One might argue that in this context, victims who alter their risky lifestyles can, in fact, reduce their likelihood of repeat victimization (what Hindelang et al., 1978, p. 129 referred to as the "once bitten, twice shy" hypothesis). Hindelang et al. (1978) were among the first to theorize that lifestyle patterns manifest as individual- and group-level adaptations to various aspects of social structure (as well as to role expectations). That is, individuals learn attitudes and behaviors in response to their social environment and, once learned, they become incorporated into their routine activities. Returning to the importance of the broader structural context, communities that suffer from high levels of disadvantage are likely to restrict the ability of victims to alter their lifestyles in ways that reduce the risk of repeat victimization (Turanovic & Pratt, 2019, p. 72). The takeaway from this is that we need to understand which structural conditions of communities are most likely to lead to offenders and victims coming together in space and time, consistent with routine activities theory. Related to that, we must understand how the culture of places shape conditions under which victims and offenders come together and behave in relation to one another.

While these insights offer general suggestions for thinking about how researchers can move forward, below we offer a more detailed discussion, focusing on how cultural theory and routine activity's concept of target suitability may inform new directions in research.

### *One Example: Cultural Theory and Target Suitability*

Code of violence theories provide a cultural basis for motivations to initiate acts of violence, but do they also specify rules for choosing targets of that violence? We contend that cultural theories, particularly those emphasizing codes of violence, make assertions both about what motivates offenders to commit crimes and about what and who are suitable targets for victimization. Cultural theories imply that target suitability is not simply a reflection of the personal preferences or tastes of motivated offenders, rather they are culturally constructed images internalized through socialization. For example, in their study of bar fighting culture among white working class males in the southern U.S., Copes et al. (2013) report on rules guiding when it is appropriate to engage in physical fighting and who is or is not an appropriate opponent. Violating these rules may elicit dishonor. Contrary to the belief that violent confrontation is required against all insults, Copes et al. argue that adherence to bar fighter's code would lead to nonviolent toleration of certain insults or potential conflict situations. Insults that are inadvertent, insults made by others who are clearly physically inferior, insults followed by clear attempts at de-escalation, or insults coming from excessively inebriated or otherwise incompetent opponents are several of the circumstances in which walking away is considered merciful and honorable. In other words, the cultural code described by Copes et al. identifies individuals in these circumstances as unsuitable targets. Fights initiated in these circumstances do not garner respect and honor, but may warrant its loss.

Beyond addressing factors that influence whether a target is suitable to an offender, cultural theories may contribute to answering the question: What makes individuals more vulnerable to victimization? While typical answers include characteristics like small physical size or weakness, cultural theory directs our attention to whether cultural exposures and socialization protect us from, or expose us to, victimization risks. As we reviewed in earlier sections, one expectation derived from Anderson's work is that street code adoption is protective, enacted in part to convey invulnerability. Yet research finds the opposite is true—adopting the code increases victimization risk (Berg et al., 2012; Schreck et al., 2012; Stewart et al., 2006). Still, studies examining the culture–victimization relationship are sparse and we know relatively little about how various dimensions of culture affect vulnerability to crime.

One possibility is that cultural socialization impacts victim vulnerability because it builds awareness of, and commitments to, value orientations and associated action strategies that can limit or enhance victimization risk. For example, in their ethnographic research in Cape Town, South Africa, Lindegaard and colleagues (Lindegaard & Zimmerman, 2017; Lindegaard et al., 2013) found that individuals with "flexible repertoires" were able to shift deftly between interactions with others who exhibited "gangster" and "decent" repertoires, adapting to their present company and social situations. Their findings show that individuals who adopt these flexible cultural repertoires experienced less victimization than those who employed either the "gangster" or the "decent" repertoire. In fact, study participants exhibiting flexible repertoires generally avoided becoming victims of crime while those who exhibited the "gangster" and "street" repertoires were more often crime victims: "...exclusively claiming decent or gang repertoires made young men extraordinarily at risk of victimization. Strategically incorporating a bit of both while avoiding offending worked protectively" (Lindegaard & Zimmerman, 2017, p. 215). Interestingly, Lindegaard and Zimmerman note that the protective effects of the flexible cultural repertoire did not occur because its practitioners were peace brokers between opposing cultural orientations but because "they melted in as urban chameleons" (p. 216) who could adopt the different interactional styles and perform strategically and as needed, when in the company of a "gangster" or "decent" audience.

For those employing a "gangster" cultural repertoire, victimization vulnerability was high and linked to a commitment to a "gangster" cultural orientation, and the dangerous activities associated with it, including a willingness to initiate violence as well as engage in other dangerous activities like drug use. Victimization rates were also high for the "decent" group, but their vulnerability resulted from the fact that their "decent" value orientation and behavioral repertoire challenged the worldview of those with a "gangster" orientation, especially their notions of appropriate masculinity. Indeed, Lindegaard and Zimmerman (2017) suggest violent acts committed by those with "gangster" repertoires against those with "decent" repertoires were intended to "re-establish social hierarchies by punishing and rejecting attempts [by those exhibiting the 'decent repertoire'] to redefine" what it meant to be a "real man" (p. 214).

In light of these findings, we believe victimology would advance by research exploring more deeply if and how cultural concepts like "flexible repertoires" (Lindegaard & Zimmerman, 2017; Lindegaard et al., 2013), "street efficacy" (Gibson, Fagan, & Antle, 2014; Sharkey, 2006), or "code switching" (Anderson, 1999) impact victimization. Returning to the discussion of flexible repertoires, for example, several important questions need answers: (1) Is repertoire flexibility associated with lower risks of victimization?; (2) Under what contextual circumstances does such flexibility provide protection?; (3) Are individuals lacking in flexible cultural repertoires aware of the vulnerability created by their inflexibility?; (4) Would awareness of this vulnerability lead to efforts to acquire these skills?; and (5) Do strong commitments to a conventional culture orientation preclude some individuals from making efforts to perform "street" culture (i.e., code-switch or pretend) even if it could reduce their vulnerability in street settings? If so, is their refusal a strategy of action selected because it reaffirms their personal value commitments and because it signifies the importance of their moral/cultural position to others wrestling with how to behave in similar circumstances?

The discussion above has focused on cultural theories and one element of routine activities theory—target suitability. A similar approach could be taken with respect to another of routine activity's concepts—capable guardianship. Much could be studied on this topic. Just to offer one example, returning to the concepts of "flexible repertoires" and "code switching," we might consider the extent to which individuals who flex between cultural orientations or toolkits differ in their willingness to intervene, and whether that may depend, to some extent, on broader neighborhood structure and culture. In neighborhoods where cultural heterogeneity exists, passing as "decent" or "gangster" represents a delicate balance that involves not only managing perceptions during direct interactions with others, but also managing perceptions when one is a "third party" to a conflict or crime. Willingness to intervene, therefore, is a reflection of place-based culture.

Researchers could also pursue questions around how capable guardianship may be informed by neighborhood collective efficacy, or shared values around crime-control. We might expect that the convergence of motivated offenders and suitable targets in places of high collective efficacy should result in lower prevalence of victimization compared to places with low collective efficacy, due to expectations around capable guardianship. Alternatively, frameworks emphasizing cultural heterogeneity and cultural attenuation both suggest a weakening in the ethic of intervention. Cultural heterogeneity arguments suggest the encroachment of alternative ideas might create doubt or ambiguity, thereby weakening collective efficacy. Cultural attenuation arguments suggest that residents become disconnected from the mainstream (e.g., looking out for the greater good). Weakened conventional culture means that third party observers are less committed to intervention individually and less certain that intervention is a shared value.

## Conclusion

This chapter is an effort at reinvigoration of victimization theory. We began the chapter by reviewing extant victimization theory and scholarship, highlighting its important contributions to the field. We then discussed critiques of this body of work, focusing on the limitations hindering theoretical development beyond existing frameworks of lifestyles and routine activities explanations. Our position is that victimization theory and research would benefit from the input of additional criminological theory frameworks. Toward that end, we introduced cultural theories, explaining why these popular theories of offending may be fruitful. Drawing on and expanding a small but important literature on the street codes–victimization link, we identified various ways that cultural frameworks may inform the study of victims and victimization, emphasizing connections among various cultural theories, neighborhood context, and routine activities.

Without restating our arguments here, we recognize the wide array of complex factors that must converge for victimization to occur. These include the choices victims make and the ways in which they evaluate information at hand and weigh the consequences of various behavioral alternatives; how offenders approach a similar set of decision processes; how the broader structure of the environment sets the stage for a victimization event itself; and, most relevant to our focus, how cultural pressures, expectations, scripts, and codes push all parties toward conflict. In short, many things have to happen in order for victims and offenders to converge in time and space and the result of that convergence is often dictated by factors—culture included—specific to the situation itself. Our hope is that the ideas presented in this chapter will stimulate additional theoretical debate and encourage scholars to further develop these lines of inquiry.

## Notes

1 See related critiques of Luckenbill's (1977) situated transaction perspective and feminist perspective (Turanovic & Pratt, 2019, p. 52–56).
2 For overviews, historical perspectives, and typologies of cultural theory see Berg et al. (2012:413–415); Harding and Hepburn (2014); Kubrin (2015); Sampson and Bean (2006); and Wilcox, Cullen and Feldmeyer (2018).
3 For related research on the role of victims' actions in robberies see Katz (1991) and Wright and Decker (1997).
4 These findings are consistent with the literature on gangs and victimization. Decker and van Winkle (1996), for example, observed that gang members

reported joining gangs for protection and social status. However, instead of offering protection, joining gangs seemed to increase their probability of victimization (see also Rich & Grey, 2005).

## References

Anderson, E. (1999). *Code of the streets: Decency, violence, and the moral life of the inner city*. New York: W. W. Norton.

Baumer, E., Horney, J., Felson, R., & Lauritsen, J. L. (2003). Neighborhood disadvantage and the nature of violence. *Criminology*, *41*(1), 39–72.

Berg, M. T. (2012). The overlap of violent offending and victimization: Assessing the evidence and explanations. In M. DeLisi & P. Conis (Eds.), *Violent offenders: Theory, research, policy and practice, 2nd Edition*. Burlington, MA: Jones & Bartlett Learning.

Berg, M. T. (2014). Accounting for racial disparities in the nature of violent victimization. *Journal of Quantitative Criminology*, *30*(4), 629–650.

Berg, M. T., & Loeber, R. (2011). Examining the neighborhood context of the violent offending-victimization relationship: A prospective investigation. *Journal of Quantitative Criminology*, *27*(4), 427–451.

Berg, M. T., Stewart, E. A., Brunson, R. K., & Simons, R. L. (2012). Neighborhood cultural heterogeneity and adolescent violence. *Journal of Quantitative Criminology*, *28*(3), 411–435.

Blumstein, A. (1995). *Youth violence, guns, and the illicit-drug industry. Journal of Criminal Law and Criminology*, *86*(1), 10–36.

Brezina, T., Agnew, R., Cullen, F. T., & Wright, J. P. (2004). The code of the street: A quantitative assessment of Elijah Anderson's subculture of violence thesis and its contribution to youth violence research. *Youth Violence and Juvenile Justice*, *2*(4), 303–328.

Browning, C. R. (2002). The span of collective efficacy: Extending social disorganization theory to partner violence. *Journal of Marriage and Family*, *64*(4), 833–850.

Cloward, R. A., & Ohlin, L. E. (1960). *Delinquency and opportunity: A theory of delinquent gangs*. New York: Free Press.

Cohen, A. K. (1955). *Delinquent boys: The culture of the gang*. Glencoe, IL: Free Press.

Cohen, A. K., Lindesmith, A. R., & Schuessler, K. (Eds.). (1956). *The Sutherland papers*. Bloomington: Indiana University Press.

Cohen, L. E., & Felson, M. (1979). Social change and crime rate trends: A routine activity approach. *American Sociological Review*, *44*, 588–608.

Cohen, L. E., Kluegel, J. R., & Land, K. C. (1981). Social inequality and predatory criminal victimization: An exposition and test of a formal theory. *American Sociological Review*, *46*, 505–524.

Copes, H., Hochstetler, A., & Forsyth, C. J. (2013). Peaceful warriors: Codes for violence among adult male bar fighters. *Criminology*, *51*(3), 761–794.

Decker, S. H., & van Winkle, B. (1996). *Life in the gang: Family, friends, and violence*. New York: Cambridge University Press.

Felson, R. B., Liska, A. E., South, S. J., & McNulty, T. L. (1994). The subculture of violence and delinquency: Individual vs. school context effects. *Social Forces*, *73*(1), 155–173.

Finkelhor, D., & Asdigian, N. L. (1996). Risk factors for youth victimization: Beyond a lifestyles/routine activities theory approach. *Violence and victims*, *11*(1), 3–19.

Gibson, C. L., Fagan, A. A., & Antle, K. (2014). Avoiding violent victimization among youths in urban neighborhoods: The importance of street efficacy. *American Journal of Public Health*, *104*(2), e154–e161.

Harding, D. J. (2007). Cultural context, sexual behavior, and romantic relationships in disadvantaged neighborhoods. *American Sociological Review*, *72*(3), 341–364.

Harding, D. J., & Hepburn, P. (2014). Cultural mechanisms in neighborhood effects research in the United States. *Sociol Urbana Rurale*, *103*, 37–73.

Hindelang, M. J., Gottfredson, M. R., Garofalo, J. (1978). *Victims of personal crime: An empirical foundation for a theory of personal victimization*. Cambridge, MA: Ballinger.

Jennings, W. G., Piquero, A. R., & Reingle, J. M. (2012). On the overlap between victimization and offending: A review of the literature. *Aggression and Violent behavior*, *17*(1), 16–26.

Katz, J. (1991). The motivation of the persistent robber. *Crime and Justice*, *14*, 277–306.

Kennedy, L. W., & Forde, D. R. (1990). Routine activities and crime: An analysis of victimization in Canada. *Criminology*, *28*(1), 137–152.

Kornhauser, R. R. (1978). *Social sources of delinquency: An appraisal of analytic models*. Chicago: University of Chicago Press.

Kubrin, C. E. (2015). Cultural disorganization and crime. In F. T. Cullen, P. Wilcox, R. J. Sampson, and B. Dooley (Eds.), *Challenging criminological theory: The legacy of Ruth Kornhauser* (pp. 193–213). New Jersey: Transaction Publishers.

Kubrin, C. E., & Weitzer, R. (2003). New directions in social disorganization theory. *Journal of Research in Crime and Delinquency*, *40*(4), 374–402.

Lauritsen, J. (2001). The social ecology of violent victimization: Individual and contextual effects in the NCVS. *Journal of Quantitative Criminology*, *17*, 3–32.

Lee, M. R., & Ousey, G. C. (2011). Reconsidering the culture and violence connection: Strategies of action in the rural south. *Journal of Interpersonal Violence*, *26*(5), 899–929.

Lindegaard, M. R., & Zimmermann, F. (2017). Flexible cultural repertoires: Young men avoiding offending and victimization in township areas of Cape Town. *Ethnography*, *18*(2), 193–220.

Lindegaard, M. R., Miller, J., & Reynald, D. M. (2013). Transitory mobility, cultural heterogeneity, and victimization risk among young men of color: Insights from an ethnographic study in Cape Town, South Africa. *Criminology*, *51*(4), 967–1008.

Luckenbill, D. F. (1977). Homicide as a situated transaction. *Social Problems*, *25*, 176–186.

McNeeley, S. (2015). Lifestyle-routine activities and crime events. *Journal of Contemporary Criminal Justice*, *31*(1), 30–52.

McNeeley, S., & Wilcox, P. (2015a). The code of the street and violent versus property crime victimization. *Violence and Victims*, *30*(6), 1049–1067.

McNeeley, S., & Wilcox, P. (2015b). Street codes, routine activities, neighborhood context and victimization. *British Journal of Criminology*, *55*, 921–943.

Merton, R. K. (1938). Social structure and anomie. *American Sociological Review*, *3*, 672–682.

Miethe, T. D., & McDowall, D. (1993). Contextual effects in models of criminal victimization. *Social Forces*, *71*(3), 741–759.

Miethe, T. D., & Meier, R. F. (1994). *Crime and its structural context: Towards a theory of offenders, victims and situations.* Albany, NY: State University of New York Press.

Miller, W. B. (1958). Lower class culture as a generating milieu of gang delinquency. *Journal of Social Issues, 14*, 5–19.

Piquero, A., Farrington, D. P., & Blumstein, A. (2003). Criminal career paradigm. In Michael Tonry (Ed.), *Crime and Justice: A Review of Research* (pp. 359–406). Chicago: University of Chicago Press.

Piquero, A. R., Moffitt, T. E., & Lawton, B. (2005). Race and crime: The contribution of individual, familial, and neighborhood-level risk factors to life-course-persistent offending. In D. F. Hawkins & K. Kempf-Leonard (Eds.), *Our children, their children: Confronting racial and ethnic differences in American juvenile justice* (p. 202–244). Chicago: University of Chicago Press.

Pratt, T. C., & Turanovic, J. J. (2016). Lifestyle and routine activity theories revisited: The importance of "risk" to the study of victimization. *Victims & Offenders*, *11*(3), 335–354.

Rich, J. A., & Grey, C. M. (2005). Pathways to recurrent trauma among young black men: Traumatic stress, substance use, and the "code of the street." *American Journal of Public Health*, *95*, 816–824.

Rountree, P. W., Land, K. C., & Miethe, T. D. (1994). Macro-micro integration in the study of victimization: A hierarchical logistic model analysis across Seattle neighborhoods. *Criminology*, *32*(3), 387–414.

Sampson, R. J. (1985). Neighborhood and crime: The structural determinants of personal victimization. *Journal of Research in Crime and Delinquency*, *22*, 7–40.

Sampson, R. J., & Bean, L. (2006). Cultural mechanisms and killing fields: A revised theory of community-level racial inequality. In R. Peterson, L. Krivo, & J. Hagan (Eds.), *The many colors of crime: Inequalities of race, ethnicity and crime in America*. New York: New York University Press.

Sampson, R. J., & Lauritsen, J. L. (1990). Deviant lifestyles, proximity to crime, and the offender-victim link in personal violence. *Journal of Research in Crime and Delinquency*, *27*(2), 110–139.

Sampson, R. J., & Wooldredge, J. D. (1987). Linking the micro-and macro-level dimensions of lifestyle-routine activity and opportunity models of predatory victimization. *Journal of Quantitative Criminology*, *3*(4), 371–393.

Schreck, C. J. (1999). Criminal victimization and low self-control: An extension and test of a general theory of crime. *Justice Quarterly*, *16*(3), 633–654.

Schreck, C. J., Stewart, E. A., & Osgood, D. W. (2008). A reappraisal of the overlap of violent offenders and victims. *Criminology*, *46*(4), 871–906.

Schreck, C. J., Ousey, G. C., Fisher, B. S., & Wilcox, P. (2012). Examining what makes violent crime victims unique: Extending statistical methods for studying specialization to the analysis of crime victims. *Journal of Quantitative Criminology*, *28*(4), 651–671.

Sharkey, P. T. (2006). Navigating dangerous streets: The sources and consequences of street efficacy. *American Sociological Review*, *71*(5), 826–846.

Shaw, C. R., & McKay, H. D. (1942). *Juvenile delinquency and urban areas*. Chicago: University of Chicago Press.

Sellin, T. (1938). *Culture conflict and crime*. New York: Social Science Research Council.

Sheley, J. F., & Wright, J. D. (1995). *In the line of fire: Youth, guns, and violence in urban America*. Hawthorne, NY: Aldine de Gruyter Publishing Co.

Smith, D. A., & Jarjoura, G. R. (1989). Household characteristics, neighborhood composition and victimization risk. *Social Forces*, *68*(2), 621–640.

St. Jean, P. K. B. (2007). *Pockets of crime: Broken windows, collective efficacy, and the criminal point of view*. Chicago, IL: University of Chicago Press.

Stewart, E. A., & Simons, R. L. (2006). Structure and culture in African American adolescent violence: A partial test of the "code of the street" thesis. *Justice Quarterly*, *23*(1), 1–33.

Stewart, E. A., Schreck, C. J., & Simons, R. L. (2006). "I Ain't Gonna Let No One Disrespect Me" Does the Code of the Street Reduce or Increase Violent Victimization among African American Adolescents?. *Journal of Research in Crime and Delinquency*, *43*(4), 427–458.

Swartz, K., Wilcox, P., & Ousey, G. C. (2017). Culture as values or culture in action? Street codes and student violent offending. *Victims & Offenders*, *12*(6), 868–890.

Swidler, A. (1986). Culture in action: Symbols and strategies. *American Sociological Review*, *51*, 273–286.

Turanovic, J. J., & Pratt, T. C. (2019). *Thinking about victimization: Context and consequences*. New York: Routledge.

Van Wilsem, J., Wittebrood, K., & De Graaf, N. D. (2006). Socioeconomic dynamics of neighborhoods and the risk of crime victimization: A multilevel study of improving, declining, and stable areas in the Netherlands. *Social Problems*, *53*(2), 226–247.

Velez, M. B. (2001). The role of public social control in urban neighborhoods: A multilevel analysis of victimization risk. *Criminology*, *39*(4), 837–864.

Villarreal, A., & Silva, B. F. (2006). Social cohesion, criminal victimization and perceived risk of crime in Brazilian neighborhoods. *Social Forces*, *84*(3), 1725–1753.

von Hentig, H. (1948). *The criminal and his victim: Studies in the sociobiology of crime*. New Haven, CT: Yale University Press.

Wacquant, L. (2002). Scrutinizing the street: Poverty, morality, and the pitfalls of urban ethnography. *American Journal of Sociology*, *107*, 1468–1532.

Warner, B. D. (2003). The role of attenuated culture in social disorganization theory. *Criminology*, 41, 73–97.

Wilcox, P., Cullen, F. T., & Feldmeyer, B. (2018). *Communities and crime: An enduring American challenge*. Philadelphia: Temple University Press.

Wilcox, P., Land, K. C., & Hunt, S. A. (2003). *Criminal circumstance: A dynamic muticontextual criminal opportunity theory*. Hawthorne, NY: Aldine de Gruyter Publishing Co.

Wilcox, P., Madensen, T. D., & Tillyer, M. S. (2007). Guardianship in context: Implications for burglary victimization risk and prevention. *Criminology*, *45*(4), 771–803.

Wolfgang, M. E. (1958). *Patterns of criminal homicide*. Oxford: Oxford University Press.

Wolfgang, M. E., & Ferracut, F. (1967). *The subculture of violence: Towards an integrated theory in criminology*. London: Tavistock.

Wright, R., & Decker, S. (1997). *Armed robbers in action: Stickups and street culture*. Boston, MA: Northeastern University Press.

# 4

# Environmental Criminology, Design, and Victimization: What We Know, How We Have Failed, and Where We Need to Go

*Martin A. Andresen and Tarah Hodgkinson*

Victimization does not occur in a vacuum. It occurs in particular places and spaces. Unsurprisingly then, victimization concentrates in certain parts of the urban landscape. Environmental criminology is useful for understanding how and why victimization concentrates in some places and not others and for guiding policy and practice to reduce victimization and make these places safer.

The first wave of research that investigated the spatial and temporal (where and when) dynamics of crime and victimization date back almost 200 years to the work of Adolphe Quetelet (1831, 1842) and Andre-Michel Guerry (1832, 1833). They found that concentrations of crime varied across French departments (approximately the size of a US county), and differently for property versus violent crime; Quetelet (1842) also found that crime and victimization varied across the seasons.

The second wave of spatial criminology emerged out of the Chicago School. Here, local practitioners and academics investigated neighborhood level crime and victimization. Research in this second wave generally found that crime and victimization was highest in "socially disorganized" neighborhoods characterized by population turnover, ethnic heterogeneity, and low socio-economic status (Shaw & McKay, 1942). This formative work in social disorganization theory investigated juvenile delinquency, not crime or victimization, but had important implications for the research of both.

The third wave of research that investigated spatial and temporal dynamics of crime is now referred to as environmental criminology, a term coined by Jeffery (1971). According to Brantingham and Brantingham (1981a), this third wave differentiated itself from the first two by specifically having a geographical rather than a sociological imagination—the fundamental focus of the research changed. When discussing this shift, Brantingham and Brantingham (1981a) stated that there were four fundamental dimensions necessary for understanding the phenomena of crime: the legal dimension, the offender dimension, the victim dimension, and the place (or situational) dimension. The legal dimension is concerned with the creation, formation, and interpretations of laws; the offender dimension is concerned with understanding the motivation of offenders, how that motivation changes across time, and why different people may have different degrees of motivation to commit crime; the victimization dimension is concerned with understanding why particular people are victims of crime; and the place, or situational, dimension is dominantly concerned with the spatial and/or temporal aspects of crime.

This third wave led to notable theoretical and empirical advancements within criminology, discussed below, but they primarily focused on opportunity structures. We argue that focusing on opportunity structures had unintended consequences that, in some cases, led to increased victimization particularly for marginalized populations. In this chapter, we outline the primary theoretical perspectives within environmental criminology (routine activity approach, geometry of crime, rational choice) and crime prevention through environmental design, discussing how victimization is accounted for, or more often ignored, by this research. We then discuss where environmental criminology has contributed to understanding victimization, where it has failed, and where it needs to go.

## Theories and Perspectives Within Environmental Criminology

As noted above, there are three theories, or perspectives, within environmental criminology: routine activity approach, geometry of crime, and rational choice. Ironically, these theories or perspectives emerged almost a decade or more after C. Ray Jeffery (1971) coined the term in the context of crime prevention.

*Routine Activity Approach*

The routine activity approach, Cohen and Felson (1979), originally emerged to investigate the sociological paradox: crime was increasing while the standard metrics of social well-being (unemployment, after-tax income, education, and so on) improved. In their influential paper, Cohen and Felson (1979) stated that in order for a crime occur, there needed to be a motivated offender, a suitable target, and the lack of a capable guardian converging in time and space. They argued that if there were more opportunities for these three components to converge, crime rates would increase.

With regard to victimization, the routine activity approach directly refers to suitable targets. In fact, one of the primary interests of Cohen and Felson (1979) is the increase in target suitability in the post-1950s era, particularly in the development of (relatively) lightweight electronics that continues to impact crime patterns today (Brimicombe, 2012; Mailley, Garciab, Whitehead, & Farrell, 2008; Whitehead & Farrell, 2008). However, in their empirical assessment, Cohen and Felson (1979) found that changes in routine activities were the drivers of increases in crime patterns. This relates to both property and personal victimization. Individuals, in particular women who had increasing opportunities to participate in the workforce, were spending more time outside of the relatively protective environment of the home and placing themselves and their property at greater risk of the above-mentioned convergences. Kennedy and Forde (1990) showed this more definitively measuring individual level activity patterns and self-report victimization data. Specifically, those who spent more time away from home had greater levels of victimization—bars and pubs for violent crime, and most other activities for property crime.

Most of the research within environmental criminology that has used the routine activity approach has operationalized suitable targets in an indirect manner. This has commonly been in the context of (spatial) regression analyses of crime in places (neighborhoods, census tracts, and other administrative units) using variables that measure the presence of suitable targets, relative to other areas: measures of income or housing value, single parent households, the presence of youth, and so on. Most often, strong support is found for these correlates, indicating that places with more suitable targets have more crime—see, for example, Andresen (2011). However, this empirical support for the routine activity approach, though instructive and useful in some crime prevention contexts, does not directly advance scholarship on victimization. From a victimization perspective, stating that places with more suitable targets, or people with particular routine activities, have higher rates of victimization is an empty statement that can be interpreted as victim-blaming, though that was not its intent.

*Geometry of Crime*

The geometry of crime (Brantingham & Brantingham, 1981b, 1993a) is effectively a spatial version of the routine activity approach—it is important to distinguish the geometry of crime from crime pattern theory (Brantingham & Brantingham, 1993b), the latter being an attempt at meta-theory to bring together the various approaches within environmental criminology. In the geometry of crime, our routine activities are presented spatially by the concepts of activity and awareness spaces. Our activity space is the area we spend most of our time at particular places (nodes) and the pathways between those nodes. Our awareness space extends some (albeit small) distance beyond our activity space; because one must deviate from their traditional paths at times, they tend to learn about the immediate areas around the nodes and pathways we routinely travel. Because of the planned nature of our built environments we share a lot of our activity nodes and pathways with other people: central business districts, shopping centers, and entertainment zones.

The geometry of crime has a number of predictions regarding the locations of criminal events, based on the above (see Brantingham & Brantingham, 1981b), but the critical message from this perspective is that criminal victimization is neither randomly nor uniformly distributed: it is concentrated in both space and time. With regard to victimization, the geometry of crime does not state anything specifically. Rather, criminal events (victimization) will occur when the activity spaces of motivated offenders overlap with the activity spaces of suitable targets. Consequently, people are most often victims of criminal events when they are in places that they routinely spend their time.

These locations for criminal victimization become most apparent within this perspective from the concepts of crime generators and crime attractors (Brantingham & Brantingham, 1995). Crime generators are places that generate a lot of criminal events because there is the presence of a large number of motivated offenders and suitable targets converging in time and space. This convergence will be at an activity node, such as a transit station or transfer point. Crime attractors, on the other hand, attract motivated offenders because of their criminal opportunities. Therefore, motivated offenders will actually modify their activity and awareness spaces to take advantage of such opportunities.

*Rational Choice*

Rationality is an assumed aspect of both the routine activity approach and the geometry of crime, but rational choice is also specifically used as a perspective within environmental criminology (Clarke & Cornish, 1985; Cornish & Clarke, 1986). Within the rational choice perspective, motivated offenders make a sequence of choices that effectively involve costs (probability of being caught and punished) and benefits (the value(s) of the outcome of the offense) when deciding if they should act at all, if a particular offense should be undertaken, and when they should desist from such behavior. Most often, people do not contest property crimes as being the outcome of a "rational choice," but violent crimes tend to be more difficult to interpret in that context. However, different people have different preferences, resources, and constraints that lead to different choices. In other words, what is rational for one, might be irrational to another. What is important to understand is that people are making the best choices they can to reach *their* goals, while considering their constraints relating to time, money, and so on. And (violent) crime is simply another choice. Beauregard, Rossmo, & Proulx (2007) has found this to be the case for violent sexual crimes with offenders making as many as nine (rational) choices for their being able to complete their criminal events.

One of the criticisms of this approach is that it is impossible to have enough information all the time to make decisions in a "rational" manner. Gathering and processing information is costly, particularly in a criminological context, and may not even be considered possible. In an effort to address this issue, the field of limited or bounded rationality emerged. Herbert Simon (1957, 1982) argued that we make our decisions heuristically by seeking out pleasure and avoiding pain, making rational choices based on the best available information.

The most common application of the rational choice perspective within criminology is in the context of crime prevention and reduction. The rational choice perspective was used to show that different criminal opportunities were not functionally equivalent and that if the "easy" targets for criminal victimization were removed or reduced, the "second best" targets would not be worth the effort for many motivated offenders. Consequently, though *some* criminal activities *may be* displaced, this was not an expectation *en masse* (Felson & Clarke, 1998). With regard to the displacement of crime, the expectation from this perspective is that it will be minimal, if it even exists. In a recent and sophisticated experimental analysis of the existence of crime displacement, Weisburd, Wyckoff, Ready, Eck, Hinkle, & Gajewski (2006) found no evidence for this phenomenon. In fact, these authors found that the benefits of crime prevention initiatives diffused into surrounding areas—this was commonly found in other literature as well, but not using a sophisticated experimental methodology—see Barr and Pease (1990), Eck (1993), Hesseling (1994), and Guerette and Bowers (2009) for reviews of this literature that find very little evidence for crime displacement. However, Hodgkinson, Saville, & Andresen (2020) found that crime displacement can occur further away than originally expected by previous research and can lead to more violent and detrimental victimizations.

As such, the rational choice literature within criminology has had little to say with regard to victimization. From a prevention standpoint, it has highlighted many circumstances in which (situational) prevention has been successful (Clarke, 1992, 1997) that can then be inverted as advice to prevent victimization, but its focus is on changing opportunity structures that subsequently change offender behavior with regard to criminal victimizations.

### *Crime Prevention Through Environmental Design and Situational Crime Prevention*

Crime prevention through environmental design, commonly referred to as CPTED, had its modern beginnings with the work of C. Ray Jeffery (1969, 1971) and Oscar Newman (1972). The "environment" in this context is meant broadly, referring to not only the built/physical environment that much of CPTED practices follow today, but also the legal and social environment. These various environments influence both opportunities and motivations for criminal activity. As such, modifications to our environment can either facilitate or mediate opportunities for crime. For obvious reasons, crime prevention focuses on modifications to our various environments in order to reduce criminal occurrences and victimizations but has also been used to outline how environments can be built to reduce criminal victimizations, *a priori* rather than *post hoc*.

How and when CPTED is implemented is of particular importance in determining the timing of the expected reductions in criminal victimizations. Brantingham and Faust (1976) utilized the primary-secondary-tertiary (PST) model from public health to crime prevention: primary prevention is implemented before a problem emerges (good social service policies, for example, to reduce motivation), secondary prevention is implemented when a target (person, object, or place) is identified as being at a greater level of risk than expected, and tertiary prevention is implemented after some form of victimization has occurred and stakeholders act to (hopefully) reduce future victimizations.

Tertiary prevention is the most common form of CPTED implementation. Rather than creating detailed development plans that identify potential opportunities for crime and redesign to prevent these opportunities (City of Saskatoon, 2010), most developers simply wait until a problem has occurred. For example, if an apartment building is dealing with a rash of auto-theft from their underground parking lot, they will likely put in methods of access control (boom gates and key fobs) to prevent further victimizations. This is particularly true in a time of neoliberalism with the trend being the reduction of social service provision (development planning) corresponding with an increase in formal control mechanisms (security) (Harvey, 2010).

More often, tertiary prevention is framed in the context of situational crime prevention (Clarke, 1980, 1983, 2012). Situational crime prevention, as the term indicates, focuses its crime prevention techniques considering the situation within which crime is occurring. As such, situational crime prevention techniques vary across crime types, time of day, places, and victim; examples of these techniques, and their broader classification, can be organized under increasing the effort, increasing the risks, reducing the rewards, reducing provocations, and removing excuses. These techniques have been shown to have success (Clarke, 1992, 1997), but these successes are often viewed, we argue, from a rather myopic perspective reducing criminal victimization here and now without the consideration of increasing victimizations there and later.

## Environmental Criminology and Victimization: What We Know

As noted above, the field of environmental criminology has not significantly contributed to the understanding of victimization patterns. However, there are a handful of areas within environmental criminology with contributions that relate to the understanding of victimization. The contributions, often understood as empirical regularities in the patterns of victimization, relate to the journey to crime/victimization, mobility triangles, repeat victimization, near-repeat victimization, and the temporal patterns of victimization.

*The Journey to Crime and Victimization*

The journey to crime actually includes two journeys: the journey of the motivated offender to the location of the criminal event and the journey of the target/victim to the location of the criminal event. We will refer to these as the journey to crime and the journey to victimization, respectively.[1] The overall finding is that the journeys to crime and victimization are short, particularly for violent crime: though there are variations across studies, the journey to violent crime is typically 1 kilometer, whereas the journey to property crime is typically 2 kilometers. These journeys are explained within environmental criminology because the metric used to assess these journeys is distance (part of the spatial dimension).

Because people spend most of their time, by definition, undertaking their routine activities in activity nodes and the pathways between them, their journeys to crime and victimization are expected to be in those spaces and the times they are there. As such, given that we attempt to minimize the effort to undertake our activities (why go to a grocery store across town when there is one two blocks away?), following Zipf's (1949) principle of least effort, our expectation for the journeys to crime and victimization are that these distances are relatively short. And this is precisely what has been found in the empirical research. Dating back almost 90 years, White (1932) found that the journey to crime was short, particularly for violent crime. This empirical regularity has been found repeatedly across a number of different property and violent crime types, national contexts, and ages of offender (Andresen, Frank, & Felson, 2014; Costello & Wiles, 2001; and Wiles & Costello, 2000).

When considering specific details regarding the types of crime being committed, research has shown that distances to crime lengthen when the reward is greater (Morselli & Royer, 2008; Vandeviver, van Daele, & vander Beken, 2015) and when a higher degree of planning is necessary (Capone & Nichols, 1976; Gabor & Gottheil, 1984; van Koppen & Jansen, 1997; White, 1932). This is consistent with the rational choice perspective with regard to expected rewards. Andresen et al. (2014)

and Ackerman and Rossmo (2015) both found that the journey to crime increases with age, peaking around 20 and then declining; this is consistent with changes in activity spaces for individuals as they age—Drawve, Walker, and Felson (2015) also showed this increase with juveniles, but had no data for adult offenders to confirm or deny the subsequent decrease found in these other studies. Additionally, Ackerman and Rossmo (2015) found that the journeys to crime in lower socio-economic neighborhoods are shorter than in higher socio-economic neighborhoods—Costello and Wiles (2001) found similar results within the context of the journeys to crime and victimization.

With regard to the journey to victimization, specifically, we are only aware of two studies. Costello and Wiles (2001) compared both the journey to crime and the journey to victimization within the context of property crime. They found that the journey to crime was relatively short, consistent with previous and subsequent research. However, they also found that the journey to victimization was even shorter, often half the distance for the journey to crime. Moreover, they found that areas with lower socio-economic status had high levels of in-area victimization with, as one would expect, shorter journeys to that victimization. Block, Galary, and Brice (2007) also found that the journey to victimization is shorter than the journey to crime for robbery and aggravated assault, but the journey is longer for sexual assault. Clearly, the victimization component of these journeys is different from the offending component. However, there is a clear lack of research in this area. The most fruitful applications with regard to distance traveled in the context of victimization is in the mobility triangle subfield of research.

### *Mobility Triangles*

A mobility triangle refers to the three geographic points that are necessary for a criminal event to occur: the starting point of the offender's journey, the starting point of the victim's journey, and the point at which they meet. As such, this research brings the journey to crime and the journey to victimization together in one construct. As a social construct, it was first put forth by Burgess (1925), when writing about sexual promiscuity. Using more criminological terms, Burgess put forth three types of triangles: delinquency triangles (offender's residence, victim's residence, and crime location all in the same neighborhood/community), mobility triangles (offender's and victim's residence in the same neighborhood, but the crime location is elsewhere), and promiscuity triangles (all points are in different neighborhoods)—Lind (1930) was the first to apply this construct to crime, finding that the delinquency triangle (the least amount of travel for both parties) was the most common in lower socio-economic neighborhoods and that the mobility of offenders increased with age—this is consistent with the journey to crime literature, discussed above.

Close to 40 years later, Normandeau (1968) expanded this typology to include five types of triangles that have been used by most researchers since this publication: crime neighborhood triangle (all in the same neighborhood), offender mobility triangle (victim and event in same neighborhood), victim mobility triangle (offender and event in same neighborhood), offense mobility triangle (offender and victim in same neighborhood), and total mobility triangle (all locations in different neighborhoods). The early work in this area found that victims were often victimized close to their home or the home of the offender (Amir, 1971; Groff & McEwen, 2007; Normandeau, 1968)—hence the short journey to crime and victimization. However, it is important to note that these patterns do vary across crime types (Rand, 1986), characteristics of the criminal event such as offender–victim relationship and the characteristics of the offender and victim (Tita & Griffith, 2005; Cosaro, Pizarro, & Shafer, 2017), and when there is more than one offender and/or victim involved in the criminal event (Andresen, Felson, & Frank, 2012; Frank, Andresen, and Felson, 2012).

Collectively, the journey to crime/victimization and mobility triangle literature has shown that, more often than not, victimization occurs close to the home of the victim. This is also useful information about offenders because they tend to live close to the criminal event location as well. Such knowledge can be used by investigators (police or otherwise) in order to identify suspect lists. For victimization, the implications are less clear. Effectively, with this knowledge in hand, suitable targets/victims only know that their risk of criminal victimization increases as they get closer to their home, which should be a safe place. The situational crime prevention literature, discussed above, would state that modifications in routine activities or the provision of guardianship in these spaces (if possible) could reduce the risk of their victimization, but is not likely to provide much solace for those at risk of victimization for the first time or if they are repeatedly victimized where they should feel safest.

*Repeat and Near-Repeat Victimization*

Repeat victimization is quite simply the phenomenon of repeatedly being a target of criminal victimization. One can be the repeated victim of the same crime type (e.g. domestic violence or hate crimes) or repeatedly a victim of different crime types. Using the International Crime Victims Survey, scholars have found that, overall, 41.5 percent of victims are re-victimized (Farrell & Bouloukos, 2001).[2] Probably the most important aspect of repeat victimization to grasp here is that the vast majority of people are not victims of crime, but once an individual has been victimized, their odds of being victimized again are quite high. As such, this is probably one of the most applicable aspects of environmental criminology for understanding the victimization aspects within criminology.

With regard to the characteristics of repeat victimization of property crimes, Johnson, Bowers, and Hirschfield, (1997) and Trickett, Osborn, Seymour, and Pease, (1992) found that residential burglary victimizations tended to occur in neighborhoods with lower socio-economic status. As such, the costs of repeat victimization tend to be borne by those who are more likely to be marginalized in society. When repeat victimization does occur, it usually occurs within 4 weeks of the initial victimization (Johnson et al., 1997; Melo, Andresen, & Matias, 2018).

An obvious question to ask at this point is: why do repeat victimizations happen? Farrell, Phillips, and Pease (1995) outlined a number of specific examples of why repeat victimizations occur, but there are two general explanations that are important to consider: the flag effect and the boost effect. The flag effect, sometimes referred to as risk heterogeneity, simply states that some targets are more suitable than others, leading to repeat victimization. This is a common explanation in the repeat victimization of residential burglary such that some neighborhoods are more suitable than others so the number of potential targets is actually quite small. The boost effect states that once an offender has completed a victimization, they have learned what worked in that particular context. As such, they may return to victimize that person/target again. The flag effect has been shown to be constant, whereas the boost effect has been shown to dissipate over time (Pease, 1998). This is unsurprising for property victimization, as the victim would only be able to replace their stolen items so many times. However, as shown by Johnson (2008) in a computer simulation, both effects were necessary to generate the repeat victimization patterns found in the empirical research.

The implications from this research for understanding, and reducing, victimization is much more direct and practical than other research in environmental criminology. Specifically, if risk heterogeneity is present then those areas with a higher risk profile should be identified and provided with crime prevention initiatives. The costs of crime are greater than the costs of providing crime prevention (Waller, 2014). Because victimization risk tends to be highest in lower socio-economic status neighborhoods, investments in crime prevention using public funds in those places simply make sense. Also using an argument regarding the efficient allocation of resources, Farrell and Pease (1993) argued for crime prevention initiatives to be put in place for those who have already been a victim of a criminal event in order to prevent their subsequent victimization that is a much high probability than someone in the general public—Grove, Farrell, Farrington, & Johnson (2012) found that crime prevention techniques reduced repeat victimization upwards of 15 percent. However, there are moral implications of this approach. In order to implement prevention against repeat victimization, the strategies have to allow for the victim to be victimized first to be able to be identify them for intervention.

An interesting spatial twist to repeat victimization is the phenomenon of near-repeat victimization: when a target is victimized (usually in the context of residential burglary) not only is that same target at greater risk of re-victimization within a short period of time, but so are other similar targets nearby (Johnson et al., 2007; Morgan, 2001; Townsley, Homel, & Chaseling, 2003). The most common test of near-repeat victimization is in the context of residential burglary; this is primarily because the (at least once) suitable target does not move so the identification of "near" repeat victimization is relatively easy to test.

Interestingly, Townsley et al. (2003) found that near-repeat victimization only occurred in certain places. Namely, they found that places with a high degree of housing homogeneity led to increases in the risk of near-repeat victimization—they also found that the presence of more motivated offenders led to increases in the probability of near-repeat victimization, but we are focusing on spatial factors that impact victimization here. As such, neighborhoods that had similar types of homes, such as more recent suburban housing developments that are completed by one builder, have been found to have higher rates of near-repeat victimization. Bowers and Johnson (2005) investigated the characteristics of near-repeat victimization in residential burglary further, finding that near-repeats are more likely in more affluent areas of the city, homes particularly close to the original victim (literally the next door neighbor was at the greatest risk), homes on the same side of the street, and homes with similar floorplans that are a common feature in more recent large-scale residential developments, as mentioned above.

Despite most of this research being centered on residential burglary, primarily for pragmatic reasons, there has been research investigating near-repeat victimization in other contexts, but this research tends to investigate near-repeat victimization at places rather than victimization of persons. This research has investigated shootings (Ratcliffe & Rengert, 2008), street robberies (Haberman & Ratcliffe, 2012; Melo et al., 2018), insurgent activity (Townsley, Johnson, & Ratcliffe, 2008), as well as motor vehicle theft (Melo et al., 2018). In these various contexts, the risk of near-repeat victimization is greatest within a relatively short timeframe (often up to 4 weeks, but as short as 1 week) and within a relatively short distance (often up to only a few hundred meters).

With regard to explanations for near-repeat victimizations, they are similar to those regarding repeat victimization, discussed above, but tend to focus on the boost effect. Bowers and Johnson (2004) found that near-repeat residential burglaries tended to have similar modus operandi, indicating near-repeat victimization by the same offender—this is further developed with the concept of optimal foraging strategies (minimizing effort while maximizing gain from criminal events) by Johnson, Summers, and Pease (2009). And Bernasco (2008) was able to show that near-repeat victimizations for residential burglary were committed by the same offender in a substantial portion of those criminal events.

### *Temporal Dimensions of Victimization*

Lastly, we will discuss the temporal dynamics of criminal events that relate to victimization. However, most of the results from this research relates to providing (potential) victims of crime with information on when they are at greatest risk. Though important, this type of "victimization" study places the onus of victimization prevention on the (potential) victims themselves.

Seasonal patterns have a history in spatial criminology that dates back close to 200 years. The temporal dynamics of criminal victimization date back to the beginning of spatial criminology with the work of Quetelet (1842) and continues today. Overall, it has been found that criminal victimizations peak in the summer and are at their lowest in the winter, particularly for violent crime types (Andresen, 2020). However, it is important to note that these general patterns do have some variations in different geographies. Research undertaken in England (Farrell & Pease, 1994; Field, 1992), Israel (Landau & Fridman, 1993), the United States (Cohn & Rotton, 2000; Rotton & Cohn, 2003), Brazil (Ceccato, 2005), The Netherlands (van Koppen & Jansen, 1999), and Scotland (Semmens, Dillane, & Ditton, 2002) found that this seasonal pattern emerges most of the time, but its magnitude varies from place to place and crime type to crime type.

Perhaps more interesting, in the context of seasonal crime patterns, is where these victimizations occur. For example, notable research has found that areas with lower socio-economic status tend to be disproportionately impacted by seasonal fluctuations in the context of homicide (Ceccato, 2005; Harries & Stadler, 1983; Harries, Stadler, & Zdorkowski, 1984) and assaults (Breetzke & Cohn, 2012). This result has been explained by noting that those with lower socio-economic status have fewer resources to escape summer heat through air conditioning—increases in temperature lead to increases in aggression. Additionally, Andresen and Malleson (2013) not only found that many crime types exhibit this seasonal pattern, but the spatial pattern of victimization shifts during the summer months to those places more frequented during those months: parks, popular beaches, and the summer fair. Similarly, Brunsdon, Corcoran, Higgs, and Ware (2009) found that victimizations tended to occur outside of the central business district during the summer months.

Temporal research of crime has also been undertaken over longer time periods such as the international crime drop (Farrell, Tilley, Tseloni, & Mailley, 2014), and weekly and daily temporal dynamics of criminal victimization. Weekly patterns of crime most often indicate that criminal events are at their greatest frequencies on Friday and Saturday (Andresen & Malleson, 2015; Corcoran, Zahnow, Kimpton, Wickes, & Brunsdon, 2019). This is most common for violent crime types, particularly assaults, but also for thefts from vehicles and criminal victimizations in commercial districts. However, it is also important to note that some crime types peak during the week when there is less guardianship present due to peoples' routine activities leaving homes unguarded for many hours of each work day—Andresen & Malleson (2015) found this to be the case for residential burglary and theft. Perhaps most interesting in their research was the change in spatial patterns of particular crime types for different days of the week.

These researchers found that assaults not only had a peak on Saturdays, but had a spatial concentration in the entertainment district that bordered on the central business district in Vancouver, Canada; a similar spatial result was found in the context of theft from vehicles within or close to parks and shopping centers. Though this information is not particularly surprising, it is predictable given these crime types, so providing (potential) victims with information as to not only which day is most likely to lead to a victimization, but where that victimization is most likely to take place, similar to the result for seasonal patterns of crime.

Lastly, research on daily temporal crime patterns brings forth an interesting measurement issue (Felson & Poulsen, 2003; Tompson & Townsley, 2010)—this would measure weekly and seasonal effects as well, but not to the same degree. That issue is the arbitrary cut-off of midnight as the change of a day. With "Friday night" and "Saturday night" running over to the next day, this could give a false sense of the risk of victimization. Friday may come across as less risky than Saturday because it does not include a few hours of that night; Saturday likely comes across at a risk level that is appropriate because it misses the last few hours of Saturday night, but does include those hours from Friday night; and Sunday may come across as greater risk than it should because any victimization counts include part of the "night" before. As such, because of this measurement issue, (potential) victims of crime may have incorrect information to base their judgments on with regard to actual risk.

Regardless of this measurement issue, there has been notable consistency in the research that has investigated daily crime patterns. Generally speaking, both property and violent crime tend to peak on Friday and Saturday nights, particularly in the context of violence that is alcohol-related (Andresen & Malleson, 2015; Newton & Hirschfield, 2009). This is the case for both street level crime and crime on transit systems (Ceccato & Uittenbogaard, 2014; Uittenbogaard & Ceccato, 2012). However, it is important to note that police interactions with the public do not always increase on Friday and Saturday nights. For example, Vaughan, Hewitt, Hodgkinson, Andresen, & Verdun-Jones (2019) found that police interactions with the mentally ill peaked during the middle of the week (Wednesday) and in the middle of the afternoon.

Though instructive for understanding patterns of crime and victimization, this literature does not tell us much about the consequences and costs of victimization. Rather, it focuses on what victims can do to reduce or minimize the risk of (further) victimization. This advice is not framed in the context of victim-blaming, but providing information for people to make "better" choices, such as the ability to alter routine activities, change the places and pathways individuals move through, and purchase safer places to live and work. However, these are not options for all. In this way, the field of environmental criminology has indirectly failed to further scholarship on victimization.

## Environmental Criminology and Victimization: How We Have Failed

Much of the environmental criminology scholarship focuses on the spatial and temporal nature of crime in order to reduce crime. However, many of these strategies that label themselves as "crime prevention" can actually victimize already victimized and marginalized populations. This is what Cozens and Love (2017) call the "dark side of CPTED," or "Crime Prevention through EXCLUSIONARY Design." They explain that these types of crime prevention strategies focus on target hardening while not considering local context or people. These strategies create a "fortress mentality" in which crime can be controlled by keeping out all potential threats through the use of increasingly advanced security technologies. Examples include the proliferation of CCTV in the downtown of almost any city, which increases control and surveillance of poor and powerless peoples in those spaces who supposedly threaten the safety and security of downtown businesses and "upstanding citizens." Local associations like Downtown Business Improvement Districts (BIDs) will use the logic of CPTED to implement private security services (Sleiman and Lippert, 2010) or new technologies that are essentially employed to remove "undesirable" people who are bad for business (Wood and McKinnon. 2019). Raymen (2016) argues that these strategies effectively "design-in" crime by creating places that focus solely on consumption and are devoid of humanity and social efficacy, further propagating offender motivation.

Never is the dark side of CPTED more evident than in the treatment of the homeless in the name of crime prevention. Target hardening strategies, which largely emerge from situational crime prevention, and not CPTED, have produced horrific outcomes such as homelessness spikes (spikes placed in entryways and under bridges) and public bench bars (bars in the middle of public benches) to discourage rough sleeping. Petty (2016) refers to this as "spatialized violence" in which target hardening serves to victimize already victimized and marginalized populations by literally attacking the places where the homeless sleep.

Second and third generation CPTED have emerged in response to the unintended consequences of the over emphasis on target hardening. The work of Saville and Cleveland (2013) reemphasizes the social and contextual nature of CPTED. They argue that in its original conception, people, not technologies, provided natural surveillance, provided territorial control, and created cohesive neighborhoods in which neighbors knew each other and would intervene if someone was behaving problematically. Second generation CPTED focuses on integrating first generation techniques (natural surveillance, access control, territoriality, and image/maintenance) with those that incorporate context and the social, including culture, cohesion, connectivity, and capacity. Mihinjac and Saville (2019) extend this notion into third generation CPTED which acknowledges that these strategies need to create inclusive and livable spaces that meet higher order needs such as belonging, esteem, and self-actualization.

If the focus of environmental criminology is to create specific and effective prevention strategies, these strategies need to be inclusive of all people. Thus, the use of target hardening alone, while ignoring local context and social needs, can lead not only to spatialized victimization (Petty, 2016) but also to spaces that discourage connection and encourage further offending (Raymen, 2016). For example, planning methodologies such as SafeGrowth® integrate the learnings of environmental criminology with social and contextual concerns to create inclusive strategies with and by local residents that shift away from crime control for the few and toward inclusion, safety, and most importantly livability for the many (Saville, 2017).

## Environmental Criminology and Victimization: Where We Need to Go

Having reviewed the spatial and temporal patterns of criminal victimization and how a myopic application of environmental criminology and crime prevention through environmental design can lead to subsequent victimization, particularly of marginalized people, we now turn to where we believe the field needs to go in order to move forward, particularly in the context of the study of victimization.

First and foremost, the focus on offenders and places clearly needs to be supplemented with victim studies. As outlined above, victimization is rarely the sole focus of study within environmental criminology, often only being tangential in the research. The research on the journey to victimization and mobility triangles, for example, tells us how far and in which areas people are victimized, but what is the impact of these spatial and temporal dynamics? Repeat and near-repeat victimization identifies the spatial and temporal patterns of re-victimization, likely explanations for these patterns, and strategies to reduce this re-victimization, but what is the impact of these repeat victims? How does this impact fear and what are the implications of changes to routine activities if they are even possible? These types of directions for future research are necessary to move the field of environmental criminology forward.

In the context of crime prevention, environmental criminologists need to move beyond considering places without considering their broader social context. Not only is the broader social context consistent with the original work on crime prevention through environmental design (Jeffery, 1971; Newman, 1972), but the empirical literature has shown that we must consider areas larger than micro-places to truly understand spatial patterns of crime (O'Brien et al., 2017; Schnell, Braga, & Piza, 2017; Steenbeek & Weisburd, 2016)—this latter empirical result is not directly related to crime prevention but shows that focusing solely on places means valuable information is lost regarding these patterns. As we have discussed, there are already efforts to integrate the social context into crime prevention research (Saville & Cleveland, 2013); however, this needs to be expanded in environmental criminology more broadly.

Additionally, in the context of crime displacement that may result from a crime prevention initiative, much of the literature in this area shows that crime does not displace or that any displaced crime is less than the volume of crime reduced in other places (Weisburd et al., 2006). However, as shown by Hodgkinson et al. (2020), crime displacement may occur further away than originally thought or measured, and that displaced crime may lead to more harmful victimizations. Clearly, more work is necessary in this area.

Lastly, research within environmental criminology and crime prevention focuses on urban settings. Patterns of crime in rural areas are different than urban areas (Donnermeyer, 2016) and need to be understood to reduce victimization in those contexts. Though populations in most countries continue to move into urban spaces, even in the United States approximately 20 percent (60 million people) live in rural areas. This is an area of research that could have implications for millions of people even in the small number of countries typically analyzed in the field of environmental criminology—billions globally.

Finally, to move forward in expanding victimological research within environmental criminological theories, this research requires better data and rigorous methodologies. Most of the research in spatial-temporal criminology uses some form of police data because these data contain spatial and temporal information for relatively larger (urban) areas such that spatial and temporal crime patterns can be identified. However, in order to generate better research within these areas on the topic of victimization, environmental criminologists need to gather data from individuals again. In the context of victimization, this means talking to, listening to, and advocating for the victims of crime generating knowledge from spatial and temporal perspectives to reduce (the impacts of) victimization. The field of environmental criminology has a lot to offer victimization studies, but in order to do so we must shift our focus to "suitable targets."

## Notes

1 There are a number of methodological issues regarding the proper measurement of these journeys, but we will not be discussing them here (see, e.g., van Koppen and de Keijser, 1997; Rengert, Piquero, and Jones, 1999; and Townsley and Sidebottom, 2010).

2 Generally speaking, repeat victimization is more common for violent crimes and in North America, Latin America, and Africa.

## References

Ackerman, J. M., & Rossmo, D. K. (2015). How far to travel? A multilevel analysis of the residence-to-crime distance. *Journal of Quantitative Criminology*, *31*(2), 237–262.

Amir, M. (1971). *Patterns of forcible rape*. Chicago, IL: University of Chicago Press.

Andresen, M. A. (2011). The ambient population and crime analysis. *Professional Geographer*, *63*(2), 193–212.

Andresen, M. A. (2020). *Environmental criminology: Evolution, theory, and practice* (2nd ed.). New York, NY: Routledge.

Andresen, M. A., & Malleson, N. (2013). Crime seasonality and its variations across space. *Applied Geography*, *43*, 25–35.

Andresen, M. A., & Malleson, N. (2015). Intra-week spatial-temporal patterns of crime. *Crime Science*, *4*(1), 1–11.

Andresen, M. A., Felson, M., & Frank, R. (2012). The geometry of offending and victimization. *Canadian Journal of Criminology and Criminal Justice*, *54*(4), 495–510.

Andresen, M. A., Frank, R., & Felson, M. (2014). Age and the distance to crime. *Criminology & Criminal Justice*, *14*(3), 314–333.

Barr, R., & Pease, K. (1990). Crime placement, displacement and deflection. *Crime and Justice: A Review of Research*, *12*, 277–318.

Beauregard, E., Rossmo, D. K., & Proulx, J. (2007). A descriptive model of the hunting process of serial sex offenders: A rational choice perspective. *Journal of Family Violence*, *22*(6), 449–463.

Bernasco, W. (2008). Them again? Same offender involvement in repeat and near repeat burglaries. *European Journal of Criminology*, *5*(4), 411–431.

Block, R., Galary, A., & Brice, D. (2007). The journey to crime: Victims and offenders converge in violent index offences in Chicago. *Security Journal*, *20*(2), 123–137.

Bowers, K. J., & Johnson, S. D. (2004). Who commits near repeats? A test of the boost explanation. *Western Criminology Review*, *5*(3), 12–24.

Bowers, K. J., & Johnson, S. D. (2005). Domestic burglary repeats and space-time clusters: The dimensions of risk. *European Journal of Criminology*, *2*(1), 67–92.

Brantingham, P. J., & Brantingham. P. L. (1981a). Introduction: The dimensions of crime. In P. J. Brantingham & P. L. Brantingham (Eds.), *Environmental criminology* (pp. 7–26). Prospect Heights IL, Waveland Press.

Brantingham, P. L., & Brantingham, P. J. (1981b). Notes on the geometry of crime. In P. J. Brantingham & P. L. Brantingham (Eds.), *Environmental criminology* (pp. 27–54). Prospect Heights IL, Waveland Press.

Brantingham, P. L., & Brantingham, P. J. (1993a). Nodes, paths and edges: Considerations on the complexity of crime and the physical environment. *Journal of Environmental Psychology*, *13*(1), 3–28.

Brantingham, P. L., & Brantingham, P. J. (1993b). Environment, routine, and situation: Toward a pattern theory of crime. In R. V. Clarke & M. Felson (Eds.), *Routine activity and rational choice, volume 5* (pp. 259–294). New Brunswick, NJ: Transaction publishers.

Brantingham, P. L., & Brantingham, P. J. (1995). The criminality of place: Crime generators and crime attractors. *European Journal on Criminal Policy and Research*, *3*(3), 5–26.

Brantingham, P. J., & Faust, F. L. (1976). A conceptual model of crime-prevention. *Crime and Delinquency*, *22*(3), 284–296.

Breetzke, G. D., & Cohn, E. G. (2012). Seasonal assault and neighborhood deprivation in South Africa: Some preliminary findings. *Environment & Behavior*, *44*(5), 641–667.

Brimicombe, A. (2012). Did GIS start a crime wave? SatNav theft and its implications for geo-information engineering. *Professional Geographer*, *64*(3), 430–445.

Brunsdon, C., Corcoran, J., Higgs, G., & Ware, A. (2009). The influence of weather on local geographical patterns of police calls for service. *Environment and Planning B: Planning and Design*, *36*(5), 906–926.

Burgess, E. W. (1925). Can neighborhood work have a scientific basis? In R.E. Park, E.W. Burgess, & R.D. McKenzie (Eds.), *The City: Suggestions for investigation of human behaviors in the urban environment* (pp. 142–155). Chicago, IL: University of Chicago Press.

Capone, D. L., & Nichols Jr., W. W. (1976). Urban structure and criminal mobility. *American Behavioral Scientist*, *20*(2), 199–213.

Ceccato, V. (2005). Homicide in San Paulo, Brazil: Assessing spatial-temporal and weather variations. *Journal of Environmental Psychology*, *25*(3), 307–321.

Ceccato, V., & Uittenbogaard, A. C. (2014). Space–time dynamics of crime in transport nodes. *Annals of the Association of American Geographers*, *104*(1), 131–150.

City of Saskatoon (2010). Safe growth and crime prevention through environmental design (CPTED). Saskatoon, SK: City of Saskatoon.

Clarke, R. V. (1980). Situational crime prevention: Theory and practice. *British Journal of Criminology*, *20*(2), 136–147.

Clarke, R. V. (1983). Situational crime prevention: Its theoretical basis and practical scope. *Crime and Justice: An Annual Review of Research*, *4*, 225–256.

Clarke, R. V. (1992). *Situational crime prevention: Successful case studies*. New York, NY: Harrow and Heston.

Clarke, R. V. (1997). *Situational crime prevention: Successful case studies* (2nd ed.). Monsey, NY: Criminal Justice Press.

Clarke, R. V. (2012). Opportunity makes the thief. Really? And so what? *Crime Science*, *1*, Article 3.

Clarke, R. V., & Cornish, D. B. (1985). Modeling offenders' decisions: A framework for research and policy. *Crime and Justice: An Annual Review of Research*, *6*, 147–185.

Cohen, L. E., & Felson, M. (1979). Social change and crime rate trends: A routine activity approach. *American Sociological Review*, *44*(4), 588–608.

Cohn, E. G., & Rotton, J. (2000). Weather, seasonal trends and property crimes in Minneapolis, 1987–1988: A moderator-variable time-series analysis of routine activities. *Journal of Environmental Psychology*, *20*(3), 257–272.

Corcoran, J., Zahnow, R., Kimpton, A., Wickes, R., & Brunsdon, C. (2019). The temporality of place: Constructing a temporal typology of crime in commercial precincts. *Environment and Planning B: Urban Analytics and City Science*. DOI: https://doi.org/10.1177%2F2399808319846904

Cornish, D. B., & Clarke, R. V. (1986). *The reasoning criminal: Rational choice perspectives on offending*. New York, NY: Springer-Verlag.

Cosaro, N., Pizarro, J. M., & Shafer, J. (2017). The influence of planned aggression on the journey to homicide: An examination across typology classifications. *Homicide Studies*, *21*(3), 179–198.

Costello, A, & Wiles, P. (2001). GIS and the journey to crime: An analysis of patterns in South Yorkshire. In A. Hirschfield & K. Bowers (Eds.), *Mapping and analyzing crime data: Lessons from research and practice* (pp. 27–60). London, UK: Taylor and Francis.

Cozens, P., & Love, T. (2017, March 29). The dark side of Crime Prevention Through Environmental Design (CPTED). *Oxford Research Encyclopedia of Criminology*. Retrieved 02 April 2020, from https://oxfordre.com/criminology/view/10.1093/acrefore/9780190264079.00 1.0001/acrefore-9780190264079-e-2.

Donnermeyer, J. F. (2016). *The Routledge international handbook of rural criminology*. New York, NY: Routledge.

Drawve, G., Walker, J. T., & Felson, M. (2015). Juvenile offenders: an examination of distance-to-crime and crime clusters. *Cartography and Geographic Information Science*, *42*(2), 122–133.

Eck, J. E. (1993). The threat of crime displacement. *Criminal Justice Abstracts*, *25*(3), 527–546.

Farrell, G., & Bouloukos, A. C. (2001). International overview: A cross-national comparison of rates of repeat victimization. *Crime Prevention Studies*, *12*, 5–25.

Farrell, G., & Pease, K. (1993). *Once bitten, twice bitten: Repeat victimization and its implications for crime prevention*. London, UK: Police Research Group, Home Office.

Farrell, G., & Pease, K. (1994). Crime seasonality: Domestic disputes and residential burglary in Merseyside 1988–90. *British Journal of Criminology*, *34*(4), 487–498.

Farrell, G., Phillips, C., & Pease, K. (1995). Like taking candy: Why does repeat victimization occur? *British Journal of Criminology*, *35*(3), 384–399.

Farrell, G., Tilley, N., Tseloni, A., & Mailley, J. (2014). Why the crime drop? *Crime and Justice: A review of Research*, *43*(1), 421–490.

Felson, M., & Clarke, R. V. (1998). *Opportunity makes the thief: Practical theory for crime prevention*. London, UK: Home Office, Policing and Reducing Crime Unit Research, Development and Statistics Directorate.

Felson, M., & Poulsen, E. (2003). Simple indicators of crime by time of day. *International Journal of Forecasting*, *19*(4), 595–601.

Field, S. (1992). The effect of temperature on crime. *British Journal of Criminology*, *32*(3), 340–351.

Frank, R., Andresen, M. A., & Felson, M. (2012). The geodiversity of crime: evidence from British Columbia. *Applied Geography*, *34*, 180–188.

Gabor, T., & Gottheil, E. (1984). Offender characteristics and spatial mobility: An empirical study and some policy implications. *Canadian Journal of Criminology*, *26*(3), 267–281.

Groff, E. R., & McEwen, T. (2007). Integrating distance into mobility triangle typologies. *Social Science Computer Review*, *25*(2), 210–238.

Grove, L. E., Farrell, G., Farrington, D. P., & Johnson, S. D. (2012). *Preventing repeat victimization: A systematic review*. Stockholm, Sweden: The Swedish National Council for Crime Prevention.

Guerette, R. T., & Bowers, K. J. (2009). Assessing the extent of crime displacement and diffusion of benefits: A review of situational crime prevention evaluations. *Criminology*, *47*(4), 1331–1368.

Guerry, A-M. (1832). La statistique compare de l'état de l'instruction et du nombre des crimes. *Revue Encyclopédique*, *55*, 414–424.

Guerry, A-M. (1833). *Essai sur la statistique morale de la France*. Paris: Crochard.

Harvey, D. (2010). *A brief history of neoliberalism*. New York, NY: Oxford University Press.

Haberman, C. P., & Ratcliffe, J.H. (2012). The predictive policing challenges of near repeat armed street robberies. *Policing: A Journal of Policy and Practice*, *6*(2), 151–166.

Harries, K. D., & Stadler, S. (1983). Determinism revisited: Assault and heat stress in Dallas. *Environment & Behavior*, *15*(2), 235–256.

Harries, K. D., Stadler, S., & Zdorkowski, R. (1984). Seasonality and assault: Explorations in inter-neighborhood variation, Dallas 1980. *Annals of the Association of American Geographers*, *74*(4), 590–604.

Hesseling, R. B. P. (1994). Displacement: a review of the empirical literature. *Crime Prevention Studies*, *3*, 197–230.

Hodgkinson, T., Saville, G., & Andresen, M.A. (2020). The diffusion of detriment: Tracking displacement using a city-wide mixed methods approach. *British Journal of Criminology*, *60*(1), 198–218.

Jeffery, C. R. (1969). Crime prevention and control through environmental engineering. *Criminologica*, *7*(3), 35–58.

Jeffery, C. R. (1971) *Crime prevention through environmental design*. Beverly Hills, CA: Sage Publications.

Johnson, S. D. (2008). Repeat burglary victimisation: A tale of two theories. *Journal of Experimental Criminology*, *4*, 215–240.

Johnson, S. D., Bernasco, W., Bowers, K. J., Elffers, H., Ratcliffe, J., Rengert, G., & Townsley, M. (2007). Space-time patterns of risk: A cross national assessment of residential burglary victimization. *Journal of Quantitative Criminology*, *23*(3), 201–219.

Johnson, S. D., Bowers, K., & Hirschfield, A. (1997). New insights into the spatial and temporal distribution of repeat victimization. *The British Journal of Criminology*, *37*(2), 224–241.

Johnson, S. D., Summers, L., & Pease, K. (2009). Offender as forager? A direct test of the boost account of victimization. *Journal of Quantitative Criminology*, *25*(2), 181–200.

Kennedy, L. W., & Forde, D. R. (1990). Routine activities and crime: an analysis of victimization in Canada. *Criminology*, *28*(1), 137–152.

Landau, S. F., & Fridman, D. (1993). The seasonality of violent crime: The case of robbery and homicide in Israel. *Journal of Research in Crime and Delinquency*, *30*(2), 163–191.

Lind, A. W. (1930). Some ecological patterns of community disorganization in Honolulu. *American Journal of Sociology*, *36*(2), 206–220.

Mailley, J., Garciab, R., Whitehead, S., & Farrell, G. (2008). Phone theft index. *Security Journal*, *21*(3), 212–227.

Melo, S. N., Andresen, M. A., & Matias, L. F. (2018). Repeat and near-repeat victimization in Campinas, Brazil: New explanations from the Global South. *Security Journal*, *31*(1), 364–380.

Mihinjac, M., & Saville, G. (2019). Third-generation Crime Prevention Through Environmental Design (CPTED). *Social Sciences*, *8*(6), 182.

Morgan, F. (2001). Repeat burglary in a Perth suburb: Indicator of short-term or long- term risk? *Crime Prevention Studies*, *12*, 83–118.

Morselli, C., & Royer, M-N. (2008). Criminal mobility and criminal achievement. *Journal of Research in Crime and Delinquency*, *45*(1), 4–21.

Newman, O. (1972) *Defensible space: Crime prevention through urban design*. New York, NY: Macmillan.

Newton, A., & Hirschfield, A. (2009). Measuring violence in and around licensed premises: The need for a better evidence base. *Crime Prevention & Community Safety*, *11*(3), 171–188.

Normandeau, A. (1968). Patterns in robbery. *Criminology*, *6*(3), 2–16.

O'Brien, D. T., & Winship, C. (2017). The gains of greater granularity: The presence and persistence of problem properties in urban neighborhoods. *Journal of Quantitative Criminology*, *33*(3), 649–675.

Pease, K. (1998). *Repeat victimisation: Taking stock* (Vol. 90). London, UK: Home Office Police Research Group.

Petty, J. (2016). The London spikes controversy: Homelessness, urban securitisation and the question of 'hostile architecture'. *International Journal for Crime, Justice and Social Democracy*, *5*(1), 67–81.

Quetelet, L. A. J. ([1831] 1984). *Research on the propensity for crime at different ages* (S. F. Sylvester, Trans.). Cincinnati, OH: Anderson Publishing.

Quetelet, L. A. J. (1842). *A Treatise on man and the development of his faculties*. Edinburgh: W. and R. Chambers.

Rand. A. (1986). Mobility triangles. In R. M. Figlio, S. Hakim, & G. F. Rengert (Eds.), *Metropolitan crime patterns* (pp. 117–126). Monsey, NY: Criminal Justice Press.

Ratcliffe, J. H., & Rengert, G. F. (2008). Near repeat patterns in Philadelphia shootings. *Security Journal*, *21*(1–2), 58–76.

Raymen, T. (2016). Designing-in crime by designing-out the social? Situational crime prevention and the intensification of harmful subjectivities. *British Journal of Criminology*, *56*(3), 497–514.

Rengert, G. F., Piquero, A., & Jones, P. (1999). Distance decay re-examined. *Criminology*, *37*(2), 427–445.

Rotton, J., & Cohn, E. G. (2003). Global warming and U.S. crime rates: An application of routine activity theory. *Environment & Behavior*, *35*(6), 802–825.

Saville, G. (2017). The missing link in CPTED theory. In B. Teasdale & M. S. Bradley (Eds.), *Preventing crime and violence* (pp. 297–307). Cham, Switzerland: Springer International Publishing.

Saville, G., & Cleveland, G. (2013). Second-generation CPTED: Rise and fall of opportunity theory. In R. I. Atlas (Ed.), *21st century security and CPTED: Designing for critical infrastructure protection and crime prevention* (pp. 91–106). Boca Raton, FL: CRC Press.

Schnell, C., Braga, A. A., & Piza, E. L. (2017). The influence of community areas, neighborhood clusters, and street segments on the spatial variability of violent crime in Chicago. *Journal of Quantitative Criminology*, *33*(3), 469–496.

Semmens, N., Dillane, J., & Ditton, J. (2002). Preliminary findings on seasonality and the fear of crime: A research note. *British Journal of Criminology*, *42*(4), 798–806.

Shaw, C. R., & McKay, H. D. (1942). *Juvenile delinquency and urban areas: A study of rates of delinquency in relation to differential characteristics of local communities in American cities*. Chicago, IL: University of Chicago Press.

Simon, H. A. (1957). *Models of man, social and rational: Mathematical essays on rational human behavior in a social setting*. New York, NY: John Wiley & Sons.

Simon, H. A. (1982). *Models of bounded rationality* (Three Volumes). Cambridge, MA: MIT Press.

Sleiman, M., & Lippert, R. (2010). Downtown ambassadors, police relations and 'clean and safe' security. *Policing & Society*, *20*(3), 316–335.

Steenbeek, W., & Weisburd, D. (2016). Where the action is in crime? An examination of variability of crime across different spatial units in The Hague, 2001–2009. *Journal of Quantitative Criminology*, *32*(3), 449–469.

Tita, G., & Griffiths, E. (2005). Traveling to violence: the case for a mobility-based spatial typology of homicide. *Journal of Research in Crime and Delinquency*, *42*(3), 275–308.

Tompson, L., & Townsley, M. (2010). (Looking) back to the future: Using space-time patterns to better predict the location of street crime. *International Journal of Police Science & Management*, *12*(1), 23–40.

Townsley, M., & Sidebottom, A. (2010). All offenders are equal, but some are more equal than others: Variation in journeys to crime between offenders. *Criminology*, *48*(3), 897–917.

Townsley, M., Homel, R., & Chaseling, J. (2003). Infectious burglaries: A test of the near repeat hypothesis. *British Journal of Criminology*, *43*(3), 615–633.

Townsley, M., Johnson, S. D., & Ratcliffe, J. H. (2008). Space time dynamics of insurgent activity in Iraq. *Security Journal*, *21*(3), 139–146.

Trickett, A., Osborn, D. Seymour, J., & Pease, K. (1992). What is different about high crime areas? *British Journal of Criminology*, *32*(1), 81–90.

Uittenbogaard, A., & Ceccato, V. (2012). Space-time clusters of crime in Stockholm, Sweden. *Review of European Studies*, *4*(5), 148.

van Koppen, P. J., & de Keijser, J. W. (1997). Desisting distance decay: On the aggregation of individual crime trips. *Criminology*, *35*(3), 505–515.

van Koppen, P. J., & Jansen, R. W. J. (1999). The time to rob: Variations in time of number of commercial robberies. *Journal of Research in Crime and Delinquency*, *36*(1), 7–29.

Vandeviver, C., van Daele, S., & vander Beken, T. (2015). What makes long crime trips worth undertaking? Balancing costs and benefits in burglars' journey to crime. *British Journal of Criminology*, *55*(2), 399–420.

Vaughan, A. D., Hewitt, A. N., Hodgkinson, T., Andresen, M. A., & Verdun-Jones, S. (2019). Temporal patterns of Mental Health Act calls to the police. *Policing: A Journal of Policy and Practice*, *13*(2), 172–185.

Waller, I. (2014). *Smarter crime control: A guide to a safer future for citizens, communities, and politicians*. Lanham, MD: Roman & Littlefield.

Weisburd, D., Wyckoff, L. A., Ready, J., Eck, J. E., Hinkle, J. C., & Gajewski, F. (2006). Does crime just move around the corner? A controlled study of spatial displacement and diffusion of crime control benefits. *Criminology*, *44*(3), 549–591.

White, R. C. (1932). The relation of felonies to environmental factors in Indianapolis. *Social Forces*, *10*(4), 498–509.

Whitehead, S., & Farrell, G. (2008). Anticipating mobile phone 'smart wallet' crime: Policing and corporate social responsibility. *Policing: a Journal of Policy and Practice*, *2*(2), 210–217.

Wiles, P., & Costello, A. (2000). *The 'road to nowhere': The evidence for traveling criminals*. Home Office Research Study 207. London, UK: Research, Development and Statistics Directorate.

Wood, D. M., & Mackinnon, D. (2019). Partial platforms and oligoptic surveillance in the smart city. *Surveillance & Society*, *17*(1/2), 176–182.

Zipf, G. (1949). *Human behavior and the principle of least effort: An introduction to human ecology*. Cambridge, MA: Addison-Wesley Press.

# Part II

## Victimization and Vulnerable Populations

# 5

# Victims of Atrocity Crimes

*Hollie Nyseth Brehm and Laura C. Frizzell*

In the wake of World War II, criminologists joined the chorus of social scientists who sought to understand what motivated the concentration camp guards, SS members, and many others who perpetrated the Holocaust. Criminologists also theorized how to bring these individuals and organizations to justice (Glueck, 1942),[1] which required addressing the myriad consequences affecting the millions of people who were victimized by their crimes (Hentig, 1948; Mendelsohn, 1956). In fact, concern regarding the far-reaching impacts of the Holocaust served as a major catalyst for the field of victimology (Walklate, 2016; Wemmers, 2009).

Despite its roots in assessing victimization during genocide and war, the victimology of genocide, crimes against humanity, and war crimes—collectively known as atrocity crimes—has developed more slowly than other subfields of victimology. This fact is particularly surprising given the relative prevalence and impact of atrocity crime. More people were killed by their governments than in all of the international wars of the 20th century (Harff, 2003; Rummel, 1997), and more people were also killed by their governments than in all of the homicides, manslaughters, and related murders that unfolded during the century (Savelsberg, 2010). The 21st century has likewise witnessed numerous atrocity crimes, with violence harming millions of people in China, Colombia, Myanmar, Syria, and Sudan, among many other places.

Motivated by the disturbing pervasiveness of these crimes, as well as criminology's and victimology's relative lack of attention to them, this chapter addresses the victims of atrocity crimes. We begin by briefly explaining state crime and situating atrocity crime within this context, followed by an assessment of atrocity crime and victimhood status. We then examine how to measure victimization of atrocity crime and the determinants of such victimization. We conclude by analyzing research on victims'[2] experiences with justice processes in the aftermath of atrocity crime, and throughout the chapter, we highlight emerging research and suggestions for promising research going forward.

## Conceptualizing the Victims of Atrocity Crime

Although it may seem easy to conceptualize a "victim," this task is anything but simple when it comes to atrocity crime (Pemberton, Letschert, Brouwer, & Haveman, 2015). We suggest this difficulty stems from the fact that states are meant to protect their citizens, such that even international criminal law relies on states for its definition and enforcement. The difficulty is likewise tied to the notion of an "ideal victim," the politicization and hierarchization of victims, and the collective nature of victimhood.

### *State Crime and Atrocity Crime*

In order to define victimhood of atrocity crime, we must first define the crime itself. Defining atrocity crime, which is often a type of state crime, has been an ongoing challenge for criminologists. States are responsible for defining and codifying traditional crimes, and they have a monopoly on the (supposed) legitimate use of force and violence (Weber, 1965). As such, scholars have moved beyond legal definitions to consider state crime as any deviant act committed by the state which violates human rights and which *civil* society categorizes as illegal or immoral (Green & Ward, 2004). State crimes therefore encompass a wide variety of acts, including corruption, state-corporate crime, state-led terrorism, torture, war crimes, and genocide.

With regard to atrocity crime in particular, prior to the Holocaust, states and their leaders were not systematically held accountable for committing large-scale violence.[3] However, following the Holocaust and later widespread violence in Rwanda and Bosnia-Herzegovina at the end of the 20th century, an international norm shift occurred that some have termed the "justice cascade" (Sikkink, 2011; but see Hinton, 2018). Essentially, the justice cascade represents a global change from immunity for state leaders and other powerful actors toward a new model of accountability.[4] The inception of the International Criminal Court (ICC) in 2002 further solidified this justice cascade and led to a clearer conceptualization and definition of atrocity crime.

Specifically, the ICC has jurisdiction over four types of crimes that are collectively known as atrocity crimes. These include war crimes (i.e., crimes that violate the laws of war), crimes against humanity (i.e., widespread and/or systematic attacks on civilians), genocide (i.e., actions taken with intent to destroy a social group), and crimes of aggression (i.e., other unlawful state violence using military force) (Scheffer, 2006). These crimes are often, yet not always, committed by states (The Stanley Foundation, 2015). Genocide is generally committed with active or tacit approval of the state (Verdeja, 2012), though there have been instances—such as ISIL's genocide against the Yazidi—when non-state actors commit genocide without state involvement. War crimes are generally committed by soldiers and thus by agents of the state, but they could likewise be committed by members of militias that are not sanctioned by states. The same is true of crimes against humanity and crimes of aggression, though power and authority are typically needed to commit widespread violence, meaning that state actors have typically been the major perpetrators of atrocity crimes (Pemberton et al., 2015).

### *States as Creators, Protectors, and Enforcers of Law*

The fact that states often commit atrocity crimes is one of the major reasons behind the difficulty conceptualizing the victims of these crimes. Dating back to Hobbes's (1651) theory of the social contract, philosophers concerned with violence and crime have suggested that states protect their citizens from victimization. States create law, police forces, and armies; in return for this security, citizens[5] yield some of their rights to the state. When states inflict unlawful violence, this over-simplified notion of states as protectors therefore becomes problematic. For instance, during episodes of genocide, states have codified victimization against certain groups into law, such as the anti-Jewish legislation in pre-World War II Germany or the laws excluding the Rohingya as a recognized ethnic group in present-day Myanmar. Indeed, state actors regularly view the victims of atrocity crime as outside of the universe of obligation[6] (Fein, 1979), as subhuman or not human (Haslam, 2006), and/or as responsible for their own victimization (Pemberton et al., 2015). These views are frequently linked to boundary drawing via us/them thinking (Wimmer, 2008) and ideological campaigns brimming with propaganda. Such strategies place the victims of atrocity crime in a rather unique position because their fellow citizens often do not perceive them as victims at the time of their victimhood (Pemberton et al., 2015).

What is more, as states retain much of the power in the international system, international criminal law is largely dependent on states for its definition and reinforcement. The ICC was created through a treaty that can only be ratified by states—states that must be willing to subject themselves to its jurisdiction and to incorporate atrocity crimes into their domestic laws. As such, people acting on behalf of states created all legal definitions of atrocity crime, often through politicized processes. For instance, the Soviet Union advocated against the inclusion of political groups in the legal definition of genocide, only to then commit violence against political dissidents within their borders (Weiss-Wendt, 2017). The ICC also does not have its own police force, meaning that it relies on domestic forces at the behest of state actors to enforce warrants.

Consequently, while researchers studying atrocity crime employ the international legal definitions of these crimes, others create their own definitions to ensure that state definitions do not dictate the boundaries of scholarship. This choice has mirrored other work in victimology that has advocated for studying social harm rather than restraining the discipline to strict legal definitions (e.g., Hillyard & Tombs, 2007). We likewise suggest that victimologists should study all social harm that occurs during atrocity, which we define as acts that result in widespread and systematic human suffering. Accordingly, we invoke international criminal law throughout this chapter but likewise consider research on atrocities that were never tried in a court or that may not constitute atrocity crime under the Rome Statute of the ICC.

### *Ideal Victims*

Regardless of one's definition of crime or the social harms it entails, all people do not have equal chances of claiming victimhood or of being accorded victim status by peers, governments, researchers, journalists, justice systems, and others who wield the power to label individuals as "victims." In his foundational article, Christie (1986) theorized that there is an "ideal victim" of street crime, essentially arguing that some victims are more sympathetic than others. For Christie, the ideal victim is a (1) weak woman (2) carrying out a respectable project (3) who is not at fault for her victimization.[7] For instance, a "little old lady" getting robbed after walking back from caring for her ill sister would likely have no trouble claiming victim status and, accordingly, being seen as a victim by the public, justice systems, and other actors. Though this particular example is admittedly extreme, research on who is able to effectively claim or receive victimhood status has largely confirmed that certain people more easily access victimhood status than others[8] (Doherty & Anderson, 2004; Miers, 1989).

This research on ideal victims should be extended to atrocity crime, though only a few researchers have done so to date. Most prominently, van Wijk (2013) theorized that ostensibly weak victims more easily attain victim status from international observers, journalists, and others. Weak victims could be older women as in Christie's example and as van Wijk affirms, though children are likely especially sympathetic victims of atrocity crime due to their perceived innocence and helplessness (Keck & Sikkink, 1998).

Rather than "respectable projects," victims of atrocity crime generally carry out "neutral projects," like simply going about their daily business (van Wijk, 2013). However, there are also instances in which people engage in non-neutral projects, such as anti-government protest, and are subsequently victims of retaliatory atrocity crime. This does not make them any less of a victim in terms of international law and does not mean they are at fault for their victimization. Yet, it nevertheless may alter how observers view them—a problem in part because atrocity crime often follows perceived threats to a government. In Rwanda, for instance, atrocity crimes targeting Tutsi occurred after a mostly-Tutsi army waged a civil war against the government (Straus, 2006). In Darfur, atrocity crimes began after a rebel group attacked government military barracks, prompting the government to attack the rebel groups' communities (Hagan & Rymond-Richmond, 2008). In each of these instances, many more people than those involved in the anti-government attacks were victimized, and the rebel groups were responding to intense state-led discrimination, ultimately blurring the notion of the purely "innocent" victim.

In fact, the line between victim and perpetrator is often unclear when it comes to atrocity crime (e.g., Campbell, 2009; Fujii, 2009; Luft, 2015). For instance, many concentration camp prisoners were forced to perpetrate acts of violence against Jews and other minorities in the camps (Chelouche, 2005). Child soldiers who are recruited against their will and commit horrific acts of violence also illustrate how mutually exclusive victim and perpetrator categories can be problematic (Bouris, 2007; Drumbl, 2012). Criminologists have long recognized that people who commit violence often suffer victimization as well, a phenomenon known as the victim–offender overlap (e.g., Berg, Stewart, Schreck, & Simons, 2012; Jennings, Higgins, Tewksbury, Gover, & Piquero, 2010). While researchers have suggested that this overlap also exists for atrocity crime, little work has empirically examined the prevalence of the overlap across atrocity crimes; how the overlap varies by gender, ethnic group, age, or other aspects of social location; or how it impacts public perceptions of victimization.

Looking forward, much more research could be devoted to understanding victim status and atrocity crime. First, international observers are not monolithic, and it is likely that some governments—such as those with diplomatic ties to the government perpetrating or allowing the violence—more readily withhold victimhood status in favor of their country's interests. Often, this withholding involves refusing to label violence as criminal in the first place, given that observers must first label a crime as such before those harmed can be labeled victims. Researchers could also address whether and how news media, human rights organizations, humanitarian organizations, and many others differentially frame victimization and the associated crimes, as framing by these actors would likewise impact public perceptions of victimhood (Benford & Snow, 2000; Savelsberg, 2015).

Furthermore, *when* people are recognized as victims may also vary. This applies to recognition of victimization as it occurs or recognition of past victimization. For instance, do certain types of violence or prominent global events that bring attention to a certain country influence when people are labeled victims? The timing of victim status recognition may also coincide with regime change, such that victims of the past regime are only recognized when a new regime is in power. This may be true in the country where the crimes occurred or in other countries, as new governments often bring new ways of viewing the past. Furthermore, given the widespread nature of atrocity crime, is there a tipping point for according victim status? Put another way, must a certain number of observers—or *powerful* observers—deem people victims?

The types of violence inflicted on individuals may also impact recognition of victimhood. Researchers have long known that gender-based violence—which can constitute a war crime, crime against humanity, or genocide in different contexts—garners less recognition overall and for men and boys in particular (for early exceptions, see Carpenter, 2006; Jones, 2006; Sivakumaran, 2007; Žarkov, 2001). We know little about how the affordance of victim status varies by other types of atrocity crime, however, and researchers should analyze how gender, race, class, sexuality, and other aspects of identity intersect with the type of violence to impact who claims or is granted victim status. Finally, as atrocity crimes often occur during conflict, aspects of the broader conflict may also shape labels of victimhood. For instance, van Wijk (2013) suggests conflicts that are not complex (so victimization is clearly sold to the media in a neatly packaged narrative), unique (and thus garner attention), short (and thus sustain attention), and well-timed (and are not competing with other events for attention) produce situations where people are more readily granted victim status. These theoretical propositions have yet to be empirically tested, however, and researchers could also assess how other aspects of the conflict (e.g., historical legacies of violence, location in the Global North or Global South, major types of violence inflicted) impact accordance of victimhood status.

### *Hierarchies of Victimhood and the Collective Nature of Victimhood*

Although there are conceptual issues with according people victim status, these issues have real ramifications for peoples' lives. In instances of atrocity crime, journalists, aid workers, diplomats, and/or researchers often suggest that only certain people—often those seen as "completely innocent"—can be considered victims. This assertion results in what McEvoy and McConnachie (2012) term "hierarchies of victimhood," a notion that results in the implication that certain victims are more deserving of assistance than others (Berry, 2018).

For instance, during the 1994 genocide and civil war in Rwanda, both Hutu and Tutsi were victimized. Tutsi were targeted in the genocide, and many more Tutsi died, bore the brunt of sexualized violence, and were displaced than Hutu. Nevertheless, it is well established that many Hutu were harmed protecting Tutsi, in the war that unfolded alongside the genocide, or even because they were mistaken for Tutsi (Straus, 2019). Yet, the Government of Rwanda labels the Tutsi as the victims of the genocide, meaning that Tutsi can generally claim survivor status, while Hutu generally cannot (Berry, 2018). This labeling not only has symbolic consequences, but it also impacts who can access certain services explicitly created for genocide survivors. Others have relatedly theorized "competitive victimhood," whereby victim groups compete for symbolic and material recognition and resources tied to their suffering (Jensen, 2002; Noor, Brown, Gonzalez, Manzi, & Lewis,

2008; Woolford & Wolejszo, 2006; Young & Sullivan, 2016), though this social psychological work has not been fully extended to contexts of atrocity crime.

Furthermore, during the collective violence in Bosnia-Herzegovina in the early 1990s, Serbs, Croats, and Bosniaks fought in armies and ran internment camps. Yet, many researchers' narratives of the violence cast Serbs as the perpetrators and Bosniaks as the victims. This characterization is not untrue, as a disproportionate amount of the violence was committed by Serbs against Bosniaks (Bećirević, 2014). Nonetheless, the categorization of an entire group of people as perpetrators excludes their suffering, which again can have significant material consequences. For instance, many Serb women who were raped and harmed often were not given services by international organizations due to misconceptions about their victimhood status (Berry, 2018).

Creating knowledge is power (Foucault, 1978), and in this case, scholars studying atrocity crimes must take seriously this power. As the study of victimology related to atrocity crimes remains nascent, scholars will have enormous power in shaping other scholars' knowledge on this topic as well as the information used by policy makers and, in essence, the world. Their work will influence whom the world sees as victims, and as such can influence who has access to national and international resources following victimization. Scholars also have the power to shape knowledge of best practices for recovering from victimization that can directly translate into on-the-ground action.

Going forward, we therefore call for researchers to consider this power when theoretically developing and analyzing these hierarchies. What situations more readily produce hierarchies of victimhood? How do these hierarchies shape victims' lived experiences? Moreover, is it possible to recognize that some peoples have experienced systematic crimes while others' victimization is more individualized without creating hierarchies? Does recognizing that a genocide targeted a certain group yet also that other people were harmed take away from the targeted peoples' claim to victimhood? We suggest it does not, as victimhood claims need not be zero-sum. Nevertheless, researchers could assess whether and how international observers understand such dynamics.

## Measuring and Documenting Atrocity Crime Victimization

To this point, we have addressed that researchers and others engaging with violence need to think critically when they label someone as a victim of atrocity crime. With this information in mind, we now consider efforts to measure victimization. Just as with labeling, it is imperative to recognize the power inherent in measuring victimization. There are myriad ways to gauge and document victimization, and we begin by exploring types of victimization that constitute atrocity crime, followed by how researchers have organized this victimization into conceptual levels.

### *Types of Victimization*

Atrocity crimes have numerous components, and victimization can take various forms. Specifically, the Rome Statute of the ICC—which we rely on for a foundation but again also transcend—delineates myriad acts that can constitute atrocity crime. The crime of genocide can involve murder, infliction of serious bodily or mental harm, rape and related sexualized violence,[9] actions intended to lead to the loss of life (e.g., forced starvation), measures to prevent births, and forced internment, among other types of violence (Rome Statute, 1998, Article 6). Crimes against humanity can likewise involve murder, deportation/forcible transfer of a population, and rape, sexual slavery, and other sexualized violence (Rome Statute, 1998, Article 7). They can also include enforced disappearances, as was the case with the disappearance of tens of thousands of people during Argentina's Dirty War; Apartheid, as was infamously illustrated in South Africa's race laws; and torture, imprisonment, or enslavement, alongside other acts that cause great suffering and injury to physical or mental health.

Much as with crimes against humanity and genocide, war crimes can *also* involve murder, bodily harm, torture, unlawful deportation, and hostage taking, which is often similar to internment. War crimes can likewise constitute other specific breaches of international humanitarian law, such as harming a soldier who had declared a truce or intentionally attacking buildings dedicated to religion, art, education, or related purposes (Rome Statute, 1998, Article 8). Finally, crimes of aggression involve the use of an armed force in a manner that violates the Charter of the United Nations. For instance, this could involve invasions, blockades, or the employment of mercenaries (Kampala Amendment, 2010).

It is consequently clear that atrocity crimes involve numerous types of violence, though to date, researchers have primarily focused on measuring victimization in terms of murder. This emphasis stems from the fact that it is typically easier to track bodies as compared to other types of violence. Even so, counting deaths is generally challenging (Andreas & Greenhill, 2010). The widespread chaos that accompanies atrocity crime makes typical sources of mortality data, like civilian registration systems, unreliable. There are also rarely criminal justice responses to atrocity crime as it unfolds, meaning that arrest or conviction data that criminologists regularly rely upon are often unavailable. Consequently, mortality estimates tied to atrocity crimes often vary widely. For instance, during the war and genocide in Darfur, many researchers disagreed about the number of people who had been killed, with citations ranging between 36,000 deaths and 530,000 deaths during the first few years of the conflict (Degomme & Guha-Sapir, 2010).

Occasionally, national or international organizations engage in direct efforts to count deaths due to atrocity crime (Brunborg, forthcoming). The Bosnian Book of the Dead, for instance, attempted to obtain information on every person who died during the war and genocide in Bosnia-Herzegovina. The vast majority of causalities in the database are direct deaths. These include people who died or were unaccounted for and whose death or disappearance was caused by direct violence, including deportation to and imprisonment in concentration camps. The database also classifies deaths by combatant and noncombatant status. Combatant status was ascertained using official military lists, and the organization spearheading the initiative also visited hundreds of military and civilian cemeteries and gathered books and photos from military memorials. Once they had compiled their list of deaths, the organization invited Bosnian citizens to assess the database and submit names of anyone they had missed (Nettelfield, 2010).

Data like the Bosnian Book of the Dead are called micro data, as they contain information regarding individuals. These data are often ideal, though since these data are constructed after violence ends, it becomes difficult to ascertain which deaths were due to atrocity crimes and which were not. Micro data on deaths are also estimates at best, as entire families may be killed such that no one remains to report their deaths. Furthermore, researchers and practitioners disagree over whether to restrict micro data to direct deaths, as was done with the Bosnian Book of the Dead, or to expand the data to include people who die due to disease in refugee camps after fleeing violence (typically called excess mortality). This particular decision often depends on the goal of the organization collecting the data. For instance, humanitarian organizations generally aim to assess all people affected by the violence, including the lasting impacts in refugee camps. Criminal courts, however, typically have a much higher burden of proof when it comes to counting deaths tied to atrocity crime (Hagan, Schoenfeld, & Palloni, 2006).

Researchers regularly use macro data, or aggregated data, to assess deaths as well. These data commonly stem from media reports of deaths (see, for instance, the UCDP and ICEWS datasets), though it is notably difficult to differentiate which deaths stem from atrocity crimes unless databases include the specific circumstances surrounding the violence. For instance, attacks on civilians would typically constitute atrocity crimes, while battlefield deaths may not, meaning that the location of the violence and the combatant status of the victims are important information. Ideally, these reports of circumstances include precise numbers of deaths, though it is also possible to measure aggregate attacks on communities. For example, the US State Department tracked attacks on Darfurian villages, noting if the village was damaged or destroyed by the soldiers and militias (US Department of State, 2011). This information stemmed from satellite imagery and, consequently, does not inform death tolls, though a community-level analysis of violence may nonetheless use this information to assess community victimization.

In other cases, researchers must rely upon indirect measures to assess death tolls. To assess how many people were killed during the wars and genocide in Cambodia during the 1970s, for example, researchers have used population censuses taken before and after the violence, as well as surveys of segments of the population in the aftermath (e.g., Neupert & Prum, 2005; see also Tabeau & Zwierzchowski, 2013). These sources enable assessment of what the population size may have been had violence not occurred and thus can be used to obtain a crude measure of deaths (see also Obermeyer, Murray, & Gakidou, 2008; Price & Ball, 2014; as well as the work of Patrick Ball and the Human Rights Data Analysis Group).

Beyond deaths, other forms of violence have proven even more difficult to measure, and much more research is needed to better operationalize the many other types of victimization that constitute atrocity crime. Data on forced displacement may be available and reliable if an organization is tracking peoples' movements or if people cross international borders, invoking the involvement of the United Nations High Commissioner for Refugees in organizing and maintaining refugee camps. Even then, however, numbers of displaced peoples are often imprecise approximations, especially since millions of people are regularly displaced by conflicts and remain transient. Forced internment is likewise difficult to assess, in large part because governments generally hide this internment from the public eye. Some researchers have begun to use innovative methods such as satellite data (Checchi, Stewart, Palmer, & Grundy, 2013) and a combination of satellite imagery and mobile phone records (Bharti, Lu, Bengtsson, Wetter, & Tatem, 2015) to estimate displacement. More research should seek to apply these strategies to other conflicts, as well as develop further methods for analyzing displacement in varied contexts.

Furthermore, sexualized violence is particularly challenging to document and enumerate, as many survivors of the violence do not want their survivorship status known due to stigma (Ahrens, 2006; Fleming & Kruger, 2013). This may be especially true for survivors who have multiple marginalized identities (Koo, Nguyen, Andrasik, & George, 2015; McGuffey, 2013; Washington, 2001), as may be the case with sexualized violence against minority ethnic groups. Additionally, people are routinely sexually victimized prior to being killed, making accurate victim counts of sexualized violence almost impossible to ascertain. There are also myriad forms of sexualized violence, and researchers sometimes disagree over what makes violence sexual. For many decades, research largely focused on forcible, penetrative vaginal rape with a male perpetrator, though definitions of sexualized violence have since expanded. For instance, sexualized violence can include purposefully infecting someone with a sexually transmitted infection, mutilation or removal of genitalia or breasts, and sexualized verbal domination and humiliation. Those who perpetrate sexualized violence also use tools during the violence to further intimidate their victims, such as machetes and whips, and researchers have expanded their consideration of sexualized violence to include men and boys as victims.[10,11]

Atrocity crimes often occur during conflict, meaning that many people witness death, sexualized violence, and property destruction, often on a daily basis. As such, Walklate (2016) argues that people can suffer from indirect victimization, or witnessing violence committed against another person. For this reason, surveys or interviews administered during periods of widespread violence often ask people about the violence that they saw or heard about. Using one such survey (i.e., the Atrocities Documentation Survey in Darfur), Ferrales, Nyseth Brehm, and McElrath (2016) differentiate between primary victimization, or violence perpetrated directly against an individual, and proximate victimization, or witnessing violence perpetrated against others. The latter was particularly prominent in their study, as members of militias known as the Janjaweed purposefully harmed peoples' families while they helplessly watched.

Finally, the pain, trauma, and psychological harm stemming from atrocity crime is just as important to document as the physical harms inflicted, yet such victimization is especially difficult to measure. For instance, many survivors of atrocity crimes bore witness to horrific acts of violence even if they did not directly experience violence, and assessments of trauma following mass violence typically include several indicators of witnessing violence. Many survivors also experience significant trauma from prolonged periods of hiding and a perpetual fear of being harmed or killed. All of these types of trauma can result in symptoms of Post-Traumatic Stress Disorder and other debilitating mental illnesses (Schaal & Elbert, 2006; Yehuda, Schmeidler, Siever, Binder-Brynes, & Elkin, 1997). As such, researchers should consistently consider trauma in measurements of victimization. And, while we have been unable to consider all types of victimization stemming from atrocity crime, it is likewise important to expand considerations of victimization following atrocity crimes to include crime more broadly conceived, including the destruction of property, the imposition of poverty, and other violations of social, economic, or cultural rights (Hagan, Kaiser, Rothenberg, Hanson, & Parker, 2012).

### *Levels of Victimization*

Researchers have also organized victimization into conceptual levels. Notably, conceptual levels are not hierarchical but rather focus on relative temporal or physical proximity to violence. For instance, Walklate (2016) theorizes that primary victimization is the direct impact of being a victim, while secondary victimization is the subsequent contact that the primary victim has with the criminal justice system.

Govier (2015) likewise conceptualizes levels of victimhood for atrocity crime, among other crime types. She suggests that primary victims are the individuals who immediately experience violence, aligning with Walklate's conceptualization. For Govier, however, secondary victimization does not pertain to the impact of the criminal justice system but rather extends to the family of the primary victim, while tertiary victims include the primary victim's community. For example, a child forced to leave their family in order to attend a residential school for First Nations children in Canada would be a primary victim. The child's parents would be secondary victims adversely affected by the government taking their family member, and the entire community of First Nations peoples would constitute tertiary victims given the detrimental cultural impact of boarding schools.

This conceptualization makes clear that a person's victimization often affects their family members. Yet, while scholars have studied the impacts of victimization on families for many types of crimes (e.g., Davis, Taylor, & Bench, 1995; Morrall, Hazelton, & Shackleton, 2011), they have seldom analyzed the effects of atrocity crime victimization on families and other close members of social networks. Future scholarship should thus address how families are impacted by their loved ones' victimization during atrocity crime, both in the immediate aftermath and as they experience co-victimization via the victim's long-term victimization.

Govier's conception of tertiary victimhood is likewise important for atrocity crimes, though the notion of the community is not always clear-cut. Communities may be spatial in nature, though since some atrocity crimes (e.g., genocide) target an entire identity or social group, a victim's community may also involve their ethnic, religious, national, or other related group. To date, scholarship assessing the community impacts of atrocity crime victimization has generally focused on community bereavement (e.g., Gupta, 1999), group or cohort-specific collective memories (e.g., Alexander, 2004; DeGloma, 2009; Longman & Rutagengwa, 2004), or on how individuals perceive in-group victimization (e.g., Pennekamp, Doosje, Zebel, & Fischer, 2007). Victimologists of atrocity crime should therefore expand upon this existing work by defining tertiary victims across a variety of atrocity crimes and analyzing the effects of such indirect victimization.

As mentioned above, the impacts of victimization may also be felt for generations to come, meaning levels may not just be spatial but rather temporal. Intergenerational transmission of trauma has been documented across numerous atrocity crimes, such as the Holodomor in Ukraine (Bezo & Maggi, 2015) and the Holocaust (Alford, 2019), although some studies suggest this relationship stems from the impacts of parental trauma on childrearing practices (Roth, Neuner, & Elbert, 2014). Intergenerational health impacts may be felt in other ways as well. Many studies have used data from the Development and Health Surveys (DHS)—which USAID launched in 1984 to monitor population and health trends in developing countries—or similar survey data to assess the lasting consequences of atrocity crimes (Barel, 2010; Munyandamutsa, Nkubamugisha, Gex-Fabry, & Eytan, 2012.) For example, Akresh and de Walque (2008) use DHS data to show the negative effect of genocide on subsequent educational attainment in Rwanda. Additional research should analyze the myriad other ways that the consequences of atrocity crimes extend across time, such as by impacting community social cohesion, intergenerational health outcomes, relationship formation and stability, and community crime rates. Research going forward should further assess how collective memories of atrocity crimes differ across generations, in line with scholarship on how generational cohorts remember the Holocaust (see Paez & Liu, 2011) or how conceptions of trauma change over time (e.g., Fassin & Rechtman, 2009).

### *Victimality and Atrocity Crime*

Documenting victimization is important in its own right, though documentation data can also allow researchers to assess the factors associated with being victimized, or what researchers have varyingly referred to as "victim proneness," "victim precipitation," or "victimality."[12] A rich body of research has assessed victim proneness for many other types of crimes, though researchers have yet to fully address the individual and social factors associated with higher odds of victimization of atrocity crime. Nevertheless, existing studies point toward several factors that operate at multiple conceptual levels (Vollhardt, 2012).

As many atrocity crimes target groups in particular, Rafter and Walkate (2012) suggest that scholars should pay attention to the group level by assessing what they call a group's victimality, or a group's potential to be a victim of a genocide or a related atrocity crime. The term victimality moves away from earlier terms such as "victim precipitation" and "victim proneness," which can be easily manipulated to apply fault to a victim. To illustrate this concept, they focus on the case of Armenia, arguing that prior massacres of Armenian peoples well before the genocide serve as a primary indicator of the group's victimality. Scholars have indeed documented prior discrimination of groups as a risk factor of mass atrocity (see Harff, 2003), though since many groups suffer from long histories of abuse, a focus on groups' victimality must be complemented by an examination of other factors. What more, some atrocity crimes do not target identity-based groups but instead target groups that are particularly context-dependent, such as political opponents or diverse civilians living together in a refugee camp, indicating that identity-based group-level factors may not always impact the risk of victimization.

Subnational and national factors may also impact victimization. Many researchers have illustrated that certain settings are associated with more atrocity crime victimization within communities. Nyseth Brehm (2017) highlights, for instance, that socially disorganized communities experienced greater levels of killing in 1994 Rwanda, while McDoom (2014) illustrates that this violence started earlier in more divided communities. A flurry of research in political science has begun to address the subnational factors associated with many types of violence as well. This work has ascertained that civil conflict is more likely in subnational spaces marked by low economic growth and capacity (Buhaug, Gates, & Lujala, 2009) or climate variability (Fjelde & von Uexkull, 2012), as well as in sparsely populated regions near borders and comparatively far from capital cities (Rustad, Rød, Larsen, & Gleditsch, 2008), though it remains to be seen whether atrocity crime is also more likely in such contexts. Hagan, Rymond-Richmond, and Palloni (2009) further suggest that the people perpetrating the attacks within communities shape community victimization as well, illustrating that joint attacks from the government and militias (rather than one or the other) were associated with racialized epithets during sexualized violence in Darfur.

Finally, state-level factors likewise play a role in contributing to victimization, though these factors may be less useful in predicting which civilians would be victimized and are more beneficial for understanding the occurrence of atrocity crime. Nevertheless, it is still valuable to assess whether citizens of certain countries are comparatively more at risk of atrocity crime. Anderton and Ryan (2016) find, for instance, that low-level attacks against civilians are predictors of high-level attacks against civilians,[13] and many others have studied how the type of government, the power structure within a society, or the presence of other state-level factors are associated with the onset of atrocity crime (e.g., Goldsmith, Butcher, Semenovich, & Sowmya, 2013; Harff, 2003; Krain, 1997; Uzonyi, 2018).[14] Much of this scholarship has focused on genocide, with limited research also addressing the conflict or country determinants of sexualized violence (Cohen, 2013; Wood, 2006, 2010). Moving forward, additional work should assess whether and how such state-level factors are associated with levels and types of many forms of victimization, as well as whether such factors shape the likelihood of victimization.

Although group-level factors (alongside subnational and national factors) are critical to comprehending victimization during atrocity crimes, understanding within-group differences is equally as important to studying and predicting victimization. At the individual level, age, gender, race, ethnicity, nationality, sexuality, and other sociodemographic factors are associated with the likelihood of any crime victimization (e.g., Cohen & Cantor, 1981; Hindelang, Gottfredson, & Garofalo, 1978; Vest, Catlin, Chen, & Brownson, 2002). However, researchers have not yet identified how victimization stemming from atrocity crimes varies across these individual-level sociodemographic factors (for one exception, see De Walque & Verwimp, 2010). Given that atrocity crimes target large numbers of people, the impact of these factors is likely to differ from that of traditional crime, suggesting an urgent area for future research.

This research should also address how sociodemographic factors are associated with the *severity* of victimization. For instance, Hagan and Rymond-Richmond (2008) show that the severity of adult victimization in Darfur decreased with age. They also find that women and members of certain ethnic groups experienced more severe violence. Furthermore, researchers should analyze how individual-level factors are associated with the *type* of violence. Scholarship has suggested, for instance, that gender-based violence is more likely to target women during identity-related atrocity crime given conceptions of women as carriers of the nation (Mullins, 2009). Moreover, Jones (2006) argues that some atrocity crimes involving deaths target noncombatant males of an imputed "battle age," while others are "root-and-branch" slaughters, meaning that the violence targets all members of the victim group.

Given the critical nature of both group-level and individual-level factors for risk of victimization during atrocity crime, we argue that researchers should move toward the integration of these factors in future studies. What group-level and individual-level factors are important in vulnerability to victimization? How do individual-level risk factors differ across groups, and how do these factors diverge across communities and states faced with violence? Studies have shown the importance of simultaneous examination of individual, group, and community-level factors for predicting violent victimization in the US (e.g., Sampson, Raudenbush, & Earls, 1997), but studies have yet to do so regarding victimization during atrocity crime. Future studies should simultaneously integrate these three levels of analysis by employing either multi-level models or comparisons of individual- and group-level victimization across different subnational spaces. Doing so will result in critical information needed to create a new, integrated theoretical model of victimization during atrocity crime.

*Experiences with Justice and Beyond*

Finally, although the impacts of victimization are multifaceted, numerous researchers have paid particular attention to how criminal justice exposure continues to affect victims of atrocity crime (Walklate, 2016). As illustrated in our brief discussion of the justice cascade, the range of justice responses to atrocity crime are relatively new. As such, existing research on victims and criminal justice has emphasized assessing (1) the types of justice that are theoretically most appropriate for atrocity crime, (2) victims' notions of the most suitable criminal justice response, (3) the impact of exposure to these responses, and (4) victims' post-hoc assessments.

Atrocity crime is often, though certainly not always, followed by a transitional justice response. The term transitional justice initially referred to the legal strategies that international and national political actors employed to aid transitions to democracy (Kritz, 1995). Over the last few decades, however, this concept expanded to include new types of mechanisms used to reconcile violent or repressive pasts (Teitel, 2002). Today, governments and organizations often implement transitional justice mechanisms in the wake of atrocity crime, though it is important to note that many atrocity crimes are not followed by transitional justice and that research should address the impact of the *absence* of transitional justice on victims as well.

Trials have been a prominent transitional justice mechanism since Nuremberg (Sikkink, 2011; see also Roht-Arriaza, 2006), and they can occur within communities (like Rwanda's post-genocide *gacaca* courts), at the state-level (such as the now-ongoing Extraordinary Chambers in the Courts of Cambodia), or even at the international level (like the ICC). Given the emphasis on punishment at trials as well as the historical failure to include victims (Karstedt, 2010), however, several scholars have questioned whether they actually address the needs of victims (e.g., Dembour & Haslam, 2004). For instance, Rothe and Kauzlarich (2014) suggest that international criminal justice is not designed to respond to victim needs (see also Pemberton et al., 2015). Though this may be the case, transitional justice trials have notably become progressively more responsive to victims. Victims were not present in the courtrooms, generally did not give testimony, and were essentially silenced in post-World War II trials (Karstedt, 2010), though norms about victim involvement have begun to shift, and today the ICC is the first tribunal to explicitly address victims' rights (Wemmers, 2009).

Beyond trials, truth and reconciliation commissions (TRCs) are another prominent transitional justice mechanism that can occur within communities or at the national level. TRCs strive to create a truthful record of events that occurred during a period of violence, and they generally do so by incorporating victims' testimonies in a public setting. Notably, TRCs must be sanctioned by states. Though there are multiple ideas of what a TRC should entail, most involve the following five elements: (1) discover, clarify, and acknowledge past abuses, (2) respond to the needs of victims, (3) contribute to justice and accountability, (4) outline institutional responsibility and recommend reforms, and (5) promote reconciliation (Hayner, 2011).

Amnesties and vetting constitute two other prominent transitional justice mechanisms. Amnesties allow guilty parties to escape punishment through cooperation; as such, some advocates argue that amnesties encourage impunity (Pensky, 2008; though see Olsen, Payne, & Reiter, 2010). Yet, amnesties may be useful solutions when a leader responsible for atrocities remains in power because they encourage expedient bargains (Goldsmith & Krasner, 2003; Vinjamuri & Snyder, 2004), though scholars have yet to fully assess how victims generally view amnesties (though see Gibson, 2002). Vetting (also known as lustration) is the purging of anyone connected to the old regime from the new government. While vetting is not a criminalizing measure, it nonetheless focuses largely on the perpetrators of atrocity crime rather than centering victims' needs. Inaccuracies when deciding whom to purge are common (Schwartz, 1995), and again, little research has theorized or analyzed how vetting impacts victims (Horne, 2014).

Finally, reparations, or compensation offered to the victims of abuses, are also common transitional justice mechanisms that, unlike many others, place emphasis squarely on the victims and their needs. There is a general consensus that victims of atrocity crime should receive compensation, although there is little agreement regarding the form that compensation should take or whom in particular should receive reparations following atrocity crime (Lutz, 1995; Torpey, 2006). Reparations can include both material (e.g., money, property) and nonmaterial (e.g., formal apologies or recognition of acts) goods, though redress and reparations movements generally urge for apologies to accompany material reparations.

Though some scholarship has theorized which transitional justice mechanisms are best suited to addressing victims' needs, a growing body of scholarship has empirically analyzed which mechanisms victims themselves desire, as well as how victims conceive of peace and justice. Weinstein, Fletcher, Vinck, and Pham (2010), for example, examined surveys from five countries to assess variation in attitudes regarding justice by culture, geography, experience with violence, and type of intervention. Others have likewise surveyed those affected to ascertain their thoughts about future transitional justice processes. For instance, when Darfurian Voices (2011) surveyed over 1,800 Darfuri refugees, they found that the majority of participants favored International Criminal Court intervention. By contrast, Samii (2013) found that many Burundians hoped to essentially forgive and forget. He attributed this sentiment to the potential for renewed violence and the intense competition for political power among competing factions. Researchers at the Human Rights Center at Berkeley and at the International Center for Transitional Justice have similarly conducted surveys in many countries that experienced atrocity crime to assess perspectives on key concepts (e.g., justice, peace) as well as on transitional justice mechanisms.

This line of research is incredibly promising for the centering of victims following atrocity crimes, but it remains in its infancy. Going forward, researchers must also analyze what determines transitional justice preferences among victimized populations. Nussio, Rettberg, and Ugarriza (2015) found that there were little to no statistically significant differences between transitional justice preferences of victims and non-victims in Colombia following the demobilization of more than 50,000 armed non-state actors. Yet, Hall, Kovras, Stefanovic, and Loizides (2018) found that those who were victimized in Bosnia-Herzegovina were more likely to prefer retributive measures than those who were not victimized. More broadly, in a study of determinants of attitudes about transitional justice in Spain, Aguilar, Balcells, and Cebolla-Boado (2011) identified that older respondents, especially those living in small towns, were less likely to support the creation of TRCs. They likewise documented that people who held comparatively more religious and more right-wing views were also less likely to support TRCs, illustrating that numerous individual, family, and sociodemographic factors shape transitional justice views (see also Backer, 2010; David & Choi, 2006; Nalepa, 2010).

Moving forward, this scholarship should draw from criminological studies of punitive attitudes (e.g., Costelloe, Chiricos, & Gertz, 2009; Johnson, 2001) and political science work on enemy images (e.g., Alexander, Brewer, & Hermann, 1999; Caiani, 2017) to further analyze the individual and social determinants of transitional justice preferences. Furthermore, as most research has been cross-sectional in nature, researchers should analyze how transitional justice preferences and meanings tied to these preferences change over time, as well as the factors associated with such changes.

Finally, researchers should assess which mechanisms actually have the best outcomes for victims. To be certain, some researchers have analyzed the impacts of transitional justice participation, including more immediate effects as well as impacts that may last well beyond the transitional justice mechanisms (Stover, 2011). For instance, scholars have analyzed how participation in truth telling influences victims' wellbeing. Although truth telling is not necessarily part of local transitional justice efforts, many mechanisms do involve an element of truth telling. Desmond Tutu (quoted in Kiss, 2000, p. 72) and other prominent practitioners have suggested that "there is no healing without truth," and many have similarly argued that truth telling yields therapeutic benefits (see Mendeloff, 2004, 2009). However, researchers examining this claim have generally found no relationship between truth telling and mental health (e.g., Kaminer, Stein, Mbanga, & Zungu-Dirwayi, 2001) or, more prominently, a negative relationship (Brounéus, 2010; Cilliers, Dube, & Siddiqi, 2016; Rimé, Kanyangara, Yzerbyt, & Paez, 2011).

Going forward, researchers could once again address the many other possible impacts of transitional justice mechanisms and how those impacts vary across factors such as sociodemographic variables, type of victimization, location of the mechanism (e.g., within or outside of the victim's own community), and the time between violence and transitional justice implementation. To do so, scholars can draw on research examining the impacts of victim participation in traditional criminal justice proceedings (e.g., Orth & Maercker, 2004). Ultimately, scholars must integrate transitional justice mechanisms into emerging theories of victimization during atrocity crimes in order to achieve a comprehensive, victim-centered understanding of victimization in this context.

## Conclusion

Atrocity crimes are prominent and serious crimes that affect millions of people. Yet, while victimology originated in the wake of the Nazi Holocaust, criminologists have been relatively slow to develop a victimology of atrocity crime. In this chapter, we have surveyed existing interdisciplinary literature on victims of atrocity crime and have illuminated how theories and tools from victimology could expand this literature in numerous meaningful ways.

Studying the victims of atrocity crime involves labeling certain individuals as victims in the first place. We have suggested that criminologists must take seriously the power they wield when they assign such labels and have illustrated that labeling victims of atrocity crime can be particularly difficult due to the fact that states are meant to protect their citizens, the notion of an "ideal victim," the politicization and hierarchization of victims, and the collective nature of victimhood. Future scholarship should analyze the factors that shape the "ideal victims" of atrocity crime, the victim–perpetrator overlap for atrocity crime, and the factors associated with and resulting from hierarchies of victimhood.

We likewise suggest that victimologists should create and employ new tools to measure the myriad forms of atrocity crimes that can affect people. Though research to date has largely focused on documenting mortality, we illustrate the importance of documenting sexualized violence, trauma, and indirect victimization via witnessing violence. We likewise suggest victimologists should consider documenting victimization that occurs at multiple conceptual levels, such as ripple effects to family and community members or across time.

This documentation is important in its own right, but it is likewise important to measure victimization in order to assess the victimality, or victim proneness, of atrocity crime. Very little research has applied traditional research on victim proneness to atrocity crime, indicating a ripe area for future inquiry. We accordingly suggest that researchers should analyze the individual sociodemographic factors associated with the occurrence, type, and severity of atrocity crime victimization and that such inquiries should simultaneously address the group, subnational, and national factors that likewise play a role. A comprehensive theory of victimization during atrocity crime will need to simultaneously assess predictors of victimization at all of these conceptual levels.

Finally, atrocity crimes are often followed by a transitional justice response. We argue that victimologists should analyze the responses that victims prefer and, importantly, assess the factors associated with these preferences. Such analyses could integrate existing literature on punitive attitudes and enemy images. What is more, research on how transitional justice impacts victims has largely emphasized impacts on wellbeing and social capital, meaning that a more holistic model of the myriad ways that transitional justice affects individuals and communities—in the immediate aftermath of atrocity crime and well beyond it—is warranted.

Though this research has clear theoretical import, it likewise has practical implications for the lives of millions of people who currently are afflicted by atrocity crime. It is our hope that our discipline continues to expand toward answering important questions about these individuals' lived experiences, as well as how their experiences impact families, communities, and nations for generations to come.

## Notes

1 For instance, Glueck published *War Criminals: Their Prosecution and Punishment,* which presented a plan for prosecuting war crimes committed during World War II.

2 Although many people who have experienced violence, especially sexualized violence, prefer the term "survivor" to "victim," we use the term "victim" in line with the volume and the field of victimology.

3 See Bass (2000) for more on Nuremberg and other trials related to the crimes perpetrated during World War II and the Holocaust, as well as for information on pre-World War II trials that began to lay the foundation for the eventual shift in norms.

4 To be certain, we do not suggest that a shifting norm pertaining to accountability means that state actors are always or even often actually held accountable.

5 As Arendt (1951) and many others have poignantly illustrated, stateless peoples can often be particularly vulnerable to victimization.

6 For Fein (1979), the universe of obligation constitutes the people and groups to whom rules apply and whose injuries call for amends.

7 Christie also suggested that the victimizer is "big, bad, and unknown." This may be the case with atrocity crime, but there are numerous examples of individuals who became notorious for perpetrating violence (e.g., Joseph Kony of the Lord's Resistance Army in Uganda) and whose victims garnered international attention (see also Maruna, 2001). Indeed, if the public recognizes the actor perpetrating the violence as "bad," such as violence perpetrated by ISIL, they may more readily label such violence as criminal. When states commit violence, however, members of the public may be more hesitant to label such violence as criminal unless the state reputation already has a negative or questionable reputation within a given society. In other words, labeling the violence of a powerful or globally respected state as criminal is likely comparatively more challenging.

8 Claiming victimhood and receiving recognition as a victim do not always co-occur. In this chapter, we focus primarily on situations where third parties have afforded the victim label to people who have been harmed in recognition that scholars wield substantial power in determining who is or is not labeled a victim.

9 Sexualized violence was not originally included in the international legal definition of genocide. Case law, such as the 1998 International Criminal Tribunal for Rwanda judgment of the Akayesu trial, has since recognized the crime of rape as a form of genocide.

10 Although gender is fluid, many societies worldwide conceive of gender as binary. As such, most studies of sexualized and gender-based violence to date have likewise conceptualized gender as binary—a false binary that should be expanded upon in future research.

11 Earlier scholarship often framed violence against men or boys as torture rather than as sexual in nature or overlooked it all together. Again, for early exceptions, see Žarkov (2001), Carpenter (2006), Jones (2006), and Sivakumaran (2007).

12 Studies assessing victim proneness have generally examined the factors associated with victimization, though it is important to note that a victim is never to blame for their victimization. Rafter and Walklate (2012) suggest the term victimality instead, though as this term in their conceptualization focuses on the determinants of group victimization, we employ both.

13 See pages 546–547 of Anderton and Ryan (2016) for the operationalization of low- and high-level attacks.

14 What is more, certain types of violence within countries may be more associated with atrocity crime. For instance, Valentino, Huth, and Balch-Lindsay (2004) argue that mass killing is more prominent in conflicts where guerrilla armies oppose governments. Yet, Krcmaric (2018) finds that mass killing is more probable during conventional wars than during guerilla wars, suggesting that additional research is needed on the relationship between the type of violence and the atrocity crimes that may unfold alongside it.

## References


Aguilar, P., Balcells, L., & Cebolla-Boado, H. (2011). Determinants of attitudes toward transitional justice: An empirical analysis of the Spanish case. *Comparative Political Studies*, *44*(10), 1397–1430.

Ahrens, C. E. (2006). Being silenced: The impact of negative social reactions on the disclosure of rape. *American Journal of Community Psychology*, *38*(3–4), 31–34.

Akresh, R., & De Walque, D. (2008). *Armed conflict and schooling: Evidence from the 1994 Rwandan genocide*. The World Bank.

Alexander, J. C. (2004). Toward a theory of cultural trauma. In J. C. Alexander, R. Eyerman, B. Giesen, N.J. Smelser, & P. Sztompka (Eds.), *Cultural trauma and collective identity* (pp. 1–30). Berkeley, CA: University of California Press.

Alexander, M. G., Brewer, M. B., & Hermann, R. K. (1999). Images and affect: A functional analysis of out-group stereotypes. *Journal of Personality and Social Psychology*, *77*(1), 78–93.

Alford, C. F. (2019). Intergenerational transmission of trauma: Holocaust Survivors, their children and their children's survivors. *Journal of Psychosocial Studies*, *12*(1–2), 145–155.

Anderton, C. H., & Ryan, E. V. (2016). Habituation to atrocity: Low-level violence against civilians as a predictor of high-level attacks. *Journal of Genocide Research*, *18*(4), 539–462.

Andreas, P., & Greenhill, K. M. (Eds.). (2010). *Sex, drugs, and body counts: The politics of numbers in global crime and conflict*. Ithaca, NY: Cornell University Press.

Arendt, H. (1951). *Final act of the United Nations Conference of Plenipotentiares on the status of refugees and stateless persons*. Retrieved from https://digitallibrary.un.org/record/696128?ln=en

Backer, D. (2010). Watching a bargain unravel? A panel study of victims' attitudes about transitional justice in Cape Town, South Africa. *International Journal of Transitional Justice*, *4*(3), 443–456.

Barel, E. (2010). Surviving the Holocaust: A meta-analysis of the long-term sequelae of a genocide. *Psychological Bulletin*, *136*(5), 677–698.

Bass, G. J. (2000). *Stay the hand of vengeance: The politics of war crimes tribunals*. Princeton, NJ: Princeton University Press.

Bećirević, E. (2014). *Genocide on the Drina River*. New Haven, CT: Yale University Press.

Benford, R. D., & Snow, D. A. (2000). Framing processes and social movements: An overview and assessment. *Annual Review of Sociology*, *26*(1), 611–639.

Berg, M. T., Stewart, E. A., Schreck, C. J., & Simons, R. L. (2012). The victim–offender overlap in context: Examining the role of neighborhood street culture. *Criminology*, *50*(2), 359–390.

Berry, M. E. (2018). *War, women, and power: From violence to mobilization in Rwanda and Bosnia-Herzegovina*. New York, NY: Cambridge University Press.

Bezo, B., & Maggi, S. (2015). Living in "survival mode:" Intergenerational transmission of trauma from the Holodomor genocide of 1932–1933 in Ukraine. *Social Science & Medicine*, *134*, 87–94.

Bharti, N., Lu, X., Bengtsson, L., Wetter, E., & Tatem, A. J. (2015). Remotely measuring populations during a crisis by overlaying two data sources. *International health*, *7*(2), 90–98.

Bouris, E. (2007). *Complex political victims*. Bloomfield, CT: Kumarian Press, Inc.

Brounéus, K. (2010). The trauma of truth telling: Effects of witnessing in the Rwandan Gacaca courts on psychological health. *Journal of Conflict Resolution*, *54*(3), 408–437.

Brunborg, H. (Forthcoming). Victimization surveys and mortality estimates. In B. Hola, H. Nyseth Brehm, & M. Weerdesteijn (Eds.), *The Oxford handbook of atrocity crime*.

Buhaug, H., Gates, S., & Lujala, P. (2009). Geography, rebel capability, and the duration of civil conflict. *Journal of Conflict Resolution*, *53*(4), 544–569.

Caiani, M. (2017). Between contextual opportunities and discursive resources. Understanding the politics of the enemy in Central and Eastern Europe. *East European Politics and Societies*, *3*(3), 14–40.

Campbell, B. (2009). Genocide as social control. *Sociological Theory*, *27*(2), 150–172.

Carpenter, C. R. (2006). Recognizing gender-based violence against civilian men and boys in conflict situations. *Security Dialogue*, *37*(1), 83–103.

Checchi, F., Stewart, B. T., Palmer, J. J., & Grundy, C. (2013). Validity and feasibility of a satellite imagery-based method for rapid estimation of displaced populations. *International journal of health geographics*, *12*(4), 1–12.

Chelouche, T. (2005). Some ethical dilemmas faced by Jewish doctors during the Holocaust. *Medicine and Law*, *24*(4), 703–716.

Christie, N. (1986). The ideal victim. In E. A. Fattah (Ed.), *From crime policy to victim policy* (pp. 17–30). London: Palgrave Macmillan.

Cilliers, J., Dube, O., & Siddiqi, B. (2016). Reconciling after civil conflict increases social capital but decreases individual well-being. *Science*, *352*(6287), 787–794.

Cohen, D. K. (2013). Explaining rape during civil war: Cross-national evidence (1980–2009). *The American Political Science Review*, *107*(3), 461–477.

Cohen, L. E., & Cantor, D. (1981). Residential burglary in the United States: Lifestyle and demographic factors associated with the probability of victimization. *Journal of Research in Crime and Delinquency*, *18*(1), 113–127.

Costelloe, M. T., Chiricos, T., & Gertz, M. (2009). Punitive attitudes toward criminals: Exploring the relevance of crime salience and economic insecurity. *Punishment & Society*, *11*(1), 25–49.

Darfurian Voices. (2011). *Darfurian voices: Documenting Darfurian refugees' views on issues of peace, justice, and reconciliation*. Retrieved from https://static1.squarespace.com/static/52920ed5e4b04a0741daa89c/t/529224ffe4b049dd0ca09a3f/1385309439460/Darfurian+Voices+-+Report+-+English.pdf

David, R., & Choi, S. Y. P. (2006). Forgiveness and transitional justice in the Czech Republic. *The Journal of Conflict Resolution*, *50*(3), 339–367.

Davis, R., Taylor, B., & Bench, S. (1995). Impact of sexual and nonsexual assault on secondary victims. *Violence and victims*, *10*(1), 73–84.

De Walque, D., & Verwimp, P. (2010). The demographic and socio-economic distribution of excess mortality during the 1994 genocide in Rwanda. *Journal of African Economies*, *19*(2), 141–162.

Degloma, T. (2009). Expanding trauma through space and time: Mapping the rhetorical strategies of trauma carrier groups. *Social Psychology Quarterly*, *72*(2), 105–122.

Degomme, O., & Guha-Sapir, D. (2010). Patterns of mortality rates in Darfur conflict. *Lancet*, *375*(9711), 294–300.

Dembour, M.-B, & Haslam, E. (2004). Silencing hearings? Victim-witnesses at war crimes trials. *European Journal of International Law*, *15*(1), 151–177.

Doherty, K., & Anderson, I. (2004). Making sense of male rape: Constructions of gender, sexuality and experience of rape victims. *Journal of Community & Applied Social Psychology*, *14*(2), 85–103.

Drumbl, M. A. (2012). *Reimagining child soldiers in international law and policy*. New York, NY: Oxford University Press.

Fassin, D., & Rechtman, R. (2009). *The empire of trauma: An inquiry into the condition of victimhood*. Princeton University Press.

Fein, H. (1979). *Accounting for genocide: National responses and Jewish victimization during the Holocaust*. Chicago, IL: Free Press.

Ferrales, G., Nyseth Brehm, H., & McElrath, S. (2016). Gender-based violence against men and boys in Darfur: The gender-genocide nexus. *Gender & Society*, *30*(4), 565–589.

Fjelde, H., & von Uexkull, N. (2012). Climate triggers: Rainfall anomalies, vulnerability and communal conflict in Sub-Saharan Africa. *Political Geography*, *31*(7), 444–453.

Fleming, K., & Kruger, L. (2013). "She keeps his secrets": A gendered analysis of the impact of shame on the non-disclosure of sexual violence in one low-income South African community. *African Safety Promotion: A Journal of Injury and Violence Prevention*, *11*(2), 107–124–124.

Foucault, M. (1978). *The history of sexuality*. New York, NY: Pantheon Books.

Fujii, L. A. (2009). *Killing neighbors: Webs of violence in Rwanda*. Ithaca, NY: Cornell University Press.

Gibson, J. L. (2002). Truth, justice, and reconciliation: Judging the fairness of amnesty in South Africa. *American Journal of Political Science*, *46*(3), 540–556.

Glueck, S. (1942). By what tribunal shall war offenders be tried. *Harvard Law Review*, *56*, 1059.

Goldsmith, B. E., Butcher, C. R., Semenovich, D., & Sowmya, A. (2013). Forecasting the onset of genocide and politicide: Annual out-of-sample forecasts on a global dataset, 1988–2003. *Journal of Peace Research, 50*(4), 437–452.
Goldsmith, J., & Krasner, S. D. (2003). The limits of idealism. *Daedalus, 132*(1), 47–63.
Govier, T. (2015). *Victims and victimhood.* Peterborough, Ontario: Broadview Press.
Green, P., & Ward, T. (2004). *State crime: Governments, violence and corruption* (Vol. 31). London: Pluto Press.
Gupta, L. (1999). Bereavement recovery following the Rwandan genocide: A community-based intervention for child survivors. *Bereavement Care, 18*(3), 40–42.
Hagan, J., Kaiser, J., Rothenberg, D., Hanson, A., & Parker, P. (2012). Atrocity victimization and the costs of economic conflict crimes in the battle for Baghdad and Iraq. *European Journal of Criminology, 9*(5), 481–498.
Hagan, J., & Rymond-Richmond, W. (2008). The collective dynamics of racial dehumanization and genocidal victimization in Darfur. *American Sociological Review, 73*(6), 875–902.
Hagan, J., Rymond-Richmond, W., & Palloni, A. (2009). Racial targeting of sexual violence in Darfur. *American Journal of Public Health, 99*(8), 1386–1392.
Hagan, J., Schoenfeld, H., & Palloni, A. (2006). The science of human rights, war crimes, and humanitarian emergencies. *Annual Review of Sociology, 32*, 329–349.
Hall, J., Kovras, I., Stefanovic, D., & Loizides, N. (2018). Exposure to violence and attitudes towards transitional justice. *Political Psychology, 39*(2), 345–363.
Harff, B. (2003). No lessons learned from the Holocaust? Assessing risks of genocide and political mass murder since 1955. *American Political Science Review, 97*(1), 57–73.
Haslam, N. (2006). Dehumanization: An integrative review. *Personality and Social Psychology Review, 10*(3), 252–264.
Hayner, P. B. (2011). *Unspeakable truths: Transitional justice and the challenge of truth commissions* (2nd ed.). New York, NY: Routledge.
Hentig, H. V. (1948). *The criminal & his victim: Studies in the sociobiology of crime*. New Haven, CT: Yale University Press.
Hillyard, P., & Tombs, S. (2007). From 'crime' to social harm? *Crime, Law and Social Change, 48*(1–2), 9–25.
Hindelang, M. J., Gottfredson, M. R., & Garofalo, J. (1978). *Victims of personal crime: An empirical foundation for a theory of personal victimization.* Pensacola, FL: Ballinger Publishing Co.
Hinton, A. (2018). *The justice facade: Trials of transition in Cambodia.* Oxford, UK: Oxford University Press.
Hobbes, T. (1651). *Leviathan, or the matter, forme and power of a commonwealth ecclesiasticall and civil.*
Horne, C. M. (2014). Lustration, transitional justice, and social trust in post-communist countries. Repairing or wresting the ties that bind? *Europe-Asia Studies, 66*(2), 225–254.
Jennings, W. G., Higgins, G. E., Tewksbury, R., Gover, A. R., & Piquero, A. R. (2010). A longitudinal assessment of the victim-offender overlap. *Journal of Interpersonal Violence, 25*(12), 2147–2174.
Jensen, R. (2002). "No Irish need apply": A myth of victimization. *Journal of Social History, 36*(2), 405–429.

Johnson, D. (2001). Punitive attitudes on crime: Economic insecurity, racial prejudice, or both? *Sociological Focus*, *34*(1), 33–54.

Jones, A. (2006). Straight as a rule: Heteronormativity, gendercide, and the noncombatant male. *Men and Masculinities*, *8*(4), 451–469.

Kaminer, D., Stein, D. J., Mbanga, I., & Zungu-Dirwayi, N. (2001). The truth and reconciliation commission in South Africa: Relation to psychiatric status and forgiveness among survivors of human rights abuses. *British Journal of Psychiatry*, *178*(4), 373–377.

Kampala Amendment to the Rome Statute. (2010). Accessed at https://asp.icc-cpi.int/en_menus/asp/crime%20of%20aggression/Pages/default.aspx.

Karstedt, S. (2010). From absence to presence, from silence to voice: Victims in international and transitional justice since the Nuremberg trials. *International Review of Victimology*, *17*(1), 9–30.

Keck, M. E., & Sikkink, K. (1998). *Activists beyond borders: Advocacy networks in international politics*. Ithaca, NY: Cornell University Press.

Kiss, E. (2000). Moral ambition within and beyond political constraints: Reflections on restorative justice. In R. I. Rotberg & D. F. Thompson (Eds.), *Truth v. justice: The morality of truth commissions* (pp. 68–98). Princeton, NJ: Princeton University Press.

Koo, K. H., Nguyen, H. V., Andrasik, M. P., & George, W. H. (2015). The cultural context of nondisclosure of alcohol-involved acquaintance rape among Asian American college women: A qualitative study. *The Journal of Sex Research*, *52*(1), 55–68.

Krain, M. (1997). State-sponsored mass murder: The onset and severity of genocides and politicides. *Journal of Conflict Resolution*, *41*(3), 331–360.

Krcmaric, D. (2018). Varieties of civil war and mass killing: Reassessing the relationship between guerrilla warfare and civilian victimization. *Journal of Peace Research*, *55*(1), 18–31.

Kritz, N. (1995). *Transitional justice: How emerging democracies reckon with former regimes*. Washington, DC: United States Institute of Peace Press.

Longman, T., & Rutagengwa, T. (2004). Memory, identity, and community in Rwanda. In E. Stover & H. Weinstein (Eds.), *My neighbor, my enemy: Justice and community in the aftermath of mass atrocity* (pp. 162–182). New York, NY: Cambridge University Press.

Luft, A. (2015). Toward a dynamic theory of action at the micro level of genocide: Killing, desistance, and saving in 1994 Rwanda. *Sociological Theory*, *33*(2), 148–172.

Lutz, E. (1995). After the elections: Compensating victims of human rights abuses. In N. J. Kritz (Ed.), *Transitional justice: How emerging democracies reckon with former regimes* (pp. 551–565). Washington, DC: United States Institute of Peace Press.

Maruna, S. (2001). *Making good: How ex-convicts reform and rebuild their lives*. American Psychological Association.

McDoom, O. S. (2014). Predicting violence within genocide: A model of elite competition and ethnic segregation from Rwanda. *Political Geography*, *42*, 34–45.

McEvoy, K., & McConnachie, K. (2012). Victimology in transitional justice: Victimhood, innocence and hierarchy. *European Journal of Criminology*, *9*(5), 527–538.

McGuffey, C. S. (2013). Rape and racial appraisals: Culture, intersectionality, and black women's accounts of sexual assault. *Du Bois Review: Social Science Research on Race*, *10*(1), 109–130.

Mendeloff, D. (2004). Truth-seeking, truth-telling, and postconflict peacebuilding: Curb the enthusiasm? *International Studies Review*, *6*(3), 355–380.

Mendeloff, D. (2009). Trauma and vengeance: Assessing the psychological and emotional effects of post-conflict justice. *Human Rights Quarterly*, *31*, 592–623.

Mendelsohn, B. (1956). A new branch of bio-psychological science: La victimology. *Revue Internationale De Criminologie Et De Police Technique*, *10*, 782–789.

Miers, D. (1989). Positivist victimology: A critique. *International Review of Victimology*, *1*(1), 3–22.

Morrall, P., Hazelton, M., & Shackleton, W. (2011). Homicide and its effect on secondary victims. *Mental Health Practice*, *15*(3), 14–19.

Mullins, C. W. (2009). "He would kill me with his penis": Genocidal rape in Rwanda as a state crime. *Critical Criminology*, *17*(1), 15–33.

Munyandamutsa, N., Nkubamugisha, P.M., Gex-Fabry, M., & Eytan, A. (2012). Mental and physical health in Rwanda 14 years after the genocide. *Social Psychiatry and Psychiatric Epidemiology*, *47*(11), 1753–1761.

Nalepa, M. (2010). *Skeletons in the closet: Transitional justice in post-communist Europe*. New York, NY: Cambridge University Press.

Nettelfield, L. J. (2010). Research and repercussions of death tolls: The case of the Bosnian Book of the Dead. In P. Andreas & K. M. Greenhill (Eds.), *Sex, drugs, and body counts: The politics of numbers in global crime and conflict* (pp.159–187). Ithaca, NY: Cornell University Press.

Neupert, R. F., & Prum, V. (2005). Cambodia: Reconstructing the demographic stab of the past and forecasting the demographic scar of the future. *European Journal of Population / Revue Européenne de Démographie*, *21*(2), 217–246.

Noor, M., Brown, R., Gonzalez, R., Manzi, J., & Lewis, C. A. (2008). On positive psychological outcomes: What helps groups with a history of conflict to forgive and reconcile with each other? *Personality and Social Psychology Bulletin*, *34*(6), 819–832.

Nussio, E., Rettberg, A., & Ugarriza, J. E. (2015). Victims, nonvictims and their opinions on transitional justice: Findings from the Colombian case. *International Journal of Transitional Justice*, *9*(2), 336–354.

Nyseth Brehm, H. (2017). Subnational determinants of killing in Rwanda. *Criminology*, *55*(1), 5–31.

Obermeyer, Z., Murray, C. J. L., & Gakidou, E. (2008). Fifty years of violent war deaths from Vietnam to Bosnia: Analysis of data from the world health survey programme. *BMJ*, *336*(7659), 1482–1486.

Olsen, T. D., Payne, L. A., & Reiter, A. G. (2010). The justice balance: When transitional justice improves human rights and democracy. *Human Rights Quarterly*, *32*(4), 980–1007.

Orth, U., & Maercker, A. (2004). Do trials of perpetrators retraumatize crime victims? *Journal of Interpersonal Violence*, *19*(2), 212–227.

Paez, D., & Liu, J. H. (2011). Collective memory of conflicts. *Intergroup conflicts and their resolution: A social psychological perspective*, 105–124. Accessed at www.researchgate.net/profile/Dario_Paez/publication/285735981_Collective_memory_of_conflicts/links/566aed6808ae1a797e39669c/Collective-memory-of-conflicts.pdf.

Pemberton, A., Letschert, R. M., Brouwer, A. M. de, & Haveman, R. H. (2015). Coherence in international criminal justice: A victimological perspective. *International Criminal Law Review*, *15*(2), 339–368.

Pennekamp, S. F., Doosje, B., Zebel, S., & Fischer, A. H. (2007). The past and the pending: The antecedents and consequences of group-based anger in historically and currently disadvantaged groups. *Group Processes & Intergroup Relations*, *10*(1), 41–55.

Pensky, M. (2008). Amnesty on trial: Impunity, accountability, and the norms of international law. *Ethics & Global Politics*, *1*(1–2), 1–40.

Price, M., & Ball, P. (2014). Big data, selection bias, and the statistical patterns of mortality in conflict. *SAIS Review of International Affairs*, *34*(1), 9–20.

Rafter, N., & Walklate, S. (2012). Genocide and the dynamics of victimization: Some observations on Armenia. *European Journal of Criminology*, *9*(5), 514–526.

Rimé, B., Kanyangara, P., Yzerbyt, V., & Paez, D. (2011). The impact of Gacaca tribunals in Rwanda: Psychosocial effects of participation in a truth and reconciliation process after a genocide. *European Journal of Social Psychology*, *41*, 695–706.

Roht-Arriaza, N. (2006). *The Pinochet effect: Transnational justice in the age of human rights*. Philadelphia, PA: University of Pennsylvania Press.

Rome Statute of the International Criminal Court. (1998). Accessed at www.icc-cpi.int/resource-library/documents/rs-eng.pdf.

Roth, M., Neuner, F., & Elbert, T. (2014). Transgenerational consequences of PTSD: risk factors for the mental health of children whose mothers have been exposed to the Rwandan genocide. *International journal of mental health systems*, *8*(1), 1–12.

Rothe, D., & Kauzlarich, D. (Eds.). (2014). *Towards a victimology of state crime*. Abingdon: Routledge.

Rummel, R. J. (1997). *Death by government*. Livingston, NJ: Transaction Publishers.

Rustad, S. C. A., Rød, J. K., Larsen, W., & Gleditsch, N. P. (2008). Foliage and fighting: Forest resources and the onset, duration, and location of civil war. *Political Geography*, *27*(7), 761–782.

Samii, C. (2013). Who wants to forgive and forget? Transitional justice preferences in postwar Burundi. *Journal of Peace Research*, *50*(2), 219–233.

Sampson, R. J., Raudenbush, S. W., & Earls, F. (1997). Neighborhoods and violent crime: A multilevel study of collective efficacy. *Science*, *277*(5328), 918–924.

Savelsberg, J. (2010). *Crime and human rights: Criminology of genocide and atrocities*. London: SAGE.

Savelsberg, J. (2015). *Representing mass violence: Conflicting responses to human rights violations in Darfur*. Oakland, CA: University of California Press.

Schaal, S., & Elbert, T. (2006). Ten years after the genocide: Trauma confrontation and posttraumatic stress in Rwandan adolescents. *Journal of Traumatic Stress*, *19*(1), 95–105.

Scheffer, D. (2006). Genocide and atrocity crimes. *Genocide Studies and Prevention*, *1*(3), 229–250.

Schwartz, H. (1995). Lustration in Eastern Europe. In N. J. Kritz (Ed.), *Transitional justice: How emerging democracies reckon with former regimes* (pp. 461–483). Washington, DC: United States Institute of Peace Press.

Sikkink, K. (2011). *The justice cascade: How human rights prosecutions are changing world politics.* New York, NY: W. W. Norton & Company.

Sivakumaran, S. (2007). Sexual violence against men in armed conflict. *European Journal of International Law*, *18*(2), 253–276.

Stover, E. (2011). *The witnesses, war crimes and the promise of justice in the Hague*. Philadelphia, PA: University of Pennsylvania Press.

Straus, S. (2006). *The order of genocide: Race, power, and war in Rwanda*. Ithaca, NY: Cornell University Press.

Straus, S. (2019). The limits of a genocide lens: Violence against Rwandans in the 1990s. *Journal of Genocide Research*, *21*(4), 504–524.

Tabeau, E., & Zwierzchowski, J. (2013). A review of estimation methods for victims of the Bosnian War and the Khemr Rouge Regime. In T. B. Seybolt, J. D. Aronson, & B. Fischhoff (Eds.), *Counting civilian casualties: An introduction to recording and estimating nonmilitary deaths in conflict* (p.213–243). New York, NY: Oxford University Press.

Teitel, R. G. (2002). Humanity's law: Rule of law for the new global politics. *Cornell International Law Journal*, *35*(2), 3.

The Stanley Foundation. (2015). *Violent Nonstate Actors as Perpetrators and Enablers of Atrocity Crimes*. Retrieved from https://academic.oup.com/english/article-lookup/doi/10.1093/english/23.116.57-a

Torpey, J. C. (2006). *Making whole what has been smashed: On reparations politics*. Boston, MA: Harvard University Press.

U.S. Department of State–Humanitarian Information Unit. (2011). Darfur, Sudan update: Confirmed damaged and destroyed villages February 2003—December 2010 (as of 28 January 2011). Retrieved from https://reliefweb.int/map/sudan/darfur-sudan-update-confirmed-damaged-and-destroyed-villages-february-2003-december-2010-0

Uzonyi, G. (2018). Interstate rivalry, genocide, and politicide. *Journal of Peace Research*, *55*(4), 476–490.

Valentino, B. A., Huth, P., & Balch-Lindsay, D. (2004). "Draining the sea": Mass killing and guerrilla warfare. *International Organization*, *58*(2), 375–407.

van Wijk, J. (2013). Who is the 'little old lady' of international crimes? Nils Christie's concept of the ideal victim reinterpreted. *International Review of Victimology*, *19*(2), 159–179.

Verdeja, E. (2012). The political science of genocide: Outlines of an emerging research agenda. *Perspectives on Politics*, *10*(2), 307–321.

Vest, J., Catlin, T. K., Chen, J. J., & Brownson, R. C. (2002). Multistate analysis of factors associated with intimate partner violence. *American Journal of Preventive Medicine*, *22*(3), 156–164.

Vinjamuri, L., & Snyder, J. (2004). Advocacy and scholarship in the study of international war crime tribunals and transitional justice. *Annual Review of Political Science*, *7*(1), 345–362.

Vollhardt, J. R. (2012). Collective victimization. In L. R. Tropp (Ed.), *The Oxford Handbook of Intergroup Conflict* (pp. 136–157). Oxford: Oxford University Press.

Walklate, S. (2016). The metamorphosis of the victim of crime: From crime to culture and the implications for justice. *International Journal for Crime, Justice and Social Democracy*, *5*(4), 4–16.

Washington, P. A. (2001). Disclosure patterns of black female sexual assault survivors. *Violence Against Women*, *7*(11), 1254–1283.

Weber, M. (1965). *Politics as a vocation*. Philadelphia, PA: Fortress Press.

Weinstein, H. M., Fletcher, L. E., Vinck, P., & Pham, P. N. (2010). Stay the hand of justice: Whose priorities take priority? In L. Shaw, L. Waldorf, & P. Hazan (Eds.), *Localizing transitional justice: Interventions and priorities after mass violence* (pp. 27–48). Stanford, CT: Stanford University Press.

Weiss-Wendt, A. (2017). *The Soviet Union and the gutting of the UN Genocide Convention*. Madison, WI: The University of Wisconsin Press.

Wemmers, J.-A. (2009). Victim reparation and the International Criminal Court. *International Review of Victimology*, *16*(2), 123–126.

Wimmer, A. (2008). The making and unmaking of ethnic boundaries: A multilevel process theory. *American Journal of Sociology*, *113*(4), 970–1022.

Wood, E. J. (2006). Variation in sexual violence during war. *Politics & Society*, *34*(3), 307–342.

Wood, E. J. (2010). Sexual violence during war: Toward an understanding of variation. In *Gender, war, and militarism: Feminist perspectives*. Santa Barbara, CA: ABC-CLIO.

Woolford, A., & Wolejszo, S. (2006). Collecting on moral debts: Reparations for the Holocaust and Pořajmos. *Law & Society Review*, *40*(4), 871–902.

Yehuda, R., Schmeidler, J., Siever, L. J., Binder-Brynes, K., & Elkin, A. (1997). Individual differences in posttraumatic stress disorder symptom profiles in Holocaust survivors in concentration camps or in hiding. *Journal of Traumatic Stress*, *10*(3), 453–463.

Young, I. F., & Sullivan, D. (2016). Competitive victimhood: A review of the theoretical and empirical literature. *Current Opinion in Psychology*, *11*, 30–34.

Žarkov, D. (2001). The body of the other man: Sexual violence and the construction of masculinity, sexuality and ethnicity in Croatian media. In C. O. N. Moser & F. C. Clark (Eds.), *Victims, perpetrators or actors? Gender, armed conflict and political violence* (pp. 69–82). London: Zed Books.

# 6

# Theoretical Perspectives on the Victimization of Women

*Candace Kruttschnitt and Timothy Kang*

In order to understand the relevance of various theories put forth to explain women's victimization we need to know how often, and under what circumstances, women are victimized. Simply put, these data allow us to assess whether there are specific contexts in which our extant theories of victimization do, or do not, apply to women.

The majority of information we have on the victimization of women focuses on violent victimization and is derived from the National Crime Victimization Survey (NCVS).[1] NCVS data are based on self-reports from individuals age 12 or older living in households. Violent crimes included in the survey are rape or sexual assault, robbery, aggravated assault, and simple assault. NCVS also reports on domestic violence (victimizations by family members and intimate partners) and violent crimes that involved weapons or injury. Although information on domestic violence, intimate partner violence (IPV), and violence involving injury are reported, they are subsets, or not mutually exclusive, of the four main violent crimes (Morgan & Truman, 2018).

Generally, these data show few gender differences in the rates of non-lethal violent victimization. In 2017, 49% of the males and 51% of the females reported a non-fatal violent incident (Morgan & Truman, 2018, table 10). Moreover, unlike the gender gap in offending, this gender parity in victimization has remained relatively stable over the past decade while tipping slightly toward more female victimizations (see Rand, 2008).[2]

This picture of rough gender parity in violent victimizations changes when we look at the most serious type of victimization, homicide, and two types of victimization that disproportionately involve women: Intimate partner violence and rape and sexual assaults. In the case of homicide, men represent about 80% of the victims and this has remained relatively stable over time and place (Gartner, 2011; Lauritsen & Heimer, 2008).[3] However, when we turn to homicides involving intimate partners, females make up 70% of the victims. Declines in the rates of intimate partner homicides have occurred for both sexes, but the declines have been greater for males relative to females (Catalano, Smith, Synder, & Rand, 2009; Lauritsen & Heimer, 2008).

Women's victimization by intimate partners is less frequent than their victimization by either acquaintances or strangers and these intimate victimizations have declined over time (Catalano et al., 2009; Lauritsen & Heimer, 2008; Xie, Heimer, & Lauritsen, 2012).[4] Although it is assumed that women's rates of intimate partner victimization exceed those of men, the use of different measures of violence have complicated this issue. When researchers use the Conflict Tactics Scale to measure intimate violence, which does not tap the nature or extent of injury, men are more likely to be victims of intimate partner violence than women (Straus, 2004). However, surveys that capture more serious forms of violence that result in injury find that women are more likely to be victimized than men are (Tjaden & Thoennes, 2000).

Sexual assaults and rape measured by the NCVS include completed, attempted, or threatened acts. Roughly 91% of the victims are females and 78% of the women report that the offender was a family member, intimate partner, friend, or acquaintance (Planty, Langton, Krebs, Berzofsky, & Smiley-McDonald, 2013). Although NCVS reports substantial declines in reported rapes and sexual assaults between 1993 and 2011 and some increases thereafter (Morgan & Trumann, 2018), concerns have been raised about the accuracy of their estimates of these offenses relative to the estimates derived from health surveys (Kruttschnitt, Kalsbeek, & House, 2014).

Summarily, although there is some parity in the rates of victimization women and men encounter, there are notable differences in how they experience these offenses. Women are much more likely to be victimized by someone they know (an intimate partner or acquaintance) than are men (Catalano, 2007; Gartner, 2011) regardless of the type of offense (Lauritsen & Heimer, 2008).[5] This suggests that as we evaluate our extant theories of victimization to determine how applicable they are for women, we need to keep in mind that much of the victimization women experience occurs at the hands of an intimate partner (23%) or, to an even greater extent, an acquaintance (44%).

## Social Status and Patriarchy

Explanations for the violent victimization of women have been dominated by work on the gender structure of society (women's status relative to that of men's) and, by association, patriarchy.[6] On the one hand, the "ameliorative" hypothesis suggests that gender inequalities and violence against women are accepted in patriarchal societies (Whaley & Messner 2002); as such, while gender inequality fosters violence, reductions in gender inequality (or increases in the relative status of women) should reduce their rates of victimization. On the other hand, the "backlash" hypothesis suggests that as inequality is reduced, violence against women will increase as men feel threatened by the relative gains women are making. Xie, Heimer, and Lauritsen (2012) reviewed much of this research and found no conclusive results supporting either of these hypotheses. As a result, they drew attention to the import of examining (i) the inequality–violence relationship in the context of the victim–offender relationship and, (ii) both absolute and relative changes in inequality over time. Focusing on non-lethal victimizations in 40 US metropolitan areas over the period 1980–2004, they found that women's absolute economic and political gains reduced intimate partner victimization. Some support appeared for the backlash hypothesis as women's relative increases in the labor force increased their intimate partner victimization; but the effects of their absolute gains in reducing violence were as large or larger than their relative gains. The only strong support found for women's labor force participation increasing their rates of victimization occurred in the context of violence involving strangers and acquaintances (consistent with the routine activities perspective).

Other scholars interested in how women's relative status relates to their risks of violent victimization have focused on particular types of intimate partner violence. The findings, for studies conducted in the US, indicate that gender inequality is positively related to all types of intimate partner violence and adolescent dating violence for women, but not for men (Gessard, Swahn, & Tharp, 2015; Willie & Kershaw, 2019). Similar results have been shown in cross-national studies that examine both intimate partner sexual violence and partner violence (Heise & Kotsadam, 2015; LeSuer, 2019; Yodanis, 2004). If we turn to studies of lethal violence, an important early work underscores these more recent IPV findings. Bailey and Peterson (1995) studied the effects of gender inequality on different types of homicides in 130 US cities. Estimating separate models by victim–offender relationship, they found significant positive relationships between the rate of women being killed by their husbands and the rate of women killed by acquaintances and various measures of gender inequality.

Taken together, these studies clearly support the ameliorative hypothesis but subsequent studies of female homicide victimization that do not address the victim–offender relationship find support for the backlash hypothesis particularly among White females and in southern regions of the US (Pridemore & Freilich, 2005; Vieraitis & Williams, 2002; Whaley & Messner, 2002). By including stranger homicides in their analyses and measuring gender equality with employment and earnings, they may well be tapping into lifestyle changes that increase women's risk of victimization.

## Routine Activities

Like the backlash hypothesis, routine activity theory predicts that the increases in women's educational attainment and labor force participation as a result of broader structural changes will increase opportunities for crime and victimization (Cohen & Felson, 1979). These changes associated with modernization increase the time women spend outside the safety of the home and increase their interactions in time and space with potential offenders and without the capable guardianship of family. Decades of research have, in general, found support for these predictions for women's property crime victimization (Bennett, 1991; Bunch, Clay-Warner, & Lei, 2015; Franklin, Franklin, Nobles, & Kercher, 2012; Mustaine, 1997), sexual victimization (Clodfelter, Turner, Hartman, & Kuhns, 2010; De Coster, Estes, & Mueller, 1999; Felson & Burchfield, 2004; Fisher, Daigle, & Cullen, 2010; Franklin et al., 2012), stalking (Fisher, Cullen, & Turner, 2002; Mustaine & Tewksbury, 1999; Reyns, Henson, Fisher, Fox, & Nobles, 2016), violent victimization (Belknap, 1987; Felson & Burchfield, 2004; Lauritsen & Heimer, 2008; Like-Haislip & Miofsky, 2011; Miethe, Stafford, & Long, 1987; Mustaine, 1997; Stein, 2010; Stewart, Elifson, & Sterk, 2004), homicide (Gartner, Baker, & Pampel, 1990), and rape (Maume, 1989; Whaley, 2001).[7]

However, several scholars note that routine activity is inadequate for explaining victimization at the hands of intimates and acquaintances

(Belknap, 1987; Gartner & McCarthy, 1991; Schwartz, Dekeseredy, Tait, & Alvi, 2001). Dugan and Apel (2005) highlight that routine activity applies most appropriately when offenders select targets opportunistically based on their perceived situational attractiveness. When offenders deliberately select targets or share common private space with the victim, as in the case of intimates, family members, and acquaintances, the home no longer provides a safe haven against victimization for women and those typically responsible for guardianship against crime transform into potential victimizers. This is where theoretical attempts to merge feminist and routine activity theories have the most promise. For example, Schwartz and his colleagues (Schwartz et al., 2001; Schwartz & Pitts, 1995) suggest that in the case of sexual victimization, the traditional predictions of routine activity theory have difficulty explaining why sexual assaults on campuses predominantly involve male offenders and female victims. They argue that feminist perspectives can enhance routine activity approaches by explaining the presence of motivated offenders of sexual violence and a lack of effective guardianship. The "rape-supportive culture" in North America fosters motivation and deters guardianship by providing an abundance of excuses that normalize sexual aggression among men and breeds tolerance among criminal justice officials, college officials, bystanders, and even victims. Moreover, some male peer groups encourage and perpetuate the sexual exploitation of intoxicated women, which can explain why motivations for sexual aggression are widespread on campus and why campuses are "effective-guardian-absent" (2001, p. 630). Using data from college and university students, Schwartz and colleagues (Schwartz et al., 2001; Schwartz & Pitts, 1995) show that having more friends that support violence against women and that get women drunk or high to have sex with them significantly increases the likelihood that men will be sexually aggressive against intimates and women will be sexually victimized.

Mustaine and Tewksbury (2002) also advocate for the synthesis of feminist and routine activity theories to better understand variation in rape and sexual assault victimization among women. They argue that although feminist theory highlights why gender inequality and the broader patriarchal structures of society put women at greater risk for rape and sexual assault compared with men (between-gender variation), routine activity theory can explain why some women are at greater risk than others (within-gender variation). Using data from college and university students, they show that activities that increase their exposure to potential offenders (involved in campus activities, hanging out, going out at night for leisure, buying drugs) and using drugs in public (target attractiveness) increase the likelihood of sexual assault. They also show that self-guardianship behaviors (carrying protection on their person) are not effective in preventing sexual assault, likely because women are less likely to anticipate needing them when they are with people they know or with intimate partners.

These bodies of literature demonstrate that theoretical integration is important for understanding the victimization of women. While routine activity perspectives help us understand how societal changes have increased opportunities for women's victimization, they may be best suited for understanding relatively opportunistic crimes (Dugan & Apel, 2005). Incorporating feminist perspectives with routine activity theory, however, can refine our understanding of the motivations of offenders, the suitability of targets, and the times and places that may or may not provide guardianship against the victimization of women particularly at the hands of intimate partners and acquaintances.

## Structural Factors

If guardianship, or the lack thereof, is important to understanding women's vulnerability to both stranger and intimate partner violence, then we need to know if efforts to increase guardianship have affected the victimization of women. Attempts to determine this have focused primarily on community interventions to prevent domestic violence. Generally, while this research indicates that legislative policies aimed at gender violence and increased social services reduce intimate violence (Dugan 2003; Sanz-Barbero, Corradi, Otero-Garcia, Ayala, & Vives-Cases, 2018; Xie, Lauritsen, & Heimer, 2012), the effect of police actions are less clear. Evidence suggests that increasing the number of sworn officers in a city lowers women's victimization but the effect of mandatory arrest policies is less clear; in some contexts they appear to have no effect, in others they impede the likelihood that the police will be notified about an instance of IPV and, in the case of lethal violence, their effects may be contingent on the race and marital status of the parties involved (Dugan, 2003; Dugan, Nagin, & Rosenfeld 2003; Xie, Lauritsen, and Heimer 2012). While this comports well with what we know about battered Black women's reluctance to call the police (Potter, 2008), it also points to the import of considering more carefully the variations in neighborhoods and community contexts that make some women (and men) more vulnerable to victimization.

Research on the predictors of violence in neighborhoods and community contexts relies primarily on census tract data as proxies for neighborhood areas and derives indices to measure the levels of social disorganization (e.g., the level of poverty, residential instability, percent of single-female-headed households). While these studies almost uniformly find that neighborhoods with concentrated poverty, residential instability, and high rates of male unemployment have high rates of intimate partner violence (Miles-Doan, 1998; Vioth & Brondino, 2017; Wright & Benson, 2010), they provide less insight into whether these factors are unique to women's experiences of IPV and the degree to which they are gender-specific. Powers, Chamberlain, and Boggess (2018) shed some light on these questions as they looked at how neighborhood characteristics impact assault and robbery victimizations for males and females. They find that neighborhood disadvantage, residential instability, and vacancy rates affect both male and female victimizations but the effects are greater for males than females. The percentage of female-headed households was also significantly related to female, but not male, assault victimizations. This latter finding is somewhat surprising in that we would expect that women's risk of assault victimization might be reduced in neighborhoods with a high concentration of female-headed households because of the potential for protective networks and collective efficacy (neighborhood cohesion and informal social controls). Research on the effects of collective efficacy on women's risk of violent victimization is based primarily on data from the Project on Human Development in Chicago Neighborhoods and focuses on IPV. The findings strongly suggest a conditional effect. That is, while collective efficacy reduces intimate partner violence, non-lethal severe partner violence, and dating violence, the size of this reduction hinges on the presence of neighborhood norms about not intervening in family conflicts, the level of neighborhood poverty or social disorganization, and women's collective economic resources (Browning, 2002; Jackson, 2016; Jain, Buka, Subramanian, & Molnar, 2010; Wright & Benson, 2011). This suggests that the level of neighborhood cohesion and control may be a necessary condition for reducing women's likelihood of experiencing IPV but, in and of itself, it is not a sufficient condition.

The question of how much individual factors and family factors contribute to women's (and men's) risk of violence in particular communities has generated a number of important multi-level studies. Van Wyk, Benson, Fox, and DeMaris (2003), extending the work on IPV, modeled individual factors (race and social support), family characteristics (e.g., marital status, subjective financial well-being), and community characteristics. Similar to the findings for collective efficacy, they found that the effects of social support were contingent on neighborhood disadvantage: In neighborhoods that were extremely disadvantaged and had few social supports, levels of IPV were higher. They also found that race interacted with neighborhood disadvantage. Race had no effect on IPV in highly disorganized neighborhoods, but in neighborhoods that were characterized as having a medium level of disorganization, non-Whites experienced more IPV than Whites. Others have found that the association between race in IPV disappears when White women and Black women are living in similar communities and that individual-level risk factors are racially invariant (Benson, Wooldredge, & Thistlethwaite, 2004). The contribution of individual, as opposed to community, factors to IPV is also important because it speaks to whether high rates of IPV are due to the kinds of people that move into particular neighborhoods (compositional effects) or how the characteristics of a neighborhood affect its residents (contextual effects). Studies that have examined women's risk of IPV, non-stranger violence, and stranger violence suggest that both compositional and contextual effects impact women's risk of violent victimization (Benson, Fox, DeMaris, & Van Wyk, 2003; Lauritsen & Schaum, 2004). Additionally, Lauritsen and Schaum (2004), using NCVS data on non-lethal violence, considered whether the victim–offender relationship conditions the effects of individual, family, and community predictors of violence against women. In so doing, they found that regardless of the victim–offender relationship, "younger women, single women with children, women who are relatively new to their address, and women who live in areas where greater proportions of families with children headed by women are most likely to be victimized" (p. 345). Although there are some differences in predictors across victim–offender relationships, the commonalities in the individual, family, and community factors were greater than the differences. This suggests that young, highly mobile women living in areas with relatively little guardianship are particularly vulnerable to violence. Is this combination of factors unique to women's victimization? A subsequent analysis by Lauritsen and Carbone-Lopez (2011), again using NCVS data, addresses this issue by examining whether gender moderates victim–offender relationships in the context of individual, family, and neighborhood characteristics. They found that, generally, age (older), marriage, and household income protect both men and women from being victimized, regardless of the offender's relationship to them. However, in the case of stranger victimizations length of residence (mobility) and single parenthood appear to put women at more risk than men whereas neighborhood disadvantage makes men particularly vulnerable to stranger victimizations. In the case of IPV, women who are younger, single parents, and mobile are at the greatest risk.

Overall, these findings underscore the import of considering whether and how women's victimization experiences differ from men's. Both women and men reduce their risks of non-lethal victimization by being older, married, and increasing their household income. However, where women's vulnerability to violence exceeds that of men, in the case of IPV, it is their individual and family characteristics that put them at greatest risk. While their neighborhoods can provide supports (both formal and informal) that condition the effects of economic disadvantage on IPV, they are unlikely to alter the statuses (single parenthood, and the attending lack of guardianship) that make women particularly vulnerable to IPV.

## Consequences of Victimization Over the Life Course

Not only can the experiences of victimization differ between men and women, but the effects of victimization vary by gender as well. A large body of literature, focusing almost exclusively on IPV and sexual assault, documents the range of negative effects victimization can have on women. For instance, IPV and sexual assault victimization have been linked to depressive symptoms (Bonomi et al., 2006; Flanagan, Jaquier, Overstreet, Swan, & Sullivan, 2014; Lövestad, Löve, Vaez, & Krantz, 2017; Mechanic, Weaver, & Resick, 2008), post-traumatic stress disorder (Flanagan et al., 2014; Maddoux, McFarlane, Symes, Fredland, & Feder, 2018; Mechanic et al., 2008; Ullman & Peter-Hagene, 2016), health problems (Bonomi et al., 2006), substance use (Bonomi et al., 2006; Flanagan et al., 2014; Lynch et al., 2017; Rhew, Stappenbeck, Bedard-Gilligan, Hughes, & Kaysen, 2017), and offending (Lynch et al., 2017) among women. To assess gender differences in the effects of victimization, however, studies including both women and men in samples are necessary. Some research finds similarities across gender. For instance, IPV is associated with increases in depressive symptoms (Coker et al., 2002; Fergusson, Horwood, & Ridder, 2005; Fletcher,

2010; Johnson, Giordano, Longmore, & Manning, 2014; Magdol et al., 1997; Porcerelli et al., 2003), substance use (Coker et al., 2002; Magdol et al., 1997), socio-emotional problems (Langton & Truman, 2014), physical health (Coker et al., 2002; Fletcher, 2010), suicidal ideation (Fergusson et al., 2005; Swahn et al., 2008), and further IPV revictimization (Exner-Cortens, Eckenrode, Bunge, & Rothman, 2017) in both men and women.

Other scholarship, however, finds that many of these consequences are more common or more serious for women as a result of IPV compared with men (for a review, see Caldwell, Swan, & Woodbrown, 2012). Women tend to experience more health issues (Porcerelli et al., 2003), depressive symptoms (Anderson, 2002; Ehrensaft, Moffitt, & Caspi, 2006; Harned, 2001; Porcerelli et al., 2003; Walton et al., 2007), post-traumatic stress disorder (Ehrensaft et al., 2006; Harned, 2001), and substance use (Anderson, 2002; Ehrensaft et al., 2006) than men as a result of IPV. These discrepant findings may be due to gender differences in exposure to, and content of, victimization experiences. Carbone-Lopez, Kruttschnitt, and Macmillan (2006) identified how patterns of IPV differed for men and women and the health-related consequences of different types of victimization. Using data from the National Violence Against Women Survey, they found that although men and women experienced similar types of IPV, the prevalence of every type of victimization was greater for women than men. Moreover, women tend to have greater odds of experiencing a broader range of health, mental health, and substance use consequences as a result of IPV compared with men. One explanation they offer is that, at the population level, men's IPV experiences may more frequently be the result of victim precipitation. If they are the primary aggressors in acts of IPV, their victimization as a result of their partner's defensive reactions may be less severe and result in fewer and less detrimental consequences.

In addition, the greater prevalence of IPV in the lives of women may cumulate and amplify negative consequences relative to men. Experiences of victimization have been shown to increase the risks of future or revictimization (Blom, Hogberg, Olofsson, & Danielsson, 2014; Daigle, Fisher, & Cullen, 2008; Exner-Cortens et al., 2017), and potentially more so for women (Ruback, Clark, & Warner, 2014; Widom, Czaja, & Dutton, 2008). It is here that life course perspectives can be most productive in understanding how the timing and sequencing of victimization experiences and their consequences increase the risk of further victimization and negative outcomes. Not only do the structural disadvantages described above increase risks of victimization, but the negative consequences of victimization, such as substance use, mental health issues, and physical problems can increase the risk of subsequent victimization and amplify the effects of negative consequences in a cumulatively disadvantageous "chain of risks" (Ferraro, Shippee, & Shafer, 2009; Kuh, Ben-Shlomo, Lynch, Hallqvist, & Power, 2003).

*The Effects of Proximal and Distal Victimization Experiences*

Research on the timing of victimization indicates that it is the more proximal events that have the most negative consequences. This research primarily focuses on the health and mental health consequences of IPV and child maltreatment. For example, Bonomi and colleagues compared women (ages 18 to 65) with and without IPV experiences (physical, sexual, or non-physical) and found that women with recent IPV experiences had higher rates of severe and minor depressive symptoms and a higher number of physical symptoms. Further, the recency of exposure to IPV appeared to be as important as the duration of exposures, since those with ten or more years of IPV had similar health outcomes to the women who were exposed to IPV over the previous five years (see also Johnson et al., 2014). Similar effects have also been observed with respect to child maltreatment among impoverished women in Wisconsin (Families and Children Thriving Study). Once adverse childhood experiences (ACE: Five indicators of child maltreatment and indicators of family dysfunction) are controlled, adult adversities (which include IPV experiences) have a stronger impact on mental health outcomes than ACE (Mersky, Janczewiski, & Nitkowski, 2018). These findings suggest that lacking information on the timing of victimization may result in erroneous estimates of the effects of various types of victimization on women's adult outcomes. In the latter case, for example, Mersky and colleagues (2018) found that the direct effect of ACE on adult mental health was not significant but it had an indirect effect through adult adversities. Consistent with a life course framework, this research suggests that early adversities like victimization may be critical to subsequent development not necessarily because of their lasting impact but because they can produce a series of cumulative disadvantages.

### *The Intervening Events Between Victimization and Life Course Outcomes*

The context of some of these disadvantages has been demonstrated by scholars who are increasingly paying attention to the mediators of the relationship between child maltreatment and subsequent problems with substance abuse, anxiety, and criminal offending. In samples that contain both males and females, the effect of child maltreatment (or exposure to violent crime) on substance use problems is attenuated when controls are introduced for mood and anxiety disorders (Afifi, Henriksen, Asmundons, & Sareen, 2012; Douglas et al., 2010; Simpson & Miller 2002). In fact, Douglas and colleagues (2010) found that the onset of mood and anxiety disorders occurred, on average, three years before a diagnosis for a substance abuse problem. The process of teasing out the intervening events between maltreatment and untoward outcomes has also been shown in qualitative studies of women offenders. Carbone-Lopez and Miller (2011) examined the life course of adult female methamphetamine users and found that childhood sexual victimization and other indicators of family dysfunction (e.g., parental drug use) were common among their study participants. Nevertheless, only two women linked these risk factors to their methamphetamine use. Instead, most of the women with histories of childhood sexual abuse indicated that this experience pushed them into precocious adult roles (living on their own and parenthood at an early age, caring for siblings, and involvement with older peers or romantic partners) which, in turn, provided the impetus for their meth use. Kruttschnitt and Kang (2019) uncovered a similar pattern in their analyses of the life histories of persistent offenders. White women, who were particularly likely to have experienced childhood sexual abuse, did not always link these experiences to their offending histories. Rather, they attributed their downfall to the bad romantic relationships that initiated a drug addiction and their subsequent crimes that supported this addiction (see also Wilson & Widom, 2010).

Studies of revictimization paint a similar picture where the initial victimization portends subsequent risk taking (including substance use), perceived threats of harm, or offending and then revictimization (Begle et al., 2011; Fargo, 2009; Jaffe, DiLillo, Gratz, & Messman-Moore, 2019; Ruback et al., 2014). Notably, however, some of this research draws attention to gender differences in the intervening and cumulative processes between initial victimization and subsequent victimization. Ruback et al. (2014) found that, for women, victimization leads to delinquency and heavy drinking which subsequently leads to revictimization, but the comparable pathway for men involves violent offending, rather than delinquency, and heavy drinking. Although this finding is consistent with the assumption that women are more likely to respond to trauma by internalizing their distress and men by externalizing it, it may also be the case that the community contexts in which these victimizations occur play a large part in how men and women respond to the victimization (see e.g., Jones, 2010). Context would also appear to be important to our understanding of gender differences in the relationship between adolescent dating violence (ADV) and IPV. Exner-Cortens and colleagues (2017) found that the relationship of ADV to adult IPV operates through young adult IPV; however, this relationship appeared to be stronger for men than women. This suggests, as other studies have (Johnson et al., 2014), that men may be particularly susceptible to the negative effects of IPV victimization in light of cisgender norms regarding vulnerability to victimization. All of this suggests that the life course outcomes of victimization are anything but straight forward. While victimization clearly presupposes individuals to additional vulnerabilities and risks, these vulnerabilities and risks are further conditioned by the contexts and societal norms in which victims reside.

## Conclusion

We started by noting the import of understanding the context that circumscribes most of the victimization experiences women encounter (assaults, sexual assaults, and rape). Reviewing the extant empirical data revealed that women are more likely than men to be victimized by someone they know (an intimate or acquaintance). This fact sets the stage for our evaluation of several prominent victimization theories and the growing body of work on the life course consequences of victimization. When we considered the work on status and patriarchy, we found strong support for the proposition that gender inequality increases women's risks of sexual assaults, IPV, and even homicides committed by their husbands and acquaintances, and conversely, in those contexts where gender inequality declines, so also do women's rates of victimization. This finding contradicts routine activity theory which holds that, and finds evidence for, the notion that as women's opportunities outside of the home increase, so also will their rates of victimization.

However, routine activities theory is unable to account for the contexts in which women are more likely to be victimized: In intimate relationships and with acquaintances, often on college campuses. It is the marrying of routine activities theory with feminist theory that provides a more plausible explanation for women's high rates of IPV and sexual assault. Work on the community and neighborhood context also extends our understanding of women's victimization by showing how disadvantaged neighborhoods, single parenthood, and residential instability place women at high risk for IPV. Taken together, we think these findings argue for the development of "context-congruent theorizing" (Nevin, 2019).

Context-congruent theorizing draws attention to the import of the context in understanding any given phenomenon. The victimization of women is distinguished primarily by its intimate nature and, as noted above, we have a fairly rich picture of the contexts that place women at high risk for IPV and sexual assault. However, unifying these findings into a single explanatory theory has yet to be done. Additionally, despite its proliferation, the research on the life course consequences of victimization has developed somewhat independently from the mainstream theories of victimization. Yet, the consequences of victimization are central to our study of victimization precisely because they can portend future victimization experiences. Some women experience discrete and isolated incidents of victimization while others are repeatedly revictimized (Kruttschnitt & Macmillan, 2006). While the life course literature gives us some clues as to the contexts that increase the risk of revictimization (risk taking behaviors, heavy alcohol or drug use), it has yet to unravel the contexts that put some women at risks for multiple victimizations across their life course and across multiple intimate relationships (cf. Carbone-Lopez & Kruttschnitt, 2010).

The role of agency in the victimization process is also not well researched but there are ample signs of its presence in the extant literature. For example, there is evidence that young girls who experience family violence and abuse, or who grow up in a particularly violent neighborhood, engage in pre-emptive violence (Batchelor, 2005; Jones, 2010). Some women who are the victims of domestic violence strike back with force, engaging in what Wolfgang (1958) referred to as victim-precipitation (Kruttschnitt & Carbone-Lopez, 2006). Others with prior IPV experience engage in tactics of de-escalation (Kruttschnitt, Yule, Alper, & Klassen, 2018) and still others disrupt the IPV cycle by moving out of violent relationships (Carbone-Lopez, Rennison, & Macmillan, 2012). Nevertheless, the contexts that facilitate these kinds of acts are not always clear. Here it may be particularly important to consider how other disadvantages can condition the life course consequences of victimization. IPV that occurs in the context of poverty and social isolation may limit a woman's ability to move out of a violent relationship or it may make her more susceptible to entering new relationships that are also violent.

Summarily, we believe that scholars need to pay more attention to the contexts that circumscribe the types of victimizations women are most likely to encounter: Those involving intimate partners and acquaintances. Our ability to develop a more comprehensive theory that addresses the victimization of women may hinge on highlighting not only the kinds of cumulative disadvantages that accrue with living in an impoverished neighborhood, or one that lacks guardianship, but also on addressing the timing of victimization experiences which has implications for subsequent aspects of the life course. We believe that such a context-contingent approach will not only lead to a richer understanding of women's victimization but also the salient differences between women and men's experiences.

## Notes

1 The National Crime Victimization Survey includes information on three property crimes: Household burglary, motor vehicle theft, and the taking of property or cash without personal contact with the victim. In these cases, the denominator is the household. Only one respondent in each household is asked the questions to avoid over-estimations of property crimes. Information on respondents living alone is one source of data on women's victimization in household property offenses but this captures only those living alone. Although information also exists on personal larceny, these numbers are extremely low and hence raise questions about the reliability for each sex.

2 An analysis of victimization rates for males and females over the period 1973–2004 reveals that male rates of aggravated and simple assaults (the vast majority of victimizations) declined faster for males than females (Lauritsen & Heimer, 2008). If this trend has continued, this may explain why rates of victimizations are tipping up for females relative to males.

3 Homicide statistics are based on the FBI's Uniform Crime Report data.

4 NCVS data classify intimate partners as spouses, ex-spouses, boyfriends, girlfriends, and ex-boyfriends or ex-girlfriends.

5 And Lauritsen and Heimer point out (2008, p. 136) robbery is somewhat of an exception. Because non-stranger robberies are extremely rare for both males and females the gender gap in this crime has fluctuated over time.

6 Most of the work reviewed here focuses on macro-level analyses of women's victimization. Hines (2011) suggests that on a micro-level, there is little support for patriarchy theory.

7 For exceptions, however, see Bailey (1999), Titterington (2006), Vieraitis, Britto, & Kovandzic (2007).

## References

Afifi, T. O., Henriksen, C. A., Asmundons, G. J. G., & Sareen, J. (2012). Childhood maltreatment and substance use disorders among men and women in a nationally representative sample. *Canadian Journal of Psychiatry*, *57*, 677–686.

Anderson, K. L. (2002). Perpetrator or victim? Relationships between intimate partner violence and well-being. *Journal of Marriage and Family*, *64*(4), 851–863.

Bailey, W. C. (1999). The socioeconomic status of women and patterns of forcible rape for major U.S. cities. *Sociological Focus*, *32*(1), 43–61.

Bailey, W. C., & Peterson, R. D. (1995). Gender inequality and violence against women. In J. Hagan & R. D. Peterson. (Eds.) *Crime and inequality.* Stanford, CA: Stanford University Press.

Batchelor, S. (2005). "Prove me the bam!": Victimization and agency in the lives of young women who commit violent offenses. *Probation Journal*, *53*(4), 358–375.

Begle, A. M., Hanson, R. F., Danielson, C. K., McCart, M. R., Ruggiero, K. J., Amstadter, A. B., … Kilpatrick, D. G. (2011). Longitudinal pathways of victimization, substance use, and delinquency: Findings from the National Survey of Adolescents. *Addictive Behaviors*, *36*, 682–689.

Belknap, J. (1987). Routine activity theory and the risk of rape: Analyzing ten years of National Crime Survey data. *Criminal Justice Policy Review*, *2*(4), 337–356.

Bennett, R. R. (1991). A cross-national assessment of a criminological perspective. *Social Forces*, *70*(1), 147–163.

Benson, M. L., Fox, G. L., DeMaris, A., & Van Wykm, J. (2003). Neighborhood disadvantage, individual economic distress and violence against women in intimate relationships. *Journal of Quantitative Criminology*, *19*(3), 207–235.

Benson, M. L., Wooldredge, J., Thistlethwaite, A. B., & Fox, G. L. (2004). The correlation between race and domestic violence is confounded with community context. *Social Problems*, *51*(3), 326–342.

Blom, H., Hogberg, U., Olofsson, N., & Danielsson, I. (2014). Strong association between earlier abuse and revictimization in youth. *BMC Public Health*, *14*, 715–725.

Bonomi, A. E., Thompson, R. S., Aderson, M., Reid, R. J., Carrell, D., Dimer, J. A., & Rivara, F. P. (2006). Intimate partner violence and women's physical, mental, and social functioning. *American Journal of Preventive Medicine*, *30*(6), 458–466.

Browning, C. R. (2002). The span of collective efficacy: Extending social disorganization theory to partner violence. *Journal of Marriage and the Family*, *64*, 833–850.

Bunch, J., Clay-Warner, J., & Lei, M. K. (2015). Demographic characteristics and victimization risk: Testing the mediating effects of routine activities. *Crime & Delinquency*, *61*(9), 1181–1205.

Caldwell, J. E., Swan, S. C., & Woodbrown, D. (2012). Gender differences in intimate partner violence outcomes. *Psychology of Violence*, *2*(1), 42–57.

Carbone-Lopez, K., & Kruttscnitt, C. (2010) Risky relationships: Assortative mating and women's experiences of intimate partner violence. *Crime & Delinquency*, *56*, 358–384.

Carbone-Lopez, K., Kruttschnitt, C., & Macmillan, R. (2006) Patterns of intimate partner violence and their associations with physical health, psychological distress, and substance use. *Public Health Reports*, *121*, 382–392.

Carbone-Lopez, K., & Miller, J. (2011). Precociious role entry as a mediating factor in women's methamphetamine use: Implications for life-course and pathways research. *Criminology*, *50*(1), 187–220.Carbone-Lopez, K., Rennison, C. M., & Macmillan, R. (2012). The transcendence of violence across relationships: New methods for understanding men's and women's experiences of intimate partner violence across the life course. *Journal of Quantitative Criminology*, *28*(2): 319–346.

Catalano, S. (2007). *Intimate partner violence in the United States*. Washington D.C.: Bureau of Justice Statistics. U.S. Department of Justice.

Catalano, S., Smith, E., Synder, H., & Rand, M. (2009). Female victims of violence. NCJ 228356. Washington D.C.: Bureau of Justice Statistics.

Clodfelter, T. A., Turner, M. G., Hartman, J. L., & Kuhns, J. B. (2010). Sexual harassment victimization during emerging adulthood: A test of routine activities theory and a general theory of crime. *Crime & Delinquency*, *56*(3), 455–481.

Coker, A. L., Davis, K. E., Arias, I., Desai, S., Sanderson, M., Brandt, H. M., & Smith, P. H., (2002). Physical and mental health effects of intimate partner violence for men and women. *American Journal of Preventive Medicine 23*(4), 260–268.

Cohen, L. E., & Felson, M. (1979). Social change and crime rate trends: A routine activity approach. *American Sociological Review*, *44*(4), 588–608.

Daigle, L. E., Fisher, B. S., & Cullen, F. T. (2008). The violent and sexual victimization of college women: Is repeat victimization a problem? *Journal of Interpersonal Violence*, *23*, 1286–1313.

De Coster, S., Estes, S. B., & Mueller, C. W. (1999). Routine activities and sexual harassment in the workplace. *Work and Occupations*, *26*(1), 21–49.

Douglas, K. R., Chan, G., Gelernter, J., Arias, A. J., Anton, R. F., Weiss, R. D., … Kranzler, H. R.. (2010). Adverse childhood events as risk factors for substance dependence: Partial mediation by mood and anxiety disorders. *Addictive Behaviors*, *35*: 7–13.

Dugan, L. (2003) Domestic violence legislation: Exploring its impact on the likelihood of domestic violence police involvement and arrest. *Criminology and Public Policy*, *2*(2), 283–312.

Dugan, L., & Apel, R. (2005). The differential risk of retaliation by relational distance: A more general model of violent victimization. *Criminology*, *43*: 697–730.

Dugan, L., Nagin, D. S., & Rosenfeld, R. (2003). Exposure reduction or retaliation? The effects of domestic violence resources on intimate-partner homicide. *Law and Society Review*, *37*(1), 169–198.

Ehrensaft, M. K., Moffitt, T. E., & Caspi, A. (2006). Is domestic violence followed by an increased risk of psychiatric disorders among women but not among men? A longitudinal cohort study. *American Journal of Psychiatry*, *163*, 885–892.

Exner-Cortens, D., Eckenrode, J., Bunge, J., & Rothman, E. (2017). Revictimization after adolescent dating violence in a matched, national sample of youth. *Journal of Adolescent Health*, *60*, 176–183.

Fargo, J. D. (2009). Pathways to adult sexual revictimization: Direct and indirect behavioral risk factors across the lifespan. *Journal of Interpersonal Violence*, *24*(11), 1771–1791.

Felson, R. B., & Burchfield, K. B. (2004). Alcohol and the risk of physical and sexual assault victimization. *Criminology*, *42*(4), 837–860.

Fergusson, D. M., Horwood, L. J., & Ridder, E. M. (2005). Partner violence and mental health outcomes in a New Zealand birth cohort. *Journal of Marriage and Family*, *67*, 1103–1119.

Ferraro, K. F., Shippee, T. P., & Shafer, M. K. (2009). Cumulative inequality theory for research on aging and the life course. In V. L. Bengston, D. Gans, N. M. Pulney, & M. Silverstein (Eds.), *Handbook of theories of aging* (pp. 413–433). New York, NY: Springer Publishing Co.

Fisher, B. S., Cullen, F. T., & Turner, M. G. (2002). Being pursued: Stalking victimization in a national study of college women. *Criminology & Public Policy*, *1*(2), 257–308.

Fisher, B. S., Daigle, L. E., & Cullen, F. T. (2010). What distinguishes single from recurrent sexual victims? The role of lifestyle-routine activities and first-incident characteristics. *Justice Quarterly*, *27*(1), 102–129.

Flanagan, J. C., Jaquier, V., Overstreet, N., Swan, S. C., & Sullivan, T. P. (2014). The mediating role of avoidance coping between intimate partner violence (IPV) victimization, mental health, and substance abuse among women experiencing bidirectional IPV. *Psychiatry Research*, *220*, 391–396.

Fletcher, J. (2010). The effects of intimate partner violence on health in young adulthood in the United States. *Social Science & Medicine*, *70*(1), 130–135.

Franklin, C. A., Franklin, T. W., Nobles, M. R., & Kercher, G. A. (2012). Assessing the effect of routine activity theory and self-control on property, personal, and sexual assault victimization. *Criminal Justice and Behavior*, *39*(10), 1296–1315.

Gartner, R. (2011). Sex, gender and crime. In M. Tonry (Ed.), *The Oxford handbook of crime and criminal justice* (pp. 348–384). New York: Oxford University Press.

Gartner, R., Baker, K., & Pampel, F. C. (1990). Gender stratification and the gender gap in homicide victimization. *Social Problems*, *37*(4), 593–612.

Gartner, R., & McCarthy, B. (1991). The social distribution of femicide in urban Canada, 1921–1988. *Law & Society Review*, *25*(2), 287–311.

Gessard, L. A., Swahn, M. H., & Tharp, A. T. (2015) A first look at gender inequality as a societal risk factor for dating violence. *American Journal of Preventive Medicine*, *49*(3): 448–457.

Harned, M. S. (2001). Abused women or abused men? An examination of the context and outcomes of dating violence. *Violence and Victims*, *16*, 269–285.

Heise, L. L., & Kotsadam, A. (2015). Cross-national and multi-level correlates of partner violence: An analysis of data from population-based surveys. *The Lancet Global Health*, *3*(6), 332–340.

Hines, D. A. (2011). Domestic violence. In M. Tonry (Ed.), *The Oxford handbook of crime and public policy* (pp. 115–139). New York: Oxford.

Jackson, A. L. (2016). The combined effect of women's neighborhood resources and collective efficacy on IPV. *Journal of Marriage and the Family*, *78*(4): 890–907.

Jain, S., Buka, S. L., Subramanian, S.V., & Molnar, B. E. (2010). Neighborhood predictors of dating violence victimization and perpetration in young adulthood: A multilevel study. *American Journal of Public Health*, *100*(9), 1737–1744.

Jaffe, A. E., DiLillo, D., Gratz, K. L., & Messman-Moore, T. L. (2019). Risk for revictimization following interpersonal and noninterpersonal trauma: Clarifying the role of posttraumatic stress symptoms and trauma related cognitions. *Journal of Traumatic Stress*, *32*, 42–55.

Johnson, W. L., Giordano, P. G., Longmore, M. A., & Manning, W. D. (2014) Intimate partner violence and depressive symptoms during adolescence and young adulthood. *Journal of Health and Social Behaviour*, *55*(1), 39–55.

Jones, N. (2010). *It's about being a survivor: African American girls, gender, and the context of inner-city violence*. In M. Chesney-Lind & N. Jones (Eds.), *Fighting for girls: New perspectives on gender and violence* (pp. 202–216). Albany, NY: SUNY Press.

Kuh, D., Ben-Shlomo, Y., Lynch, J., Hallqvist, J., & Power, C. (2003). Life course epidemiology. *Journal of Epidemiology and Community Health*, 57(10), 778–783.

Kruttschnitt, C., & Carbone-Lopez, K. (2006). Moving beyond the stereotypes: Women's subjective accounts of their violent crime. *Criminology*, *44*(2), 321–352.

Kruttschnitt, C., & Kang, T. (2019). Do intersectional variations shape prisoners' understanding of their past lives? An examination of the stock narratives of persistent offenders. *Justice Quarterly*. https://doi.org/10.1080/07418825.2019.1575456

Kruttschnitt, C., Kalsbeek, W. D., & House, C. (2014). *Estimating the incident of rape and sexual assault*. Washington, D.C. National Research Council.

Kruttschnitt, C., Yule, C., Alper, M., & Klassen, A. (2018). Situational variations in, and women's accounts of, avoided acts of serious intimate partner violence. *Violence Against Women*, *24*(4): 477–450.

Langton, L., & Truman, J. (2014). *Socio-emotional impact of violent crime*. NCJ 247076. U.S. Department of Justice.

Lauritsen, J. L., & Carbone-Lopez, K. (2011). Gender differences in risk factors for violent victimization: An examination of individual-, family-, and community-level predictors. *Journal of Research in Crime and Delinquency*, *48*(4), 538–565.

Lauritsen, J. L., & Heimer, K. (2008). The gender gap in violent victimization, 1973–2004. *Journal of Quantitative Criminology*, *24*, 125–147.

Lauritsen, J. L., & Schaum, R. J. (2004). The social ecology of violence against women. *Criminology*, *42*(2), 323–357.

LeSuer, W. (2019). An international study of the contextual effects of gender inequality on intimate partner violence against women students. *Feminist Criminology*. DOI: 10.1177/1557085119842652.

Like-Haislip, T. Z., & Miofsky, K. T. (2011). Race, ethnicity, gender, and violent victimization. *Race and Justice*, *1*(3), 254–276.

Lövestad, S., Löve, J., Vaez, M., & Krantz, G. (2017). Prevalence of intimate partner violence and its association with symptoms of depression: A cross-sectional study based on a female population sample in Sweden. *BMC Public Health*, *17*, 335–346.

Lynch, S. M., DeHart, D. D., Belknap, J. E., Green, B. L., Dass-Brailsford, P., Johnson, K. M., & Wong, M. R. (2017). An examination of the associations among victimization, mental health, and offending in women. *Criminal Justice and Behavior*, *44*(6), 796–814.

Maddoux, J., McFarlane, J., Symes, L., Fredland, N., & Feder, G. (2018). Using baseline data to predict chronic PTSD 48-months after mothers report intimate partner violence: Outcomes for mothers and the intergenerational impact on child behavioral functioning. *Archives of Psychiatric Nursing*, *32*, 475–482.

Magdol, L., Moffit, T. E., Caspi, A., Newman, D. L., Fagan, J., & Silva, P. A. (1997). Gender differences in partner violence in a birth cohort of 21-year-olds: Bridging the gap between clinical and epidemiological approaches. *Journal of Consulting and Clinical Psychology*, *65*(1), 68–78.

Maume, D. J. (1989). Inequality and metropolitan rape rates: A routine activity approach. *Justice Quarterly*, *6*(4), 513–527.

Mechanic, M. B., Weaver, T. L., & Resick, P. A. (2008). Mental health consequences of intimate partner abuse: A multidimensional assessment of four different forms of abuse. *Violence Against Women*, *14*(6), 634–654.

Mersky, J., Janczewski, C. E., & Nitkowski, J. C. (2018). Poor mental health among low-income women in the U.S.: The roles of adverse childhood and adult experiences. *Social Science and Medicine*, *206*, 14–21.

Miethe, T. D., Stafford, M. C., & Long, J. S. (1987). Social differentiation in criminal victimization: A test of routine activities/lifestyle theories. *American Sociological Review*, *52*(2), 184–194.

Miles-Doan, R. (1998). Violence between spouses and intimates: Does neighborhood context matter? *Social Forces*, *77*(2), 623–645.

Morgan, R. E., & Truman, J. L. (2018). *Criminal Victimization, 2017*. NCJ 252472. Washington D.C.: Bureau of Justice Statistics.

Mustaine, E. E. (1997). Victimization risks and routine activities: A theoretical examination using a gender-specific and domain-specific model. *American Journal of Criminal Justice*, *22*(1), 41–70.

Mustaine, E. E., & Tewksbury, R. (1999). A routine activity theory explanation for women's stalking victimizations. *Violence Against Women*, *5*(1), 43–62.

Mustaine, E. E., & Tewksbury, R. (2002). Sexual assault of college women: A feminist interpretation of a routine activities analysis. *Criminal Justice Review*, *27*(1), 89–123.

Nevin, A. D. (2019). Cyber-psychopathy revisited: An alternative framework for explaining online deviance. Paper presented at the annual meeting of the American Sociological Association, August 10–13, New York.

Planty, M., Langton, L., Krebs, C., Berzofsky, M., & Smiley-McDonald, H. (2013). *Female victims of sexual violence, 1994–2010*. NCJ 240655. Washington D.C.: Bureau of Justice Statistics.

Porcerelli, J. H., Cogan, R., West, P. P., Rose, E. A., Lambrecht, D., Wilson, K. E., … Karana, D. (2003). Violent victimization of women and men: Physical and psychiatric symptoms. *Journal of the American Board of Family Practice*, *16*, 32–39.

Potter, H. (2008). *Battle cries: Black women and intimate partner abuse*. New York, NY: New York University Press.

Powers, R. A., Chamberlain, A. W., & Boggess, L. N. (2018). The impact of structural disadvantage on the gender-gap and sex-specific rates of nonlethal violent victimization. *Crime and Delinquency*, *64*(2), 201–226.

Pridemore, W. A., & Freilich, J. D. (2005). Gender equality, traditional masculine culture, and female homicide victimization. *Journal of Criminal Justice*, *33*(3), 213–223.

Rand, M. R. (2008). *Criminal victimization, 2007.* NCJ 224390. Washington D.C.: Bureau of Justice Statistics.

Reyns, B. W., Henson, B., Fisher, B. S., Fox, K. A., & Nobles, M. R. (2016). A gendered lifestyle-routine activity approach to explaining stalking victimization in Canada. *Journal of Interpersonal Violence*, *31*(9), 1719–1743.

Rhew, I. C., Stappenbeck, C. A., Bedard-Gilligan, M., Hughes, T., & Kaysen, D. (2017). Effects of sexual assault on alcohol use and consequences among young adult sexual minority women. *Journal of Consulting and Clinical Psychology*, *85*(5), 424–433.

Ruback, B. R., Clark, V. A., & Warnter, C. (2014). Why are crime victims at risk of being victimized again? Substance use, depression and offending as mediators of the victimization–revictimization link. *Journal of Interpersonal Violence*, 29(1), 157–185.

Sanz-Barbero, B., Corradi, C., Otero-Garcia, L., Ayala, A., & Vives-Cases, C. (2018). The effect of macrosocial policies on violence against women: A multilevel study in 28 European countries. *International Journal of Public Health*, *63*(8), 901–911.

Schwartz, M. D., Dekeseredy, W. S., Tait, D., & Alvi, S. (2001). Male peer support and a feminist routine activities theory: Understanding sexual assault on the college campus. *Justice Quarterly*, *18*(3), 623–649.

Schwartz, M. D., & Pitts, V. L. (1995). Exploring a feminist routine activities approach to explaining sexual assault. *Justice Quarterly*, *12*(1), 9–31.

Simpson, T. L., & Miller, W. R. (2002). Concomitance between childhood sexual and physical abuse and substance use problems: A review. *Clinical Psychological Review*, *22*(1), 27–77.

Stein, R. E. (2010). The utility of country structure: A cross-national multilevel analysis of property and violent victimization. *International Criminal Justice Review*, *20*(1), 35–55.

Stewart, E. A., Elifson, K. W., & Sterk, C. E. (2004). Integrating the general theory of crime into an explanation of violent victimization among female offenders. *Justice Quarterly*, *21*(1), 159–181.

Straus, M. (2004). Women's violence toward men is a serious social problem. In D. R. Loseke, R. J. Gelles, & M. M. Cavanaugh (Eds.), *Current controversies on family violence*. Thousand Oaks, CA: Sage.

Swahn, M. H., Simon, T. R., Hertz, M. F., Arias, I., Bossarte, R. M., Ross, J. G. … Hamburger, M. E. (2008). Linking dating violence, peer violence, and suicidal behaviours among high-risk youth. *American Journal of Preventive Medicine*, *34*, 30–38.

Titterington, V. B. (2006). A retrospective investigation of gender inequality and female homicide victimization. *Sociological Spectrum*, *26*(2), 205–236.

Tjaden, P., & Thoennes, N. (2000). *Full report of the prevalence, incidence, and consequences of violence against women. Report from the National Institute of Justice and the Centers for Disease Control and Prevention.* Washington, DC: U.S. Department of Justice.

Ullman, S. E., & Peter-Hagene, L. C. (2016). Longitudinal relationships of social reactions, PTSD, and revictimization in sexual assault survivors. *Journal of Interpersonal Violence*, *31*, 1074–1094.

Van Wyk, J. A., Benson, M. L., Fox, G. L., & DeMaris, A. (2003). Detangling individual-, partner-, and community-level correlates of partner violence. *Crime and Delinquency*, *49*(3), 412–418.

Vieraitis, L. M., Britto, S., & Kovandzic, T. V. (2007). The impact of women's status and gender inequality on female homicide victimization rates: Evidence from U.S. counties. *Feminist Criminology*, *2*(1), 57–73.

Vieraitis, L. M., & Williams, M. R. (2002). Assessing the impact of gender inequality on female homicide victimization across U.S. cities. *Violence Against Women*, *8*(1), 35–63.

Voith, L. A., & Brondino, M. J. (2017). Neighborhood predictors of intimate partner violence: A theory-informed analysis using hierarchical linear modeling. *American Journal of Community Psychology*, *60*, 187–198.

Walton, M. A., Cunningham, R. M., Chermack, S. T., Maio, R., Blow, F. C., & Weber, J. (2007). Correlates of violence history among injured patients in an urban emergency department: Gender, substance use, and depression. *Journal of Addictive Diseases*, *26*(3), 61–75.

Whaley, R. B. (2001). The paradoxical relationship between gender inequality and rape: Toward a refined theory. *Gender and Society*, *15*(4), 531–555.

Whaley, R. B., & Messner, S. (2002). Gender equality and gendered homicide. *Homicide Studies*, *6*, 188–210.

Widom, C. S., Czaja, S. J., & Dutton, M. A. (2008). Childhood victimization and lifetime revictimization. *Child Abuse and Neglect*, *32*, 785–795.

Willie, T. C., & Kershaw, T. S. (2019). An ecological analysis of gender inequality and intimate partner violence in the United States. *Preventive Medicine*, *118*, 257–263.

Wilson, H. W., & Widom, C. S. (2010). The role of youth problem behaviors in the path from child abuse and neglect to prostitution: A prospective examination. *Journal of Research on Adolescence*, *20*(1), 210–236.

Wolfgang, M. E. (1958). *Patterns of criminal homicide*. Philadelphia, P. A.: University of Pennsylvania Press.

Wright, E. M., & Benson, M. L. (2010). Relational aggression, intimate partner violence and gender: An exploratory analysis. *Victims and Offenders*, *5*, 283–302.

Wright, E. M., & Benson, M. L. (2011). Clarifying the effects of neighborhood context on violence "behind closed doors." *Justice Quarterly*, *28*(5), 775–798.

Xie, M., Heimer, K., & Lauritsen, J. (2012). Violence against women in U.S. metropolitan areas: Changes in women's status and risk, 1980–2004. *Criminology*, *50*, 105–143.

Xie, M., Lauritsen, J. L., & Heimer, K. (2012). Intimate partner violence in U.S. metropolitan areas: The contextual influences of police and social services. *Criminology*, *50*(4), 961–992.

Yodanis (2004). Gender inequality, violence against women and fear. *Journal of Interpersonal Violence*, *19*(6), 655–675.

# 7

# Theories of Inmate Victimization

*Daniel P. Mears*

Inmate victimization commands interest for many reasons. For victims, the experience is injurious. For corrections officials, there is a moral and legal obligation to limit, if not eliminate, victimization of inmates. Not least, for scholars, too, there is the opportunity to investigate inmate victimization as a social phenomenon of interest in its own right and as a vehicle through which to illuminate and understand victimization in general.

Notwithstanding the interest that different groups have in the study of inmate victimization, relatively little systematic theoretical attention has been given to it. As one recent review noted, "the vast majority of research on prisoner victimization has been descriptive in nature" (Steiner, Ellison, Butler, & Cain, 2017, p. 17). Proponents of applied, or policy-focused, research may find that unproblematic. This view is mistaken—theory provides a platform for understanding inmate victimization, including the mechanisms that give rise to it. Without such guidance, no amount of empirical description will lead to better policy. It may lead to the ability to document differences, such as the potential for younger inmates to be victimized more so than adult inmates. But it ignores a plethora of other differences that may exist. In addition, descriptive accounts provide no foundation on which to base an intervention. For example, we might focus our attention on younger inmates, but what exactly would our intervention target?

Policy aside, the relative inattention to theorizing inmate victimization inhibits development of deeper insight into social behavior in prisons. It also deprives researchers of a chance to test and possibly modify general theories of victimization. All, though, is not bleak. Theoretical work on inmate victimization does exist. For example, some scholars have applied importation and deprivation theories to inmate victimization (e.g., Hemmens & Marquart, 1999; Lahm, 2015; Wood, 2013), and others have applied general victimization theories, such as lifestyle or routine activities theories, to inmate groups (e.g., Wooldredge & Steiner, 2014; see, generally, Pratt & Turanovic, 2016). Even so, the theoretical landscape is sparse.

In this chapter, I argue that theoretical advances in the study of inmate victimization can be useful for illuminating insights into the experiences and lives of inmates and into victimization more generally. Prisons and jails constitute unique contexts and they serve unique populations. That alone makes them interesting places where victimization may arise through context- or population-specific processes. At the same time, the possibility exists that insights about victimization in general may be gained by a focus on inmates. After developing this argument, I then extend it to argue that theoretical advances can be critical for informing policy and practice.

These arguments are developed as follows. First, I provide an overview of the emergence of scholarship on victimization theories. I then describe theories of victimization that have been developed with a particular focus on inmates as well as those that have been developed with a focus on individuals in free society. The chapter turns to the central focus of this essay, which is a description of dimensions relevant to theorizing inmate victimization. Next, I argue that consideration of these dimensions is relevant for expanding the focus of general theories of victimization. Finally, I explain how theoretical accounts of inmate victimization can be critical to developing more effective policies and practices for safeguarding inmates.

## Victimization Theories

Societies have long been concerned with addressing crime, but that concern led to informal or formal legal processes that largely excluded victims. Early policy approaches, such as the Babylonian's Code of Hammurabi that originated almost 4,000 years ago, emphasized the notion of creating equity for victims. "An eye for an eye," for example, under the Code of Hammurabi could be seen as a just response to the harm caused by an offender.

Even so, victims historically have not held center stage in the administration of justice. Their deprioritization became institutionalized during and after the Industrial Revolution. Crime came to be conceptualized as "violations against the state rather than the victim" (Daigle & Muftić, 2020:2). Victims thus became a secondary consideration. In the 1940s, this situation changed. Scholars increasingly turned their attention to victims. However, they primarily focused on victim characteristics rather than what might contribute to victimization. Meanwhile, criminology by and large remained steadfastly focused on criminals and crime.

Subsequent decades saw victimology—as a field within criminology—turn toward a broader view of victimization and its causes (see, generally, Daigle & Muftić, 2020; Karmen, 2013; Meier & Miethe, 1993; Turanovic & Pratt, 2019). Research in the 1970s and 1980s increasingly captured the complexity of victimization and veered away from studies that implicitly or explicitly blamed victims. It turned, for example, from Wolfgang's (1957) focus on "victim precipitation" and began to consider a spectrum of potential contributors to victimization.

The two most prominent theories to emerge during this transition to contemporary scholarship were the lifestyle-exposure theory of victimization (Hindelang, Gottfredson, & Garofalo, 1978) and routine activity theory (Cohen & Felson, 1979). The former argues that demographic variation in victimization stems from lifestyle differences among groups and thus exposure to conditions—such as places or times of the day or individuals—that increase the likelihood of victimization. As Meier and Miethe (1993) have emphasized, it proceeds from the premise that demographic groups vary in the expectations that exist about appropriate behavior and the structural constraints they face. In turn, "adherence to these cultural and structural expectations leads to the establishment of routine activities patterns and associations with others similarly situated"; the lifestyles and associations "enhance one's exposure to risky or vulnerable situations that increase individuals' chances of victimization" (p. 466). Routine activity theory offers a parallel explanation but uses different terminology. In Cohen and Felson's (1979) articulation of the theory, victimization is more likely to occur when three conditions converge—the simultaneous presence of motivated offenders, suitable or "attractive" targets, and the absence of capable guardianship. The theory originated with a focus on explaining over-time changes in crime, whereas lifestyle-exposure theory focused on explaining victimization differences among groups (p. 470). Eventually, though, they both came to be applied to efforts to understand variation in victimization over time and places as well as among groups.

The logic of these theories rests on the notion that victimization results from the proximity of potential victims to offenders and to opportunities for victimization that derive from social and physical environments. Certain lifestyles or routine activities—such as those that affect proximity to, and exposure of, "attractive" individuals or property to potential offenders who have limited guardianship—are anticipated to increase criminal victimization. Conversely, being viewed as a less suitable target, having less proximity or exposure to potential offenders, and experiencing some form of guardianship are anticipated to decrease the risk of it occurring. Some groups may reside in areas where these conditions may align in different ways or may change over time. In either case, lifestyles and routine activities are held to be key to explaining variation in victimization among individuals or among groups or places.

Variations on these two theories exist, but they remain the dominant theoretical accounts of victimization. A large body of research on them attests to their usefulness in explaining variation in victimization. At the same time, it highlights the need to carefully think through what key concepts may mean for certain populations or areas. For example, proximity in an urban area may mean something quite different from proximity in a highly rural or agricultural area. Or consider bars—whether in urban or rural areas, these are places where there can be considerable physical proximity between potential offenders and victims. Bars are more common in urban areas, and so one might anticipate that victimization is not only more likely in bars but also, by extension, in urban areas. (Of course, rural communities with large numbers of bars might well have victimization rates that exceed those of rural communities with fewer bars.) The more general point is that conditions in rural or agricultural areas vary so greatly from those in urban ones that concepts like target attractiveness, proximity, exposure, and guardianship likely have to be specified in a manner that makes sense in those areas (Mears, Scott, & Bhati, 2007). The issue is not unique to a focus on rural versus urban differences. And it is not per se one of identifying operational measures of these concepts. Rather, it is one of understanding what each dimension means in particular social or physical environments.

## Theoretical Accounts of Inmate Victimization

Paralleling developments in the larger field of criminology, penal scholarship traditionally has not focused on inmate victimization. Rather, it has focused on conditions of order and safety in prisons and risk factors for engaging in misconduct. The emergence of victimization theories, however, led to a natural interest in applying them to correctional settings. Wooldredge (1998) has identified the reasons: prison and jails "consist of nothing but 'potential offenders,' " places within prisons and jails may be especially risky and thus conducive to victimization, and "as in other social domains, the structure of inmate lifestyles and daily routines can vary dramatically" (p. 481; see also Ellison, Steiner, & Wright, 2018; Steiner et al., 2017).

The "lifestyles" or routine activities in prisons are shaped by such factors as the number of classes (education, vocational, rehabilitative, etc.), physical layouts of recreational compounds and dining halls, patterns of potential association governed by rules for which groups must transition from one area of the prison to another, and so on. More structured activities, such as ones where officers are present to supervise inmates closely, may decrease the risk of victimization. Less structured ones, such as the informal gatherings in recreational compounds, may increase this risk. Security levels, too, may shape opportunities for victimization. Higher-security facilities may rely more on solitary confinement and higher staff-to-inmate ratios and so reduce the likelihood that victimization will occur.

Some concepts from victimization theories have been adapted to the study of inmates. To illustrate, Wooldredge and Steiner (2014, p. 143) argue that "target antagonism" may help to explain victimization in prison and jail settings—some individuals may have attributes or act in ways that lead others to dislike or want to retaliate against them. Younger inmates, for example, may provoke older inmates to convey a sense of toughness. In a correctional setting, this potential is complemented by a different one—namely, some individuals may be more vulnerable to attack than others. Consider younger inmates—they are more likely than older inmates to be victims, a difference that may derive from being smaller and less sophisticated in their ability to mobilize peer support. As a group, then, younger inmates may be more at risk of victimization due both to "target antagonism" and to "target vulnerability."

In correctional settings, guardianship must be operationalized differently as well. It entails not only the presence of officers and staff who may deter crime or misconduct, but also the policies and practices that officers and staff follow in managing inmates. It entails as well the physical architecture of prison and jail facilities (Nadel & Mears, 2019). The design of these facilities dictates where and how interactions can occur and how easily correctional officers can monitor inmate activities. Design features include the layouts of dormitories, dining halls, recreational areas, units where programming occurs, and so on. Supermax prisons provide an illustration—by design, they restrict inmate contact with any human beings.

Separate from these theories are theoretical accounts of prison order. They tend to emphasize ways in which the administration of prisons and jails affect order and safety (DiIulio, 1987) or how the perceived legitimacy of administrators and staff, or social ecology in general, may influence inmate compliance with rules (Bottoms, 1999; Sparks, Bottoms, & Hay, 1996). Such accounts do not per se focus on victimization. But to the extent that they explain rates of disorder and violence, they simultaneously provide an explanation for variation in rates of victimization. They do not, however, necessarily provide insight into which groups are most likely to be victimized or places within facilities where victimization is most likely to occur.

Despite increasing attention on the application of victimization theories to the study of inmate victimization, the bulk of research to date consists, as Steiner et al. (2017) have emphasized, of descriptive empirical accounts. These tend to point to groups—such as younger inmates, males, and those who act out and break rules—who are more likely to be victimized. Alternatively, they point to settings (e.g., maximum-security facilities) where victimization rates may be higher (see, e.g., Kerbs & Jolley, 2007; Lahm, 2015; Pérez, Gover, Tennyson, & Santos, 2010; Reyns, Woo, Lee, & Yoon, 2018; see also Turanovic & Pratt, 2019, pp. 161–165). Exceptions are studies that apply lifestyle and routine activities theories to inmate victimization, whether at the individual or facility level (see, e.g., Caravaca-Sánchez & Wolff, 2018; Ellison et al., 2018; Wooldredge, 1998; Wooldredge & Steiner, 2014). The few studies to date suggest that victimization among incarcerated populations is more likely among certain groups for reasons that may involve lifestyle or routine activities mechanisms. For example, males' higher risk of victimization may arise because they may act more aggressively and so invite others to retaliate against them (Wooldredge & Steiner, 2014). Similarly, victimization may be lower when inmates engage in structured, supervised activities (Wooldredge, 1998). Participation in recreational activities, where there may be less supervision, has been found to be associated with a greater risk of victimization (Steiner et al., 2017).

General victimization theories increasingly began to be applied to prison and jail settings in the 1990s and thereafter. However, longstanding theories of correctional order and safety—such as those that focus on importation, deprivation, institutional management, legitimacy, or social ecology—can be viewed as offering additional grounds for explaining victimization.

Importation theory emphasizes the notion that inmates bring with them characteristics, attitudes, values, beliefs, and more that affect their conformity with prison rules (Irwin & Cressey, 1962; Jacobs, 1976; Kigerl & Hamilton, 2016). These in turn contribute to misconduct and violence, and thus necessarily the victimization of others.

Deprivation theory takes a different view—it argues that the "pains of imprisonment" (Sykes, 1958, p. 63) lead inmates to develop subcultures and adaptations that shape behavior. Some subcultures and adaptations entail aggression toward other inmates, especially those who might be weaker (Clemmer, 1950; Sykes, 1958; Thomas, Petersen, & Zingraff, 1978; Trammell, 2012).

Institutional management theoretical accounts argue that how prisons are run contributes to order and safety and, by extension, rates of victimization. DiIulio's (1987) description of three managerial strategies illustrates this idea. He identified three types: Control-oriented approaches call for rigid adherence to rules, responsibility-oriented ones call for providing inmates leeway to self-govern, and consensual models call for a balance between these two management strategies. There remains a paucity of evidence on the relative effectiveness of these or other approaches (see, e.g., Huebner, 2003; Reisig, 1998; Ricciardelli & Sit, 2016; Stohr, Lovrich, Menke, & Zupan, 2006; see also Wolff, 2018). Regardless, as with importation and deprivation theories, the logical basis for anticipating effects on order, safety, and victimization is compelling. Management strategies presumably can and do matter.

Finally, there exists a long line of scholarship that focuses on legitimacy and social ecology as critical aspects of correctional management that influence order and safety in prisons or jails (Bottoms, 1999; King, 2018; Sparks et al., 1996). This work argues that order and safety derive from the extent to which inmates believe that authority is wielded in a fair and consistent manner and from the social ecology or correctional systems (staff-to-inmate ratios, amount and quality of programming, visitation, officer and inmate cultures, etc.). For example, defiance, rule-breaking, riots, and more may occur more frequently when inmates view correctional administrators, officers, and staff exercising power in illegitimate ways.

## Dimensions of a General Theory of Inmate Victimization

Inmate victimization remains largely under-studied and under-theorized. Wolff, Blitz, Shi, Siegel, and Bachman (2007, p. 590) have highlighted that few empirical studies exist that rely on random samples of inmates to estimate the magnitude and types of victimization (e.g., staff-on-inmate, inmate-on-staff, or inmate-on-inmate) in prisons or jails (see, generally, Bottoms, 1999; Steiner et al., 2017). Extant studies, though, indicate that correctional settings entail markedly higher levels of violence and crime than exist in society at large. That fact creates an opportunity to advance science by focusing not only inmate victimization but also on how the causes of victimization may vary across different groups and contexts.

The theoretical landscape on inmate victimization is, if anything, more anemic. Some productive efforts have used lifestyle and routine activities theories to explain victimization in correctional settings (e.g., Wooldredge, 1998). However, these perspectives have not been systematically applied to prisons and jails or been applied in ways that capture well the nuances of each theory (see, however, Wooldredge & Steiner, 2014). There is, as discussed above, a longstanding literature on correctional systems management (e.g., DiIulio, 1987; Reisig, 1998), legitimacy and social ecology (e.g., Bottoms, 1999; Sparks et al., 1996), and deprivation and importation as factors that can help to explain order and safety. However, they have not been used, by and large, to explain victimization in prisons and jails; yet, as theories of order and safety, they are relevant for efforts to do so.

One strategy for improving theory and research on inmate victimization, then, is to apply these different theoretical perspectives to inmates and to jail and prison settings. I argue, though, that a more fruitful approach is to proceed in a different, more systematic manner. This approach differs in three ways. First, it emphasizes a focus on two sets of dimensions: inmate vs. prison or jail factors and the salience of different types of causal forces that may independently or in interaction with others contribute to victimization. Second, it calls for thinking about inmate victimization in a more comprehensive manner, one oriented toward developing a general theory of inmate victimization. Third, it calls for thinking about different types of causal relationships.

My central argument is that inmate victimization may stem from a variety of causal factors that involve different potential causal relationships. A general theory of inmate victimization does not have to consider all of the factors or types of causation. It might, for example, focus only on one dimension. I argue, though, that a general theory that seeks to incorporate a wider range of factors and causal relationships holds the potential to explain more variation in inmate victimization. It also can point to fruitful avenues of theorizing that otherwise would be overlooked in theories that focus only on one cause. As an example, consideration of two types of causal forces may lead to consideration of interaction effects. We then must consider a theoretical account that explains how and why the two forces may interact.

Figure 7.1 provides the contours of what a useful general theory of inmate victimization might include. The contours consist of inmate factors and prison and jail factors. The reason for this distinction is simple. Individuals in correctional settings differ markedly from those in the general population. They are more likely to come from disadvantaged backgrounds, to be less educated, to have learning disabilities, to be mentally ill, to have spotty work histories, and so on (Mears & Cochran, 2015). Theoretical accounts of inmate victimization thus should contemplate this fact and its implications. Similarly, inmates reside in a social and organizational context vastly different from what holds in conventional society. Here, again, a theory that can explain greater variation in inmate victimization likely needs to take this context into account.

Each of these two sets of causes—inmate factors and correctional factors—can be disaggregated into distinct categories of causal forces, as shown in the figure. These dimensions flow from consideration of lifestyles and routine activities theories *and* from theoretical accounts of prison order, such as those that emphasize the role of importation, deprivation, managerial strategies, social ecology, and how inmates perceive the legitimacy of prison or jail authority.

Inmate factors include four dimensions that inmates potentially "import," or bring with them, to prison or jail and that may contribute to victimization. They go well beyond standard social and demographic characteristics and, for example, include peer, home, and community contexts.

**Figure 7.1**
**Causal Factors and Dynamics Relevant to a Theory of Inmate Victimization**

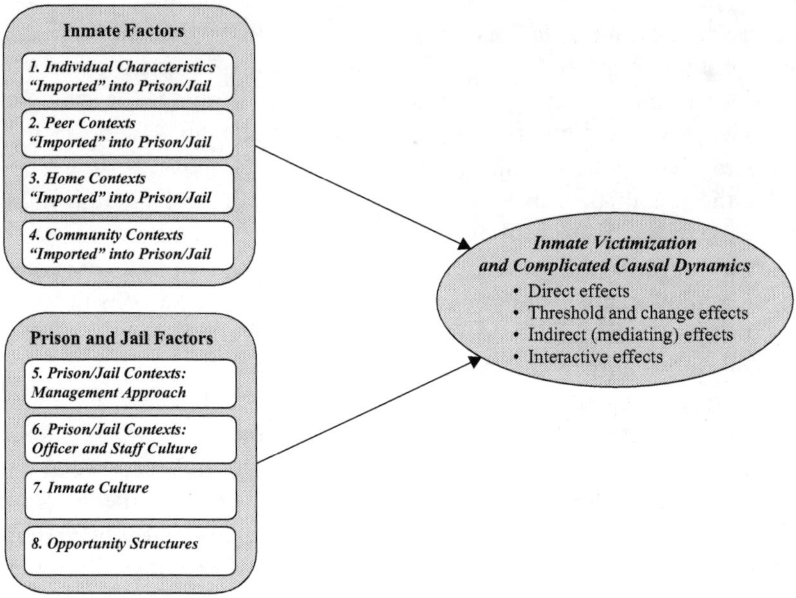


Prison and jail factors likewise include four dimensions that may influence inmate victimization. These include the management approach used by prison systems and individual prison wardens, the officer and staff culture, the inmate culture, and the opportunity structures within particular prison and jail settings.

All of these factors may contribute to inmate victimization. And they may do so in different ways and through a variety of causal dynamics. The simplest mechanism is through direct effects. There may be some influence of a given factor that directly causes victimization. A second is a threshold effect, whereby the causal force only exerts a force when it reaches a certain level. A third is an indirect, or mediating, effect. Here, a given factor leads to another, which in turn causes victimization. And, finally, there are interactive effects, where the influence of one factor amplifies that of another. Other types of causal relationships exist (Mears & Cochran, 2019). These, however, capture some of the main types that arguably are most prevalent. More pragmatically, they are more amenable to empirical tests.

Simple, single-factor general theories are helpful because they provide a clear foundation on which to develop explanations about how or why one factor contributes to an outcome. For example, revisiting deprivation theory with an eye toward how it might explain inmate victimization may be productive. However, single-factor theories come at a cost—they provide limited insight into the varied causes of an outcome or a variety of complicated causal dynamics, involving these different causes, that contribute to it.

By contrast, a multi-factor theory can provide greater insight. The cost? It can be more difficult to create a coherent integrated logic through which to tie different parts of a multi-factor theory together. It also is more difficult to test. Even so, I argue that this approach may provide the greatest potential for shedding light on inmate victimization.

The discussion that follows therefore emphasizes only that consideration of different sets of causal forces and dynamics holds the potential to explain better variation in inmate victimization and to identify avenues of insight that otherwise might be missed. I do not present a general theory but rather the dimensions of what could go into one or perhaps into multiple middle-range theories (Merton, 1968). Why? Any substantial advance in creating a general theory or set of middle-range theories is unlikely to arise without at least contemplating ways in which diverse factors may individually or in combination with one another—and through a variety of causal dynamics—contribute to inmate victimization.

Below, I sketch some of the ways in which a variety of factors may contribute to victimization. In so doing, I discuss how the factors may entail different possible causal dynamics. That is because exploring a variety of causal dynamics provides a path toward developing more powerful theories. Accordingly, the point of the discussion is not to provide a review of the literature on each factor but instead to highlight the potential importance and benefits of thinking about inmate victimization through a multi-factor, causally diverse manner.

This approach to considering inmate victimization does not privilege a focus on correlates of victimization. It also does not privilege a focus on one theory. Instead, it draws attention to constellations of factors associated with inmates and correctional settings and ways in which these factors may contribute to and interact with one another. There is necessarily a need to invoke the logic of different theories. But the theories are not the main focus. Instead, we are led to consider diverse causes and causal dynamics that may go into theoretical accounts better capable of explaining variation in victimization at micro- and macro-level units of analysis.

*Inmate Victimization: Inmate Factors*

*Dimension 1. Individual Characteristics "Imported" into Prison or Jail.* The individuals who go to prison do not arrive *tabula rasa.* They bring with them a host of characteristics that have formed over a lifetime or that they have had from birth. These individuals may vary in their level of self-control, social capital, social bonds, intelligence, personality type (e.g., introverted or extroverted), mental health, and more.

One can readily envision how such factors may influence victimization. Inmates with low self-control may provoke others, some mentally ill inmates may act in ways that confuse or anger others or that make them vulnerable, younger inmates may be smaller and less able to defend themselves, and so on (see, e.g., Ellison et al., 2018). Causation here can entail thresholds and both indirect and interactive effects. For example, perhaps individuals beyond a threshold—who may have a markedly low level of self-control—may be much more likely to be victimized; perhaps at levels of extreme low self-control individuals become far more noxious to others to the point of provoking aggressive responses (Mears, Cochran, & Beaver, 2013). Severely depressed inmates may find it difficult to make friends and in turn may be more vulnerable to attack (a mediating effect). Further, younger inmates may have less self-control and among such individuals the effects of lesser intelligence may be more acute (an interactive effect).

These causal relationships are conceptualized as occurring only among individual characteristics. However, they might as easily include other characteristics that attach to the inmates, such as peer, home, and community contexts, or prison and jail conditions.

*Dimension 2. Peer Contexts "Imported" into Prison or Jail.* Inmates are called "inmates" because that is the name that society uses for anyone sent to prison or jail. However, they are also individuals and, as such, social beings. The importance of the social dimension can be seen in the fact that inmates view separation from friends and their broader peer network as among the most concerning aspects of incarceration (Adams, 1992; Mears & Cochran, 2015).

When viewed in this light, it becomes apparent that individuals who enter prison may bring with them the beliefs, values, and attitudes of those with whom they previously associated. They also, though, may quite literally bring these people with them through visitation or arranged distribution of contraband on prison grounds or in jails. Contraband is central to prison social systems (Kalinich & Stojkovic, 1985). It may help to prevent victimization by providing individuals with something that can be exchanged with others. But it also might make individuals more vulnerable to attack because they possess something valuable.

*Dimension 3. Home Contexts "Imported" into Prison or Jail.* Home contexts also can be imported into prison or jail. The beliefs, values, and attitudes of families, like those of peers, may be carried with the inmate. They may influence how the inmate acts, talks, reacts, and adapts to incarceration. In addition, families may affect victimization or how inmates respond to it. For example, inmates with families who have resources to advocate for them might be more likely to receive needed services or appropriate placements. Family support may be helpful, too, in assisting inmates in finding ways that they can protect themselves. Ironically, those with family members who have been incarcerated might be more prepared for the risks in prisons and jails and so be better able to protect themselves while incarcerated.

In studies of inmate visitation, one question that arises is whether a visit or two really suffices to exert any type of causal effect. There has been relatively little research that systematically examines dose effects of visitation (Cochran & Mears, 2013; Mears, Cochran, Siennick, & Bales, 2012). Theoretically, it seems entirely plausible that a visit or two might have no effect, or perhaps a substantial one. It may be, for example, that a visit constitutes the equivalent of a life-line, something that helps sustain inmates through dark times. If it leads them to not give up, then, it may reduce the potential for victimization because they have something to live for. Perhaps, though, a visit does no such thing. Or perhaps there are potential interactive possibilities. For example, a visit might be especially helpful to the youngest inmates or those who have never before been incarcerated. By contrast, a much larger number of visits may be necessary for individuals who have repeatedly been in prison or jail. If some groups are more likely to be visited than others (see, e.g., Cochran, Mears, & Bales, 2017), then these interactive effects would be more pronounced for some groups than others. Such causal complexity may attach to other aspects of home contexts "imported" into prisons and jails.

*Dimension 4. Community Contexts "Imported" into Prison or Jail.* Individuals incarcerated in jail typically will be closer to their home communities than those incarcerated in prison. However, among those sent to prison, some may be closer than others to these communities. Proximity to them in turn may be associated with a diverse array of factors, such as access to social services, continuity in mental health treatment, a better ability to prepare for post-release employment and housing, and more.

Reentry studies typically view communities from the standpoint of how they may influence ex-prisoner transitions into society (Mears & Cochran, 2015; Wright & Cesar, 2013). However, communities may reach into prison and jail settings (Boessen & Cauffman, 2016). Inmates may bring beliefs, values, and attitudes from these communities with them. They also may be more likely or able to access community resources and services. Individuals and organizations in the community may be more likely to enter into prisons and jails to offer assistance. These then may promote greater inmate adaptation to incarceration and conceivably reduce the risk of victimization. Among other possibilities, friends and members of families and communities may be more aware of what occurs in prison or jail and so be able to advocate for their friends, loved ones, or clients. When, however, individuals reside in prisons or jails far from their home communities, they live in the equivalent of a black box, one where victimization may be more likely to go unnoticed and thus unchecked. Causal complexity again is possible. For example, one study points to the potential for curvilinear effects of prison distance from an inmate's home community on inmate misconduct (Lindsey, Mears, Cochran, Bales, & Stults, 2017). Misconduct itself is linked to victimization risk (Reyns et al., 2018; Wooldredge, 1998).

### *Inmate Victimization: Prison and Jail Factors*

*Dimension 5. Prison and Jail Contexts—Management Approach.* Discussions of inmates frequently locate the cause of misconduct, offending, or victimization within these individuals. However, how prisons and jails operate may influence these outcomes as well (Bottoms, 1999; DiIulio, 1987; Mears & Cochran, 2015; Morris, 2002; Morris & Rothman, 1995; Randol & Campbell, 2017; Riveland, 1999; Sparks et al., 1996). They may do so through a variety of ways. One is the management approach taken by leadership. Prison and jail administrators might adopt a no-nonsense authoritarian style that demands harsh penalties for every infraction. Others might balance this approach with one that calls for leniency and case-by-case decisions that consider the context in which some behavior occurred. Norval Morris' (2002) account of Alexander Machonochie's experiences running the prison system on Norfolk Island in the mid-1800s provides a colorful example of these contrasting approaches. These contrasts can be seen in contemporary prison systems as well (see, e.g., Golden, 2006).

Management approaches can contribute to victimization in many different ways. Lax oversight of officers allows them to take advantage of inmates with little fear of a sanction. Similarly, lax oversight of inmates can have the same effect, with some inmates being more likely to prey on weaker inmates. Strict enforcement of rules could improve matters, but it also might worsen them. If, for example, inmates collectively perceive prison authority as being wielded in an illegitimate manner, with no consideration of what is fair, balanced, or appropriate, they may be more likely to defy officers and staff (Bottoms, 1999; Sparks et al., 1996). The end result can be greater disorder and violence and a concomitant increase in victimization (Ricciardelli & Sit, 2016; see, generally, Mears & Reisig, 2006). More generally, management approaches can influence the overall social ecology of prisons and jails. Factors such as officer-to-inmate staffing ratios, the amount and quality of programming, the extent to which inmates are allowed visits and connections to family or local communities—these and more collectively contribute to the ecology of a prison or jail and in turn may influence officers and inmates alike.

*Dimension 6. Prison and Jail Contexts—Officer and Staff Culture.* I once attended a session where researchers asked the leadership of one of the largest prison systems in the country what they felt were the most critical areas where research could be helpful to them. The director responded that he wanted more information about the culture among his officers and staff.

Today, in an era in which calls for "evidence-based" policy abound, the director's comment is remarkable as a contrast to contemporary calls for narrowly focused policies. Many demands for "evidence-based" policies envision specific programs that target concrete problems, like drug abuse, and that can be evaluated using experimental designs (Mears & Cochran, 2019). "Culture" is, by contrast, a notoriously difficult concept to operationalize. It is manifest in diverse ways, many factors contribute to it, there is no simple silver-bullet approach to altering it, and evaluating the impacts of systemwide efforts to change it do not readily lend themselves to experimental design research evaluations. Yet, efforts to improve officer or staff culture might do more to improve order and safety than a large number of programs.

The director's insight is one that flows from research on prisons (see, e.g., Bottoms, 1999; Steiner & Wooldredge, 2018). It is one, more generally, that flows from a systems-based approach to thinking about prisons and jails (Mears, 2017). Such places operate like any organizational system. Written rules and unwritten norms—that flow from and define culture—guide everyday actions and decision-making. In anthropological accounts, a study of culture might focus on cuisine and customs. The focus can be much broader, however. In a correctional context, it might include the ways in which staff and officers interact with one another, agreement about the best ways to manage inmates, when and how—or if—it is acceptable to use excessive violence with some inmates, and more (see, e.g., Thompson, 2016).

To the extent that officer and staff culture shapes inmate behavior, it by extension can influence inmate victimization. One might trace victimization to the characteristics of the officers or inmates who attack or steal from another inmate, but this approach would miss the potential for the role that officer and staff culture plays in creating a setting where the involved individuals interact in the way that they do (Liebling, Price, & Shefer, 2011; Lombardo, 1989).

*Dimension 7. Prison and Jail Contexts—Inmate Culture.* Alongside of the culture among officers and staff is that of inmates. The culture might be brought into penal settings, per importation theory (Irwin & Cressey, 1962; Jacobs, 1976; Kigerl & Hamilton, 2016). Alternatively, it might arise from the conditions, including deprivations, in prisons and jails (Clemmer, 1940, 1950; Sykes, 1958; Trammell, 2012). Regardless, the penological literature is replete with accounts of how inmate culture develops, is sustained, and may affect interactions with other inmates and with officers and staff.

Inmate culture may contribute to victimization by guiding individual inmates to act in a certain manner. For example, if an inmate code exists that calls for responding to provocations with violence, then this code simultaneously may contribute to more misconduct and victimization (Mears et al., 2013). Inmate culture might dictate certain ways of interacting with officers and staff, which in turn may contribute to more or to less victimization. If the culture calls for outright defiance, inmates might be more subject to harassment or abuse from officers. Conversely, if it calls for cooperation, they might be subject to less. Such effects themselves, however, might be variable. To illustrate, first-time inmates might need to establish themselves as ready to stand up for themselves. In such cases, they might face more victimization initially from officers or inmates, but in the longer term their stance may provide a buffer against future attempts to victimize them (e.g., McCorkle, 1992).

*Dimension 8. Prison and Jail Contexts—Opportunity Structures.* Opportunities for offending or victimization to occur stem from a wide variety of factors. Outside the prison walls, crime can be seen as arising from opportunity structures (Clarke & Felson, 1993; Cohen & Felson, 1979; Land, 2003). Accordingly, crime prevention depends on shaping these structures. Criminal acts may be more likely to arise when streets are poorly lit or when expensive commodities, such as phones or jewelry, are left out and unguarded. Addressing these situations—through better lighting and more careful placement of phones and jewelry—might reduce the number of criminal acts and, by extension, victimization.

Much the same can be said about prison and jail settings. Consider inmates who are actively involved in prison programming and work. They may be protected from victimization because of the extra monitoring by officers (Wooldredge & Steiner, 2014). Similarly, activities in settings that place inmates in close proximity might increase victimization. Levels of guardianship in a given wing or unit, facility, or system also might shape the opportunities that exist for victimization to occur (Bottoms, 1999; DiIulio, 1987). Notably, these factors might interact. For example, reduced guardianship in a context in which inmates are in close proximity with one another might be more likely to contribute to victimization among more vulnerable inmates, such as younger inmates or the aged (Felson, Cundiff, & Painter-Davis, 2012).

### *Inmate Victimization and Complicated Causal Dynamics*

Many theories give little attention to causality, beyond stating that X may give rise to Y. There are, though, a wide range of potential causal dynamics that can exist. I argue here that a general theory of inmate victimization should contemplate at least four possibilities. Doing so may result in a greater ability to explain variation in inmate victimization and provide a more systematic foundation on which to understand the causal complexity of victimization.

*Direct Effects.* The first and most basic step is for a theory of inmate victimization to identify causal factors. As discussed above, there are both inmate and contextual factors that may contribute to inmate victimization. For each, the theory should be able to articulate the direction of effect (e.g., positive or negative) and the magnitude of effect.

*Threshold and Change Effects*. Theories ideally can tell us the precise way in which a causal force is related to an outcome. That goes beyond whether the association is positive or negative and includes a focus on functional form. One prominent example involves a threshold effect—X may be related to Y in one way, up to a certain point, and then after that point the effect might change. As temperatures decline, water molecules interact in different ways, but at 0 degrees Celsius a critical threshold is crossed such that the water molecules combine to create ice.

A similar possibility exists for each of the factors that may influence inmate victimization. For example, up to a certain level, a positive and professional officer culture may modestly reduce inmate victimization. This effect, though, may be much more pronounced after this culture reaches a certain level. Identifying the threshold may improve efforts to explain variation in inmate victimization. Explaining why it exists may improve theory.

A general theory of inmate victimization should identify as well how *changes* in a causal factor may contribute to a given amount of change in inmate victimization. Theories often are presented in a manner that emphasize levels—more of X is associated with more of Y. That, though, ignores the potentially different causal dynamics that arise from changes. It is, for example, one thing for higher levels of deprivation to be associated with a greater level of victimization and quite another for an inmate to be suddenly thrust from one level of deprivation (e.g., housing in a minimum-security facility) to another (e.g., housing in a supermax facility).

*Indirect (Mediating) Effects*. A theory that contemplates an X→Y effect typically has a reason for expecting one. That reason usually involves a mediating (M) effect. For example, the theory might argue that prison conditions (X) lead some inmates to become depressed (M1) and so isolate themselves from others (M2), which in turn makes them more vulnerable to attack (M3) and, ultimately, more likely to be victimized (Y). That is, X→M1→M2→M3→Y.

A general theory should identify the various mediating pathways through which a given causal force may give rise to inmate victimization. Doing so can lead to identification of ways in which different factors may involve similar causal sequences. It also can lead to identification of ways in which multiple theories may be combined to create a more general theory of victimization.

*Interactive Effects*. A benefit of theories that focus on a single causal force is simplicity and the potential for greater logical coherence. Such theories are simpler to test as well. The downside to this approach is that we miss the contribution of other causal forces. We also may miss ways in which different factors combine to produce a given outcome. A focus on interactions serves as a corrective to this problem. Meier and Miethe (1993) have argued for the importance of victimization research that examines potential interactional effects between individual lifestyle and neighborhood context measures. Similarly, Wooldredge (1998) has argued that individual and contextual-level factors may interact to influence victimization. For example, inmates with less self-control are more likely to be victimized, but this effect might be amplified in prison facilities where officers and staff are less professional or infrequently monitor inmates. Similarly, inmates who are less involved in structured activities may face a greater risk of victimization when they reside in prisons whose design allows for more proximity among inmates or less guardianship from officers and staff (Wooldredge, 1998, p. 483).

## How a Theory of Inmate Victimization May Generate Insights into All Victimization

Inmates differ from the general population in many ways. They tend to be younger, less educated, have lower intelligence and little in the way of social or economic capital, have spotty work histories, and are more likely to have learning disabilities and mental disorders (Mears & Cochran, 2015). They also differ in that they reside in institutional contexts that control their every waking moment and movement (Sykes, 1958).

Even so, that does not mean that theories of victimization do not apply to inmates. Theories that focus on opportunity structures, risky lifestyles, and routine activities clearly have the potential to explain variation in inmate victimization (see, e.g., Meier & Miethe, 1993; Wooldredge, 1998; Wooldredge & Steiner, 2014).

There is, though, the question of what studies of inmate victimization may contribute to developing general theories of victimization. One clear direction in research on importation and deprivation theories is to integrate the two perspectives (see, e.g., Hochstetler & DeLisi, 2005). Neither theory logically contradicts the other and, indeed, both may complement one another. That possibility suggests one concrete way in which a focus on inmate victimization may inform general theories of victimization. Importation and deprivation theories seek to explain inmate behavior and, in particular, misconduct and adaptation to prison.

They can be seen, though, as simultaneously identifying conditions under which victimization may be more likely to occur.

That possibility suggests an insight relevant for understanding victimization outside the prison walls. In society, analogs to deprivation might include residing in communities that experience extreme poverty and isolation or in organizations where employees have little to no say-so in their work lives. For example, as Upton Sinclair's (1906) novel, *The Jungle*, illustrated, working conditions in meat-packing houses placed employees at considerable risk of harm. A lack of oversight over any industry in which conditions create the risk of physical harm may contribute to greater rates of injury and death. Of course, some deprivations, such as the loss of liberty or the deprivation of security, may seem to be unique to prison settings. That assumption falls apart upon closer inspection. In areas of concentrated disadvantage, both deprivations arguably exist, though they manifest differently.

A focus on importation theory draws attention to the salience of what individuals may contribute to victimization. It focuses on the values, attitudes, and beliefs that individuals may have and how these may guide their conduct. The code of the street illustrates the point—it calls for retaliatory attacks in response to certain challenges or threats. In so doing, this code may contribute both to offending and to victimization. And it may do so on the streets (Stewart, Schreck, & Simons, 2006) as well as behind prison or jail walls (Mears, Stewart, Siennick, & Simons, 2013). In this sense, the insights that may arise from applying the logic of importation theory to victimization parallels those that may arise from applying theories of offending, life self-control theory, to victimization (Schreck, 1999).

Attention to inmate victimization also leads us to consider the role of contextual factors that may contribute to victimization. Peer, family, community, and organizational contexts all arguably contribute to inmate victimization. And they just as clearly may contribute to victimization in society as well. For example, communities that suffer from higher rates of disadvantage—such as high levels of poverty and unemployment and low levels of social or political capital—may have higher rates of both crime and victimization (Sampson, 2012). How criminal justice agencies and the courts operate also may affect victimization (Herman, 2010).

One insight that the study of inmates offers for general theories of victimization is the importance of systems. Alongside of peer, home, community, and organizational contexts is the manner in which prisons are run (DiIulio, 1987). More broadly, there is the overarching prison system (Adams, 1992; Bottoms, 1999; Edgar, O'Donnell, & Martin, 2003; Mears, 2017). How it operates, the culture that it promotes systemwide, and the practices and policies that it follows—these all provide a broader context that may shape the conditions at particular facilities and influence how forces inside and outside of the prison interact. As one example, prison systems that seek to promote family ties and reunification might increase the likelihood that inmates receive visitors. That might create stronger ties between inmates and these visitors and the local community. That in turn might reduce victimization. But it also might create opportunities for contraband to be brought into prisons, which could have the opposite effect.

Thinking about systems is relevant not just for understanding victimization in prisons and jails. A systems focus may improve the ability of theory and research to enhance our understanding of victimization in general. Consider the criminal justice system. It is largely just that—a system focused on criminals. It does not exist primarily to serve victims (Herman, 2010). That can result in a myriad of forces that can combine to increase victimization. For example, historically, the police and courts have not considered the needs of victims. Certain types of victimization, such as domestic violence, were given little attention or priority. Abusers could act with little concern that the police or courts would intervene. And if the police or courts did so, they proceeded in a manner that might worsen violence. If a victim called the police and the police visited a home but declined to make an arrest, the end result could be empowerment of abusers. They would know that they could abuse their spouses with little fear of reprisal. A similar risk arises if the courts seek to aggressively pursue domestic violence cases, even when victims do not want to file a complaint and when the cases are, from a prosecutorial standpoint, weak (Davis, Smith, & Taylor, 2003). The broader point? Systems may contribute to victimization. And a systems focus can help us to identify a broad range of factors that may contribute to victimization and to consider the conditional nature of many causal influences.

## Policy Relevance of Theories of Inmate Victimization

Theories of inmate victimization have considerable relevance for policy. All too frequently, policies are based on a silver-bullet strategy. Lawmakers focus on one factor and hope that doing so will appreciably improve matters. That works fine with phenomena that arise primarily from one cause. It does not when they arise from many factors.

For prisons and jails, as for society, the implication is that efforts to reduce victimization must target a diverse array of factors. Theory can aid in this endeavor. To proceed in a theoretically informed manner is to target those factors that theories say contribute to victimization. In a prison context, that can mean examining opportunity structures and routines unique to correctional settings. It can mean focusing on management strategies and inmates' perceptions of the legitimacy of prison or jail officers' authority. It can mean, too, focusing attention on those groups, such as individuals who are lower in self-control or who have fewer social supports, that theories suggest may be more at risk of harm. It can mean, not least, thinking about the unique characteristics of these groups, the contexts that they "import" with them into prisons and jails, and the unique social ecology of these places.

When viewed in this light, attention to inmate victimization highlights some of the problems with efforts to address victimization in society. In a prison or jail setting, there is little pretense that inmates are in control. Administrators, officers, and staff have a legal obligation to oversee all aspects of inmates' lives. In this sense, then, they are responsible for levels or rates of victimization and for pursuing all steps that reasonably be taken to reduce them.

By contrast, for citizens in a free society, the state does not control their every movement. That creates a situation in which no one institution or authority controls or has responsibility for addressing rates of victimization. Here, then, we can see one of the most significant policy challenges that confront efforts to prevent or reduce victimization—no one is in charge of such efforts (Herman, 2010; Mears, 2017). That results in piecemeal efforts that only tackle some causes of victimization and do so with little efficient coordination of efforts.

A more effective and cost-efficient approach then might be a *system* of victim prevention efforts. It would require the legal authority to oversee, guide, and coordinate victimization efforts, and it would require resources to implement and evaluate these efforts. Such an approach is likely the only way to create sustained and large-scale reductions in victimization in correctional settings and in society. That does not mean that certain policies and programs are not or cannot be effective, only that they will not likely generate large-scale returns. Turning our focus to correctional settings, it also means that control-oriented approaches to operating them will not greatly reduce inmate victimization. Why? They do little that systematically targets the spectrum of factors that contribute to harm to victims (Wolff, 2018).

## Conclusion

Victimization theory and research has advanced considerably in the last 50 years. Gone are the days when, at least in the research community, victimization was assumed to be purely the responsibility of the victim. Even so, much remains to be done. Writing in 1993, Meier and Miethe observed, "Only in the last two decades have victimization theories generated empirical, as well as anecdotal, support, most notably in the form of lifestyle-exposure (Hindelang et al., 1978) and routine activities theories (Cohen & Felson, 1979)" (p. 460). In the decades since, progress has continued to occur, and yet tremendous gaps in knowledge remain.

Perhaps the largest is the understanding of how different factors combine to contribute to victimization and how, in particular, individual- and contextual-level forces separately and collectively do so. Turanovic and Pratt (2019) have emphasized that "victimization does not occur in a vacuum" (p. 76). They point to the fact that victimization involves multiple contexts—family, peer, community, and more. Here, I have echoed that argument and identified ways in which various contexts can be critical for understanding inmate victimization.

If we are to more fully explain variation in victimization of all types, we will need theories that integrate insights from the broader body of victimization research. We will need, too, efforts to incorporate insights about contexts specific to prisons and those specific to jails (Ellison et al., 2018). The focus on inmate victimization illustrates the importance of this approach. Inmates bring with them and reside in multiple contexts. They reside, too, in systems designed to control all aspects of their lives. Victimization scholarship holds the key to illuminating the causes of inmate victimization and what can be done to reduce it.

A general theory of victimization will need to consider extant theories of victimization and those designed to explain order, safety, and inmate compliance in prisons and jails. It assuredly will be complicated. It will demand more and better data than currently exist. For example, it will require survey data from inmates and officers, and linking these data to administrative records data. The data must provide measures of core theoretical constructs or we will be left with descriptive accounts that shed little light on the causes of inmate victimization. And a general theory approach will require sophisticated analytic techniques capable of modeling contextual, interactive, threshold, and other such effects. The pay-off, though, will be improved understanding and greater insight into ways to reduce victimization in prisons, jails, and society.

## References

Adams, K. (1992). Adjusting to prison life. *Crime and Justice*, *16*, 275–359.

Boessen, A, & Cauffman, E. (2016). Moving from the neighborhood to the cellblock: The impact of youth's neighborhoods on prison misconduct. *Crime and Delinquency*, *62*, 200–228.

Bottoms, A. E. (1999). Interpersonal violence and social order in prisons. *Crime and Justice*, *26*, 205–282.

Caravaca-Sánchez, F., & Wolff, N. (2018). Understanding polyvictimization in prison: Prevalence and predictors among men inmates in Spain. *Journal of Interpersonal Violence*, (DOI 10.1177/0886260518775751).

Clarke, R. V., & Felson, M. (Eds.). (1993). *Routine activity and rational choice*. New Brunswick, NJ: Transaction.

Clemmer, D. (1940). *The prison community*. Boston, MA: Christopher Publishing House.

Clemmer, D. (1950). Observations on imprisonment as a source of criminality. *Journal of Criminal Law and Criminology*, *41*, 311–319.

Cochran, J. C., & Mears, D. P. (2013). Social isolation and inmate behavior: A conceptual framework for theorizing prison visitation and guiding and assessing research. *Journal of Criminal Justice*, *41*, 252–261.

Cochran, J. C., Mears, D. P., & Bales, W. D. (2017). Who gets visited in prison? Individual- and community-level disparities in inmate visitation experiences. *Crime and Delinquency*, *63*, 545–568.

Cohen L. E., & Felson, M. (1979). Social change and crime rate trends: A routine activities approach. *American Sociological Review*, *44*, 588–608.

Daigle, L. E., & Muftić, L. R. (2020). *Victimology: A comprehensive approach* (2nd edition). Thousand Oaks, CA: Sage.

Davis, R. C., Smith, B., & Taylor, B. (2003). Increasing the proportion of domestic violence arrests that are prosecuted. *Criminology and Public Policy*, *2*, 263–282.

DiIulio, J. J., Jr. (1987). *Governing prisons*. New York: Free Press.

Edgar, K., O'Donnell, I., & Martin, C. (2003). *Prison violence: The dynamics of conflict, fear and power*. Portland, OR: Willan.

Ellison, J. M., Steiner, B., & Wright, E. M. (2018). Examining the sources of violent victimization among jail inmates. *Criminal Justice and Behavior*, *45*, 1723–1741.

Felson, R. B., Cundiff, P., & Painter-Davis, N. (2012). Age and sexual assault in correctional facilities: A blocked opportunity approach. *Criminology*, *50*, 887–911.

Golden, T. (2006). The battle for Guantánamo. *The New York Times Magazine*, September 17, pp. 60–71, 140–145.

Hemmens, C., & Marquart, J. W. (1999). Straight time. *Journal of Offender Rehabilitation*, *28*, 1–21.

Herman, S. (2010). *Parallel justice for victims of crime*. Washington, D.C.: National Center for Victims of Crime.

Hindelang, M. S., Gottfredson, M., & Garofalo, J. (1978). *Victims of personal crime*. Cambridge, MA: Ballinger.

Hochstetler, A., & DeLisi, M. (2005). Importation, deprivation, and varieties of serving time: An integrated lifestyle-exposure model of prison offending. *Journal of Criminal Justice*, *33*, 257–266.

Huebner, B. (2003). Administrative determinants of inmate violence. *Journal of Criminal Justice*, *31*, 107–117.

Irwin, J., & Cressey, D. R. (1962). Thieves, convicts, and the inmate culture. *Social Problems*, *10*, 142–155.

Jacobs, J. B. (1976). Stratification and conflict among prison inmates. *Journal of Criminal Law and Criminology*, *66*, 476–482.

Kalinich, D. B., & Stojkovic, S. (1985). Contraband: The basis for legitimate power in a prison social system. *Criminal Justice and Behavior*, *12*, 435–451.

Karmen, A. (2013). *Crime victims: An introduction to victimology* (8th edition). Belmont, CA: Wadsworth.

Kerbs, J. J., & Jolley, J. M. (2007). Inmate-on-inmate victimization among older male prisoners. *Crime and Delinquency*, *53*, 187–218.

Kigerl, A., & Hamilton, Z. (2016). The impact of transfers between prisons on inmate misconduct: Testing importation, deprivation, and transfer theory models. *The Prison Journal*, *96*, 232–257.

King, R. D. (2018). A comparison of British and American policies for managing dangerous prisoners: A question of legitimacy. In J. D. Wooldredge & P. Smith (Eds.), *The Oxford handbook of prisons and imprisonment* (pp. 367–393). New York: Oxford University Press.

Lahm, K. F. (2015). Predictors of violent and nonviolent victimization behind bars: An exploration of women inmates. *Women and Criminal Justice*, *25*, 273–291.

Land, K. (2003). *Criminal circumstance: A dynamic multi-contextual criminal opportunity theory*. New York: Routledge.

Liebling, A., Price, D., & Shefer, G. (2011). *The prison officer* (2nd edition). New York: Willan.

Lindsey, A. M., Mears, D. P., Cochran, J. C., Bales, W. D., & Stults, B. J. (2017). In prison and far from home: Spatial distance effects on inmate misconduct. *Crime and Delinquency*, *63*, 1043–1065.

Lombardo, L. X. (1989). *Guards imprisoned: Correctional officers at work*. New York: Routledge.

McCorkle, R. C. (1992). Personal precautions to violence in prison. *Criminal Justice and Behavior*, *19*, 160–173.

Mears, D. P. (2017). *Out-of-control criminal justice: The systems improvement solution for more safety, justice, accountability, and efficiency*. New York: Cambridge University Press.

Mears, D. P., & Cochran, J. C. (2015). *Prisoner reentry in the era of mass incarceration*. Thousand Oaks, CA: Sage Publications.

Mears, D. P., & Cochran, J. C. (2019). *Fundamentals of criminological and criminal justice inquiry*. New York: Cambridge University Press.

Mears, D. P., Cochran, J. C., & Beaver, K. M. (2013). Self-control theory and nonlinear effects on offending. *Journal of Quantitative Criminology*, *29*, 447–476.

Mears, D. P., Cochran, J. C., Siennick, S. E., & Bales, W. D. (2012). Prison visitation and recidivism. *Justice Quarterly*, *29*, 888–918.

Mears, D. P., & Reisig, M. D. (2006). The theory and practice of supermax prisons. *Punishment and Society*, *8*, 33–57.

Mears, D. P., Scott, M. L., & Bhati, A. S. (2007). Opportunity theory and agricultural crime victimization. *Rural Sociology*, *72*, 151–184.

Mears, D. P., Stewart, E. A., Siennick, S. E., & Simons, R. L. (2013). The code of the street and inmate violence: Investigating the salience of imported belief systems. *Criminology*, *51*, 695–728.

Meier, R. F., & Miethe, T. D. (1993). Understanding theories of criminal victimization. *Crime and Justice*, *17*, 459–499.

Merton, R. K. (1968). *Social theory and social structure*. New York: Free Press.

Morris, N. (2002). *Maconochie's gentlemen: The story of Norfolk Island and the roots of modern prison reform*. New York: Oxford University Press.

Morris, N., & Rothman, D. J. (Eds.). (1995). *The Oxford history of the prison*. New York: Oxford University Press.

Nadel, M. R., & Mears, D. P. (2019). Building with no end in sight: The theory and effects of prison architecture. *Corrections* (forthcoming).

Pérez, D. M., Gover, A. R., Tennyson, K. M., & Santos, S. D. (2010). Individual and institutional characteristics related to inmate victimization. *International Journal of Offender Therapy and Comparative Criminology*, *54*, 378–394.

Pratt, T. C., & Turanovic, J. J. (2016). Lifestyle and routine activity theories revisited: The importance of "risk" to the study of victimization. *Victims and Offenders*, *11*, 335–354.

Randol, B. M., & Campbell, C. M. (2017). Macro-correlates of inmate violence: The importance of programming in prison order. *The Prison Journal*, *97*, 451–474.

Reisig, M. D. (1998). Rates of disorder in higher-custody state prisons: A comparative analysis of managerial practices. *Crime and Delinquency*, *44*, 229–244.

Reyns, B. W., Woo, Y., Lee, H. D., & Yoon, O. (2018). Vulnerability versus opportunity: Dissecting the role of low self-control and risky lifestyles in violent victimization risk among Korean inmates. *Crime and Delinquency*, *64*, 423–447.

Ricciardelli, R. & Sit, V. (2016). Producing social (dis)order in prison: The effects of administrative controls on prisoner-on-prisoner violence. *The Prison Journal*, *96*, 210–231.

Riveland, C. (1999). Prison management trends, 1975–2025. In M. H. Tonry & J. Petersilia (Eds.), *Prisons* (pp. 163–204). Chicago: University of Chicago Press.

Sampson, R. J. (2012). *Great American city: Chicago and the enduring neighborhood effect*. Chicago: University of Chicago Press.

Schreck, C. J. (1999). Criminal victimization and low self-control: An extension and test of a general theory of crime. *Justice Quarterly*, *16*, 633–654.

Sinclair, U. (1906). *The jungle*. London: Penguin Books.

Sparks, R, Bottoms, A. E., & Hay, W. (1996). *Prisons and the problem of order*. Oxford, England: Oxford University Press.

Steiner, B, Ellison, J. M., Butler, H. D., & Cain, C. M. (2017). The impact of inmate and prison characteristics on prisoner victimization. *Trauma, Violence, and Abuse*, *18*, 17–36.

Steiner, B., & Wooldredge, J. D. (2018). Prison officer legitimacy, their exercise of power, and inmate rule breaking. *Criminology*, *56*, 750–779.

Stewart, E. A., Schreck, C. J., & Simons, R. L. (2006). "I ain't gonna let no one disrespect me": Does the code of the street reduce or increase violent victimization among African American adolescents? *Journal of Research in Crime and Delinquency*, *43*, 427–458.

Stohr, M. K., Lovrich, Jr., N. P., Menke, B. A., & Zupan, L. L. (2006). Staff management in correctional institutions: Comparing DiIulio's "control model" and "employee investment model" outcomes in five jails. *Justice Quarterly*, *11*, 471–497.

Sykes, G. M. (2007) [1958]. *The society of captives: A study of a maximum security prison.* Princeton, NJ: Princeton University Press.

Thomas, C. W., Petersen, D. M., & Zingraff, R. M. (1978). Structural and social psychological correlates of prisonization. *Criminology*, *16*, 383–393.

Thompson, H. A. (2016). *Blood in the water: The Attica prison uprising of 1971 and its legacy*. New York: Random House.

Trammell, R. (2012). *Enforcing the convict code: Violence and prison culture*. New York: Lynne Rienner.

Turanovic, J. J., & Pratt, T. C. (2019). *Thinking about victimization: Context and consequences*. New York: Routledge.

Wolff, N. (2018). A general model of harm in correctional settings. In J. D. Wooldredge & P. Smith (Eds.), *The Oxford handbook of prisons and imprisonment* (pp. 288–319). New York: Oxford University Press.

Wolff, N, Blitz, C. L., Shi, J., Siegel, J., & Bachman, R. (2007). Physical violence inside prisons: Rates of victimization. *Criminal Justice and Behavior*, *34*, 588–599.

Wolfgang, M. (1957). *Patterns of criminal homicide*. Philadelphia: University of Pennsylvania Press.

Wood, S. R. (2013). Dual severe mental and substance use disorders as predictors of Federal inmate assaults. *The Prison Journal*, *93*, 34–56.

Wooldredge, J. D. (1998). Inmate lifestyles and opportunities for victimization. *Journal of Research in Crime and Delinquency*, *35*, 480–502.

Wooldredge, J. D., & Steiner, B. (2014). A bi-level framework for understanding prisoner victimization. *Journal of Quantitative Criminology*, *30*, 141–162.

Wright, K. A., & Cesar, G. T. (2013). Toward a more complete model of offender reintegration: Linking the individual-, community-, and system-level components of recidivism. *Victims and Offenders*, *8*, 373–398.

# 8

# Putting School-Based Victimization in Context

*Heather Zaykowski and Callie Marie Rennison*

News media have brought attention to violence in schools at both the secondary school and college levels. School shootings in Columbine, Sandy Hook, Virginia Tech, University of California at Santa Barbara, Parkland, and other schools have raised concern that schools are no longer safe (e.g., Rochman, 2012). Although fears about school violence have decreased since the Columbine shootings in 1999, survey data indicate that parental concern about school safety spikes following a high-profile school shooting (Reinhart, 2018). There has also been increasing attention to sexual violence on college campuses—specifically that colleges and universities are one of the most dangerous places in America for women (Booth, 2015). Consequently, a great deal of public and policy attention has been given to making schools of all kinds safe. Similarly, scholarly research has directed a great deal of effort to understand school-based victimization and conceptualized schools as uniquely risky places for young people (Butler, Lee, & Fisher, 2019; Chouhy, Madero-Hernandez, & Turanovic, 2017; Hong & Espelage, 2012).

After decades of research on victimization in secondary and post-secondary schools, we have learned that the factors explaining victimization in schools are similar to explanations of victimization in general. Among the most robust factors that increase the likelihood of victimization in schools are risky behaviors such as criminal offending, affiliations with deviant peers, and low self-control risk (for recent reviews see Butler et al. 2019; Chouhy et al., 2017). Rather than continue to explain why victimization risk varies *between* schools, which has been covered extensively in the literature already, we propose a new direction—to place school-based victimization risk within the broader context of the lives of adolescents and young adults.

To accomplish this, we must move beyond the current static application of opportunity theories and think more about how both opportunity structures and routine activities vary across the early life course (Turanovic, Hall, & Street, 2018). In this chapter, we first explain opportunity theories and how they have been applied to explain victimization in the school context. We then extend the opportunity perspective to help explain variations in victimization risk at school and away from school, age-graded differences in victimization risk, and differences in risk between students and nonstudents. We then present data from the National Crime Victimization Survey that address these factors in predicting violent victimization risk. Finally, we discuss the implications of these findings for opportunity theories, future research, and policy related to school-based victimization.

## Opportunity Theories

Opportunity theories of victimization have been the leading theoretical frameworks to explain school-based victimization. Opportunity theories are a broad group of similar perspectives rooted in lifestyle-exposure theory (Hindelang, Gottfredson, & Garofalo, 1978) and routine activity theory (Cohen & Felson, 1979). In general, lifestyle-exposure theory argues that variations across social groups could be explained by the differences in where they spend their time. Most notably, the more time spent in public places, the greater likelihood of having contact with offenders (Hindelang et al., 1978). Routine activity theory argues that the convergence of an offender, suitable target, and lack of capable guardianship (e.g., the absence of protection or surveillance) make up the pieces necessary for a crime to occur (Cohen & Felson, 1979). In opportunity theories, the motivation of offenders is often assumed, in that the theory does not seek to explain the underlying theory of offending, but instead focuses on the crime event or victimization risk (McNeeley, 2015). Suitable targets are something desired, such as expensive and portable electronics, or a target could also be a person who has characteristics that might entice an offender, such as the victim's perceived vulnerability or antagonism toward the offender (Finkelhor & Asdigian, 1996). Guardianship is the protective element—the presence of people or security measures, or the use of self-protective measures (such as weapon carrying) (McNeeley, 2015).

These ideas are integrated into the lifestyle-routine activities theory (or L-RAT), which measures four dimensions—exposure, proximity, guardianship, and target attractiveness (Cohen, Kluegel, & Land, 1981; McNeeley, 2015; Wilcox & Cullen, 2018). Exposure measures the visibility of victims to offenders, whereas proximity includes the physical locations where offenders are more likely to congregate or look for targets (Cohen et al., 1981). Although initially conceptualized as time in public places, particularly risky places, this concept has evolved to more specifically measure the risky or deviant lifestyles of the victim (Jensen & Brownfield, 1986; Lauritsen, Sampson, & Laub, 1991). In fact, a fairly large literature has supported that one of the most substantial predictors of victimization is offending (Berg & Mulford, 2020; Lauritsen & Laub, 2007).

*Opportunity Theories and the School Context*

Although opportunity theories were initially intended to explain predatory crime across neighborhoods, more recently its key concepts have been applied to school contexts (Augustine, Wilcox, Ousey, & Clayton, 2002; Bouchard, Beauregard, & Wang, 2012; Burrow & Apel, 2008; Cass, 2007; Fisher, Sloan, Cullen, & Lu, 1998; Kulig, Cullen, Wilcox, & Chouhy, 2019; Kulig, Pratt, Cullen, Chouhy, & Unnever, 2017; Mustaine & Tewksbury, 1998; Peguero, 2009; Peguero, Popp, & Koo, 2011; Peterson, Lasky, Fisher, & Wilcox, 2018; Popp & Peguero, 2011; Schreck, Miller, & Gibson, 2003; Wilcox & Cullen, 2018; Wilcox, Tillyer, & Fisher, 2009). The concept of target attractiveness or exposure has been measured a number of ways from student demographic characteristics, the physical size of students (vulnerability), delinquent behaviors, and participation in school activities (Augustine et al., 2002; Bouchard et al., 2012; Burrow & Apel, 2008; Popp & Peguero, 2011). For college students, risky lifestyles such as drug and alcohol use, particularly binge drinking, attending parties, and involvement in Greek life have served as measures of target attractiveness (Cass, 2007; Fisher et al., 1998; Mustaine & Tewksbury, 1998).

Proximity or how close victims are to motivated offenders has included the geographic location of schools (e.g., located in a city or not), the characteristics of communities (e.g., crime level, economic disadvantage), the level of delinquency and school misconduct at the school level, and for college students, the time spent on campus, or their living arrangements (Butler et al., 2019). Secondary schools, like the home, provide a heightened level of guardianship (Burrow & Apel, 2008). Therefore, scholars have addressed variation in different types of guardianship within the school context such as connections to peers and teachers, participation in school activities, personal self-protective measures, and school security measures (Burrow & Apel, 2008; Popp & Peguero, 2011; Wilcox et al., 2009). In terms of studies of college students, research has also included measures of police officers on campus and whether one lives alone or with roommates (Cass, 2007; Fisher et al., 1998).

### *Age-Graded Differences in Lifestyles and Routine Activities*

Although much of the school-based opportunity literature has focused on students' victimization risk within particular age cohorts with attention to either middle or high school, or among only college students, there are important differences in opportunity structures across these different stages of the early life course (Kruttschnitt & Macmillan, 2006; Macmillan, 2001; Turanovic, Hall, & Street, 2018). Although scholars have recognized these differences in life course criminology, they are often neglected within research on school-based victimization. This is important, however, because the nature of students' routine activities *outside* of school changes extensively through adolescence and into early adulthood.

Younger youth are less independent and spend most of their time in supervised environments such as in school, at home, or at friends' homes under parental supervision. Factors such as attachment to parents and commitment to school may help foster bonds that prevent youth from engaging in delinquency (Hirschi, 1969). As young people grow older, they spend less time with family and are less concerned about parents' approval of how they spend their time. Youth tend to place more value in their friends and spend more time in unstructured environments during mid-adolescence relative to early adolescence and pre-teen years (Moffitt, 1993; Osgood, Wilson, O'Malley, Bachman, & Johnston, 1996). Greater time spent away from supervised environments and structured routine activities increases the likelihood that young people will be exposed to criminogenic circumstances and peers

(Osgood et al., 1996). This would suggest that as young people age into adolescence, their victimization risk away from school may increase, but the risk may remain stable within the school context.

During the emerging adulthood period, when many individuals go to college, students have even more freedoms. This is also an important time in the life course characterized by instability, changes in self-identify, and experimentation with substance use—all of which influence victimization risk (Arnett, 2000). Yet college students still maintain an important level of attachment to education, which may act as a social bond through early adulthood (Sampson & Laub, 1993). College students are also more likely than nonstudents of comparable ages to come from backgrounds with greater resources (Bailey & Dynarski, 2011; Goldrick-Rab, Kelchen, Harris, & Benson, 2016; Wolniak, Wells, Engberg, & Manly, 2016). Such structural advantages also protect against adopting risky lifestyles that are closely linked to victimization (Turanovic, Pratt & Piquero, 2018). These differences suggest there would be an increasing divide in the level of risk between being on campus and off campus, and between students and nonstudents.

## Putting School-Based Victimization in Context

There are several key limitations with how opportunity theories have been applied to explain school-based victimization among young people. First, the majority of studies have focused exclusively on the school context (for an exception see Burrow & Apel, 2008). Only some parts of students' lives are actually spent within the school context. Students spend a great deal of time in places other than schools—at home, in the community, or even at work. Second, opportunity perspectives on school-based victimization have predominantly ignored age-graded differences. Although age has been recognized as an important correlate of victimization and changes in lifestyles and routine activities (Kruttschnitt & Macmillan, 2006; Macmillan, 2001; Turanovic, Hall, & Street, 2018; Turanovic, Pratt & Piquero 2018), this notion has not been applied to opportunity perspectives on victimization in schools. Finally, there has been little attention to how victimization among older students, particularly college aged students, compares to nonstudents (Rennison & Addington, 2014). This is important because nonstudents are often overshadowed in terms of public concern and policy attention, yet may have lifestyles and live in social contexts that pose greater risks than college students.

*Risk Beyond the School Context*

Although there has been some debate about risk in school contexts, the evidence is fairly clear that the odds of violent death are extremely low, and much lower in school than away from school. Data from the *Indicators of School Crime and Safety* indicate that the risk for any violent death (homicide or suicide) among youth age 5 to 18 is one death per 2.7 *million* students. Furthermore, less than 3 percent of all youth homicides occur at school. Among data on college campuses, in 2016 (the most recent year available), there were 15 murders, 3 of which occurred in residence halls—a rate of 0.010 per 10,000 full time students. Since 2004, there was an average of 17.4 murders on college campuses. However, it's important to note that these data include any incident on campus regardless of whether the victim was a student or not (Musu, Zhang, Wang, Zhang, & Oudekerk, 2019).

Although there has been less agreement as to whether youth and college students have higher risk at school or away from school for non-fatal victimizations, the difference in these studies appears to be in the types of crimes that are examined and how they are measured. In general, *total levels of victimization* appear higher in schools (for middle and high school students), but these offenses are mostly minor in nature (Burrow & Apel, 2008; Finkelhor, Vanderminden, Turner, Shattuck, & Hamby, 2016; Musu et al., 2019; Turner, Finkelhor, Hamby, Shattuck, & Ormrod, 2011). The types of victimization that have been more common in high school and middle schools include theft/larceny (Burrow & Apel, 2008) and bullying-like behaviors including minor physical harm, emotional harm, and harassment (Finkelhor et al., 2016; Turner et al., 2011). Sexual assault and rape, dating violence, and assaults with weapons have been found to be more common away from school (Finkelhor et al., 2016; Turner et al., 2011).

Among college students, some evidence suggests that nine out of ten violent student victimizations took place off campus (Baum & Klaus, 2005; Hart & Miethe, 2011). However, some victimizations that are more likely to occur on college campuses include property crimes—particularly theft and burglary—as well as harassment (Fisher et al., 1998). Although there has been a great deal of attention with regard to rape and sexual assault on campus, the evidence does not clearly support that risk is uniquely high. In a study of 12 colleges and universities, Fisher and colleagues (1998) found that rape and sexual assault was higher on campus (16.7 per 1,000 students; compared to 13.3 per 1,000 students off campus), although rape alone (excluding sexual assault) was more likely to occur off campus.

### *Age Differences in Victimization Risk*

Another factor lacking attention in the school victimization literature is age. Age is one of the most durable predictors of victimization risk (Macmillan, 2001). However, theoretical and empirical work on the age-graded nature of victimization has not received the same level of attention as offending (Daigle, Hoffman, & Johnson, (2018); Tillyer, 2014; Turanovic, Hall, & Street, 2018). In general, estimates show that younger persons have higher victimization risk than older persons. In the most recent report on *Criminal Victimization in the United States*, estimates of violent victimization were highest among the 12 to 17 and 18 to 24 age groups (Morgan & Oudekerk, 2019). Serious victimization risk increases with age until late adolescence and early adulthood, and then declines over time (Macmillan, 2001; Perkins, 1997). However, risk for more minor offenses, including bullying victimization, has been found to be more prominent among middle school rather than high school populations (Hong & Espelage, 2012). With regard to college aged populations, research has focused on "traditional" college aged students (18 to 24). Although there are some data sources that provide estimates of risk by age in general, no study to our knowledge has examined victimization risk comparing traditional college aged populations to other age groups, including older college students.

### *Comparing Risk Between Students and Nonstudents*

Some research has examined victimization risk of college students compared to nonstudents of the same ages (Baum & Klaus, 2005; Hart, 2003; Hart & Rennison, 2011). In general, these findings have suggested that violent victimization risk is lower among college students than similarly aged nonstudents (Baum & Klaus, 2005; Hart, 2003; Hart & Rennison, 2011; Rennison & Addington, 2014) or not significantly different (Buddie & Testa, 2005; Coker, Follingstad, Bush, & Fisher, 2016). Research on college campus violence also suggests that risk for victimization, including serious violence, is lower on college campuses compared to surrounding areas (Fox & Burstein, 2010).

Data from the 1995 to 2002 National Crime Victimization Survey show that participants age 18 to 24 who were enrolled in a college or university had lower rates of both serious violence (aggravated assault, robbery, and rape/sexual assault) and simple assault, compared to similarly aged nonstudents (Baum & Klaus, 2005). Hart and Rennison (2011) found no significant differences in victimization rates between Hispanic students and nonstudents of the same age, with the exception that Hispanic college students were significantly less likely to be victims of robbery. Studies looking specifically at rape and sexual assault also suggest that rates are higher for nonstudents (Rennison, 2014; Rennison & Addington, 2014; Sinozich & Langton, 2014). From 1995 to 2013, the rate of rape and sexual assault was 1.2 times greater for non-college women age 18 to 24 compared to college women (Sinozich & Langton, 2014). Other research found no significant differences in rates of sexual violence and other interpersonal violence (Buddie & Testa, 2005; Coker et al., 2016).

## Current Study

In this chapter, we move beyond the school context itself and compare: (1) violent victimization risk for students at school and away from school and (2) violent victimization risk for students compared to nonstudents. Research has shown that victimization risk varies across different age cohorts, therefore, it is important to view risk within these different stages of the life course (Turanovic, Hall, & Street, 2018). Within these areas of inquiry, we distinguish findings for different age cohorts from middle school (age 12 to 14), high school (15 to 17), and college age (18 to 24 and 25 to 34). Findings from the literature also suggest that distinguishing minor offenses and more serious offenses is important (Finkelhor et al., 2016; Fisher et al., 1998; Rennison & Addington, 2014; Turner et al., 2011). Because simple assaults make up the vast majority of violent victimizations (Morgan & Oudekerk, 2019), failure to separate these offenses may obscure findings regarding offenses that are arguably of greater public concern. This study is the first to our knowledge to examine victimization rates by age cohort, school level, and student status, and to test for significant differences at school compared to away from school, and differences between students and nonstudents. We hope by providing insights into these dynamics we can move forward with opportunity perspectives on school-based victimization by including insights about how victimization at school and among students compares to other contexts.

## Data and Methods

In order to examine victimization between students and nonstudents, and victimization at and away from school, we use 1999 to 2016 NCVS data since these years include the needed student status data. The collection of NCVS data is sponsored by the Bureau of Justice Statistics in the US Department of Justice, and is one of two official sources of national crime statistics. Data are collected both in-person and over the phone from every person age 12 or older living in a nationally representative sample of housing units. Each person age 12 and older within sampled households are asked about victimization experiences during the past six months. Households remain in the sample for six cycles. The NCVS gathers extensive details of victimizations and produces findings representative of the non-institutionalized US population (Rennison & Rand, 2007). From 1999 to 2016, the household response rate averaged 90%, and the individual response rate averaged 87%.

### *Dependent Variables*

Our research focuses on two dependent variables: serious violence and simple assault. Rates for each of these types of victimization were compared for participants by location (at or away from school), age, and by student status (student or nonstudent). The NCVS defines simple assault as assaults in which there was minor or no injury, and no weapon used by the perpetrator. Serious violence is defined as an aggregation of aggravated assault, rape/sexual assault, and robbery. Aggravated assaults included any attacks with a weapon, and attacks without a weapon that involve serious injury. Robbery included an attempted or completed theft, directly from a person by force or threat of force. Rape/sexual assault included forced sexual intercourse and unwanted touching.

### *Independent Variables*

*Student Status*. Student status was measured using variable v3079 which focuses on school attendance. We focus on three categories of respondents identified by this variable: college students, grade school students, and nonstudents. College students include any household member who has graduated high school and currently attends a two or four year college or university, or post-graduate school. Grade school students include those in attendance in "regular school" which is defined as "both public and private schools starting with kindergarten and continuing through elementary, junior or middle, and high school, regardless of whether the classes are graded or ungraded." Nonstudents are those respondents who described themselves as not attending school. Participants attending a trade or vocational school, those who did not respond, or refused to respond were excluded from the analysis.

*Age*. In order to understand the role that age plays in victimization risk, we focus on several age categories: 12 to 14; 15 to 17; 18 to 24; 25 to 34. These age categories are consistent with approximate school groupings of middle school, high school, college, and continuing education college student. These age categories are also widely used in victimization and educational research allowing comparisons across studies (e.g., Musu et al., 2019; Truman, 2011). For the first research question, whether schools are safer than being away from school, all age categories were used, and comparisons were made between them. However, for the second question, whether students are safer than nonstudents (away from school), the age brackets used were limited to 15 years and older. This decision was made because of the low sample size of 12- to 14-year-old nonstudents, and legal age when students can drop out of school. We also excluded several other age cohort/student status combinations with relatively limited cases and/or that theoretically did not contribute to our understanding of the central research questions. Specifically, we excluded 12- to 14-year-old college students, 15- to 17-year-old college students, and 25- to 34-year-old grade school students.

*Location.* Location was defined as incidents occurring "in school" or "away from school." At school victimizations included incidents occurring within the school building and occurring on school grounds. Away from school includes any other location (home, friend's house, public place) and "other" locations. Incidents occurring outside the United States were excluded from the analysis, whether they occurred at school or away from school.

### *Analytic Approach*

The current study calculates the rate of victimization per 1,000 persons age 12 or older in the United States. To estimate the rates, the incident level dataset, which contains incident details, was combined with the person-level dataset, which contains characteristics of all interviewed persons (those who have been victimized and those who have not). When combining victimization incidents, the number of incidents and incident weights are also matched to the person file using the person id and year-quarter variables in both datasets. This procedure was conducted for each victimization type (serious violence or simple assault) and location (school or away from school).

When creating the rates, the sample design, weights, and clustering need to be taken into account to ensure accurate estimates. Survey weights are also incorporated in the nested stratification of the survey design, which changes every few years and must be specified prior to the survey set command. The rates for each type of victimization are then multiplied by the adjustment factor (the weights available in the incident file) and by 1,000. Each rate is then estimated using the *means* command, over age, for each characteristic considered (grade school student, college student, nonstudent). Detailed procedures for computing rates are available in the NCVS technical assistance manual (see Shook-Sa, Couzens, & Berzofsky, 2014).

Tests of statistical significance for all estimates compared are based on specialized formulas accounting for the NCVS's complex sampling (Couzens, Shook-Sa, Lee, & Berzofsky, 2015). These significance tests use generalized variance function constant parameters to calculate variance estimates, standard errors, and confidence intervals from the original, unweighted data. Estimated rates are based on weighted data to ensure sample representativeness.

## Sample Characteristics by Age Cohort and Student Status

Before addressing the research questions, we describe the sample. Table 8.1 presents the unweighted sample characteristics by age cohort and student status. The total unweighted sample included 1,020,019 respondents. A majority of the sample were nonstudents (57.6%), and nearly half of the sample were in the age 25 to 34 age cohort (45.6%). While all of the individuals age 12 to 14 were students in our sample, students made up 92.4% of the 15 to 17 cohort, 39.7% of the 18 to 24 cohort, and 10.6% of the 25 to 34 cohort.

## Comparing Students' Victimization Risk at School and Away from School

The first research question examined whether students were less likely to be violently victimized at school compared to students who

**Table 8.1**
**Unweighted Sample Characteristics by Age Cohort and Student Status**

| Age Cohort | Students | | Nonstudents | | Totals |
|---|---|---|---|---|---|
| | *n* | % | *n* | % | |
| 12 to 14 | 140,774 | 32.6 | N/A | N/A | 140,774 |
| 15 to 17 | 136,579 | 31.6 | 11,180 | 1.9 | 147,759 |
| 18 to 24 | 105,702 | 24.4 | 160,573 | 27.3 | 266,275 |
| 25 to 34 | 49,423 | 11.4 | 415,788 | 70.8 | 465,211 |
| Totals | 432,478 | 100.0 | 587,541 | 100.0 | 1,020,019 |

Note: Students age 12 to 14 and 15 to 17 are grade school students. Students age 18 to 24 and 25 to 24 are college students. N/A indicates groupings that are not applicable and are not included in the analysis.

are away from school. To address this question, we calculated victimization rates for grade school students (age cohorts 12 to 14 and 15 to 17) and college students (age cohorts 18 to 24 and 25 to 34), by the incident location (at school, or away from school). Figure 8.1 illustrates the results for serious violence (aggravated assault, rape/sexual assault, robbery) and simple assault (physical assault with minor or no injury). The x-axis displays the age cohort, and the y-axis indicates the victimization rate per 1,000 persons in each age cohort. Rates and significance tests complementing Figure 8.1 are provided in Table 8.2.

Findings show that a global statement that a student is safer at school versus away from school is overly simplistic. Rather, this relationship depends on the age cohort and type of violence considered. When considering only serious violence, students across all age cohorts and school levels were significantly less likely to be victimized at school compared to away from school ($p<.05$). The greatest differences in risk were observed for college students, with rates of less than 1 victimization per 1,000 persons occurring at school, compared to 15.1 victimizations (age 18 to 24) and 11.9 victimizations (age 25 to 34) per 1,000 persons away from college campuses.

A somewhat different pattern is observed for simple assault. Although the pattern of simple assault risk for college students was similar to what was found for serious assault: victimization risk was significantly lower at school compared to away from schools ($p<.05$), this pattern was reversed for younger students. In the 12 to 14 age cohort, students were significantly *more* likely to be victimized at school compared to away from school (29.2 and 12.0 victimizations per 1,000 respectively,

**Figure 8.1**
**Simple Assault and Serious Violence Victimization Rates per 1,000 Persons for Students 'at School' and 'Away from School'**

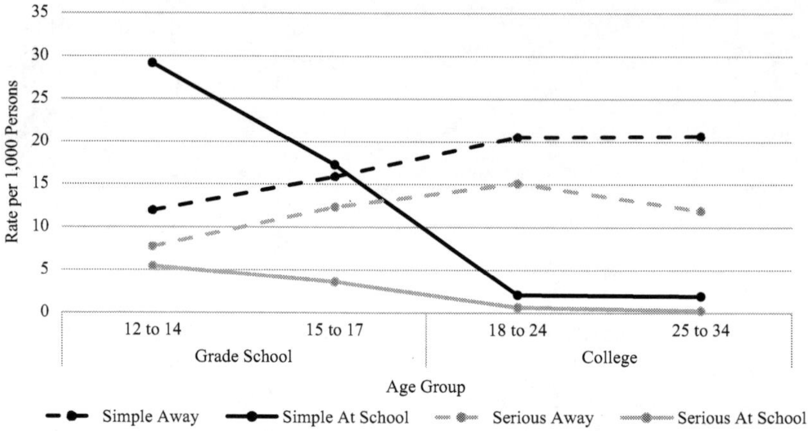


**Table 8.2**
**Victimizations Rates (per 1,000) and Significance Testing: At School v. Away from School**

| Student Status | Simple Assault Rates per 1,000 | | | Serious Violence Rates per 1,000 | | |
|---|---|---|---|---|---|---|
| | At School [95% CI] | Away [95% CI] | *p* | At School [95% CI] | Away [95% CI] | *p* |
| Grade School | | | | | | |
| 12 to 14 | 29.2 [25.7 – 32.6] | 12.0 [10.5 – 13.4] | p<.05 | 5.5 [4.2 – 6.8] | 7.7 [6.6 – 8.8] | p<.05 |
| 15 to 17 | 17.3 [14.8 – 19.8] | 15.9 [14.2 – 17.6] | NS | 3.6 [2.5 – 4.7] | 12.4 [10.6 – 14.1] | p<.05 |
| College | | | | | | |
| 18 to 24 | 2.1 [0.3 – 3.9] | 20.5 [18.0 – 23.1] | p<.05 | 0.7 [0.4 – 0.9] | 15.1 [13.1 – 17.1] | p<.05 |
| 25 to 34 | 1.9 [1.1 – 2.8] | 20.7 [17.3 – 24.0] | p<.05 | 0.3 [0.1 – 0.5] | 11.9 [9.9 – 14.0] | p<.05 |

Note: NS indicates nonsignificant results (i.e., $p > .05$). 95% CI refers to 95% confidence interval.

p<.05). Significance testing indicates no differences in the 15 to 17 age cohort victimization rates. In other words, simple assault victimization was equally likely at and away from school among 15- to 17-year-olds.

## Comparing Students' Victimization Risk with the Victimization Risk of Nonstudents

The second research question compared victimization risk between students and nonstudents away from schools. To address this question, we calculated victimization rates per 1,000 persons for students and nonstudents away from school by age cohort and level of school (grade school, college). By focusing just on rates away from school we can better tease out the effect of being a student (if any) from the location of school itself.[1] Figure 8.2 presents the results for serious violence and simple assault. Table 8.3 provides the rates and significance tests that accompany Figure 8.2. We limited the comparison to persons in the older age ranges (age 15 and older) due to compulsory schooling requirements for children. Along these lines, although the sample size was not problematic for 15- to 17-year-old nonstudents, these comparisons should be observed with some caution, as nonstudents in this age range could be not attending for a range of reasons. The evidence demonstrates, for both serious violence and simple assault, students are characterized by lower victimization rates than nonstudents away from school locations with one exception. The exception was that students and nonstudents shared statistically equal victimization rates among the 25 to 34 age cohort. These findings suggest that for individuals younger than age 25, being a student serves as a protective status, not one that elevates risk.

## Discussion

In this chapter we argued for expanding the opportunity perspective to acknowledge how victimization risk of students and within schools compares to the broader contexts of young people's lives, much of which is spent away from school. Although we were not able to measure opportunity theories directly, we were able to provide evidence that this direction of inquiry is important, if not essential. Specifically, this chapter compared students' violent victimization risk at school and away from school and students' violent victimization risk compared to nonstudents using data from the National Crime Victimization Survey. Although prior work has examined school violence, the current study

**Figure 8.2**
**Simple Assault and Serious Violence Victimization Rates per 1,000 Persons for Students and Nonstudents (Away from School)**

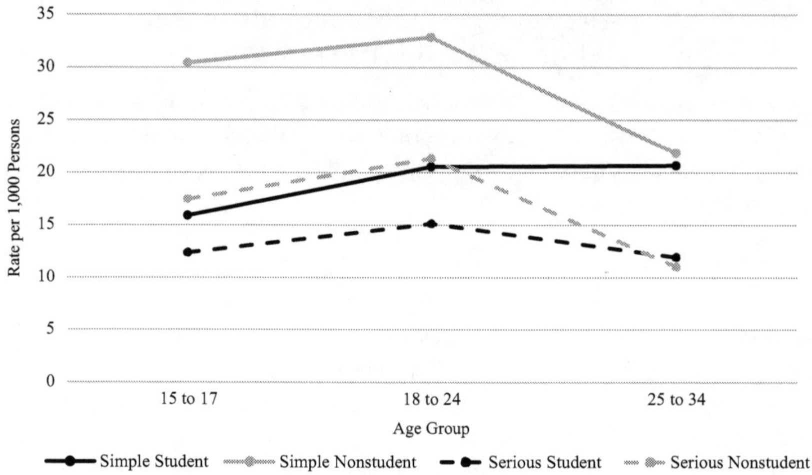


**Table 8.3**
**Victimizations Rates and Significance: Student v. Nonstudent (Away from School)**

| Student Status | Simple Assault Rates per 1,000 | | | Serious Violence Rates per 1,000 | | |
|---|---|---|---|---|---|---|
| | Student [95% CI] | Nonstudent [95% CI] | *p* | Student [95% CI] | Nonstudent [95% CI] | *p* |
| Grade School | | | | | | |
| 15 to 17 | 15.9 [14.2 – 17.6] | 30.4 [21.3 – 39.5] | p<.05 | 12.4 [10.6 – 14.1] | 17.5 [11.0 – 24.0] | p<.05 |
| College | | | | | | |
| 18 to 24 | 20.5 [18.0 – 23.1] | 32.9 [29.7 – 36.0] | p<.05 | 15.1 [13.1 – 17.2] | 21.3 [19.4 – 23.3] | p<.05 |
| 25 to 34 | 20.7 [17.3 – 24.0] | 21.8 [20.0 – 23.6] | NS | 11.9 [9.9 – 14.0] | 11.1 [10.2 – 12.0] | NS |

Note: NS indicates nonsignificant results (i.e., $p > .05$). 95% CI refers to 95% confidence interval.

addressed several important gaps in the literature by disaggregating risk by age cohorts, crime severity, student status, and location of the incident. Prior work has also predominantly failed to distinguish college students from nonstudents, and has almost exclusively ignored college students older than 24 years old who in our sample made up nearly one third of all college students.

Our findings overall point to a critical need to expand our understanding of school-based victimization as just one part of violent victimization risk among both grade school and college students. With regard to the first research question examining if students are safer at school, the results overall supported the hypothesis that students are less likely to be victimized at school. The exception to this finding was observed for the youngest age cohort, youth age 12 to 14. Although on its surface this finding may be surprising, when applying a life course and unstructured socializing frameworks, there are several possibilities for why this should be expected. Unlike older youth, young adults, and adults, young people age 12 to 14 (approximately middle school) have less freedom and time away from supervised environments (Osgood et al., 1996). At this age, youth are more likely than the other age cohorts to spend time under some form of supervision. At school, these youth are supervised by teachers and principals. Away from school, these youth spend a lot of time at home under their parents' supervision. It is possible that youth "away from school" are actually spending more time under direct supervision than at school. In other words, being away from school, they will have *more* guardianship and *fewer* opportunities for unstructured socializing with peers, except for siblings within the family context.

It is also important to address students' victimization risk within the broader context of young people overall—many of whom do not have the privilege to attend college. The second question explored how risk for victimization compared between students and nonstudents. For this analysis we focused on risk away from school for both groups. Results of this analysis also supported our hypothesis that students have lower risk than nonstudents, even when they are off campus. Although there may be something about being a student that acts as a protective factor, even when away from school, it may be that these results can be explained by other factors that have a greater influence on risk such as their socioeconomic status or proximity to high crime areas. A key argument, for example, is that college students are more financially privileged than non-college students of similar ages, and that colleges may be located in lower-risk areas in general. College students are disproportionality more affluent than non-college students, despite some efforts to reduce these inequalities (Bailey & Dynarski, 2011; Goldrick-Rab et al., 2016; Wolniak et al., 2016).

Although the NCVS collects data on a number of socio-economic indicators at the individual and household level, it would be difficult to determine whether differences seen here are due to socio-economic status. The difficulties stem in part due to the NCVS measures and in part due to the nature of students in college. At the individual level, the NCVS collects data on employment and education, and at the household level, it collects information about household income (which can be transformed into poverty status using the survey year and household size) and home ownership. College students, even those who are more affluent, may be unlikely to be employed or homeowners, and would not have completed their advanced education. Household income is measured at the household level, which in the case of some college students is a "group quarters" or college dormitory, not the parent or guardian's household income. As such, a greater proportion of college students age 18 to 24 fall in the "below poverty" range compared to nonstudents (27.0%; 20.6%, respectively). Future research is needed to better understand the differences between students and nonstudents.

A key finding here is that victimization risk for the 25 to 34 cohort was not significantly different for students and nonstudents. One possible explanation points again to the role of unstructured socializing and adult "bonds" which foster attachment, commitment, supervision, and new social role expectations (Hindelang et al., 1978; Osgood et al., 1996; Sampson & Laub, 1993). By age 34, most young adults have embarked on a career, started a family, and are generally engaged in a lifestyle that is less risky and away from potential offenders. For example, recent data from the US Census indicate that during the time period examined in this study, the median age of first marriage for males ranged from 26.9 to 29.5, and for females, the range was 25.1 to 27.4. Data from our study indicate that at age 18, less than 5% of participants were married, while by age 25, this proportion rose to 40%, with 65% of nonstudents being married by age 34. This may suggest that while students retain or reengage with the social bond of education through early adulthood, over time, nonstudents develop other types of bonds, "catching up" to their student counterparts in terms of protective factors against victimization. Future work should investigate the relationship between social bonds and unstructured socializing, and victimization risk into adulthood.

*Implications*

Research about school safety is timely given intensified public attention and calls for action. Although responses are varied, there has been an increase in school security measures such as metal detectors, security officers, and other tactics (Gumbrecht, 2012). Even more recently, there have been calls to arm teachers to protect students (Boyer, 2018; Horsley, 2018). Yet some scholars, journalists, public figures, and even teachers themselves have commented that responses have gone too far and affect the rights of the accused (Viren, 2020; Yoffe, 2014), create an environment of fear (Fox & Savage, 2009; Kupchik, 2010), disproportionately harm young people of color (Kupchik, 2010), and take away resources from areas of greater need (Boyer, 2018). These responses may be exaggerated or unwarranted, and provide a distraction from those who are more likely to be victimized, and circumstances that pose greater risks. Furthermore, in contrast to growing public concern, research tends to suggest that schools are actually safe places (Mayer & Furlong, 2010). However, some evidence suggests that risk may vary for different types of victimization (Finkelhor et al., 2016; Turner et al., 2011).

The results of this study, guided by opportunity perspectives, confirm that, overall, schools and being a student do not pose exceptional risks, despite public concern. In fact, schools are among the safest places for young people, particularly when it comes to serious violence. Of course, these results may not resonate with those who remain concerned about the safety of their children or themselves due to media attention on extreme forms of violence. If victimization risk is shaped by unstructured socializing, then the implications would be to enhance supervision within school (for younger youth) and non-school contexts. However, it is important to maintain that supervision may not necessarily mean enhancing school security (in terms of police officers, firearms, cameras, metal detectors), but rather building relationships among students and school staff and addressing victims' needs (including both response and prevention). Research suggests that school security enhancements may have unintended consequences that dissolve student trust, reduce faith in the rules, and increase punitive outcomes (Fox & Savage 2009; Kupchik, 2010). Unfortunately, the greater risk of victimization away from schools and for nonstudents is more difficult to address. Social contexts matter, and finding ways to structure socialization among these groups should also be a priority.

## Note

1 Although not included in this chapter, we also compared risk for students and nonstudents at school with each pairing away from school. The results of these analyses follow observations from the first research question, that school victimization (for both students and nonstudents) was significantly lower among those age 15 and older. The complete set of significant tests for student at school, student away from school, nonstudent at school, and nonstudent away from school are available by request.

## References

Arnett, J. J. (2000). Emerging adulthood: A theory of development from the late teens through the twenties. *American Psychologist*, *55*(5), 469–480.

Augustine, M. C., Wilcox, P., Ousey, G. C, & Clayton, R. R. (2002). Opportunity theory and adolescent school-based victimization. *Violence victimization*, 17, 233–253 Benson ML,

Bailey, M. J., & Dynarski, S. M. (2011). *Gains and gaps: Changing inequality in US college entry and completion* (No. w17633). Washington, DC: National Bureau of Economic Research.

Baum, K., & Klaus, P. (2005). *Violent victimization of college students, 1995–2002*. Washington, DC: Bureau of Justice Statistics.

Berg, M., & Mulford, C. (2020). Reappraising and redirecting research on the victim-offender overlap. *Trauma, Violence & Abuse*, *21*(1):16–30.

Booth, B. (2015, September 22). One of the most dangerous places for women in America. *CNBC News*. Retrieved from www.cnbc.com/2015/09/22/college-rape-crisis-in-america-under-fire.html.

Bouchard, M., Beauregard, E., & Wang, W. (2012). Social capital, opportunity, and school-based victimization. *Violence and Victims*, *27*(5), 656–673.

Boyer, D. (2018, February 26). States, teachers unions resist Trump's call to arm educators. *The Washington Times*. Retrieved from www.washingtontimes.com/news/2018/feb/26/trump-call-arm-teachers-resisted-teachers-unions-s/.

Buddie, A. M., & Testa, M. (2005). Rates and predictors of sexual aggression among students and nonstudents. *Journal of Interpersonal Violence*, *20*(6), 713–724.

Burrow, J. D., & Apel, R. (2008). Youth behavior, school structure, and student risk of victimization. *Justice Quarterly*, *25*, 349–380.

Butler, L. C., Lee, H., & Fisher, B. S. (2019). Less safe in the ivory tower: Campus sexual assault policy in the Trump administration. *Victims & Offenders*, *14*(8), 979–996.

Cass, A. I. (2007). Routine activities and sexual assault: An analysis of individual- and school-level factors. *Violence and Victims*, *22*(3), 350–366.

Chouhy, C., Madero-Hernandez, A., & Turanovic, J. J. (2017). The extent, nature, and consequences of school victimization: A review of surveys and recent research. *Victims & Offenders*, 12, 823–844.

Cohen, L. E., & Felson, M. (1979). Social change and crime rate trends: A routine activity approach. *American Sociological Review*, *44*, 588–608.

Cohen, L. E., Kluegel, J. R., & Land, K. C. (1981). Social inequality and predatory criminal victimization: An exposition and test of a formal theory. *American Sociological Review*, 46, 505–524. doi:10.2307/2094935

Coker, A. L., Follingstad, D. R., Bush, H. M., & Fisher, B. S. (2016). Are interpersonal violence rates higher among young women in college compared with those never attending college? *Journal of Interpersonal Violence*, *31*(8), 1413–1429.

Couzens, G. L., Shook-Sa, B., Lee, P., & Berzofsky, M. (2015). *Users' guide to the national Crime Victimization Survey (NCVS) generalized variance functions*. Research Triangle Park, NC: RTI International.

Daigle, L. E., Hoffman, C. Y., & Johnson, L. M. (2018). The extent and risk of violent victimization among international college students enrolled in the United States: A gendered analysis. *Journal of Interpersonal Violence*, *33*(19), 3053–3073.

Finkelhor, D., & Asdigian, N. L. (1996). Risk factors for youth victimization: Beyond a lifestyles/routine activities approach. *Violence and Victims*, 11, 3–19.

Finkelhor, D., Vanderminden, J., Turner, H., Shattuck, A., & Hamby, S. (2016). At-school victimization and violence exposure assessed in a national household survey of children and youth. *Journal of School Violence*, *15*(1), 67–90.

Fisher, B. S., Sloan, J. J., Cullen, F. T., & Lu, C. (1998). Crime in the ivory tower: The level and sources of student victimization. *Criminology*, *36*(3), 671–710.

Fox, J., & Burstein, H. (2010). *Violence and security on campus: From preschool through college*. Santa Barbara, CA: Praeger Publishers.

Fox, J., & Savage, J. (2009). Mass murder goes to college: An examination of changes on college campuses following Virginia Tech. *American Behavioral Scientist*, *52*(10), 1465–1485.

Goldrick-Rab, S., Kelchen, R., Harris, D. N., & Benson, J. (2016). Reducing income inequality in educational attainment: Experimental evidence on the impact of financial aid on college completion. *American Journal of Sociology*, *121*(6), 1762–1817.

Gumbrecht, J. (2012, December 15.) What really makes schools safer? *CNN News*. Retrieved from www.cnn.com/2012/12/15/us/connecticut-school-safety/

Hart, T. C. (2003). *Violent victimization of college students*. Washington, DC: Bureau of Justice Statistics.

Hart, T. C., & Miethe, T. D. (2011). Violence against college students and its situational contexts: Prevalence, patterns, and policy implications. *Victims and Offenders*, *6*(2), 157–180.

Hart, T. C., & Rennison, C. M. (2011). Violent victimization of Hispanic college students: Findings from the National Crime Victimization Survey. *Race and Justice*, *1*, 362–385.

Hindelang, M. J., Gottfredson, M. R., & Garofalo, J. (1978). *Victims of personal crime: An empirical foundation for a theory of personal victimization*. Cambridge, MA: Ballinger.

Hirschi, T. (1969). *Causes of delinquency*. Berkeley, CA: University of California Press.

Hong, J. S., & Espelage, D. L. (2012). A review of research on bullying and peer victimization in school: An ecological system analysis. *Aggression and Violent Behavior*, *17*, 311–322.

Horsley, S. (2018, February 26). Renewing call to arm teachers, Trump tells governors the NRA is 'on Our side'. *NPR*. Retrieved from www.npr.org/2018/02/26/588865775/renewing-call-to-arm-teachers-trump-tells-governors-the-nra-is-on-our-side.

Jensen, G. F., & Brownfield, D. (1986). Gender, lifestyles, and victimization: Beyond routine activity. *Violence and Victims*, *1*, 85–99.

Kruttschnitt C., & Macmillan R. (2006). The violent victimization of women: A life course perspective. In K. Heimer & K. Kruttschnitt (Eds.), *Gender and crime: Patterns in victimization and offending* (pp. 139–170). New York: New York University Press.

Kulig, T. C., Cullen, F. T., Wilcox, P., & Chouhy, C. (2019). Personality and adolescent school-based victimization: do the big five matter? *Journal of School Violence*, *18*(2), 176–199.

Kulig, T. C., Pratt, T. C., Cullen, F. T., Chouhy, C., & Unnever, J. D. (2017). Explaining bullying victimization: Assessing the generality of the low self-control/risky lifestyle model. *Victims & Offenders*, 12, 891–912.

Kupchik, A. (2010). *Homeroom security: School discipline in an age of fear*. New York: New York University Press.

Lauritsen, J. L., & Laub, J. H. (2007). Understanding the link between victimization and offending: New reflections on an old idea. In M. Hough & M. Maxfield (Eds.), *Surveying crime in the 21st century* (Vol. 22, pp. 55–76). Monsey, NY: Criminal Justice Press.

Lauritsen, J. L., Sampson, R. J., & Laub, J. H. (1991). The link between offending and victimization among adolescents. *Criminology*, 29, 265–292.

Macmillan, R. (2001). Violence and the life course: The consequences of victimization for personal and social development. *Annual Review of Sociology*, *27*(1), 1–22.

Mayer, M. J., & Furlong, M. J. (2010). How safe are our schools? *Educational Researcher*, *39*(1), 16–26.

McNeeley, S. (2015). Lifestyle-routine activities and crime events. *Journal of Contemporary Criminal Justice*, *31*, 30–52.

Moffitt, T. E. (1993). Adolescence-limited and life-course-persistent antisocial behavior: A developmental taxonomy. *Psychological Review*, *100*(4), 674–701.

Morgan, R. E., & Oudekerk, B. A. (2019). *Criminal victimization, 2018*. Washington, DC: Bureau of Justice Statistics.

Mustaine, E. E., & Tewksbury, R. (1998). Predicting risks of larceny theft victimization: Routine activity analysis using refined lifestyle measures. *Criminology*, *36*, 829–857.

Musu, L., Zhang, A., Wang, K., Zhang, J., & Oudekerk, B. (2019). *Indicators of school crime and safety: 2018*. Washington, D.C.: National Center for Education Statistics, U.S. Department of Education, and Bureau of Justice Statistics, Office of Justice Programs, U.S. Department of Justice.

Osgood, D. W., Wilson, J. K., O'malley, P. M., Bachman, J. G., & Johnston, L. D. (1996). Routine activities and individual deviant behavior. *American Sociological Review*, *61*, 635–655.

Peguero, A. A. (2009). Opportunity, involvement, and student exposure to school violence. *Youth Violence and Juvenile Justice*, *7*, 299–312.

Peguero, A. A., Popp, A. M., & Koo, D. J. (2011). Race, ethnicity, and school-based adolescent victimization. *Crime & Delinquency*, *61*, 323–349.

Perkins, C. (1997). *Age patterns of victims of serious violent crime*. Washington, DC: Bureau of Justice Statistics.

Peterson, S., Lasky, N. V., Fisher, B. S., & Wilcox, P. (2018). Gendered opportunity and school-based victimization: An integrated approach. *Youth Violence and Juvenile Justice*, *16*, 137–155.

Popp, A. M., & Peguero, A. A. (2011). Routine activities and victimization at school: The significance of gender. *Journal of Interpersonal Violence*, *26*(12), 2413–2436.

Reinhart, R. J. (2018, January 23). In the news: School shootings. *Gallup*. Retrieved from https://news.gallup.com/poll/226202/news-school-shootings.aspx

Rennison, C. M. (2014, December 22). Privilege, among rape victims who suffers most from rape and sexual assault in America? *New York Times*. Retrieved from www.nytimes.com/2014/12/22/opinion/who-suffers-most-from-rape-and-sexual-assault-in-america.html.

Rennison, C. M., & Addington, L. A. (2014). Violence against college women: A review to identify limitations in defining the problem and inform future research. *Trauma, Violence and Abuse*, 15(3), 159–169.

Rennison, C. M., & Rand, M. (2007). Introduction to the National Crime Victimization Survey. In J. P. Lynch & L. A. Addington (Eds.), *Understanding crime statistics: Revisiting the divergence of the NCVS and UCR* (pp. 17–54). New York: Cambridge University Press.

Rochman, B. (2012, December 18). School security: Why it's so hard to keep kids safe. *Time Magazine*. Retrieved from http://healthland.time.com/2012/12/18/school-security-why-its-so-hard-to-keep-kids-safe/.

Sampson, R. J., & Laub, J. H. (1993). *Crime in the making: Pathways and turning points through life*. Cambridge, MA: Harvard University Press.

Schreck, C. J., Miller, J. M., & Gibson, C. L. (2003). Trouble in the school yard: A study of the risk factors of victimization at school. *Crime & Delinquency*, *49*(3), 460–484.

Shook-Sa, B., Couzens, G. L., & Berzofsky, M. (2014). *User's guide to National Crime Victimization Survey (NCVS) direct variance estimation*. Retrieved from www.bjs.gov/content/pub/pdf/NCVS_Variance_User_Guide%2011.06.14.pdf

Sinozich, S., & Langton, L. (2014). *Rape and sexual assault victimization among college-age females, 1995–2013*. Washington, DC: Bureau of Justice Statistics.

Tillyer, M. S. (2014). Violent victimization across the life course: Moving a "victim careers" agenda forward. *Criminal Justice and Behavior*, 41(5), 593–612.

Truman, J. (2011). *Criminal victimization, 2010*. Washington, DC: Bureau of Justice Statistics.

Turanovic, J. J., Hall, E., & Street, S. C. (2018). Toward a life-course theory of victimization. In *Criminology and public policy* (pp. 85–103). Temple University Press.

Turanovic, J. J., Pratt, T. C., & Piquero, A. R. (2018). Structural constraints, risky lifestyles, and repeat victimization. *Journal of Quantitative Criminology*, 34, 251–274.

Turner, H. A., Finkelhor, D., Hamby, S. L., Shattuck, A., & Ormrod, R. K. (2011). Specifying type and location of peer victimization in a national sample of children and youth. *Journal of Youth and Adolescence*, *40*(8), 1052–1067.

Viren (2020). The Accusations Were Lies. But Could We Prove It? *New York Times Magazine*. nytimes.com/2020/03/18/magazine/title-ix-sexual-harassment-accusations.html

Wilcox, P., & Cullen, F. T. (2018). Situational opportunity theories of crime. *Annual Review of Criminology*, 1, 123–148. doi:10.1146/annurev-criminol-032317-092421

Wilcox, P., Tillyer, M. S., & Fisher, B. S. (2009). Gendered opportunity? School-based adolescent victimization. *Journal of Research in Crime and Delinquency*, *46*, 245–269.

Wolniak, G. C., Wells, R. S., Engberg, M. E., & Manly, C. A. (2016). College enhancement strategies and socioeconomic inequality. *Research in Higher Education*, *57*(3), 310–334.

Yoffe, E. (2014, December). The college rape overcorrection. *Slate*. Retrieved from www.slate.com/articles/double_x/doublex/2014/12/college_rape_campus_sexual_assault_is_a_serious_problem_but_the_efforts.html.

# Part III

## New Theoretical Applications

# 9

# Biosocial Perspectives on Victimization

*Kevin M. Beaver and Bridget Joyner*

During the past decade or so, there has been a tremendous amount of criminological research examining the genetic architecture to antisocial behaviors (Eley, Lichtenstein, & Moffitt, 2003; Moffitt, 2005; Tuvblad & Beaver, 2013). The results generated from this body of scholarship—frequently referred to as biosocial criminology—have converged to show that the behavioral outcomes studied by criminologists—such as crime, delinquency, violence, aggression, and drug use—are all under substantial genetic influence (Boisvert, Wright, Knopik, & Vaske, 2012; Tuvblad & Baker, 2011; Verweij et al., 2010). At the same time, some of the most potent criminogenic traits, including low self-control and psychopathy, also have a strong genetic component to them (Beaver, Wright, DeLisi, & Vaughn, 2008; Waldman, Rhee, LoParo, & Park, 2018). Indeed, across outcomes, studies have consistently revealed that about one-half of the variance is attributable to genetic influences (Polderman et al., 2015). This genetic effect is so robust that most other fields of study consider it a "fact" and thus have moved on to more complex questions regarding the etiology of human phenotypes (Turkheimer, 2000).

Criminologists, however, have been slow to accept the results of thousands of studies showing a genetic effect. They have been even slower to modify their theories and methodologies to account for genetic influences (Ellis & Walsh, 1999). Moreover, there have even been calls—published in the discipline's flagship journal—to *ban* criminological studies from using certain types of genetic methodologies (Barnes et al., 2014b; Moffitt & Beckley, 2015), despite the fact that these methodologies have been employed in thousands of studies and have been shown to produce highly accurate and replicable results (Barnes, Boutwell, Beaver, Gibson, & Wright, 2014a; Moffitt & Beckley, 2015). The end result of such antagonism toward, and censorship of, genetic research in criminology is that the application of genetic research to other outcomes has been somewhat stifled. One line of inquiry that has not been fully explored—either empirically or theoretically—is the role that genetics might play in the creation of personal victimization.

With that said, it is important to note that while there has been an emerging number of studies exploring the genetics–victimization nexus (Beaver, Boutwell, Barnes, & Cooper, 2009), there has been very limited systematic effort to understand this potential connection. The current chapter is designed to help address this gap in the victimology literature. Toward this end, the chapter is organized into three key components. First, since most criminologists lack an understanding of behavioral genetics, we provide an introduction to behavioral genetics, including some of the main methodologies that are used and the key findings to emerge from this body of work. Second, we discuss the main results of studies examining the genetic basis to victimization. Third, we describe the ways in which genetic research on victimology could be integrated into existing theories and explanations of victimization.

## Behavioral Genetics

Behavioral genetic research is interested in estimating the proportion of phenotypic variance (e.g., variance in personality traits or behavioral patterns) that is accounted for by genetic influences and environmental factors (Plomin, DeFries, McClearn, & McGuffin, 2008). The proportion of variance that is accounted for by genetic variance is known as heritability and heritability estimates range between .00 and 1.00. A heritability estimate of .00 would mean that zero (0) percent of the variance is accounted for by genetic influences whereas a heritability estimate of 1.00 would mean that 100 percent of the variance is accounted for by genetic influences. Although heritability estimates appear relatively straightforward to interpret, they are often interpreted incorrectly or viewed in a distorted way. To begin with, heritability estimates do not apply to individuals, but rather are mathematically designed to explain variance generated from a sample. So, trying to extrapolate a heritability estimate to an individual (e.g., Why did Ted Bundy become a serial killer?) is misguided and erroneous. Knowing, for example, that a heritability estimate is .40 for a specific behavior does not mean that 40 percent of the reason why a particular individual engaged in that behavior was due to their genes. In addition, heritability estimates are often interpreted as some fixed value that is immutable. This simply is not the case. Heritability estimates can—and do—ebb and flow over time, across places, and in response to different environmental stimuli (Bergen, Gardner, & Kendler, 2007). Taken together, heritability estimates do not represent a constant and deterministic value, but rather apply only to the sample-level variance of the measure being studied.

All too frequently, social scientists view behavioral genetic research as focusing exclusively on genetic influences and ignoring the potential contributors of environmental factors. Even a cursory understanding of heritability and heritability estimates quickly dispels this myth. After all, the proportion of variance that is not accounted for by genetics has to be accounted for by environmental factors (and/or error). As long as the heritability estimate is below 1.00, then the environmental estimate would be greater than .00. Environmental estimates are interpreted the same way as heritability estimates except that they capture the proportion of variance accounted for by environmental factors.

Unlike most social science research, including the vast majority of criminological and victimization research, behavioral genetic research divides environmental influences into two components: a shared environmental component and a nonshared environmental component (Beaver, 2019). Shared environments are environments that are the same among siblings from the same household and that make them similar to each other. Examples of some shared environments would be family-wide parenting techniques, socio-economic status, and even shared peer groups. Nonshared environments, in contrast, are environments that are dissimilar among siblings from the same household and that make siblings different from each other. Some common examples of nonshared environments are unique parent–child relationships, prenatal influences, and exposure to different friendship networks. Together, shared environmental influences and nonshared environmental influences account for 100 percent of environmental influences on phenotypic variance (Plomin et al., 2008).

Heritability, shared environmental, and nonshared environmental estimates can provide some important insight into the biosocial underpinnings to human phenotypes. But the question remains: How is it possible to generate these genetic and environmental estimates? While there are a number of methodologies that can be employed, the most commonly used approach is known as the twin-based methodology. The twin-based methodology relies on comparing monozygotic (MZ) twins to dizygotic (DZ) twins. MZ twins are identical twins who share 100 percent of their genetic material whereas DZ twins share, on average, 50 percent of their distinguishing DNA and thus are just as genetically similar as regular biological siblings. The environments between twins from MZ twin pairs and twins from DZ twins, however, should be relatively equal. In other words, twins and co-twins from MZ twin pairs should experience environments that are no more similar to each other than the environments experienced by twins and co-twins from DZ twin pairs. This assumption is known as the equal environment assumption (EEA). As long as the EEA is not violated—and there is extensive evidence to suggest that it is upheld (e.g. Barnes et al., 2014b; Cronk et al., 2002; Felson, 2012; Felson, 2014)—then the only reason that MZ twins should be more similar to each other than DZ twins is because they share twice as much genetic material. Employing this logic, it is easy to see that heritability estimates can be garnered by comparing twins and co-twins from MZ twin pairs to twins and co-twins from DZ twin pairs. If MZ twins are more similar (on whatever measure is being investigated) than DZ twins, then genetic influences, to some extent, are at play. And, as MZ twins become more similar to each other relative to DZ twins, the genetic effect (i.e., heritability) becomes larger. Overall, the twin-based approach is the most frequently used behavioral genetic research design and it has been used in thousands of studies to examine the genetic and environmental influences on virtually every measurable human characteristic (Polderman et al., 2015).

In addition to the twin-based methodology, another methodological approach that has been used to estimate genetic and environmental contributors to phenotypic variance is the adoption-based research design. The logic of the adoption-based method is relatively straightforward: If a child is adopted at birth and has no contact with their biological parents, then the only reason that they should be phenotypically similar to their biological parents is because of the genetic material that they share with them. In contrast, if the adoptive parents are not biologically related to the adopted child, then the only reason that the adoptee should be phenotypically similar to their adoptive parents is because of environmental influences. The adoption research design, while not as widely used as the twin-based research design, has been employed quite frequently to examine the genetic and environmental basis to a broad range of personality and behavioral outcomes (see Polderman et al., 2015).

One of the concerns with adoption-based methodologies and, although to a lesser extent, with twin-based methodologies, is that the results generated from such studies may not be generalizable to samples of non-adoptees and non-twins. Although there is research indicating that, at least for twins, there are no appreciable differences between them and regular siblings (Barnes & Boutwell, 2013), nonetheless this does remain a key concern with research using such genetically informative designs. Fortunately, there is yet another research design that can be used to estimate genetic and environmental influences on phenotypes that does not rely exclusively on twins or adoptees. This alternative research design is often referred to as a blended-family research design. The blended-family design is based on samples that consist of any type of sibling pair, such as full biological siblings, half siblings, biologically unrelated siblings (e.g., stepsiblings), cousins, as well as twins or any other type of sibling. By using a blended-family design, the concern of non-generalizability with only analyzing twins or adoptees becomes a non-issue. The results based on these blended-family designs could, depending on the sampling procedure, be generalizable to all sibling pairs. While this represents a key advantage over twin or adoption research designs, there are limitations with the blended-family design. One of the key concerns is that since the siblings being compared (to estimate heritability) are often of different ages, and thus may experience events at different ages, then this might be akin to comparing apples and oranges (unlike the comparison of twins which represents a clean, apples-to-apples comparison). The end result might be inaccurate and somewhat biased estimates of genetic and environmental influences. While it is possible to statistically account for such differences that exist between siblings, these sibling differences still represents the key concern with using blended-family designs. However, it is worth noting that studies analyzing blended-family samples have revealed heritability estimates that are consistent with those from twin- and adoption-based research (Plomin et al., 2008).

These three research designs are used in the overwhelming majority of all behavioral genetic research. At the same time, however, each of these three methodological approaches has its own unique limitations that may affect the estimates for heritability, shared environmental, and nonshared environmental influences. What is salient to recognize, though, is that the limitations of each methodology do not cut across all of the methodologies. As a result, it is possible to compare genetic and environmental estimates for each of the methodologies to determine whether such estimates converge or whether they vary considerably. If the estimates converge across methodologies, then the limitations of each methodology are unlikely driving the results. In contrast, if the estimates vary widely across methodologies, then there is a considerable possibility that the estimates are a function of the methodology (and the limitations inherently built into it).

## Genetic Foundation to Victimization

Thousands of studies that have examined hundreds of thousands of sibling pairs have been published to estimate the genetic and environmental underpinnings to human phenotypes (Polderman et al., 2015). The results generated from these studies have converged to show that approximately 50 percent of the variance in most human traits is due to genetic factors (Polderman et al., 2015). The remaining 50 percent of the variance is attributable to the environment, but what is interesting is that the shared environment and the nonshared environment have very different influences (Harris, 1998). The shared environment typically accounts for between 0 and 20 percent of the variance, with its effects being stronger early in life and waning in influence in adulthood. The nonshared environment, however, tends to have much stronger and more robust influence, and accounts for around 40 to 60 percent of the variance (Bezdjian, Baker, & Tuvblad, 2011; Rhee & Waldman, 2002). Bear in mind, though, that the effects of error are included in the nonshared environmental estimate so the "environmental" component captured by the nonshared environmental component is likely upwardly biased.

These results have been generated for behaviors and traits that have direct application to crime, delinquency, and violence. To illustrate, genetic influences have been found to account for about 50 percent of the variance in measures of antisocial behaviors and traits (Polderman et al., 2015). And, the more serious and violent the offense and the offender, the stronger the genetic influence (Barnes, Beaver, & Boutwell, 2011; Mason & Frick, 1994). In terms of environmental influences, one of the more surprising results to emerge from this body of literature is that the shared environment tends to account for very little of the variance in antisocial behaviors (Rhee & Waldman, 2002). Early in life and into adolescence, shared environmental influences tend to have their strongest effect, but by the time adulthood rolls around the shared environmental effect has been consistently found to be zero. Nonshared environments, however, have been found to account for around 50 percent of the variance in antisocial behaviors, with the effect becoming stronger throughout the life course (Beaver, 2019; Lyons et al., 1995).

Although the interest in understanding the genetic foundation to antisocial behaviors has grown exponentially during the past couple of decades, only relatively recently has there been much interest in examining the genetic structure of victimization. During a relatively short period of time, there has been quite a bit of literature that has examined genetic and environmental influences on various issues related to victimization. To begin with, there is emerging evidence indicating that adolescent victimization is not uniformly distributed across families, but rather concentrates within families. One study, for instance, revealed that 5 percent of all families account for somewhere between 38 and 57 percent of all victimization experiences, and 10 percent of families account for between 54 and 79 percent of all victimization experiences (Rima, Yerbol, Adlet, Sholpan, & Beaver, 2019). Nearly 100 percent of all adolescent victimization was attributable to 25 percent of all families. Having a sibling who was victimized increased significantly the odds that their co-sibling would be victimized, too.

The results of this study provide some preliminary evidence that victimization is not randomly distributed across households and that there are certain factors that make victimization more common in some families than in others. Even so, the nonrandom distribution of victimization across families does not provide any information as to whether genetic or environmental processes are at play. In order to address this question, we next turn to the results of studies that estimated the genetic and environmental influences on victimization by using the twin-based methodology. The results generated from these studies have tended to show that genetic factors are involved in the production of adolescent victimization. While the estimates vary somewhat from study-to-study, overall the heritability of victimization tends to fall in line with the heritability of most other human phenotypes and hovers around 40 to 50 percent (Beaver, Boutwell et al., 2009). It is important to note, moreover, that the adoption-based methodology has also been used to examine the genetic origins of victimization and the results have largely paralleled the results of twin-based studies (Beaver, Boutwell, Barnes, DeLisi, & Vaughn, 2013). Keep in mind, however, that there is a limited amount of research estimating the heritability of victimization and most of this research is drawn from a sample of US adolescents.

Other types of victimization, however, may be less heritable than adolescent victimization. Hines and Saudino (2004) addressed this possibility by examining the genetic and environmental influences on being a victim of psychological aggression and physical aggression when the perpetrator was an intimate partner. The results of their behavioral genetic models revealed that 25 percent of the variance in being the victim of psychological aggression was due to genetic factors and 15 percent of the variance in being the victim of physical aggression was due to genetic factors (Hines & Saudino, 2004). These heritability estimates are obviously much lower when compared to those generated for adolescent victimization. There are three points to bear in mind, however. First, the variance estimates (including heritability estimates) from behavioral genetic studies tend to have relatively large confidence intervals. As a result, the heritability estimates from this study might not be all that different from other studies. Second, this study has yet to be replicated so whether these same results would form a pattern that is robust across studies remains undetermined at this point. Third, it is quite possible that intimate partner victimization, and other types of victimization, may have different genetic etiologies underlying them. If this is the case, then it would be expected to see heritability estimates ebb and flow across different types of victimization.

Taken together, the available evidence indicates that various forms of victimization are influenced by genetic factors, at least to some degree. As a consequence, more recent research has moved beyond univariate models (wherein variance is decomposed into genetic and environmental influences for a single variable) into more advanced behavioral genetic modeling approaches that are able to address more complex issues related to the nexus between genetics and victimization. One of the key approaches that has been used in this body of work is by extending the univariate twin model into a bivariate twin model. Unlike univariate models that focus on decomposing variance in a single measure, bivariate models decompose the covariance between two measures. Just as the variance in univariate models is divided into three components (i.e., heritability, shared environmental, and nonshared environmental), the covariance in bivariate models is divided into the same three components. The resulting values for these three components indicate the percentage of covariance that is due to genetic and environmental influences.

One of the first studies to use bivariate modeling and apply it to victimization examined whether repeat victimization in adolescence (i.e., the covariance between victimization measured at two time points) was due to genetic influences (Beaver, Shutt et al., 2009). The results of these bivariate models revealed that genetic factors accounted for 64 percent of the variance in repeat victimization. The remaining 36 percent of the variance was attributable to the nonshared environment (and error). None of the variance in repeat victimization was accounted for by shared environmental influences.

Another key area where bivariate modeling has been used in victimization research pertains to the genetic architecture of the victim–offender overlap. In this line of research bivariate models are applied to examine the genetic structure of the covariance between a measure of offending and a measure of victimization. The results generated from these studies have suggested that between 20 and 98 percent of the covariance between victims and offenders is attributable to genetic factors (Barnes & Beaver, 2012; Vaske, Boisvert, & Wright, 2012). While these are the only studies to examine the genetics of the victim-offender overlap, they should provide reason for scholars to begin to consider the role that genetic influences play in accounting for certain phenomenon related to victimization and should inspire future victimology research with such an approach. Indeed, scholars have begun to take this possibility more seriously and have applied bivariate modeling strategies to other areas of victimization research. For example, genetic influences have been detected on the covariance between victimization and delinquency as well as depression (Connolly & Beaver, 2016; Kavish, Connolly, & Boutwell, 2019), attachment anxiety (Barbaro, Boutwell, & Shackelford, 2019), and intelligence (Boutwell et al., 2017). Perhaps if more research was conducted using both univariate and bivariate modeling strategies, a much more comprehensive understanding of the link between genetics and victimization would be realized.

## Integration of Genetics into Theories of Victimization

The results generated from behavioral genetics research are instructive in detailing the relative influence of genetics and environments on phenotypic variance, but these studies do not necessarily reveal anything about the processes involved in creating genetic and/or environmental influences. In order to understand the processes at play in producing victimization, the results of behavioral genetic research need to be interpreted in the context of victimization theories. Existing victimization theories and explanations, however, do not focus on genetics, thus raising the following concern: If genes are consistently found to be related to personal victimization but existing theories of victimization ignore such genetic influences, then should all existing theories of victimization be abandoned as they do not comport with the findings from existing studies? No, this would be akin to "throwing out the baby with the bathwater," as many existing victimization theories are actually compatible with the results generated from behavioral genetic research. Below we provide a relatively brief overview of how the findings from behavioral genetic research could be integrated into three groups of victimization theories.

First, and most straightforward, in recent years propensity-based theories of victimization have gained significant traction and have been the source of a considerable amount of research. For example, studies have examined whether traits, such as low levels of self-control, are linked to the probability of being victimized (Higgins, Jennings, Tewksbury, & Gibson, 2009; Schreck, 1999; Schreck, Wright, & Miller, 2002; Turanovic, Reisig, & Pratt, 2015). The results of such studies have revealed that persons who score high on such traits are at considerably greater risk for being victimized when compared to persons who score relatively lower on such traits. At the same time, there is a voluminous body of research showing that almost all personality traits—especially criminogenic traits, such as a lack of self-regulation—are under significant genetic influence (Beaver, DeLisi, Vaughn, Wright, & Boutwell, 2008; Beaver, Shutt et al., 2009; Beaver, Wright et al., 2008; Polderman et al., 2015; Willems, Boesen, Finkenauer, & Bartels, 2019). Following this logic, genetic influences on the risk for victimization would not operate directly, but rather indirectly via the effects that they have on traits that have been tied to victimization.

Second, environmental explanations of victimization have been among the most dominant explanations from which to understand and explain all types of victimization. These theories identify environments that increase the likelihood of victimization, such as residing in a high-crime neighborhood, involvement in certain lifestyles, and being embedded in criminal social networks (Browning & Erickson, 2009; Jiang, Yu, Zhang, Bao, & Zhu, 2016; Nofziger, 2009). Although these explanations may seem to be at odds with genetic influences as they tend to focus almost exclusively on environmental factors, there is actually good reason to suspect that they are compatible with the results of behavioral genetic research. To understand how this is the case, it is first imperative to recognize that there is a large body of behavioral genetic research that has used the twin-based methodology to estimate genetic influences on measures of the environment (Kendler & Baker, 2007; Plomin, Reiss, Hetherington, & Howe, 1994). The process and logic to estimate genetic influences on environmental variance is the exact same as when estimating genetic influences on behavioral phenotypes; the only difference is that the variance in environmental measures (as opposed to behavioral or personality measures) is decomposed into a genetic component, a shared environmental component, and a nonshared environmental component. An exhaustive literature review of studies that estimated genetic influences on environments was conducted and revealed that virtually all environments are under some level of genetic influence (Kendler & Baker, 2007). It is important to note, though, that the average genetic effect size was about .25 for all environments. Given that genetic effects are detected on environmental measures, this leaves open the possibility that genetic influences on victimization may be produced via the effects that genes have on structuring exposure to environments that increase the probability of victimization.

Third, and finally, genetic research findings can be synthesized with explanations of victimization that focus on the consistent finding that victims are not always innocent bystanders who are attacked randomly. Rather, there is an abundance of research showing victims often play an active role in producing their own victimization (Wolfgang, 1957). For example, there is a significant degree of overlap between criminal offenders and victimization, with offenders being significantly more likely to be victimized than non-offenders. Ethnographic research has made clear that offenders often are in close proximity to other offenders and take advantage of opportunities to exploit and victimize them, particularly when it comes to robbery and burglary (Wright & Decker, 1994, 1997, 2002). This same process appears to be at play in violent types of victimization, too. In what has become known as victim-precipitated homicide, homicide victims often are part of a transactional process, wherein they may provoke the perpetrator or be involved in some type of illegal or aggressive behavior that culminates in a murder (Luckenbill, 1977; Wolfgang, 1957).

Given that criminal, delinquent, violent, and aggressive behaviors have all been found to be quite heritable, with estimates ranging from around .50 to greater than .70 (Barnes et al., 2011; Burt, 2009; Mason &

Frick, 1994), it stands to reason that genetic influences may operate on victimization via the effects they have on structuring involvement in antisocial behaviors. The end result is that genetic influences are detected on victimization because of the effects that genes have on engaging in behaviors that increase the propensity for victimization. This is precisely what has been borne out empirically in previous behavioral genetic research (Barnes & Beaver, 2012).

Findings generated from behavioral genetic research may, at first glance, appear to be incongruent with theories and explanations of victimization. Upon further evaluation, though, it is clear that these findings could easily be integrated into certain victimization theories. Moreover, such integration would likely result in more precise and accurate theories indicating who is most likely to be victimized, under what conditions they will likely be victimized, and even how victimization unfolds. To date, however, there has not been a systematic and concerted effort to empirically evaluate the veracity of specific predictions regarding the link between genetics and victimization. Future research should move beyond decomposing variance in victimization measures or covariance between victimization and other measures and begin to more systematically examine genetics in the context of victimization theories and explanations.

## Future Directions and Conclusions

Understanding the causes of victimization is key to developing programs that might be able to limit victimization and equip people with the knowledge that could possibly reduce their individual propensity for being victimized. Although significant inroads have been made in understanding the etiology of victimization (Felson, 2002; Felson, 2006; Gottfredson, 1973), there still remains much that is unknown about the causes of personal victimization (Beaver, Boutwell et al., 2009). One area that has received relatively little attention is the genetics of victimization. As this chapter has shown, though, the available evidence indicates that victimization is under some level of genetic influence. Estimates from behavioral genetic studies show that victimization is likely around .50. Moreover, the covariance between victimization and some of the main covariates of victimization, such as being a criminal offender, has been shown to be driven partially by genetic influences. Taken together, there is clear evidence that victimization is governed, at least in part, by genetic influences, but most victimization research ignores the potential role of genetics.

Against this backdrop, we note three future directions of victimization research. First, most of the existing literature on the genetics of victimization has come from a single sample (i.e., National Longitudinal Study of Adolescent to Adult Health [Add Health]). As a result, more research is needed to ensure that the genetic results related to victimization are not unique to this sample, but rather are consistently detected across heterogeneous samples. With that said, these results converge with heritability estimates for virtually every other human phenotype (Polderman et al., 2015). Even so, replication is key to the scientific enterprise and thus it would be prudent to ensure that these genetic effects on victimization are reproducible in other samples.

Second, victimization research needs to begin to consistently take into account genetic influences. As studies have shown, failure to account for genetic influences produces studies that are misspecified, inaccurate, and sometimes completely wrong (Barnes et al., 2014a; Harden, Mendle, Hill, Turkheimer, & Emery, 2008; Haynie & McHugh, 2003). Victimization research can avoid these methodological pitfalls by simply analyzing samples that allow for the modeling of genetic influences (e.g., using twin-based sample, adoption research designs, blended-family designs, etc.).

Third, there needs to be a more concerted effort to integrate genetic influences into existing theories and then to test the propositions of such theories. Currently, behavioral genetic research that focuses on victimization is largely atheoretical and/or does not test precise hypotheses linking genetics to victimization. Instead, to date such research has focused mainly on (1) establishing the heritability of victimization and (2) estimating whether the covariance between victimization and certain covariates is accounted for by genetic influences. To move beyond simple descriptive values, there needs to be a concern with understanding the complex processes that are at play in linking genetics to victimization. This can only be accomplished through the refinement of theories to explicitly account for genetic influences.

In closing, we would like to point out that genetic explanations for human outcomes can be quite controversial, especially when they focus on negative outcomes, such as crime and delinquency (Beaver, 2019; Heylen, Pauwels, Beaver, & Ruffinengo, 2015). Genetic explanations of victimization are likely no different as they can easily lead to accusations of "blaming the victim" or, more precisely in this case, "blaming the victim's genes." Of course, explanations and theories are designed to explain some phenomenon, not to justify it or to lay the burden of responsibility on a particular person, such as the victim. Genes are only one potential causal agent in the explanation of victimization, just as are environmental factors, personality traits, and routine activities. Genes are not deterministic nor are they fatalistic; rather, they are probabilistic. They may increase or decrease a person's chances of being victimized, but they certainly do not predict with 100 percent accuracy who will and who will not be victimized. And, moreover, genetic effects (i.e., heritability) do not represent fixed, immutable values that do not change. Genetic effects can change over time, across space, and in response to different environments. If we were able to understand precisely how genes intersect with these moderating factors, then perhaps we would be in a better position to be able to reduce victimization and make society a safer place.

## References

Barbaro, N., Boutwell, B. B., & Shackelford, T. K. (2019). Associations between attachment anxiety and intimate partner violence perpetration and victimization: Consideration of genetic covariation. *Personality and Individual Differences*, *147*, 332–343.

Barnes, J. C., & Beaver, K. M. (2012). Extending research on the victim-offender overlap: Evidence from a genetically informative analysis. *Journal of Interpersonal Violence*, *27*, 3299–3321.

Barnes, J. C., Beaver, K. M., & Boutwell, B. B. (2011). Examining the genetic underpinnings to Moffitt's developmental taxonomy: A behavioral genetic analysis. *Criminology*, *49*, 923–954.

Barnes, J. C., & Boutwell, B. B. (2013). A demonstration of the generalizability of twin-based research on antisocial behavior. *Behavior Genetics*, *43*, 120–131.

Barnes, J. C., Boutwell, B. B., Beaver, K. M., Gibson, C. L., & Wright, J. P. (2014a). On the consequences of ignoring genetic influences in criminological research. *Journal of Criminal Justice*, *42*, 471–482.

Barnes, J. C., Wright, J. P., Boutwell, B. B., Schwartz, J. A., Connolly, E. J., Nedelec, J. L., & Beaver, K. M. (2014b). Demonstrating the validity of twin research in criminology. *Criminology*, *52*, 588–626.

Beaver, K. M. (2019). *Biosocial criminology: A primer* (4th ed.). Dubuque: Kendal Hunt Publishing Company.

Beaver, K. M., Boutwell, B. B., Barnes, J. C., & Cooper, J. A. (2009). The biosocial underpinnings to adolescent victimization: Results from a longitudinal sample of twins. *Youth Violence and Juvenile Justice*, *7*, 223–238.

Beaver, K. M., Boutwell, B. B., Barnes, J. C., DeLisi, M., & Vaughn, M. G. (2013). Exploring the genetic origins of adolescent victimization in a longitudinal sample of adoptees. *Victims and Offenders*, *8*, 148–163.

Beaver, K. M., DeLisi, M., Vaughn, M. G., Wright, J. P., & Boutwell, B. B. (2008). The relationship between self-control and language: Evidence of a shared etiological pathway. *Criminology*, *46*, 939–970.

Beaver, K. M., Shutt, J. E., Boutwell, B. B., Ratchford, M., Roberts, K., & Barnes, J. C. (2009). Genetic and environmental influences on levels of self-control and delinquent peer association. *Criminal Justice and Behavior*, *36*, 41–60.

Beaver, K. M., Wright, J. P., DeLisi, M., & Vaughn, M. G. (2008). Genetic influences on the stability of low self-control: Results from a longitudinal sample of twins. *Journal of Criminal Justice*, *36*, 478–485.

Bergen, S. E., Gardner, C. O., & Kendler, K. S. (2007). Age-related changes in heritability of behavioral phenotypes over adolescence and young adulthood: A meta-analysis. *Twin Research and Human Genetics*, *10*, 423–433.

Bezdjian, S., Baker, L. A., & Tuvblad, C. (2011). Genetic and environmental influences on impulsivity: A meta-analysis of twin, family, and adoption studies. *Clinical Psychology Review*, *31*, 1209–1223.

Boisvert, D., Wright, J. P., Knopik, V., & Vaske, J. (2012). Genetic and environmental overlap between low self-control and delinquency. *Journal of Quantitative Criminology*, *28*, 477–507.

Boutwell, B. B., Connolly, E. J., Barbaro, N., Shackelford, T. K., Petkovsek, M., & Beaver, K. M. (2017). On the genetic and environmental reasons why intelligence correlates with criminal victimization. *Intelligence*, *62*, 155–166.

Browning, S. & Erickson, P. (2009). Neighborhood disadvantage, alcohol use, and violent victimization. *Youth Violence and Juvenile Justice*, *7*, 331–349.

Burt, S. A. (2009). Are there meaningful etiological differences within antisocial behavior? Results of a meta-analysis. *Clinical Psychology Review*, *29*, 163–178.

Connolly, E. J., & Beaver, K. M. (2016). Considering the genetic and environmental overlap between bullying victimization, delinquency, and symptoms of depression/anxiety. *Journal of Interpersonal Violence*, *31*, 1230–1256.

Cronk, N. J., Slutske, W. S., Madden, P. A. F., Bucholz, K. K., Reich, W., & Heath, A. C. (2002). Emotional and behavioral problems among female twins: An evaluation of the equal environments assumption. *Journal of the American Academy of Child & Adolescent Psychiatry*, *41*, 829–837.

Eley, T. C., Lichtenstein, P., & Moffitt, T. E. (2003). A longitudinal behavioral genetic analysis of the etiology of aggressive and nonaggressive antisocial behavior. *Development and Psychopathology*, *15*, 383–402.

Ellis, L., & Walsh, A. (1999). Criminologists' opinion about causes and theories of crime. *The Criminologist*, *24*, 1–6.

Felson, J. (2012). *What can we learn from the twin studies? An evaluation of the equal environments assumption.* New York: Mellen Press.

Felson, J. (2014). What can we learn from twin studies? A comprehensive evaluation of the equal environments assumption. *Social Science Research*, *43*, 184–199.

Felson, M. (2002). *Crime and everyday life* (3rd ed.). Thousand Oaks: Sage.

Felson, M. (2006). *Crime and nature.* Thousand Oaks: Sage.

Gottfredson, M. R. (1973). On the etiology of criminal victimization. *The Journal of Criminal Law and Criminology*, *72*, 714–726.

Harden, K. P., Mendle, J., Hill, J. E., Turkheimer, E., & Emery, R. E. (2008). Rethinking timing of first sex and delinquency. *Journal of Youth and Adolescence*, *37*, 373–385.

Harris, J. R. (1998). *The nurture assumption: Why children turn out the way they do.* New York, NY: The Free Press.

Haynie, D. L., & McHugh, S. (2003). Sibling deviance: In the shadows of mutual and unique friendship effects? *Criminology*, *41*, 355–392.

Heylen, B., Pauwels, L. J. R., Beaver, K. M., & Ruffinengo, M. (2015). Defending biosocial criminology: On the discursive style of our critics, the separation of ideology and science, and a biologically informed defense of fundamental values. *Journal of Theoretical and Philosophical Criminology*, *7*, 83–95.

Higgins, G. E., Jennings, W. G., Tewksbury, R., & Gibson, C. L. (2009). Exploring the link between low self-control and violent victimization trajectories in adolescents. *Criminal Justice and Behavior*, *36*, 1070–1084.

Hines, D. A., & Saudino, K. J. (2004). Genetic and environmental influences on intimate partner aggression: A preliminary study. *Violence and Victims*, *19*, 701–718.

Jiang, Y., Yu, C., Zhang, W., Bao, Z., & Zhu, J. (2016). Peer victimization and substance use in early adolescence: Influences of deviant peer affiliation and parental knowledge. *Journal of Child and Family Studies*, *25*, 2130–2140.

Kavish, N., Connolly, E. J., & Boutwell, B. B. (2019). Genetic and environmental contributions to the association between violent victimization and major depressive disorder. *Personality and Individual Differences*, *140*, 103–110.

Kendler, K. S., & Baker, J. H. (2007). Genetic influences on measures of the environment: A systematic review. *Psychological Medicine*, *37*, 615–626.

Luckenbill, D. F. (1977). Criminal homicide as a situated transaction. *Social Problems*, *25*, 176–186.

Lyons, M. J., True, W. R., Eisen, S. A., Goldberg, J., Meyer, J. M., Faraone, S. V., … Tsuang, M. T. (1995). Differential heritability of adult and juvenile antisocial traits. *Archives of General Psychiatry*, *52*, 906–915.

Mason, D. A., & Frick, P. J. (1994). The heritability of antisocial behavior: A meta-analysis of twin and adoption studies. *Journal of Psychopathology and Behavioral Assessment*, *16*, 301–323.

Moffitt, T. E. (2005). Genetic and environmental influences on antisocial behaviors: Evidence from behavioral-genetic research. *Advances in Genetics*, *55*, 41–104.

Moffitt, T. E., & Beckley, A. (2015). Abandon twin research? Embrace epigenetic research? Premature advice for criminologists. *Criminology*, *53*, 121–126.

Nofziger, S. (2009). Deviant lifestyles and violent victimization at school. *Journal of Interpersonal Violence*, *24*, 1494–1517.

Plomin, R., DeFries, J. C., McClearn, G. E., & McGuffin, P. (2008). *Behavioral genetics* (5th ed.). New York, NY: Worth Publishers.

Plomin, R., Reiss, D., Hetherington, E. M., & Howe, G. (1994). Nature and nurture: Genetic contributions to measures of the family environment. *Developmental Psychology*, *30*, 32–43.

Polderman, T. J. C., Benyamin, B., de Leeuw, C. A., Sullivan, P. F., van Bochoven, A., Visscher, P. M., & Posthuma, D. (2015). Meta-analysis of the heritability of human traits based on fifty years of twin studies. *Nature Genetics*, *47*, 702–709.

Rhee, S. H., & Waldman, I. D. (2002). Genetic and environmental influences on antisocial behavior: A meta-analysis of twin and adoption studies. *Psychological Bulletin*, *128*, 490–529.

Rima, D., Yerbol, A., Adlet, Y., Sholpan, M., & Beaver, K. M. (2019). Familial concentration and distribution of adolescent victimization: An analysis of factors that promote and protect siblings from victimization. *Victims and Offenders*, *14*, 727–744.

Schreck, C. J. (1999). Criminal victimization and low self-control: An extension and test of a general theory of crime. *Justice Quarterly*, *16*, 633–654.

Schreck, C. J., Wright, R. A., & Miller, J. M. (2002). A study of individual and situational antecedents of violent victimization. *Justice Quarterly*, *19*, 159–180.

Turanovic, J. J., Reisig, M. D., & Pratt, T. C. (2015). Risky lifestyles, low self-control, and violent victimization across gendered pathways to crime. *Journal of Quantitative Criminology*, *31*, 183–206.

Turkheimer, E. (2000). Three laws of behavior genetics and what they mean. *Current Directions in Psychological Science*, *9*, 160–164.

Tuvblad, C., & Baker, L. A. (2011). Human aggression across the lifespan: Genetic propensities and environmental moderators. *Advances in Genetics*, *75*, 171–214.

Tuvblad, C., & Beaver, K. M. (2013). Genetic and environmental influences on antisocial behavior. *J Crim Justice*, *41*, 273–276.

Vaske, J., Boisvert, D., & Wright, J. P. (2012). Genetic and environmental contributions to the relationship between violent victimization and criminal behavior. *Journal of Interpersonal Violence*, *27*, 3213–3235.

Verweij, K. J. H., Zietsch, B. P., Lynskey, M. T., Medland, S. E., Neale, M. C., Martin, N. G., … Vink, J. M. (2010). Genetic and environmental influences on cannabis use initiation and problematic use: A meta-analysis of twin studies. *Addiction*, *105*, 417–430.

Waldman, I., Rhee, S. H., LoParo, D., & Park, Y. (2018). Genetic and environmental influences on psychopathy and antisocial behavior. In C. J. Patrick (Ed.), *Handbook of psychopathy* (pp. 335–353). New York: The Guildford Press.

Willems, Y. E., Boesen, N., Li, J., Finkenauer, C., & Bartels, M. (2019). The heritability of self-control: A meta-analysis. *Neuroscience & Biobehavioral Reviews*, *100*, 324–334.

Wolfgang, M. E. (1957) Victim precipitated criminal homicide. *The Journal of Criminal Law, Criminology, and Police Science*, *48*, 1–11.

Wright, R., & Decker, S. H. (1994). *Burglars on the job: Streetlife and residential break-ins*. Boston, MA: Northeastern University Press.

Wright, R., & Decker, S. H. (1997). *Armed robbers in action.* Boston, MA: Northeastern University Press.

Wright, R., & Decker, S. H. (2002). *Robbers on robbery: Prevention and the offender.* NIJ Final Report Award #94-IJ-CX-0030.

# 10

# Toward a Realist Criminology of the Internet: Considering Technology-Facilitated Crime and Victimization[1]

*Kevin F. Steinmetz and Adrienne L. McCarthy*

Online crime control solutions generally come in three varieties: technological solutions (e.g. credit-monitoring, anti-virus, and firewalls), moderation of content by online platforms and services, and specialized law enforcement units or task forces (Jewkes & Andrews, 2005; McGuire, 2016; Roberts, 2019). These strategies focus on limiting criminal opportunities, deterring criminal behavior, and encouraging self-policing. From this view, crime and victimization are a problem of improperly deterred individuals seizing criminal opportunities and little attention is needed to the conditions which gave rise to such criminals and criminal motivations in the first place (Hall, 2012). Such approaches share their classical roots with "terrestrial" crime control strategies like situational crime prevention and hot-spots policing which similarly rely on institutional coercion (or the threat thereof) to curb crime, the purchase of crime controlling technologies (e.g. surveillance cameras and callboxes), and the removal of "incivilities" from neighborhoods (e.g. Braga, Papachristos, & Hureau, 2014; Clarke, 1980; Wilson & Kelling, 1982).

Just as these terrestrial strategies have resulted in the growth and centralization of state and corporate power in the name of crime control, online deterrence and opportunity-reduction strategies have rendered the internet an increasingly securitized space with rapidly increasing government and corporate surveillance assemblages at the cost of individual privacy.[2] In the US, law enforcement agencies regularly employ surveillance technologies and are turning to big data analytic techniques for predictive policing purposes (Brayne, 2017). Intelligence agencies, often in concert with allied nations, have developed numerous surveillance programs, the most notorious being revealed following the 2013 leaks by US intelligence contractor Edward Snowden (2019). Entire industries are now dependent on the generation, collection, distribution, and analysis of personal data (Zuboff, 2015). Though not all of these surveillance technologies have been developed for the purposes of fighting crime and reducing victimization, they can easily be re-appropriated as law enforcement agencies increasingly turn to big data repositories (Rieke, Yu, Robinson, & von Hoboken, 2016).

Largely absent from online crime control models are social policies which (1) address root causes of crime and criminality, (2) ameliorate the harms experienced by the victims of such crimes, and (3) do not unduly contribute to state and corporate power and surveillance. This represents the fundamental crisis facing online governance—taking seriously the harms caused by online crime and victimization while also taking seriously the erosion of civil liberties wrought by contemporary online crime solutions. Just as Hall and Winlow (2015, p. 23) argue that "the insidious harms inflicted on society by intensive securitization and incarceration in many ways outweigh the harms caused by street crime," so too should it be concerning that the massive expansion of online surveillance in the name of crime control, national security, and other concerns concentrate power online within institutions of commerce and control, potentially causing more harm than online crimes themselves.

To date, criminology has contributed relatively little to information security policy (with notable exceptions, e.g. Brewer et al., 2019; Testa, Maimon, Sobesto, & Cukier, 2017). One particular strain of criminological theorizing that may be useful for tackling the problem of online harm with a sensitivity to social structure and power is realist criminology. Realist criminology began with the emergence of Left Realism in Britain during the 1980s. Left Realism is a strain of critical criminology which tried to reduce the harms caused by street violence through social policies designed to directly address crimes as well as the social structural inequalities at the root of many crime problems (Lea & Young, 1984). It presented a kind of "radical" or "critical victimology" that aimed to reduce the suffering disproportionately inflicted upon the poor and the marginalized (DeKeseredy & Schwartz, 1991; Jones, MacLean, & Young, 1986, pp. 2–3; Phipps, 1986; Walklate, 2015). Though significant strides have been made in advancing realist criminology (e.g. Hall & Winlow, 2015; Matthews, 2014), little work has applied realist approaches beyond traditional forms of violence or street crime. Yet, in the information age, there are many harms that can be inflicted upon the victims of online crime.

This chapter argues that realist criminology may provide a theory of victimology that allows criminologists to take such harms seriously while also being sensitive to the role of social structure and inequality, notably in the forms of power differentials structured by class, race, and gender among other considerations. Though fully detailing such a perspective is beyond the scope of a single chapter, this chapter illuminates key challenges involved in updating realist criminology to tackle online crimes, providing a roadmap forward. Before these challenges are addressed, this chapter first provides an overview of realist criminology, notably through the traditions of left, critical, and ultra-realism.

## Realist Criminology

Left Realism "with capital letters" (Currie, 2010, p. 113) emerged in 1980s Britain during a time of post-Fordist deindustrialization, a strong conservative social and economic shift under Thatcherism, and a prevailing sense of precariousness and anxiety among the general population (Brown & Hogg, 1992; Walklate, 2015; Young, 2007). During this period, there was public anxiety that crime and victimization were on the rise. Yet the results of the 1983 British Crime Survey led the UK Home Office and others to conclude that public fear of crime was "irrational" and "out of proportion with their actual risk from crime" (Walklate, 2015, p. 181). Such a conclusion from this data was misleading, however (Matthews, 2014, p. 13). Local victimization surveys like those conducted in Islington and Merseyside revealed that crime, "when situated in its local context and in relation to what people knew went on in their neighbourhood, was a problem for people" that could not be dismissed as "irrational" (Walklate, 2015, p. 181). Comparing public fears of crime with national crime trends unfairly dismissed the very real crime risks confronting certain populations in particular locations as victimization is not evenly distributed socially and geographically (Like-Hailsip & Miofsky, 2011; Walklate, 2015).

At this point, radical criminologists like John Lea and Jock Young (1984) recognized that one of the most significant problems confronting British working classes were intra-class forms of crime and victimization, particularly violence. Rather than explain such criminality as a result of poor moral character or psychological defects—as was the tendency among the conservative criminologists of the time—so-called "Left Realists" saw crime as the product of social structure and material conditions. Further, they recognized that the most socially and economically disenfranchised and marginalized were also the most likely to be victimized by street crime and violence. These criminologists saw a pressing need to create crime control policies that worked "in and against" the system to ameliorate the harms caused by crime while also addressing those caused by social structure and circumstance (Matthews, 2016, p. 3).

In taking this position, Left Realists juxtaposed themselves to "left idealists" or critical criminologists said to neglect the harms caused by intra-class forms of crime. Since the 1960s and 1970s, critical criminology has directed considerable attention to the crimes of the powerful including white collar, corporate, and state crime (Pearce, 1976; Schwartz & DeKeseredy, 2010, p. 108). To the extent that they considered street crime, left idealists were accused of romanticizing such criminals as simply downtrodden victims of circumstance or proto-revolutionary folk heroes (Lea, 2010, p. 142). Drawing from Gouldner (1968), Young (1979) criticized left idealists as the "zookeepers of deviancy"—those who would preserve deviants within a glass cage of abstraction divorced from "social and political power relations" and "define away any notion of personal integrity, autonomy and authentic existence" (Lea, 2014, p. 433). Left idealists were also attacked for their tendency to "downplay the seriousness and extent" of violent crime "because of either the fear of pathologizing the poor, 'whipping up' support for severe punishment, and supporting racist arguments," or victim blaming (DeKeseredy, 2003, p. 31). Though such concerns are not wholly unjustified, they lead to a kind of minimalist or hands-off approach to crime that offers little for the predominantly poor and working-class communities struggling with the real effects of violence. Similarly, Matthews (2014) is critical of what he terms "liberal criminologists" who make policy suggestions but limit themselves to decarceration, rehabilitation programs, and community corrections. Such an approach focuses on reducing the negative effects of sanctioning while doing little to address crime and victimization (Matthews, 2014, p. 20).

Left Realists are equally critical of "administrative criminologists" or "right realists"—conservative criminologists like James Q. Wilson, George Kelling, and Ron Clarke who advanced crime control policies while maintaining an "antagonism to the idea that social circumstances cause crime, and a lack of interest in the causes of crime" (Hough, 2014, p. 215; Matthews, 2014). From this view, crime is primarily a result of defects of personal character; either the result of biology, psychology, or the exercise of improperly restrained free will (Lea, 2010, p. 141). Thus, in their pursuit of crime control, right realists advanced policies that directly contributed to the over-policing of poor communities, adding to the structural burden such populations bear (e.g. Hough, 2014; Matthews, 2014; Meares, 2015; Young, 2007).

Eventually criminologists in the US, Canada, and Australia took up the mantle of Left Realism, becoming what Elliot Currie (2010, p. 113) terms left realism "without capitals" or "plain" left realism (e.g. Brown & Hogg, 1992; Currie, 1998; DeKeseredy & Schwartz, 1991). As its influence expanded, Currie (2010) argues that it retained certain general principles. First, he argues that, as opposed to the views of left idealists or what he terms "liberal minimalists," "crime isn't *just* a matter of social construction—not just a phantom issue stirred up by governments, right wing politicians, or the mass media, playing on the exaggerated fears of a deluded (or racist) public" (Currie, 2010, p. 114). They also resist the notion that crime rates are purely a byproduct of overzealous policing efforts (Currie, 2010; DeKeseredy & Schwartz, 1991, p. 249). Instead, left realists recognize that while fears about crime may be inflamed by moral panics or other distortions, they cannot be dismissed outright as irrational.

Second, left realists argue that victimization is not evenly distributed across space and demography. Crime—particularly serious crime—affects "some people, in some kinds of places, far more than others" (Currie, 2010, p. 114). In particular, crimes like violence tend to be disproportionately leveled against the socially, economically, and politically marginalized. From this position the failure of leftist criminologists to address crime and victimization is tantamount to complicity in structures that organize such social inequalities and their collateral consequences.

Third, left realism insists that reforms can make meaningful change as opposed to some radical scholars who assert that any reform short of a full revolution will only be absorbed into its machinations and new forms of the same oppression will manifest (Currie, 2010). While not unsympathetic to this position, left realists recognize that real harms are occurring as a result of crime here and now. As Schwartz and DeKeseredy (2010, p. 109) explain, "purposeful inattention to policing … also means dooming to misery those women and men who are right now being raped, robbed, beaten and burglarized." Left realists have been criticized for this commitment to policy. They stand accused of complicity in the social harms wrought by repressive criminal justice policies because they work with agents and agencies of the system. Yet, as Currie (2010, p. 117) argues, left realists are also critical of "repressive criminal justice strategies in controlling crime" (Lea & Young, 1984, p. 194). Such repression is one of the key reasons that left realists argue for direct involvement in crime control. Without such involvement, leftists are surrendering crime control to the right, which has repeatedly demonstrated an unwillingness to consider the role of social structure, power, inequality, and oppression in the creation of crime, criminality, and victimization (Currie, 2016, p. 25; DeKeseredy, 2018, p. 31).

Left realism is also "'social democratic' in its core analysis and implications" (Currie, 2010, p. 115). Lea (2010, p. 144) refers to this proclivity as left realism's "democratic imperative." A social democratic orientation views capitalism as inherently harmful, but argues that the damage can be ameliorated by informed democratic social policy. Further, left realism is also social democratic because it emphasizes bringing multiple parties together to generate informed, effective, and holistic crime control policy, examining the so-called "square of crime" (Jones et al., 1986) or what Lea (2002, p. 144) later described as "the social relations of crime control" (Lea, 2016a, p. 56). These concepts refer to "the interaction between law enforcement, the wider community and public, the victim and the offender" (Lea, 2010, p. 144). Any effective policy has to consider the relationships between these parties while also allowing for each party to have a voice in the process, particularly victims, offenders, and the public, who are often omitted from inclusion in the conversation typically dominated by criminal justice agencies and politicians. For left realists, the particular relations between these parties may vary depending on the particular type of crime under examination as well as the specific communities under consideration (Lea, 2016a). Thus, left realists are tasked with understanding the social relations of crime in a given context before working to reorient those relations in a more democratic fashion. The process also necessitates a sensitivity to the role of social structure and power in the contexts under scrutiny including those based on "class, gender, ethnicity, politics, law and the state and … the economy" (Lea, 2016a, p. 59).

In the decades since Left Realism crawled out from the muck of the Thatcher-Reagan era, expansions and revisions have emerged. Drawing more explicitly from the realist philosophical and social science tradition (Archer, 1995; Bhaskar, 1978/2008; Sayer, 2000) are the critical realists with the late Roger Matthews as perhaps its most prominent contemporary proponent. In his recent work *Realist Criminology*, Matthews (2014, p. 28) claims that critical realists advance left realism by placing it "upon a firmer epistemological and methodological foundation." He emphasizes that realist criminologists must adopt a methodological position that prioritizes both theory and evidence. Careful conceptualization is thus vital, particularly with key concepts like "crime" and "violence." As he explains, "where loose and sloppy abstractions are used, they are unable to bear the explanatory weight placed upon them" (Matthews, 2014, p. 31).[3] Recognizing all of the issues endemic to legal definitions of crime, for example, Matthews (2014, pp. 46–48) instead defines crime as the production of harm stemming from the violation of human rights and dignity. This definition decouples crime and social harm from the confines of the state while also providing a new basis for grounding a consistent definition of harm. Additionally, critical realism holds that theory without evidence is as useless as evidence without theory. "Naïve realists" or administrative criminologists are viewed as prioritizing evidence while applying only the most vestigial of theory whereas some left idealists might be engaged in "theoreticism" or theoretical abstraction that divorces itself from reality. Additionally, though left realists specifically drew from Marxist theory and argued for the importance of social class and political economy, Matthews (2014) firmly centers class as a key feature of the realist enterprise.

Matthews (2014, p. 14) also explicitly tackles the structure versus agency debate. Consistent with realist philosophy, he argues that structure and agency are "analytically separable" and not to be "conflated" with one another. For the purposes of temporal ordering, "structure necessarily pre-dates action, which leads to its reproduction and transformation and that structure also post-dates action sequences that have given rise to it" (Matthews, 2014, p. 39). Building from this position, realist analyses should therefore examine the situational relationships between structure and agency as well as identify factors that mediate these relationships. Relatedly, critical realists also conceptualize power beyond the two-dimensional repressive function of the state and law.

Drawing from Foucault, Matthews (2014, p. 45) argues that power incorporates "a multiplicity of forces involving ceaseless struggles and confrontations" which can be both repressive and productive. In this manner, critical realists advance a more fully formed epistemic position to advance criminological and victimological research that will inform crime-prevention policies.

One of the key challenges confronting realist criminology is a lack of a straightforward theoretical explanatory apparatus. Despite assurances that these approaches are theory driven, specific explanations for crime and victimization are generally created on an *ad hoc* basis. As Matthews (2014, p. 70) explains, the objective of realist research is to "develop *explanations* of social phenomena and processes in order to contribute to policy development [emphasis in original]." If theory presents some explanation of the social world, left and critical realism's ultimate explanation is "it depends" while pointing toward general root causes like relative deprivation, deindustrialization, and the like. Of course, such an aversion to creating a "one size fits all" explanatory apparatus is understandable considering the unique idiosyncrasies that can emerge across contexts, especially when trying to cultivate tailored solutions for crime and victimization. Such an approach to theorizing, however, leaves realist criminology feeling loose and disjointed—consistent only in general tenets.

One of the most significant advances that attempts to overcome the paucity of capital-T theorizing in the area is *ultra-realism*, which gives significant attention to the philosophical underpinnings of their position while also advancing more broadly applicable criminological concepts (e.g. Hall, 2012; Hall and Winlow, 2015). Ultra-realism constitutes an amalgamation of realist, psycho-social, and political economic theory informed by Marx, Žižek, Freud, Lacan, and Bhaskar. It takes the left realist criticisms of left idealism further, arguing that contemporary liberal criminologists have turned a blind eye to the reality of crime and victimization as a matter of political prudence. Building from Žižek, Hall (2012) thus accuses the left of engaging in "fetishistic disavowal" where "we can continue not wanting to know what we already know and therefore continue to live and act as if we don't know" (Hall, 2012, p. 93). He accuses criminologists of engaging in "political and intellectual cowardice" by failing to take seriously basic facts about crime. For instance, that criminals are not always the victims of circumstance, that moral agency has a role to play in crime, and that not all crimes can be viewed as forms of proto-revolutionary behavior (ibid). For ultra-realists, the failure to properly address crime and victimization is not just a failure of the left, but a failure of liberalism more generally (Winlow & Hall, 2019).

Ontologically, ultra-realists subscribe to *transcendental materialism*, a position influenced by Žižek and formally articulated by Johnston (2008), which holds that,

> All humans are, paradoxically, hard-wired for plasticity, which carries a natural tendency to dysfunctionality; in other words, we are *naturally unnatural*. This allows us to create various cultures and practical ways of doing things in order to adapt to widely divergent environments, some benign and some difficult and demanding. (Hall & Winlow, 2015, p. 111)

Here, crime is understood as something which humans are energized toward by social-structural circumstances, ideology, experience, emotions, and physiology (Hall, 2012, p. 253). The tendency for humans to be pliable in their circumstances make them intrinsically vulnerable to energizing forces—notably capitalism—that encourage certain kinds of self-serving and predatory behaviors, though not deterministically so.

"Criminal actions" from this view "are those of an individual who is both ideologically and neurologically motivated to *undertake* to go considerably further than the law-abiding citizen" (Hall, 2012, p. 193). "Undertakers" are people who are "functionally ruthless" and are motivated to step over others to "get things done" (Hall, 2012, p. 199). Criminal undertakers are those who direct this energy in ways not sanctioned. Both legal and illegal undertakers share ruthlessness and aggression to compete in the marketplace. Undertakers are thus imbued with what ultra-realists describe as "special liberty" or a "sense of entitlement felt by an individual who will risk harm to others in order to further his own instrumental or expressive interests," which is fostered by the logic of capital accumulation (Hall & Winlow, 2015, p. 91). Related to special liberty is the concept of *pseudo-pacification*. Contrary to the *civilizing process* advanced by theorists like Norbert Elias (2000), Hall (2012) argues that violence has declined over time not because humans have become more civil, but that the individualist and self-serving behaviors energized by capitalism have found alternative avenues to be exercised, such as through cutthroat participation in competitive markets (hence *pseudo*-pacification).

Similar to critical realism, ultra-realism is zemiological, focusing on crime as the creation of harm rather than rule-violation. From this perspective, regardless of how crime is defined, it should be grounded in how such actions “inflict harm on individuals, their environments and their fragile social systems,” with harm being defined as “action that leaves whatever it impacts in a worse condition” (Hall & Winlow, 2018, pp. 47–48). This particular orientation is what makes ultra-realism victimological—it centers the conceptualization of crime on damage caused. Since the drive to harm is informed by characteristics like “special liberty,” ultra-realists thus argue that the engine of contemporary harm and social inequality is the capitalist mode of production and neoliberalism (Hall, 2012; Hall & Winlow, 2018; Winlow & Hall, 2019). In this sense, ultra-realists more firmly place capitalism and class as central to crime and crime control. Any failure to address these root causes reduces criminology, according to ultra-realists, to “symptomology rather than aetiology” (Winlow & Hall, 2016, p. 88).

Importantly, ultra-realists differ from left realists in their orientation toward policy. Both embrace the need for effective policy solutions to address the harms caused by crime. Left realism, however, was criticized for being too pragmatic in its policy approaches, focusing primarily on short-term policy achievements and neglecting long-term solutions. Ultra-realists argue that the “pragmatic investigation of what *can* be done must be replaced by the realistic investigation of what *must* be done to effect long-term transformation of the system in such a way as to reduce its propensity for multiple harms” (Hall & Winlow, 2018, p. 51; Winlow & Hall, 2019). Additionally, ultra-realists argue that policy should be secondary to critique because the “imperative to be ‘policy relevant’ enforces firm limits on what can be thought and said” (Winlow, 2019, p. 47).

## A Realist Criminology of the Internet

Drawing from the precepts laid forth by realist criminologies of the past, a realist criminology of the internet should be dedicated to three central objectives. First, it should center itself on the variegated harms to individual victims (and the environment) created or amplified by internet-based or -facilitated crimes. Second, it should be directed at generating theoretically and empirically sound explanations of the crimes and harms in question while working toward solutions aimed at harm reduction. Third, these solutions should be mindful of the role of power and structure in the organization of the social relations of the internet. In this vein, proposed solutions should be careful about promoting policies and programs which contribute to the erosion of online civil liberties and unnecessarily concentrate power into the hands of governments and corporations (at least without proper social democratic regulations and oversight). Of course, creating a realist criminology of the internet that meets these demands is easier said than done. In particular, key challenges exist including the problems of (1) defining "harm" with online crimes, (2) establishing locality and community, (3) mapping the social relations of crime, (4) the centering or decentering of class, and (5) deciding between piecemeal reforms or structural changes. The complex nature of these issues means that any account will undoubtedly be fractured and incomplete, at least in what can be handled within the scope of a single chapter. Yet we hope to provide some glimpses of insight into these issues that will pave the way toward more thorough articulations of a realist criminology of the internet.

### *The Problem of "Harm"*

Much like critical and ultra-realists, we argue that a realist criminology of the internet should be zemiological, focusing on "harm" rather than "crime." Yet, drawing parameters around the kinds of harms that should be considered "fair game" for criminologists and victimologists is difficult (Hall & Winlow, 2015, p. 89). To this end, Hall (2012, p. 15) provides a useful—though necessarily broad—definition of harm:

> The meaning of this term relates directly, through exploitation and irresponsibility towards the fate of others and their environments, to practices of domination in social, economic, cultural and technological practices, all of which leave some others in conditions worse than those in which they are found. Harm can be physical, social, psychological or environmental.

Considered here are a wide assortment of harms that cut across social strata both horizontally and vertically. Though providing a thorough typology of relevant harms, however, is beyond the scope of this analysis, this chapter details at least some of the harms that should be considered within the scope of a realist criminology of the internet.[4]

The harms considered are necessarily variegated and broad. Consider, for example, internet-mediated frauds like advanced fee frauds, romance scams, investment frauds, and the like. Financial damage from such frauds can be enormous. The Internet Crime Complaint Center (IC3, 2019, p. 3) reported financial losses from reported frauds to be in excess of $2.7 billion in 2018. Individual costs for frauds can be in the tens of thousands of dollars lost on average. Research indicates that victims of fraud may suffer emotional and psychological effects like anxiety, sadness, anger, shame, grief, post-traumatic stress, and even suicidal ideation (Cross, 2019; Cross, Richards, & Smith, 2016; Whitty & Buchanan, 2016). Their sense of self-worth and confidence may be sundered (Whitty & Buchanan, 2016). Physical consequences may result like sleep troubles, nausea, and weight loss (Cross, 2019; Cross et al., 2016). They may suffer lifestyle and livelihood consequences such as homelessness, unemployment, strains on their relationships with family and friends, and struggles to find support (Cross, 2019; Cross et al., 2016; Whitty & Buchanan, 2016). Similar harms to mind, body, lifestyle, and livelihood are found for crimes like online child sexual abuse images (e.g. Domhardt, Münzer, Fegert, & Goldbeck, 2015, p. 476; Gewirtz-Meydan, Walsh, Wolak, & Finkelhor, 2018), cyberstalking and harassment (e.g. Dreβing, Bailer, Anders, Wagner, & Gallas, 2014; Marganski, 2018), and others. Additionally, a realist approach to online crimes should also consider the "crimes of the powerful" (Hall, 2012; Hall & Winlow, 2015; Pearce, 1976) which include, but are not limited to, the harms caused by surveillance regimes and content control strategies as well as environmental damage created by internet use and technological development such as plundering of natural resources, exploitation of child labor, toxic materials, and resource consumption (Department of Labor, 2018, pp. 8–14; Snowden, 2019; Stretesky, Long, & Lynch, 2014; Zuboff, 2015).

What differentiates a realist approach to harm from other solutions-oriented perspectives is an explicit desire to avoid the collateral consequences that the punitive logics of other victimological harm-reduction strategies might bring (though, admittedly, realist criminology has not always lived up to this ideal). Recent critiques of "carceral feminism" provide a useful parallel to consider. Phillips and Chagnon (2020, p. 50) describe carceral feminism as "a view that promotes state-based responses to sexual violence (and gender violence more generally), primarily through the traditional criminal justice system and other appendages of the carceral state" (see also: Bernstein, 2012; Bumiller, 2008; Law, 2014). These scholars argue that punitive solutions of violence against women, as well-intended as they might be, contribute to the expansion of the carceral state and encourage a reliance on state control and coercion as the corrective. Considering the myriad social problems attributed to mass incarceration, the expansion of "community corrections," and the increased policing of poor communities (particularly communities of color) (Hough, 2014; Matthews, 2014; Meares, 2015; Young, 2007), efforts to curtail crime that rely on state coercion may not reduce net social harm but may instead displace or redirect that harm (Cohen, 1979). Realist criminologists should bear such possible collateral consequences in mind.

*Locality and Community*

Though often not explicit, realist criminology is a criminology of place. Likely because of its general focus on street crime and violence, its analyses and policies tend to focus on particular communities in particular locations (e.g. DeKeseredy & Schwartz, 1991, p. 256; Matthews, 2014, p. 4). At the same time, realist criminology must transcend locality as "the forces that shape local crime problems are never just local in provenance" (Hogg, 2016, p. 72). As Donnermeyer (2016, p. 36) explains, place "represents a micro-expression or microcosm of all the inequalities found in the larger society." He adds that "within a specific locality … are multiple forms of collective efficacy, buttressed by overlapping networks or forms of social capital" (ibid). Place is a nexus point where the structural and the situational collide. It also provides a starting point for mapping the social relations of crime (a point to which we will return momentarily). For many crimes, particularly street crimes, victims, offenders, police, community leaders, and other relevant parties tend to be geographically concentrated. This proximity facilitates interaction and cooperation to create social democratic solutions.

Place presents a challenge for online crimes. In the words of Gertrude Stein, "there is no there there." Yet, the concepts of space and place are not useless in analyses of the internet and online crime—they need only be reconceptualized. Scholars have devoted significant time to understanding how place manifests in the digital realm (e.g. Castells, 1996; Futrell & Simi, 2004). While each of these conceptualizations is useful in its own right, this chapter details the four concepts Hayward (2012, p. 455) uses to orient criminologists grappling with "virtual/networked spaces": convergence, virtuality, telepresence, and presence. *Convergence* refers to the intersection between technological change and regulatory processes—that new technologies may create situations that may test current regulations or create strange and contradictory legal situations. *Virtuality* denotes the creation of electronic, artificial, or simulated persons and environments. In particular, Hayward (2012) highlights how the "virtual" may blur and intersect with "the actual," rendering the distinction between online and offline increasingly tenuous (see also: Brown, 2006). Indeed, this is supported by recent research which argues that online crimes may actually involve significant offline components and locally situated social networks (Lusthaus & Varese, 2017). *Telepresence* is the ability of telecommunications technologies to "alter the way we experience the sense of *being* in an environment" (ibid, p. 456). Phenomenologically, humans may exist in virtual and physical environments simultaneously and thus the experiences of these spaces may be inseparable. *Presence*, on the other hand, speaks to the ability of an identity to endure and exist in the form of scattered fragments across online profiles, account registrations, blogs, social media posts, and other interactional markers that creates a "quasi-private disembodied virtual 'persona' that exists at various points across the spatial architecture of the internet." (ibid, p. 457).

These concepts, and others, speak to the complexities of "place" when the experiences of space become less dependent on physicality; technology can change the known terrain and create new interactional environments; the actual and the virtual become increasingly inseparable; people can now "exist" in two spaces simultaneously; and identities may persist in virtual spaces long after people have left (Powell, Stratton, & Cameron, 2018). Each of these dimensions may need to be considered when thinking about viable solutions to online harms and generating realist explanations of online victimization problems.

### *Mapping the Social Relations of Crime Control*

Related to the problem of locality is the problem of community—the organizing concept through which we map the social relations of crime and crime control. Implied in this concept is a view that communities are composed of *networks* of relationships among offenders, victims, state actors, and members of the public (the "square of crime"). In the age of the internet, viewing social organizations and communities as networks is useful considering the role technologies play in mediating such relationships. In working toward a realist criminology of the internet, it is worth ruminating more deeply the types of social networks engendered by contemporary telecommunications technologies, the methods through which such networks can be mapped, and how realist notions of social organization and structure may need to be loosened to deal with the unique problems presented by the internet.

According to Rainie and Wellman (2012, p. 8) the internet age is marked by "networked individualism." Referring to a time before the rise of global telecommunications networks, they argue that "in generations past, people usually had small, tight social networks … where a few important family members, close friends, neighbors, leaders and community groups (churches and the like) constituted the safety net and support system for individuals" (ibid, p. 8). Today, people are increasingly embedded in multiple diffuse social networks mediated through communications technologies. These social networks give tremendous freedom to individuals to curate and expand their relationships. On the other hand, they also create pressure for the individual to generate and maintain these relationships. In other words,

> They must actively network. They need to expend effort and sometimes money to maintain their ties near and far; choose whether to phone, visit, or electronically connect with others; remember which members of their network are useful for what sorts of things (including just hanging out); and forge useful alliances among network members who might not previously have known each other. In short, networked individualism is both socially liberating and socially taxing. (ibid, p. 9)

The implications of this work for realist criminology is that addressing crime problems through traditionally spatially bound concepts like social solidarity, social capital, collective efficacy, or similar mechanisms may require a reimagination of what these concepts mean across these new networks. For instance, Sampson, Raudenbush, and Earls (1997, p. 919) conceptualize collective efficacy as "the linkage of mutual trust and the willingness to intervene for the common good that defines the neighborhood context of collective efficacy." In the case of internet-mediated social networks, how does one generate "mutual trust" and "willingness to intervene for the common good?" These are instrumental problems confronting a realist criminology of the internet. It also means that mapping the social relations of crime requires expanding the scope of relevant actors when determining the boundaries of the relevant "community." The communities impacted by online crimes are less bound by geography compared to high-violence neighborhoods. Instead, researchers will be required to trace the diffuse and possibly expansive network of actors involved. One useful perspective for this enterprise is Actor-Network Theory (ANT) (Latour, 2005; Powell et al., 2018).

Despite its name, ANT is best understood as a methodological orientation concerned with the "tracing of associations" among "actors" (Latour, 2005, p. 5). For ANT, human action is always shaped by relationships with other actors within an "actor-network." Actors can be both human and non-human entities (objects, like technologies)—anything capable of acting or being acted upon. Networks are therefore dynamic entities constantly created and recreated through action. Further, an actor becomes more significant within a network when the volume and quality of attachments to other actors increases. ANT is useful for a realist criminology of the internet because it avoids common assumptions about non-human agency. Non-human entities like technologies, non-human animals, environmental features, law, policy, prior experience, and knowledge are capable of becoming socially active players within a network, driving and being driven by other actors (Callon, 1991; Latour & Woolgar, 1986).

Yet, an actor-network-theory approach to mapping the social relations of crime control presents a problem for realist criminology—specifically in its view of social structure. For Latour (2005, p. 165), tracing associations within actor networks requires the researcher to "keep the social flat" or resist the urge to project upward and rely on structural formations like "capitalism" and "patriarchy" to perform explanatory heavy lifting. Instead, the researcher should stick to what manifests within the context of the network—if capitalism, for instance, is a problem then it should manifest within the actions of the network, not as some esoteric spiritual force permeating the interstitial spaces of the network. As Latour (2005, p. 64) explains, "power and domination have to be produced, made up, composed. Asymmetries exist, yes, but where do they come from and what are they made out of?"

Realist criminology, on the other hand, mandates that the researcher remain sensitive to both the situational and the structural. Indeed, that consideration of the structural context is necessary to properly address crime and victimization. We suggest, however, these two perspectives are not wholly irreconcilable. In mapping the social relations of crime, realist criminologists should only consider the role of any given structure if it is made manifest in their data. Their existence should not be assumed *a priori* as a causative factor. Thus the realist criminologist needs to be able to sustain a contradiction: be sensitive to the role of structure but only insofar as structure makes itself apparent. This also will allow the researcher to respond to the particular kinds of structures most relevant for a given crime problem rather than assuming one structure is master of all.

*Centering or Decentering Class?*

Critical perspectives that draw on Marxist thought tend to be critiqued as economic reductionists, distilling myriad social harms to problems of class relations. As previously discussed, both critical and ultra-realism specifically make a point to privilege class in their analyses. While not diminishing the importance of class, a realism of the internet necessitates robust consideration of social stratification beyond the economic. In their criticism of cultural criminology, Hall and Winlow (2007, p. 83) claim that cultural criminology and other "liberal" criminologies had decided that "it was no longer hip to posit the capitalist economy and its relations of production as the bedrock of social life." Ferrell (2007, p. 92), however, retorted that it was not that "it was no longer hip" but, instead, "no longer sufficient." Though the material conditions and social relations of production undoubtedly play a significant role in the creation of criminal contexts and motivations, like Ferrell we are unconvinced that crime and victimization are *exclusively* the products of the contradictions and consequences of capitalist class relations.

For instance, consider online harassment. One study by Lenhart, Ybarra, Zickuhr, and Price-Feney (2016, p. 4) indicates that while both men and women were equally likely to be harassed online, "women experience a wider variety of online abuse, including more serious violations." Such abuse includes "brigading," "dogpiling," or "virtual mobs" which involve offenders forming online mobs where they will "dogpile" onto a victim, en masse, in a concentrated harassment campaign (Lenhart et al., 2016, p. 24; Quinn, 2017, p. 52). It would be difficult to explain the form and intensity of such abuse through pseudo-pacification or the exercise of special liberty, as might be argued by ultra-realists. Class may help explain the particular struggles triggering the abuse (e.g. the subject of "women in games"), the creation and maintenance of the vectors through which such abuse is transmitted (e.g. Twitter and Facebook), and even the underlying feelings of powerlessness or precariousness by male abuses that may be misdirected toward women. Yet, a purely economic analysis may be insufficient to explain why gender becomes a lightning rod for such issues in the first place. Or why certain men hold so much ire for women online in general. This is not to say that there is no relationship between class and gender, only that gender cannot be reduced to an "epiphenomenon" of the political economy (Wood, Anderson, & Richards, 2019, p. 3).

The point is that the tendency of realist criminologists (particularly of the critical and ultra-realist varieties) to attribute crime and victimization to capitalism diminishes the importance of other variables of social stratification like gender, race, and sexuality. To be fair, realist criminologists have attempted to bridge the gaps between left realism, feminist criminology, and other perspectives to address this shortcoming (e.g. Schwartz & DeKeseredy, 2010; Hall & Winlow, 2015). Still, a paucity remains (Renzetti, 2016). The underlying concern appears to be epistemological and ontological in nature—perhaps driven by some concern that a failure to explain other mechanisms of social stratification through the political economy will render the Marxist core of the perspective untenable. Yet, perhaps this anxiety is overstated. Though Marx was principally concerned with the political economy as the primary mechanism through which material conditions and their subsequent social relations were structured, perhaps other factors can enter the equation without the dialectical materialist foundations of the analysis falling apart. Indeed, whereas critical realists and ultra-realists have been steadfast in their commitment to class-above-all approaches, left realists have appeared at least amenable to flexibility. Perhaps there is a need to return to that flexibility, though admittedly more work will be needed to shore up the ontological and epistemological foundations of the theory were this to be done—heavy lifting that is, unfortunately, beyond this chapter.

### *Piecemeal Reform or Structural Change?*

Traditionally, left and critical realist criminologists have embraced piecemeal reform as such strategies have more immediate potential for the alleviation of harm. Ultra-realists, on the other hand, ask us to consider "what *must* be done" to create long-term harm reduction, leaning more toward the revolutionary proclivities of other critical criminologists (Hall & Winlow, 2018, p. 51). Having established that the objective of a realist criminology of the internet is to reduce the harms of online crimes while not unduly contributing to the concentration of power in the hands of the powerful, it follows that the position advanced in this chapter sits between these poles—embracing piecemeal reform when possible while keeping an eye on long-term change.

Though a dirty word for some, addressing the age-old question of "reform or revolution?" necessitates a somewhat *pragmatic* approach. The outcome of revolutions are desired but the sudden structural change often alienates the middle class and deals much collateral damage to the working class. Philosopher André Gorz (1962) argues that revolutionary reform will not out-pace capitalism's tendency to absorb change so long as the reform itself does not directly change the capitalist relationship between the worker and the mode of production. Gorz's resolution then is a slow progressive conquest of power for workers (albeit this does not exclude the possibility of revolutionary seizure). This will show that the new system (socialism in Gorz's case) is feasible and already at work—thus there will be an intermediate stage. Similarly, Madfis and Cohen (2016, p. 2) explain that:

> A left realist focus on short-term practical reform efforts represents a form of pragmatism that is necessary when attempting to bring about change in light of very real institutional barriers. This pragmatism must be directly informed and animated by the broader, more radical vision of structural change offered by left idealism.

A realist criminology of the internet recognizes that the ideological power of the state is imbedded within social relations and thus structural changes must ultimately be made. Intermediate steps can be taken, however, to prove that crime control can be handled outside of the state apparatus or in a more democratic fashion through the state.

Pursuing both short-term and long-term changes to reduce the social harms endemic to contemporary internet use is likely to be a difficult task. This chapter cannot provide a catalog of possible solutions to such problems, particularly as there is still a need to theorize these problems further. Yet, there are some promising leads which give hope for a realist approach. Consider, for example, current efforts to curtail the proliferation of hate speech and misinformation across social networks by holding online platforms accountable, such as Facebook who facilitated the proliferation of hate speech in Myanmar, which incited violence against the Rohingya ethnic minority (Wong, 2019). Efforts to generate support networks for the victims of online abuse such as the Crash Override Network may also be of interest (Quinn, 2017). The point is that these strategies, and others, show both long- and short-term efforts to deal with the harms of the internet that either challenge contemporary loci of online power or at least avoid empowering them further.

## Conclusion

This chapter constitutes tentative steps toward a realist criminology of crime, victimization, and the internet. Few definitive claims are made here about the specific propositions and contours such an approach may take. Instead, we identify five problems endemic to creating a pragmatic-yet-critical approach to technology-facilitated victimization and, when possible, gesture to possible resolutions. This chapter makes no claims to providing a definitive list of challenges necessary to overcome in the creation of a realist criminology of the internet. It only tries to start a conversation.

As described here, a realist criminology of the internet should be zemiological and embrace a wide range of harms, including financial, physical, psychological, emotional, environmental, and exploitive. Considering that the experience of crime and victimization is heavily rooted in conceptions of space and place, such a realist approach should also consider how the local manifests for those affiliated with and affected by internet-facilitated crimes. Relatedly, a realist criminology of the internet should embrace network-oriented perspectives toward community, particularly important when considering the role of non-human actors (e.g. telecommunications technologies) in mediating, influencing, and propelling human action. It should also embrace explanatory pluralism in the kinds of structures and experiences involved in crime and victimization. Though there is a pressing need to consider the importance of class and political economy in the role of crime and victimization, particularly as so much criminology has seemed content to ignore such considerations (Lynch, 2015), this should not mean exchanging one myopticism for another. Instead, a realist criminology of the internet should remain open to alternative structures—be they gender, race, sexuality, and others—as important loci of social inequality and oppression important for understanding crime and victimization. Finally, a realist criminology of the internet is challenged with the need to embrace short-term solutions to help those struggling with the harms of internet-facilitated crimes here and now while being mindful of the long-term consequences such policies may yield in addition to the possibilities of long-term reforms.

To fully formulate a realist criminology of the internet, scholars should consider drawing from a diversity of theoretical influences. Some were included in this analysis such as Actor-Network Theory (e.g. Latour, 2005) and Digital Criminology (Powell et al., 2018). The latter could prove particularly useful as it works toward a criminology encompassing of the social and cultural complexities created by the increasing pervasiveness of technology in everyday life. It is an amalgam perspective that draws from theorizing on the "digital society," Brown's (2006) work on hybridization, Actor-Network Theory, cultural criminology, and other perspectives. Though it suffers from theoretical chimerism—drawing from an assortment of theoretical influences that may or may not conflict with one another—it does show the kind of flexibility that a contemporary realist approach needs. Similarly, cultural criminology may prove useful, particularly its focus on the role of the "politics of meaning" in driving contemporary crime and victimizations issues—politics which have become all the more intense and celeritous in the age of the internet (Ferrell, 2013). We are aware that a tension exists between cultural criminology and realist criminology, particularly ultra-realism (e.g. Ferrell, 2007; Hall & Winlow, 2007). That said, we are unconvinced that the two orientations are wholly incompatible. Even Matthews (2014) has suggested that there are points of congruence between realism and cultural criminology, pointing toward the possibility of a cultural realism. Last but certainly not least, this chapter echoes previous efforts by realists to embrace feminist criminology, particularly as feminist criminologists have likely been the most active in mapping the harms created by various internet-facilitated crimes (Marganski, 2018).

## Notes

1 The authors would like to thank Travis Linnemann for his suggestions on an earlier draft of this chapter.

2 Countries and international bodies have adopted statutory measures which attempt to curb potential abuses of mass personal data collection by both governments and corporations like the EU's General Data Protection Regulation. Unfortunately, such measures appear to have done little to curb the expansion and intrusiveness of surveillance.

3 In this capacity, though critical realists criticize social constructionists for minimizing the harms caused by crime, they also recognize that social constructionism can be useful for problematizing such taken-for-granted concepts (Matthews, 2014, p. 37).

4 Hall & Winlow (2015, p. 89) similarly indicate the difficulty of providing a thorough typology of relevant harms for consideration from a realist perspective.

## References

Archer, M. (1995). *Realist social theory: The morphogenic approach.* Cambridge, England: Cambridge University Press.

Bernstein, E. (2012). Carceral politics as gender justice? The "traffic in women" and neoliberal circuits of crime, sex, and rights. *Theory and Society*, *41*, 233–259.

Bhaskar, R. (1978/2008). *A realist theory of science.* New York, NY: Routledge.

Braga, A. A., Papachristos, A. V., & Hureau, D. M. (2014). The effects of hot spots policing on crime: An updated systematic review and meta-analysis. *Justice Quarterly*, *31*(4), 633–663.

Brayne, S. (2017). Big data surveillance: The case of policing. *American Sociological Review*, *82*(5), 977–1008.

Brewer, R., De Vel-Palumbo, M., Hutchings, A., Holt, T., Goldsmith, A., & Maimon, D. (2019). *Cybercrime prevention: Theory and applications.* New York: Springer Nature.

Brown, D., & Hogg, R. (1992). Essentialism, radical criminology and left realism. *Australian and New Zealand Journal of Criminology*, *25*, 195–230.

Brown, S. (2006). The criminology of hybrids: Rethinking crime and law in technosocial networks. *Theoretical Criminology*, *18*(2), 176–197.

Bumiller, K. (2008). *In an abusive state: How neoliberalism appropriated the feminist movement against sexual violence.* Durham, NC: Duke University Press.

Callon, M. (1991). Techno-economic network and irreversibility. In J. Law (Ed.), *A sociology of monsters: Essays on power, technology and domination* (pp. 132–161). London: Routledge.

Castells, M. (1996). *The rise of the network society.* New York, NY: Blackwell.

Clarke, R. V. G. (1980). "Situational" crime prevention: Theory and practice. *British Journal of Criminology*, *20*(2), 136–147.

Cohen, S. (1979). The punitive city: Notes on the dispersal of social control. *Contemporary Crises*, *3*, 339–363.

Cross, C. (2019). Is online fraud just fraud? Examining the efficacy of the digital divide. *Journal of Criminological Research, Policy and Practice*, *5*(2), 120–131.

Cross, C., Richards, K., Smith, R. G. (2016). The reporting experiences and support needs of victims of online fraud. *Trends & Issues in Crime and Criminal Justice*, *518*, 1–14.

Currie, E. (1998). *Crime and punishment in America.* New York, NY: Metropolitan Books.

Currie, E. (2010). Plain left realism: An appreciation, and some thoughts for the future. *Crime, Law and Social Change*, *54*, 111–124.

Currie, E. (2016). The violence divide: Taking "ordinary" crime seriously in a volatile world. In R. Matthews (Ed.), *What is to be done about crime and punishment? Towards a "public criminology"* (pp. 9–30). London, England: Palgrave MacMillan.

Department of Labor. (2018). *U.S. Department of Labor's 2018 list of goods produced by child labor or forced labor.* Washington, D.C. Retrieved from www.dol.gov/sites/dolgov/files/ILAB/ListofGoods.pdf.

DeKeseredy, W. S. (2003). Left realism on inner-city violence. In M. D. Schwartz & S. E. Hatty (Eds.), *Controversies in Critical Criminology* (pp. 29–41). Cincinnati, OH: Anderson.

DeKeseredy, W. S. (2018). Left realism: A new look. In W. S. DeKeseredy & M. Dragiewicz (Eds.), *Routledge handbook of critical criminology* (pp. 30–42). New York, NY: Routledge.

DeKeseredy, W. S., & Schwartz, M. D. (1991). British and U.S. Left Realism: A critical comparison. *International Journal of Offender Therapy and Comparative Criminology*, *35*(3), 248–262.

Domhardt, M., Münzer, A., Fegert, J.M., & Goldbeck, L. (2015). Resilience in survivors of child sexual abuse: A systematic review of the literature. *Trauma, Violence, & Abuse*, *16*(4), 476–493.

Donnermeyer, J. F. (2016). Without place, is it real? *International Journal for Crime, Justice and Social Democracy*, *5*(3), 27–40.

Dreβing, H., Bailer, J., Anders, A., Wagner, H., & Gallas, C. (2014). Cyberstalking in a large sample of social network users: Prevalence, characteristics and impact upon victims. *Cyberpsychology, Behavior, and Social Networking*, *17*(2), 61–67.

Elias, N. (2000). *The civilizing process* (Rev. ed.). Hoboken, NJ: Wiley-Blackwell.

Ferrell, J. (2007). For a ruthless cultural criticism of everything existing. *Crime Media Culture*, *3*(1), 91–100.

Ferrell, J. (2013). Cultural criminology and the politics of meaning. *Critical Criminology*, *21*, 257–271.

Futrell, R., & Simi, P. (2004). Free spaces, collective identity, and the persistence of U.S. white power activism. *Social Problems*, *51*(1): 16–42.

Gewirtz-Meydan, A., Walsh, W., Wolak, J., & Finkelhor, D. (2018). The complex experience of child pornography survivors. *Child Abuse & Neglect*, *80*, 238–248.

Gorz, A. (1962). Avant-propos. *Les Temps Modernes*, *196–197*, 386–400.

Gouldner, A. (1968). The sociologist partisan. *American Sociologist*, *3*(2): 103–116.

Hall, S. (2012). *Theorizing crime and deviance: A new perspective*. Thousand Oaks, CA: Sage.

Hall, S., & Winlow, S. (2007). Cultural criminology and primitive accumulation: A formal introduction for two strangers who should really become more intimate. *Crime Media Culture*, *3*(1), 82–90.

Hall, S., & Winlow, S. (2015). *Revitalizing criminological theory: Towards a new ultra-realism.* New York, NY: Routledge.

Hall, S., & Winlow, S. (2018). Ultra-realism. In W. S. DeKeseredy & M. Dragiewicz (Eds.) *Routledge handbook of critical criminology* (pp. 43–56). New York, NY: Routledge.

Hayward, K. (2012). Five spaces of cultural criminology. *British Journal of Criminology*, *52*, 441–462.

Hogg, R. (2016). Left realism and social democratic renewal. *International Journal for Crime, Justice and Social Democracy*, *5*(3), 66–79.

Hough, M. (2014). Confessions of a recovering "administrative criminologist": Jock Young, quantitative research, and policy research. *Crime Media Culture*, *10*, 215–226.

IC3 (Internet Crime Complaint Center). (2019). *2018 internet crime report.* Washington D.C.: Federal Bureau of Investigation. Retrieved from https://pdf.ic3.gov/2018_IC3Report.pdf.fic3.

Jewkes, Y., & Andrews, C. (2005). Policing the filth: The problems of investigating online child pornography in England and Wales. *Policing and Society*, *15*(1), 42–62.

Johnston, A. (2008). *Žižek's ontology: A transcendental materialist theory of subjectivity*. Evanston, IL: Northwestern University Press.

Jones, T., MacLean, J., & Young, J. (1986). *The Islington crime survey.* Aldershot, England: Gower.

Latour, B. (2005). *Reassembling the social: An introduction to actor-network theory.* New York, NY: Oxford University Press.

Latour, B., & Woolgar, S. (1986). Laboratory life: The construction of scientific facts. Princeton, NJ: Princeton University Press.
Law, V. (2014). Against carceral feminism. *Jacobin*. Retrieved from www.jacobinmag.com/2014/10/against-carceral-feminism/.
Lea, J. (2002). *Crime and modernity*. London, England: Sage.
Lea, J. (2010). Left Realism, community and state-building. *Crime, Law and Social Change*, *54*, 141–158.
Lea, J. (2014). New deviancy, Marxism and the politics of left realism: Reflections on Jack Young's early writings. *Theoretical Criminology*, *18*(4), 432–440.
Lea, J. (2016a). Left realism: A radical criminology for the current crisis. *International Journal for Crime, Justice and Social Democracy*, *5*(3), 53–65.
Lea, J., & Young, J. (1984). *What is to be done about law and order?* New York, NY: Penguin.
Lenhart, A., Ybarra, M., Zickuhr, K., & Price-Feney, M. (2016). *Online harassment, digital abuse, and cyberstalking in America*. Data & Society Research Institute. Retrieved from www.datasociety.net/pubs/oh/Online_Harassment_2016.pdf.
Like-Haislip, T. Z., & Miofsky, K. T. (2011). Race, ethnicity, gender, and violent victimization. *Race and Justice*, *1*(3), 254–276.
Lusthaus, J., & Varese, F. (2017, Online First). Offline and local: The hidden face of cybercrime. *Policing: A Journal of Policy and Practice*.
Lynch, M. J. (2015). The classlessness state of criminology and why criminology without class is rather meaningless. *Crime, Law & Social Change*, *63*, 65–90.
Madfis, E., & Cohen, J. (2016). Critical criminologies of the present and future: Left realism, left idealism, and what's left in between. *Social Justice*, *43*(4), 1–21.
Marganski, A. (2018). Feminist theory and technocrime. In K.F. Steinmetz & M.R. Nobles (Eds.), *Technocrime and criminological theory*. New York, NY: Routledge.
Matthews, R. (2014). *Realist criminology*. London, England: Palgrave Macmillan.
Matthews, R. (2016). Realist criminology, the new aetiological crisis and the crime drop. *International Journal for Crime, Justice and Social Democracy*, *5*(3), 2–11.
McGuire, M. (2016). Cybercrime 4.0: Now what is to be done? In R. Matthews (Ed.), *What is to be done about crime and punishment: Towards a "public criminology"* (pp. 251–279). London, England: Macmillan Publishers Ltd.
Meares, T. (2015). Broken windows, neighborhoods, and the legitimacy of law enforcement or why I fell in and out of love with Zimbardo. *Journal of Research in Crime and Delinquency*, *52*(4), 609–625.
Pearce, F. (1976). *Crimes of the powerful: Marxism, crime, and deviance*. London, England: Pluto Press.
Phillips, N. D., & Chagnon, N. (2020). "Six months is a joke": Carceral feminism and penal populism in the wake of the Stanford sexual assault case. *Feminist Criminology*, *15*(1), 47–69.
Phipps, A. (1986). Radical criminology and criminal victimization. In R. Matthews & J. Young (Eds.), *Confronting Crime* (pp. 97–117). London, England: Sage.
Powell, A., Stratton, G., & Cameron, R. (2018). *Digital criminology: Crime and justice in digital society*. New York, NY: Routledge.
Quinn, Z. (2017). *Crash override: How GamerGate [nearly] destroyed my life and how we can win the fight against online hate*. New York, NY: Public Affairs.
Raine, L., & Wellman, B. (2012). *Networked: The new social operating system*. Cambridge, MA: The MIT Press.
Renzetti, C. M. (2016). Critical realism and feminist criminology: Shall the twain ever meet? *International Journal for Crime, Justice and Social Democracy*, *5*(3), 41–52.

Rieke, A., Yu H., Robinson, D., & von Hoboken, J. (2016). *Data brokers in an open society.* London, England: Open Society Foundation. Retrieved from www.opensocietyfoundations.org/uploads/42d529c7-a351-412e-a065-53770cf1d35e/data-brokers-in-an-open-society-20161121.pdf..

Roberts, S. T. (2019). *Behind the screen: Content moderation in the shadows of social media.* New Haven, CT: Yale University Press.

Sampson, R., Raudenbush, S. W., & Earls, F. (1997). Neighborhoods and violent crime: A multilevel study of collective efficacy. *Science*, *277*(5328), 918–924.

Sayer, A. (2000). *Realism and social science.* Thousand Oaks, CA: Sage.

Schwartz, M. D., & DeKeseredy, W. S. (2010). The current health of left realist theory. *Crime, Law & Social Change*, *54*, 107–110.

Snowden, E. (2019). *Permanent record.* New York, NY: Metropolitan Books.

Stretesky, P. B., Long, M. A., & Lynch, M. J. (2014). *The treadmill of crime: Political economy and green criminology.* New York, NY: Routledge.

Testa, A., Maimon, D., Sobesto, B., & Cukier, M. (2017). Illegal roaming and file manipulation on target computers: Assessing the effect of sanction threats on system trespassers' online behaviors. *Criminology & Public Policy*, *16*(3), 689–726.

Walklate, S. (2015). Jock Young, Left Realism and critical victimology. *Critical Criminology*, *23*, 179–190.

Whitty, M. T., & Buchanan, T. (2016). The online dating romance scam: The psychological impact on victims–Both financial and non-financial. *Criminology & Criminal Justice*, *16*(2), 176–194.

Wilson, J. Q., & Kelling, G. L. (1982, March). The police and neighborhood safety: Broken windows. *The Atlantic Monthly*, *249*, 29–38.

Winlow, S. (2019). What lies beneath? Some notes on ultra-realism, and the intellectual foundations of the "deviant leisure" perspective. In T. Raymen & O. Smith (Eds.), *Deviant Leisure* (pp. 45–65). London: Palgrave Macmillan.

Winlow, S., & Hall, S. (2016). Realist criminology and its discontents. *International Journal for Crime, Justice and Social Democracy*, *5*(3), 80–94.

Winlow, S., & Hall, S. (2019). Shock and awe: On progressive minimalism and retreatism, and the new ultra-realism. *Critical Criminology*, *27*(1), 21–36.

Wong, J. C. (2019, February 7). "Overreacting to failure": Facebook's new Myanmar strategy baffles local activists. *The Guardian.* Retrieved from www.theguardian.com/technology/2019/feb/07/facebook-myanmar-genocide-violence-hate-speech.

Wood, M. A., Anderson, B., & Richards, I. (2019, Online First). Breaking down the pseudo-pacification process: Eight critiques of ultra-realist crime causation theory. *British Journal of Criminology.*

Young, J. (1979). Left idealism, reformism, and beyond: From new criminology to Marxism. In B. Fine, R. Kinsey, J. Lea, S. Picciotoo, & J. Young (Eds.), *Capitalism and the rule of law: From deviancy theory to Marxism* (pp. 1–28). London, England: Hutchinson.

Young, J. (2007). *The exclusive society: Social exclusive, crime and difference in late modernity.* Thousand Oaks, CA: Sage.

Zuboff, S. (2015). Big other: Surveillance capitalism and the prospects of an information civilization. *Journal of Information Technology*, *30*, 75–89.

# 11

# A Theory of Sex Trafficking Victimization

*Teresa C. Kulig and Francis T. Cullen*

In 2000, the Victims of Trafficking and Violence Protection Act was passed that invented a new legal category in the United States—the offense of "sex trafficking." This federal legislation provided an explicit definition of actions that constituted trafficking while also creating a new way to envision these crimes. What was once only considered prostitution now became the crime of sex trafficking—involving a victim in need of rescue and a perpetrator deserving of punishment (Kulig & Butler, 2019).

The federal law is commonly referred to as the Trafficking Victims Protection Act (TVPA). This act defines sex trafficking as the recruitment, harboring, transportation, provision, obtaining, patronizing, or soliciting of a person through the use of force, fraud, or coercion for the purpose of commercial sex. Minors are considered to be sex trafficking victims regardless of whether any means were used to compel them to engage in commercial sex. Since its original inception, the TVPA has been reauthorized multiple times to provide support services for victims, increase punishments for perpetrators, and implement resources for prevention purposes (U.S. Department of Justice, 2017).

Although different pieces of international and U.S. state legislation have also been passed, the federal law offers one comprehensive definition to contextualize these offenses through particular actions (e.g., recruitment, harboring) and means (i.e., force, fraud, coercion) (Goździak & Vogel, 2020; U.S. Department of Health and Human Services, 2017). The specific behaviors that constitute sex trafficking, however, can be defined in different ways depending on jurisdiction. For example, some U.S. states vary from the federal TVPA more than others—especially in the level of proof required to classify minors as victims (Gies, Healy, Green, & Bobnis, 2020; Polaris Project, 2014). Regardless of the definition being applied, people compelling others to engage in exploitive behaviors can be captured under a variety of offenses (e.g., kidnapping, assault, promoting prostitution). By now classifying trafficking as a separate offense, these crimes and the sentences they carry are elevated by more serious responses. This new classification of crime domestically and abroad also has had implications for the fields of criminology and victimology.

In response to this new category of crime, scholars now had a novel object of study. The increasing amounts of attention received by sex trafficking has been vital to inform our understanding of these offenses (e.g., Rajaram & Tidball, 2018; Rothman et al., 2020). Although there are now hundreds of research articles on the topic, much of the attention has highlighted four main issues. First, scholars and practitioners have strived to illuminate the prevalence of sex trafficking (e.g., Anderson, Kulig, & Sullivan, 2019). The methods used to estimate known (e.g., identified by services providers or law enforcement officials) and unknown (i.e., never coming to the attention of service providers) cases of sex trafficking have increased over time to try and determine how many victims are affected (Farrell & de Vries, 2020; Kulig, 2020). Despite these efforts, the true estimates of these events are largely unknown (Farrell et al., 2019; Finkelhor, Vaquerano, & Stranski, 2017). The hidden nature of the crime coupled with concerns about identification by first responders or other service providers is believed to hinder the ability to discover victims (Farrell, McDevitt, & Fahy 2010; Newton, Mulcahy, & Martin, 2008; Reid & Jones, 2011).

Second, research has largely focused on the harms or consequences of sex trafficking victimization. During exploitation, victims can be subjected to abuse that is emotional (e.g., threats of violence, name calling), physical (e.g., restrictions of personal freedoms), and sexual (e.g., rape). The long-term effects of these violations can be accompanied by financial insecurity, substance use, strained relationships, psychological trauma (e.g., anxiety, post-traumatic stress disorder), physical injuries (e.g., muscle damage, dental damage), and neurological impairments (e.g., headaches, memory problems) (Lederer & Wetzel, 2014; Ottisova, Hemmings, Howard, Zimmerman, & Oram, 2016; Sukach, Gonzalez, & Pickens, 2018; Zimmerman et al., 2008).

The broader point here is that trafficking victimization can result in substantial and lasting harms that require appropriate responses to reduce the risk of revictimization (e.g., Adams, 2011; Busch-Armendariz, Nsonwu, Heffron, Hernandez, & Garza, 2009; Reid, 2010).

Third, studies have examined the nature of sex trafficking experiences, showing that this offense differs in unique ways from most crimes examined in criminology or victimology. Most of the research on victimization studies crime events, such as a physical assault, which oftentimes occurs at a specific time and in a particular place. Similar types of predatory offenses (e.g., robbery, sexual assault) are generally limited to a single incident that is confined to one context (Oudekerk & Truman, 2017). But sex trafficking is not a crime "event." Rather, it is a qualitatively different kind of victimization that occurs over time and place, unfolding in stages. In this way, sex trafficking is similar to other ongoing or recurrent offenses, including intimate partner violence (Oudekerk & Truman, 2017; Reid, Richards, & Kulig, 2021). It is thus important to consider the unique aspects of sex trafficking victimization in defining how these crimes are facilitated.

Fourth, more theoretical works have attempted to explain the conditions necessary for sex trafficking to occur. This literature often seeks to unpack the sex trafficking enterprise into stages, focusing on the process from onset to desistance (e.g., Aronowitz & Dahal, 2014; Aronowitz, Theuermann, & Tyurykanova, 2010; Greenbaum, 2014; Hammond & McGlone, 2014; Lopez & Minassians, 2017; Lutya & Lanier, 2012; Preble, 2019, 2020; Reid, 2012; Salt & Stein, 1997; Sanchez & Stark, 2014; Tyldum & Brunovskis, 2005; Zimmerman et al., 2003). The current chapter seeks to build on these works, as well as on the prior research detailing the nature of this offense (Kulig, 2018), to present a systematic theory of sex trafficking. Although sex trafficking offenders can include those individuals who purchase sex from a victim, the sections to follow focus on individuals who actively seek out victims to exploit and profit. As a prelude to developing this conceptual framework, we first set a broader context in which sex trafficking victimization occurs.

## A Theoretical Model of Sex Trafficking Victimization

Two theoretical approaches can be taken when explaining sex trafficking. The first approach is to examine the structural or macro conditions that create a market for sex trafficking. Macro-level theories seek to understand the origins of sex trafficking. In particular, this offense is oftentimes referred to as a "business" that involves the product (i.e., victims), supplier (i.e., the trafficker), and consumers (i.e., sex buyers) (Hammond & McGlone, 2014; Shelley, 2003). The concept behind this framework is that sex trafficking would not exist unless there was a demand for cheap sexual services (Kara, 2009). This demand thus creates a market for traffickers to supply victims from which they can benefit—of which the profits can be lucrative (Dank et al., 2014). Of course, there are ongoing debates on whether trading something of value for sexual services sex is inherently exploitive (e.g., Gerassi, 2015; Weitzer, 2010a). The focus of this chapter is on those cases where some level of force (e.g., physical restraint, violence), fraud (e.g., manipulation, lies), or coercion (e.g., threats of violence, threats to use the legal system against victim) is used to compel an individual to engage in commercial sex, per the federal TVPA definition.

Inherent in this business framework are structural inequalities that facilitate the victimization of some individuals more than others. More specifically, globalization, poverty, and gender discrimination are believed to be underlying issues that contribute to sex trafficking victimization (Abu-Ali & Al-Bahar, 2011; Kara, 2009; Lopez & Minassians, 2017; Wheaton, Schauer, & Galli, 2010; Williams, 1997). As inequalities between people grow, fewer viable employment opportunities are available for non-skilled or disadvantaged laborers. They face chronic, inescapable economic insecurity, especially women who have the added burden of gender discrimination blocking access to education and skilled employment. Scholars argue that these social conditions create environments where disadvantaged individuals are left with few options to survive through legitimate means—making them more vulnerable to traffickers' manipulative tactics to induce them to engage in commercial sex (Gerassi, 2015). These external circumstances may also foster organized crime operations to maximize profits for traffickers (Williams, 1997). Given the market for female sex partners, economically marginalized women seem to be at an elevated risk of being targeted by traffickers (e.g., Banks & Kyckelhahn, 2011; Jordan, Patel, & Rapp, 2013; Reid, 2012).

Although this business perspective is invaluable, it does not elaborate fully the ways in which trafficking occurs—or the actions that are needed to facilitate these crimes on an individual level. The second theoretical approach addresses this very issue, examining how individuals become sex trafficking victims. This perspective aligns closely with the concept of a crime script, or the step-by-step account of stages and decision points for a crime to occur (e.g., Savona, Giommoni, and Mancuso, 2014; Reid & Fox, 2019). The two types of theories can be integrated, of course, but the focus of the current chapter is on the individual experience of sex trafficking. The following theory thus provides an overview of the stages of sex trafficking victimization at the micro level.

Similar to explanations of other victimization types, a theory of sex trafficking must start with how potential victims (or targets) are initially selected and then how offenders carry out the particular offense. As noted, the prototypical predatory street crime occurs when offenders and unguarded victims intersect in time and space only for as much time as it takes for the crime event to be concluded (Cohen & Felson, 1979). But, sex trafficking victimization is rarely a one-time, situationally delimited offense (Adams, 2011; Reid, 2014; Rothman et al., 2020). As a business enterprise in which victims are marketed repeatedly for sex in the pursuit of profit, an individual's sex trafficking experiences can occur over an extended period of time as part of an ongoing process of exploitation (see also Greenbaum, 2014; Hammond & McGlone, 2014; Lutya & Lanier, 2012; Reid, 2012). Any theory thus needs to account not only for the onset of trafficking but also for the factors that allow for this victimization to persist.

A theoretical model of the descriptive recipe for trafficking to occur involves four stages: (1) recruitment, (2) exploitation, (3) control and ongoing inducement, and (4) closure. Notably, these stages often have overlapping components (e.g., controlling tactics applied during the recruitment stage), and they can look differently based on any given individual's unique trafficking experience. For a trafficking offense to be carried out, however, these general stages need to be present. Note that, although there can be multiple offenders involved in a single case of sex trafficking, the sections below will generally refer to a single trafficker for simplicity. All of the stages are presented in Figure 11.1 and discussed below to unpack the sex trafficking enterprise.

## Stage 1: Recruitment

As outlined in Figure 11.1, the first step in sex trafficking victimization is recruiting would-be victims. Similar to any crime, offenders must acquire a target before carrying out an offense (Cohen & Felson, 1979; Hindelang, Gottfredson, & Garofalo, 1978). After locating an individual to recruit, the trafficker then needs to establish a relationship

**Figure 11.1**
**Stages of Sex Trafficking Victimization**

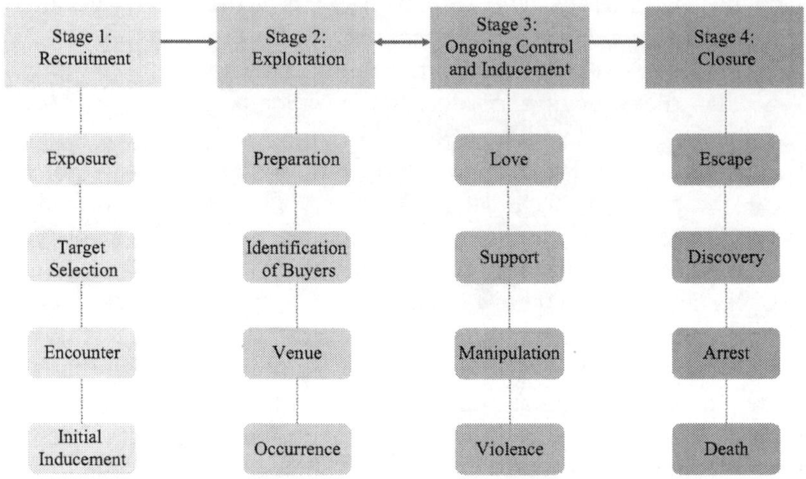


that ultimately leads to exploitation. In this way, the offender could work to recruit the individual quickly (e.g., over one day) or over a longer period of time (e.g., over six months) (Kennedy, Klein, Bristowe, Cooper, & Yuille, 2007). Additional considerations when examining how victims are recruited include the role of exposure, target selection, first encounter, and initial inducement.

*Exposure*

In victimology more broadly, individuals who are more exposed—or who are physically visible and accessible—to would-be offenders are more likely to be victimized (Cohen, Kluegel, & Land, 1981). Scholars suggest that particularly “risky” lifestyles can increase exposure to traffickers, or routines that regularly overlap with the daily activities of offenders (Pratt & Turanovic, 2016). In the context of sex trafficking, individuals who are more exposed to potential traffickers are at greater risk of being exploited (Cockbain & Wortley, 2015; Kenyon & Schanz, 2014). But what increases exposure to traffickers? Research in this area is generally limited to the experiences of minors who are trafficked for sex, identifying a number of risk indicators that could put someone in the general vicinity of offenders. More specifically for increasing exposure, individuals who use substances, who associate with criminals, who are involved in the justice system for their own offenses, or who run away from home are at an elevated risk of sex trafficking (Chohaney, 2016; Reid, 2011; Reid & Piquero, 2014; Varma, Gillespie, McCracken, & Greenbaum, 2015). It is possible that these high-risk behaviors or lifestyles increase exposure to traffickers in the pursuit of substances or during their own offenses if they associate with other offenders (Cohen & Felson, 1979; Hindelang et al., 1978). Running away from home may indicate a vulnerability to traffickers who are in search of targets with few resources to care for themselves (e.g., lack of social support, shelter, food).

Notably, who individuals live with can also have implications for their overall level of exposure and risk of victimization. For example, being part of a family with members in the sex trade can increase the likelihood of sex trafficking (Reid, 2012). Living with friends or romantic partners—particularly if they are older—has also been associated with victimization (e.g., Moore, Houck, Hirway, Barron, & Goldberg, 2020; Reid, 2012). Some children or adolescents are even trafficked by their caregivers (e.g., parents, relatives), which clearly is beyond the control of those individuals and would have nothing to do with their lifestyles (Reid, Huard, & Haskell, 2015). Although an important area of consideration, this situation of caregiver-traffickers likely does not represent the vast majority of sex trafficking cases (Kulig, 2018; Reid, 2016). Overall, exposure may be related to lifestyle choices, but could also be constant beyond any lifestyle factor if the trafficker is located in the home with the victim.

### *Target Selection*

Although lifestyle choices or living arrangements may increase exposure to potential traffickers, it is important to recognize that traffickers are also actively searching for victims to exploit (Brantingham & Brantingham, 1991, 1981). To be successful at selecting a target that they can control, traffickers need to locate individuals with certain characteristics that make them easier to manipulate or coerce—effectively more attractive targets (Cohen & Felson, 1979; Hindelang et al., 1978). In other words, research suggests that not everyone is equally likely to be selected by traffickers. This concept of offenders carefully selecting targets aligns with the target congruence framework (Finkelhor & Asdigian, 1996), whereby certain victim characteristics are perceived as making them an easier target for an offender.

Although males can be exploited (Dank et al., 2015), research suggests that younger females may be particularly vulnerable to sex trafficking (Anderson et al., 2019; Banks & Kyckelhahn, 2011; Reid, 2011, 2016). Beyond this demographic profile, research shows that other individual characteristics make potential targets more attractive selections or susceptible to traffickers' tactics (Cockbain & Wortley, 2015; Kenyon & Schanz, 2014). Thus, individuals who have experienced family dysfunction, childhood abuse or neglect, child protective services involvement, mental health concerns, poverty, low self-esteem or self-worth, or lack of prosocial attachments are more likely to be trafficked for sex (de Vries et al., 2019; Macias-Konstantopoulos, Munroe, Purcell, Tester, & Burke, 2015; Pasko & Chesney-Lind, 2016; Raymond, Hughes, & Gomez, 2001; Reid, 2011; Reid, Baglivio, Piquero, Greenwald, & Epps, 2017; Rothman, Bazzi, & Bair-Merritt, 2015). Individuals with these backgrounds may be more likely to run away from home, possibly increasing exposure (e.g., Greenbaum, 2014). Traffickers may also seek out individuals with disabilities or foreign nationals who may not be familiar with the local laws or language (Banks & Kyckelhahn, 2011; Reid, 2018; Shandro et al., 2016). Potential targets with these backgrounds may not have the resources or social support needed to act as protective factors against traffickers. As will be discussed, traffickers can exploit this vulnerability through tactics such as love, shelter, food, employment, or other acts that create a false sense of security to facilitate their offenses (e.g., Reid, 2016).

*Encounter*

An important aspect of any crime is where the victim and target intersect—or the place where the trafficker can gain access to the victim to begin the recruitment stage (Weisburd et al., 2016). Given that traffickers are targeting individuals with select backgrounds or experiences, it makes sense that they are often noted as identifying victims at certain places. More specifically, traffickers will make efforts to encounter victims outside of juvenile detention centers, group homes, schools, substance abuse clinics, or other public spaces (Kulig, 2018; Pasko & Chesney-Lind, 2016; Reid & Fox, 2019; Williamson & Prior, 2009). Traffickers today may also rely on the internet, including chat rooms and social media sites to target victims (Greenbaum, 2014; Reid & Fox, 2019; Sapiro, Johnson, Postmus, & Simmel, 2016). In this way, new advances in technology have removed the need for traffickers to encounter victims in a specific location, but still provide the means to facilitate their crimes. And as previously noted, traffickers may even seek out targets that they already know and in shared spaces (e.g., home), including friends, relatives, or their own children (Curtis, Terry, Dank, Dombrowski, & Khan, 2008; Moore et al., 2020; Reid, 2012; Reid et al., 2015). It is possible that, in addition to having exposure to targets, certain characteristics of potential victims (e.g., history of abuse) make them easier to access, control, and exploit—especially if there are no capable guardians around to intervene (Cohen et al., 1981).

### *Initial Inducement*

Beyond encountering and selecting a target to exploit, traffickers then have to consider how to induce victims into commercial sex (e.g., Kennedy et al., 2007; Rajaram & Tidball, 2018; Williams & Frederick, 2009; Williamson & Prior, 2009). Inducement is not necessarily a single act but can be an ongoing set of behaviors that the trafficker must employ to establish and maintain control over the victim. Traffickers might start out using affection to secure cooperation (e.g., intimate relationship) but then later use coercion (e.g., bargaining, bribes) and/or violent threats or actions. Traffickers thus face the ongoing challenge to continue to induce their selected target to engage in profit-making commercial sex.

Note, however, that it is not sufficient to describe the stages by which sex trafficking occurs. Also relevant are the different pathways that shape the experiences of victims and the level of inducement that they experience that initially draw them into commercial sex (e.g., Hammond & McGlone, 2014). Again, the legal federal definition of sex trafficking includes the use of force, fraud, or coercion to compel an individual to engage in commercial sex. But existing research suggests that different methods can be used to persuade someone to sell sex for something of value. Although there can be variation in experiences, the research describes three main pathways into exploitation.

The first pathway is a *voluntary* agreement to engage in commercial sex. Voluntary in this context refers to individuals choosing to sell sex as a way of asserting their human agency (Kennedy et al., 2007). As previously noted, there are ongoing debates on whether someone can ever make a choice to engage in sex work voluntarily (Gerassi, 2015), but research suggests that some individuals do make a conscious decision to sell sex (e.g., Bass, 2015; Weitzer, 2010b). Thus, some individuals may initially choose to engage in commercial sex either on their own or in collaboration with another person who serves a distinct role (e.g., security, transportation). Again, minors who sell sex for anything of value are legally classified as trafficking victims by the federal TVPA—regardless of whether they assert it was "voluntary."

Notably, research suggests that even before someone agrees to engage in commercial sex, a grooming period can occur where traffickers attempt to build trust or convey that sex with a variety of partners is not disreputable but normal (Reid & Fox, 2019). In particular, traffickers may show the individual pornography, normalize commercial sex work in their conversations, or discuss how glamorous and lucrative sex work can be (Hammond & McGlone, 2014; Kennedy et al., 2007). Individuals in these circumstances may still be asserting some agency in choosing to engage in commercial sex, but the trafficker would have made efforts to facilitate this decision.

The second pathway involves some *exchange inducement* where an individual agrees to sell sex due to some need or belief that they will get something in return. This strategy is sometimes referred to as "finesse" trafficking or pimping to try and persuade the victim that it is ultimately their decision to sell sex (e.g., Serie et al., 2018; Williamson & Prior, 2009). Within this pathway, the trafficker can use exchanges in a couple of different ways to form a bond with the victim. For example, someone might make a decision to engage in commercial sex because they need money quickly, a place to stay, transportation, food, clothes, drugs, or alcohol (Kennedy et al., 2007; Pasko & Chesney-Lind, 2016; Williamson & Prior, 2009). In particular, minors have been found to engage in "survival sex" as a way to provide for themselves without the assistance of caregivers (Dank et al., 2015; Perkins & Ruiz, 2017). The implication here is that the victim needs something and the trafficker will provide them with or bribe them with the requested resources in exchange for selling sex (Kulig, 2018; Marcus, Horning, Curtis, Sanson, & Thompson, 2014; Reid, 2016).

In another scenario, traffickers can use the guise of love or a relationship to create this exchange. Victims may believe they are in a romantic relationship with their trafficker, who may have been providing for them for some time. The victim may be coerced into exploitation to benefit the couple as a way to pay for things or as reimbursement for any gifts and getaways given to the victim during the relationship (Kennedy et al., 2007; Raphael, Reichert, & Powers, 2010; Reid, 2016; Williams

& Frederick, 2009; Williamson & Prior, 2009). Love—or the appearance of love—in this context can be a particularly powerful way for traffickers to induce victims to do what they want, especially if the trafficker had originally provided for the victim without any request for assistance (e.g., buy clothes, salon visits, meals).

Finally, victims may initially be coerced through false jobs (e.g., modeling), with the promise of a different life if they work enough. As an example, the victim may be told that they could be a professional model, only to show up and find out that the trafficker actually runs an escort business (Kulig, 2018; Williamson & Prior, 2009). The victim may agree to work as an escort under the guise that the business will turn to modeling once enough money is made. Of course, the trafficker has no intention on creating a modeling business, and the exchange here is built on manipulation and false promises. Victims may even be initiated through other sexual acts (e.g., stripping) in exchange for love or other needs; unbeknownst to them, it is also in preparation for commercial sex (Raymond et al., 2001; Rothman et al., 2015).

The third pathway is to *violently or physically induce* victims to engage in commercial sex—otherwise known as "guerilla" trafficking or pimping (Williamson & Prior, 2009). Traffickers using this tactic are generally verbally or physically aggressive from the onset. Victims may be intimidated or threatened, have their family or friends threatened, experience physical, emotional, or sexual abuse, or witness the victimization of others (Kennedy et al., 2007; Perkins & Ruiz, 2017; Raphael et al., 2010; Reid, 2016; Williams & Frederick, 2009; Williamson & Prior, 2009). Some victims may even be photographed or recorded in sexually explicit positions as blackmail to facilitate compliance (Raymond et al., 2001). Severe cases of violence may even include kidnapping and forcibly drugging victims to ensure compliance (Kulig, 2018). Although the most heinous and violent cases oftentimes make the news and are adapted for major motion pictures (e.g., *Taken*; Morel, 2008), it is not necessarily in the trafficker's best interest to be extremely violent early on. Emotional and psychological manipulation can be effective inducement strategies absent any hint of violence (e.g., Kulig, 2018; Williamson & Prior, 2009).

The pathways described here are not necessarily mutually exclusive—someone may experience one or more of these tactics when being recruited and induced to engage in commercial sex. Notably, inducement types can also change forms over time. The broader issue here is how traffickers—after initially inducing victims during recruitment—continue to compel victims to engage in commercial sex, which will be discussed in more detail in Stage 3.

## Stage 2: Exploitation

After the target has been recruited by the trafficker, the next stage involves the actual exploitation—or the involvement of selling sex for something of value (see Figure 11.1). This phase can happen shortly after recruitment or over a period of time. This shift into sex trafficking requires some preparation on the part of the trafficker and the presence of the victim. The main phases of exploiting another person involve preparation, identification of buyers, selecting a venue, and the occurrence. Each of these phases is described in more detail below.

### *Preparation*

An important step in the trafficking enterprise is the preparation phase prior to exploitation. In this context, preparation can refer to getting the victim ready to sell commercial sex and involving any partners in the criminal enterprise. When preparing the victim, the trafficker may have to purchase clothes, makeup, and/or condoms. Note that these purchases may have been made during the recruitment phase as "gifts" and before the victim knew they were going to be induced to engage in commercial sex (Williamson & Prior, 2009). The trafficker or an associate would also set prices for sexual acts and coach the victim on how to make the transaction with the sex buyer if they were not going to facilitate that interaction themselves (Raymond et al., 2001; Williamson & Prior, 2009). Another aspect of preparation may include "seasoning" or the use of violence, manipulation, isolation, and/or intimidation to break victims' wills before they sell sex (Greenbaum, 2014).

Relatedly, if there were other individuals involved in the operation, then those details would have to be organized for the exploitation to be carried out successfully. For example, the trafficker may not work alone but could involve other actors to assist with coaching the victim on how to engage in sex work, transporting the victim, acting as security, collecting payment, and/or watching the victim to ensure they do not escape or seek help (Burke & Bruijn, 2018; Denton, 2010; Williamson & Prior, 2009). Each of these roles must be coordinated—whether by one or multiple actors—for the victim to be exploited and the commercial sex exchange to occur.

### *Identification of Buyers*

To make a profit, the trafficker must also have someone to purchase sex. The "johns" or sex buyers must be solicited, which can happen in a few ways (Kulig, 2018). Traffickers can take out advertisements online, in local newspapers, or in tabloids to facilitate commercial sex. Or traffickers can rely on impromptu in-person meetings at select streets, hotels, truck stops, gas stations, or even strip clubs. Depending on the location, word of mouth might also be an effective strategy for drawing in buyers (e.g., existing clientele, friends). Regardless of which advertisement method is used to locate buyers, the trafficker will need to organize the advertisement of the victim or delegate that responsibility to another co-offender in the criminal enterprise.

For example, if posting online, then someone needs to write the advertisement, pay the fee to post it, and place it in a location where potential buyers will find it. A recent hotspot for online commercial sex advertisements was Backpage.com, which has since been shut down and seized by the U.S. government (Savage & Williams, 2018). Yet anyone who wanted to purchase sex from an advertisement on a site like Backpage.com would need the necessary contact information (e.g., phone number) and would expect that someone would answer the phone or respond to a text message to schedule the arrangement. The trafficker would need to ensure that the phone number was active, someone was going to answer it, and the arrangement would be scheduled so the buyer did not get suspicious that it was a law enforcement sting (Greenbaum, 2014; Roe-Sepowitz, 2019). In another example, the trafficker could locate a street or location known for prostitution and drop off the victim for sex buyers to approach. Depending on the city, it may be more difficult to locate such an area for street interactions to occur.

### *Venue*

Beyond attracting buyers, the trafficker needs to identify a location where the sexual acts for profit can take place (Kulig, 2018; Swaner, Labriola, Rempel, Walker, & Spadafore, 2016). The victim may plan to travel to the buyer or the buyer may plan to travel to the victim. If the victim is soliciting on the street, the buyer may just pick up the person directly and take them to a location of their choosing. Otherwise, the trafficker would have to arrange for a specific location for the sexual act to occur, such as a hotel, bar, car, park, or residence.

*Occurrence*

Once the terms and operations of the exploitation are organized, the victim will then engage in commercial sex. Again, this occurrence may be arranged from the initial inducement (e.g., some exchange between the victim and trafficker), or the trafficker may have to engage in additional strategies as outlined in Stage 3 to compel the victim to sell sex. In other words, the victim may be somewhat in agreement to sell sex, or they may only be engaging in commercial sex under duress from the trafficker. After the sexual act, the victim may or may not be allowed to keep some of the "value" (e.g., money, drugs, food) that was arranged (Greenbaum, 2014).

### Stage 3: Ongoing Control and Inducement

The third stage is focused on how traffickers maintain control over victims and continue to induce them into commercial sex (see Figure 11.1). As previously noted, this stage can overlap with Stages 1 and 2, including the types of tactics that are used. Traffickers may use a variety of strategies to induce someone to sell sex initially and immediately before exploitation, but to develop an ongoing inducement is a victimization enterprise. The fundamental aspect throughout this whole process is for traffickers to gain and maintain control over victims.

Although some individuals may initially agree to engage in commercial sex (i.e., prostitution), this sex-for-profit act is transformed into sex trafficking when the trafficker has to use strategies to compel the individual to sell sex. Traffickers cannot continue to profit from the exploitation if they cannot control the victim and induce them to do what they want. Thus, control tactics are an integral component of "successfully" trafficking another person for sex. In fact, the tactics described in Stage 3 actions can show the means by which Stage 2 exploitation is accomplished over time (see Figure 11.1). By federal legal standards, for someone to be labeled officially as a "trafficker," they must use force, fraud, or coercion against adult victims. (Recall that minors engaging in commercial sex are classified as sex trafficking victims by federal legislation regardless of whether these means are used.) The trafficker needs to employ tactics that allow them to maintain power, including love, support, manipulation, and violence. Of course, these categories are not mutually exclusive; traffickers can employ multiple tactics in any given case. Each of these strategies is described in more detail below.

*Love*

A relatively common strategy used by traffickers to initially recruit victims is through sentiments of love (Curtis et al., 2008; Dank et al., 2014; Greenbaum, 2014; Hammond & McGlone, 2014; Reid, 2012; Sanchez & Stark, 2014; Williams & Frederick, 2009; Williamson & Prior, 2009). This connection is generally developed through an ongoing romantic relationship (e.g., Rothman et al., 2015). However, traffickers can also use these tactics to maintain control over victims throughout their exploitation, and they may even use it as a form of a bribe that obtains some "buy in" from the victim. For example, a trafficker might tell a victim that they will marry them only if they engage in commercial sex (Kulig, 2018). Or, the trafficker may use their existing relationship or marriage to advocate that the victim continues to sell sex to support the couple and their basic needs. This strategy can be particularly effective if the victim had been provided with gifts or social support and now is being asked to "return the favor" to benefit the couple—an exchange of sorts (Kennedy et al., 2007). These "relationships" are often a ruse by the trafficker from the beginning and a form of *fraud* (Dank et al., 2014). Still, love can prove to be an efficient tactic to maintain control.

*Support*

Another tactic used by traffickers is exploiting support, which is similar to love in that there is often some exchange between the trafficker and victim. As previously noted, victims may engage in commercial sex so they obtain shelter, food, drugs, clothes, or even money (Curtis et al., 2008; Dank et al., 2014; Kennedy et al., 2007; Williams & Frederick, 2009). Traffickers may rely on this connection so that victims are compelled to comply with demands in order to survive or satisfy personal needs. Victims may even be told that commercial sex is glamorous and will provide a better life—possibly leading to other employment opportunities or a way to become self-sustaining if they sell sex for long enough (Kennedy et al., 2007; Kulig, 2018; Reid, 2016). Other victims may be informed that selling sex is only temporary until they "get on their feet." Yet victims may not always realize that the exchange being made is not entirely truthful. The trafficker may not allow them to share in any profits and may provide only some of their promised support (Kulig, 2018; Raphael et al., 2010). Some victims may also be told that they must settle a debt to leave. This financial obligation might initially have been portrayed as a "gift" from the trafficker that the victim is now told must be paid off, or it could be an agreed-upon exchange that becomes an ever-increasing amount the victim can never pay down (Raymond et al., 2001; Reid, 2016).

This strategy of support can be particularly compelling if the victim has a substance addiction—or develops one due to the trafficker—that the trafficker can exploit by acting as the dealer. The more dependent victims are on their trafficker, the easier it is to compel them to sell sex and profit from their exploitation. In this way, the trafficker is able to assert ongoing control on victims so as to secure a steady supply of profits, all the while victims become more and more reliant on the trafficker. Because the trafficker in these situations is generally deceiving the victim in some way (e.g., lucrative pay in sex work, debt, promise of a better life), this tactic could be considered a form of *fraud*.

### *Manipulation*

A related strategy that traffickers employ is manipulation. A trafficker may use psychological or emotional *coercion* as a way to break down the victim mentally and to convince them of some distorted reality. This tactic can involve falsifying information, using threats of violence, or inaccurately stating that the victim owes the trafficker in some way. As an example, traffickers might make victims feel worthless or like they do not have viable alternatives to commercial sex (Kulig, 2018). Traffickers will use name calling, mocking, or other degrading actions (e.g., sign a contract to stay with trafficker until death, blackmail) to convince victims that they will likely never escape their current situation (Raphael et al., 2010; Reid, 2016; Reid & Fox, 2019). The shame may be overwhelming for some victims, and they may believe that they have no option but to sell sex. Victims may also have their personal items (e.g., identification, cell phone, documents) confiscated or be threatened with deportation or other legal action to induce compliance (Dank et al., 2014; Dovydaitis, 2010; Kulig, 2018). Verbal threats of violence or forcing victims to witness violence against others can also be a warning that, if they do not obey requests, then they will be harmed next. A trafficker might even brand their victim to show ownership over them and emotionally ingrain in them that they are property (Kulig, 2018).

*Violence*

Another way that traffickers control victims is through violence. Traffickers can use various violent tactics, including isolation from support systems, physical restraint or guarding of victims, physical or sexual assault, forced drug use, or particularly cruel punishments (e.g., control food intake or sleep, force ice cold showers, shave victim's head with knives) (Dank et al., 2014; Hammond & McGlone, 2014; Kulig, 2018; Raphael et al., 2010; Raymond et al., 2001; Reid, 2016; Troshynski & Blank, 2017). These forms of control generally fall under the concept of *force*, whereby the victim is physically harmed in some way to ensure that they continue selling sex to provide profits for their trafficker.

Victims who are harmed are generally in fear for their lives or for the lives of those individuals close to them (e.g., family, children). Similar to the other strategies noted, traffickers may use violence from the beginning of recruitment or phase in violent actions if seen as required to maintain control throughout the exploitation (e.g., Reid, 2016). Regardless of when the violence begins, it can escalate into severe injury or even death—as will be discussed in Stage 4. Notably, many victims acknowledge experiencing at least some violent acts while they are exploited for sex (Greenbaum, 2014; Kulig, 2018; Williamson & Prior, 2009).

## Stage 4: Closure

Closure is the final stage of any sex trafficking enterprise—the exploitation ends (see Figure 11.1). On average, individuals can be trafficked for approximately six months, but some are exploited for years (Kulig, 2018). Victims may also be retrafficked after escaping initially—possibly by the same trafficker or a new one (e.g., Adams, 2011; Hammond & McGlone, 2014). Although trafficking can continue for an extended length of time, it ends for every individual at some point. Yet how trafficking victimization comes to a close varies, and the frequency of each of these outcomes is unclear. Because existing studies struggle to measure the unreported cases—the so-called "hidden figure" of this crime—the true prevalence of trafficking victims remains unknown (e.g., Anderson et al., 2019; Finkelhor et al., 2017; Kulig, 2020). Still, various ways to achieving closure have been documented. Thus, a victim could escape their trafficker, be discovered and rescued, be arrested, or ultimately die. Note that the closure of this one case does not mean that the trafficker's enterprise comes to an end—they could still be exploiting other individuals. These outcomes instead refer to individual victims. Each of these experiences is described in more detail below.

### *Escape*

Some trafficking victims may be fortunate enough to escape their trafficker by running away (Kulig, 2018). Other victims, however, may attempt to escape, be caught, and be punished (Troshynski & Blank, 2017). For example, a victim who makes an unsuccessful escape attempt may be subjected to sexual assault, beatings, and ongoing abuses to prevent a future attempt (Kulig, 2018; Troshynski & Blank, 2017). Given the violent and/or manipulative nature of many trafficking enterprises, it is evident why so few victims are able or willing to successfully leave on their own (Zimmerman et al., 2003).

### *Discovery*

Closure can occur when someone discovers that a person is a trafficking victim and facilitates their rescue from the trafficker. Such discoveries can be made by law enforcement officers (e.g., during prostitution sting, as a victim of another crime), by doctors or staff during medical appointments (e.g., treatment for injuries or sexually transmitted diseases), by service providers (e.g., child welfare), by an observant neighbor, or by family or friends who notice something is wrong (e.g., Farrell & Pfeffer, 2014; Jimenez, Jackson, & Deye, 2015; Roe-Sepowitz, 2019; Sprang & Cole, 2018). In these instances, it is crucial that these external actors (e.g., police, service providers) recognize the signs of sex trafficking and offer assistance when required. However, researchers suggest that first responders and other actors who may come into contact with sex trafficking victims (e.g., police) require additional training to identify the signs and know when to intervene (e.g., Farrell et al., 2019). In response to these concerns, ongoing efforts are under way to facilitate trainings and responses to sex trafficking victims (Powell, Dickins, & Stoklosa, 2017; Wilson & Dalton, 2008).

*Arrest*

Another pathway to closure is when victims are arrested. Due to the nature of sex trafficking, traffickers often compel victims to engage in illegal conduct, thus exposing them to arrest (e.g., substance use, prostitution) (Diaz, Lumpkin, & Lizano, 2018; Fernandez, 2013; Love, Hussemann, Yu, McCoy, & Owens, 2018). When arrests occur, victims are at risk of being misclassified as criminal offenders rather than as victims of sex trafficking. If this misclassification occurs—which in the past has been common—the victim is likely to receive a punitive response (as any regular offender would) rather than receive needed assistance (Farrell & Reichert, 2017). In this way, victims are being punished for actions they committed while they were being exploited by their trafficker. Thus, rather than police officers discovering victims, they may just arrest them as perpetrators and process them through the criminal justice system (e.g., Kulig, Fissel, Anderson, & Fisher, 2020).

The recognition that sex trafficking victims may be arrested and treated as offenders has resulted in the development of sex trafficking specialty courts (Kulig & Butler, 2019). These courts are meant to take the victim's unique vulnerabilities (e.g., addiction, poverty, mental health disorders) into account and provide services rather than punishment. The individuals who are arrested are thus known as victim-defendants so as to recognize that they have been exploited even if they also committed a crime. The ultimate goal is to reduce subsequent vulnerability for trafficking through the formal processes of a court. However, few evaluations have been conducted on these courts to assess their ability to achieve their goals (Kulig & Butler, 2019). Additionally, there are relatively few courts throughout the United States, which means that other convicted offenders may be victims of sex trafficking without ever being labeled as such.

*Death*

Another potential outcome of sex trafficking is death. Because trafficking often involves the use of violence, some victims can be murdered while they are exploited (Kulig, 2018; Malarek, 2003). The death of the victim could be due to a variety of causes, including the trafficker, a sex buyer, or an overdose. Although it is ultimately not in the best interest of the trafficker to kill someone who brings in a profit, some victims may be seen as problematic if they continuously try to escape or do not conform to the rules (Troshynski & Blank, 2017). Sex buyers can be violent as well, creating dangerous conditions for victims when they are isolated with them to sell sex (Curtis et al., 2008; Greenbaum, 2014). And drugs are not uncommon in trafficking enterprises, which could lead to overdoses that are intentional or unintentional (Roberson, 2017). Another possibility—which is difficult to estimate given the hidden nature of these crimes—is that some victims may commit suicide during their exploitation. The conditions under which victims are compelled to endure can be severe (e.g., lack of food, substances, injuries) (Reid, 2016; Zimmerman et al., 2003). It is possible that the only exit some individuals see is by taking their own life.

## Conclusion

Unlike most other predatory crimes, sex trafficking is an enterprise that occurs over time and unfolds in stages. No claim is being made that the conceptual model offered is definitive. Still, our theory of sex trafficking provides a coherent means through which these offenses can be understood. Exploitation does not just happen but operates through a systematic process. Two insights can be gleaned from our efforts to unpack the nature of sex trafficking victimization.

First, outlining the stages of criminal victimization allows for an objective assessment of the perpetrator's planning process (e.g., Savona et al., 2014). In turn, this understanding illuminates possible strategies for crime prevention (e.g., Aronowitz et al., 2010; Newman, 2006). Thus, the stages presented here offer distinct targets for intervention during an ongoing trafficking experience. The goal is to determine how to prevent these events from happening—and how to mitigate the harms once someone is involved. In other forms of victimization, crime prevention has provided insights into ways to intervene (Cornish & Clarke, 2003; Smith & Clarke, 2012). Situational crime prevention (SCP) techniques in particular have proven effective at reducing crime through environmental modifications that alter or remove opportunities for crime to occur (Clarke, 1997).

In this context, the SCP strategy might include increasing the risks of the offender being caught at any stage of the trafficking enterprise. The risks of a trafficking offense can be heightened by spreading awareness of these crimes so as to elevate the subsequent likelihood of detection. There are ongoing efforts to increase awareness and training for potential first responders, including police, medical personnel, child welfare providers, and flight attendants (e.g., Farrell et al., 2012). Training could also target members of the general public to maximize efforts and to implement a form of bystander intervention (e.g., Nichols, 2016). Individuals in these roles could disrupt ongoing cases of exploitation if they recognize the signs of trafficking and report their concerns to the appropriate authorities. To prevent traffickers from gaining access to victims at the recruitment phase, additional training could be mandated for staff at locations where traffickers tend to search for vulnerable victims (e.g., homeless shelters, foster care).

Another way to increase risks is by relying on place managers (Cornish & Clarke, 2003). Such managers can influence whether a place facilitates or inhibits criminal behavior (Eck, 1994; Madensen & Eck, 2013). For example, victims can be trafficked at hotels or motels. Place managers at these locations could mandate staff training on trafficking, hire security guards, or encourage patrons to report any suspicious activity related to trafficking (see also Eck & Madensen, 2018). Ultimately, the place managers of potential trafficking recruitment locations (e.g., bus stations, retail stores, casinos, laundry mats) have considerable authority over how their businesses operate and can influence whether anti-trafficking efforts are implemented (Kulig, 2018; Williamson & Prior, 2009). Other managers at locations where victims might be taken during their exploitation (e.g., retailers, salons) could implement policies to identify and disrupt these events (e.g., staff trainings, post informational signs).

Beyond environmental modification to disrupt sex trafficking operations, another potential avenue would be to target high-risk populations who may be perceived as attractive targets to offenders. As noted, traffickers search out potential targets that they can control and exploit, oftentimes targeting vulnerable individuals (e.g., history of abuse, substance addiction, running away). However, offering services to at-risk individuals could remove the opportunity for traffickers to fill those needs, especially if programs are established to assist individuals early on and over time (e.g., Dank et al., 2017; Rothman et al., 2020). If there are no viable targets to recruit into the criminal enterprise, then traffickers will struggle to exploit individuals successfully.

Second, legislative mandates in place can have real consequences for how victims are treated once they are identified. Although federal legislation defines sex trafficking victimization, all 50 states have adopted their own laws, with some aligning with the federal definition more than others. Any identification of potential victims will be affected by the legislation and regulations guiding those service providers within a given context. Without adequate legislation that removes the potential for punitive responses, it is likely that some victims will continue to be arrested as offenders for crimes they committed during their exploitation (Kulig et al., 2020). A more effective strategy, however, would be to address the underlying vulnerabilities and circumstances that made someone susceptible to trafficking in the first place. Victims are not responsible for the actions of traffickers who exploited them, but they likely require services to reduce their risk of revictimization and to facilitate reintegration into society (Adams, 2011; Hammond & McGlone, 2014). Relatedly, it will be vital that scholars are able to track the long-term outcomes of victims to ensure treatments can be adapted to their needs and in ways that reduce their vulnerability over time (e.g., Rothman et al., 2020).

The goal of studying any offense is to prevent future harms; sex trafficking victimization is no different. Research indicates that the harms associated with these offenses are substantial and can be long lasting (Williamson & Prior, 2009; Zimmerman et al., 2003). Scholars, practitioners, and legislators have continued to make efforts to offer resources and responses to these crimes. As we learn more about the nature of these offenses, the stages under which they are carried out, the vulnerabilities of victims, and the processes of traffickers, there will be more guidance on how best to employ evidence-based practices. It will be critical to avoid punitive legal responses that penalize individuals for their exploitation. By understanding the nature of this victimization, the challenge will be to develop responses to sex trafficking victims that emphasize the delivery of human services while simultaneously taking into account their individual circumstances and ambitions.

## References

Abu-Ali, A., & Al-Bahar, M. (2011). Understanding child survivors of human trafficking: A micro and macro level analysis. *Social and Behavioral Sciences*, *30*, 791–796.

Adams, C. (2011). Re-trafficked victims: How a human rights approach can stop the cycle of re-victimization of sex trafficking victims. *George Washington International Law Review*, *43*, 201–234.

Anderson, V. R., Kulig, T. C., & Sullivan, C. J. (2019). Estimating the prevalence of human trafficking in Ohio, 2014–2016. *American Journal of Public Health, 109*, 1396–1399.

Aronowitz, A. A., & Dahal, P. (2014). *Report to the government of Nepal on the situation of human trafficking: An exploratory study*. Utrecht, Netherlands: University College Utrecht.

Aronowitz, A. A., Theuermann, G., & Tyurykanova, E. (2010). *Analysing the business model of trafficking in human beings to better prevent the crime*. Vienna, Austria: OSCE.

Banks, D., & Kyckelhahn, T. (2011). *Characteristics of suspected human trafficking incidents, 2008–2010*. Washington, DC: U.S. Department of Justice.

Bass, A. (2015). *Getting screwed: Sex workers and the law*. Lebanon, NY: ForeEdge.

Brantingham, P. J., & Brantingham, P. L. (Eds.). (1991). *Environmental criminology*. Prospect Heights, IL: Waveland Press.

Brantingham, P. L., & Brantingham, P. J. (1981). Notes on the geometry of crime. In P. J. Brantingham & P. L. Brantingham (Eds.), *Environmental criminology* (pp. 27–54). Beverly Hills, CA: Sage.

Burke, M. C., & Bruijn, B. (2018). Introduction to human trafficking: Definitions and prevalence. In M. C. Burke (Ed.), *Human trafficking: Interdisciplinary perspectives* (2nd ed., pp. 3–24). New York, NY: Routledge.

Busch-Armendariz, N. B., Nsonwu, M. B., Heffron, L. C., Hernandez, M., & Garza, J. (2009). *A research study on human trafficking victims: Survivors speak out about long-term needs*. Austin: University of Texas at Austin.

Chohaney, M. L. (2016). Minor and adult domestic sex trafficking risk factors in Ohio. *Journal of the Society for Social Work and Research, 7*, 117–141.

Clarke, R. V. (Ed.). (1997). *Situational crime prevention: Successful case studies* (2nd ed.). Monsey, NY: Criminal Justice Press.

Cockbain, E., & Wortley, R. (2015). Everyday atrocities: Does internal (domestic) sex trafficking of British children satisfy the expectations of opportunity theories of crime? *Crime Science, 4*, 1–12.

Cohen, L. E., & Felson, M. (1979). Social change and crime rate trends: A routine activity approach. *American Sociological Review, 44*, 588–608.

Cohen, L. E., Kluegel, J. R., & Land, K. C. (1981). Social inequality and predatory criminal victimization: An exposition and test of a formal theory. *American Sociological Review, 46*, 505–524.

Cornish, D. B., & Clarke, R. V. (2003). Opportunities, precipitators and criminal decisions: A reply to Wortley's critique of situational crime prevention. In M. J. Smith & D. B. Cornish (Eds.), *Theory for practice in situational crime prevention* (pp. 41–96). Monsey, NY: Criminal Justice Press.

Curtis, R., Terry, K., Dank, M., Dombrowski, K., & Khan, B. (2008). *The commercial sexual exploitation of children in New York City, volume one: The CSEC population in New York City: Size, characteristics, and needs*. New York, NY: Center for Court Innovation, John Jay College of Criminal Justice.

Dank, M., Khan, B., Downey, P. M., Kotonias, C., Mayer, D., Owens, C., … Yu, L. (2014). *Estimating the size and structure of the underground commercial sex economy in eight major US cities*. Washington, DC: Urban Institute.

Dank, M., Yahner, J., Madden, K., Bañuelos, I., Yu, L., Ritchie, A., … Conner, B. (2015). *Surviving the streets of New York: Experiences of LGBTQ youth, YMSM, and YWSW engaged in survival sex*. Washington, DC: Urban Institute.

Dank, M., Yahner, J., Yu, L., Vasquez-Noriega, C., Gelatt, J., & Pergamit, M. (2017). *Pretesting a human trafficking screening tool in the child welfare and runaway and homeless youth systems*. Washington, DC: Urban Institute.

Denton, E. (2010). International news coverage of human trafficking arrests and prosecutions: A content analysis. *Women and Criminal Justice*, *20*, 10–26.

de Vries, I., Kafafian, M., Goggin, K., Bouchard, E., Goldfarb, S., & Farrell, A. (2019). Enhancing the identification of commercial sexual exploitation among a population of high-risk youths using predictive regularization models. *Child Maltreatment*. Advance online publication. doi: 10.1177/1077559519889178

Diaz, A., Lumpkin, C. L., & Lizano, E. (2018). *Practice implications for commercially sex trafficking youth: Examining data and outcomes*. Los Angeles, CA: Coalition to Abolish Slavery & Trafficking.

Dovydaitis, T. (2010). Human trafficking: The role of the health care provider. *Journal of Midwifery & Women's Health*, *55*, 462–467.

Eck, J. E. (1994). *Drug markets and drug places: A case-control study of the spatial structure of illicit drug dealing* (Doctoral dissertation). Retrieved from ProQuest Dissertations Publishing (9514517).

Eck, J. E., & Madensen, T. D. (2018). Place management. In G. J. N. Bruinsma & S. D. Johnson, *The Oxford handbook of environmental criminology* (pp. 629–663). New York, NY: Oxford University Press.

Farrell, A., Dank, M., Kafafian, M., Lockwood, S., Pfeffer, R., Hudges, A., & Vincent, K. (2019). *Capturing human trafficking victimization through crime reporting*. Washington, DC: U.S. Department of Justice.

Farrell, A., & de Vries, I. (2020). Measuring the nature and prevalence of human trafficking. In J. Winterdyk & J. Jones (Eds.), *The Palgrave international handbook of human trafficking* (pp. 147–162). New York, NY: Palgrave Macmillan, Cham.

Farrell, A., McDevitt, J., & Fahy, S. (2010). Where are all the victims? Understanding the determinants of official identification of human trafficking incidents. *Criminology & Public Policy*, *9*, 201–233.

Farrell, A., McDevitt, J., Pfeffer, R., Fahy, S., Owens, C., Dank, M., & Adams, W. (2012). *Identifying challenges to improve the investigation and prosecution of state and local human trafficking cases*. Boston, MA: Institute on Race and Justice, Northeastern University.

Farrell, A., & Pfeffer, R. (2014). Policing human trafficking: Cultural blinders and organizational barriers. *Annals of the American Academy of Political and Social Science*, *653*, 46–64.

Farrell, A., & Reichert, J. (2017). Using U.S. law-enforcement data: Promise and limits in measuring human trafficking. *Journal of Human Trafficking*, *3*, 39–60.

Fernandez, K. M. (2013). Victims or criminals? The intricacies of dealing with juvenile victims of sex trafficking and why the distinction matters. *Arizona State Law Journal*, *45*, 859–890.

Finkelhor, D., & Asdigian, N. L. (1996). Risk factors for youth victimization: Beyond a lifestyles/routine activities theory approach. *Violence and Victims*, *11*, 3–19.

Finkelhor, D., Vaquerano, J., & Stranski, M. (2017). *Sex trafficking of minors: How many juveniles are being prostituted in the US?* Durham, NH: Crimes against Children Research Center.

Gerassi, L. (2015). A heated debate: Theoretical perspectives of sexual exploitation and sex work. *Journal of Sociology and Social Welfare*, *42*, 79–100.

Gies, S. V., Healy, E., Green, B., & Bobnis, A. (2020). From villain to victim: The impact of safe harbor laws on minors involved in commercial sexual exploitation. *Criminology & Public Policy.* Advance online publication. doi: 10.1111/1745–9133.12497

Goździak, E. M., & Vogel, K. M. (2020). Palermo at 20: A retrospective and prospective. *Journal of Human Trafficking, 6*, 109–118.

Greenbaum, V. J. (2014). Commercial sexual exploitation and sex trafficking of children in the United States. *Current Problems in Pediatric and Adolescent Health Care, 44*, 245–269.

Hammond, G. C., & McGlone, M. (2014). Entry, progression, exit, and service provision for survivors of sex trafficking: Implications for effective interventions. *Global Social Welfare, 1*, 157–168.

Hindelang, M. J., Gottfredson, M. R., & Garofalo, J. (1978). *Victims of personal crime: An empirical foundation for a theory of personal victimization.* Cambridge, MA: Ballinger.

Jimenez, M., Jackson, A. M., & Deye, K. (2015). Aspects of abuse: Commercial sexual exploitation of children. *Current Problems in Pediatric and Adolescent Health Care, 45*, 80–85.

Jordan, J., Patel, B., & Rapp, L. (2013). Domestic minor sex trafficking: A social work perspective on misidentification, victims, buyers, traffickers, treatment and reform of current practice. *Journal of Human Behavior in the Social Environment, 23*, 356–369.

Kara, S. (2009). *Sex trafficking: Inside the business of modern slavery.* New York, NY: Columbia University Press.

Kennedy, M. A., Klein, C., Bristowe, J. T. K., Cooper, B. S., & Yuille, J. C. (2007). Routes of recruitment. *Journal of Aggression, Maltreatment & Trauma, 15*, 1–19.

Kenyon, S. D., & Schanz, Y. Y. (2014). Sex trafficking: Examining links to prostitution and the routine activity theory. *International Journal of Criminology and Sociology, 3*, 61–76.

Kulig, T. C. (2018). *Understanding the nature of human trafficking: A content analysis approach* (Doctoral dissertation). Retrieved from ProQuest Dissertations and Theses (UMI No. 11011146).

Kulig, T. C. (2020). *Measuring sex trafficking: A national-level victimization survey of non-college educated women* [Working paper]. School of Criminology and Criminal Justice, University of Nebraska at Omaha.

Kulig, T. C., & Butler, L. C. (2019). From "whores" to "victims": The rise and status of sex trafficking courts. *Victims & Offenders, 14*, 299–321.

Kulig, T. C., Fissel, E. R., Anderson, V. R., & Fisher, B. S. (2020). Victim or prostitute? The classification of commercial sex events involving minors in the national-incident based reporting system. *Violence and Victims, 35*, 331–353.

Lederer, L. J., & Wetzel, C. A. (2014). The health consequences of sex trafficking and their implications for identifying victims in healthcare facilities. *Annals of Health Law, 23*, 61–91.

Lopez, D. A., & Minassians, H. (2017). The sexual trafficking of juveniles: A theoretical model. *Victims & Offenders, 13*, 257–276.

Love, H., Hussemann, J., Yu, L., McCoy, E., & Owens, C. (2018). *Justice in their own words: Perceptions and experiences of (in)justice among human trafficking survivors.* Washington, DC: Urban Institute.

Lutya, T. M., & Lanier, M. (2012). An integrated theoretical framework to describe human trafficking of young women and girls for involuntary prostitution. In J. Maddock (Ed.), *Public health: Social and behavioral health* (pp. 555–570). Rijeka, Croatia: InTechOpen.

Macias-Konstantopoulos, W. L., Munroe, D., Purcell, G., Tester, K., & Burke, T. F. (2015). The commercial sexual exploitation and sex trafficking of minors in the Boston metropolitan area: Experiences and challenges faced by frontline providers and other stakeholders. *Journal of Applied Research on Children: Informing Policy for Children at Risk*, *6* 1–21.

Madensen, T. D., & Eck, J. E. (2013). Crime places and place management. In F. T. Cullen & P. Wilcox (Eds.), *The Oxford handbook of criminological theory* (pp. 554–578). New York, NY: Oxford University Press.

Malarek, V. (2003). *The Natashas: Inside the new global sex trade*. New York, NY: Arcade Publishing.

Marcus, A., Horning, A., Curtis, R., Sanson, J., & Thompson, E. (2014). Conflict and agency among sex workers and pimps: A closer look at domestic minor sex trafficking. *Annals of the American Academy of Political and Social Science*, *653*, 225–246.

Moore, J. L., Houck, C., Hirway, P., Barron, C. E., & Goldberg, A. P. (2020). Trafficking experiences and psychosocial features of domestic minor sex trafficking victims. *Journal of Interpersonal Violence*, *35*, 3148–3163.

Morel, P. (Director). (2008). *Taken* [Film]. 20th Century Fox.

Newman, G. R. (2006). *Problem-oriented guides for police, guide no. 38: The exploitation of trafficked women*. Washington, DC: Office of Community Oriented Policing Services, U.S. Department of Justice.

Newton, P. J., Mulcahy, T. M., & Martin, S. E. (2008). *Finding victims of human trafficking*. Bethesda, MD: National Opinion Research Center.

Nichols A. J. (2016). *Sex trafficking in the United States: Theory, research, policy, and practice*. New York, NY: Columbia University Press.

Ottisova, L., Hemmings, S., Howard, L. M., Zimmerman, C., & Oram, S. (2016). Prevalence and risk of violence and the mental, physical and sexual health problems associated with human trafficking: An updated systematic review. *Epidemiology and Psychiatric Sciences*, *25*, 317–341.

Oudekerk, B. A., & Truman, J. L. (2017). *Repeat violent victimization, 2005–14*. Washington, DC: Bureau of Justice Statistics.

Pasko, L., & Chesney-Lind, M. (2016). Running the gauntlet: Understanding commercial sexual exploitation and the pathways perspective to female offending. *Journal of Developmental and Life-Course Criminology*, *2*, 275–295.

Perkins, E. B., & Ruiz, C. (2017). Domestic minor sex trafficking in a rural state: Interviews with adjudicated female juveniles. *Child and Adolescent Social Work Journal*, *34*, 171–180.

Polaris Project. (2014). *2014 state ratings on human trafficking laws*. Washington, DC: Polaris Project. Retrieved from https://polarisproject.org/wp-content/uploads/2019/09/2014-State-Ratings.pdf

Powell, C., Dickins, K., & Stoklosa, H. (2017). Training US health care professionals on human trafficking: Where do we go from here? *Medical Education Online*, *22*, 1–12.

Pratt, T. C., & Turanovic, J. J. (2016). Lifestyle and routine activity theories revisited: The importance of "risk" to the study of victimization. *Victims & Offenders*, *11*, 335–354.

Preble, K. M. (2019). Under their "control": Perceptions of traffickers' power and coercion among international female trafficking survivors during exploitation. *Victims & Offenders*, *14*, 199–221.

Preble, K. M. (2020). Influence of survivors' entrapment factors and traffickers' characteristics on perceptions of interpersonal social power while being recruited to be trafficked. *Violence Against Women*. Advance online publication. doi: 10.1177/1077801220920376

Rajaram, S. S., & Tidball, S. (2018). Survivors' voices—complex needs of sex trafficking survivors in the Midwest. *Behavioral Medicine*, *44*, 189–198.

Raphael, J., Reichert, J. A., & Powers, M. (2010). Pimp control and violence: Domestic sex trafficking of Chicago women and girls. *Women & Criminal Justice*, *20*, 89–104.

Raymond, J. G., Hughes, D. M., & Gomez, C. J. (2001). *Sex trafficking of women in the United States*. New York, NY: Coalition Against Trafficking in Women.

Reid, J. A. (2010). Doors wide shut: Barriers to the successful delivery of victim services for domestically trafficked minors in a Southern U.S. metropolitan area. *Women & Criminal Justice*, *20*, 147–166.

Reid, J. A. (2011). An exploratory model of girl's vulnerability to commercial sexual exploitation in prostitution. *Child Maltreatment*, *16*, 146–157.

Reid, J. A. (2012). Exploratory review of route-specific, gendered, and age-graded dynamics of exploitation: Applying life course theory to victimization in sex trafficking in North America. *Aggression and Violent Behavior*, *17*, 257–271.

Reid, J. A. (2014). Risk and resiliency factors influencing onset and adolescence-limited commercial sexual exploitation of disadvantaged girls. *Criminal Behavior and Mental Health*, *24*, 332–344.

Reid, J. A. (2016). Entrapment and enmeshment schemes used by sex traffickers. *Sexual Abuse: A Journal of Research and Treatment*, *28*, 491–511.

Reid, J. A. (2018). Sex trafficking of girls with intellectual disabilities: An exploratory mixed methods study. *Sexual Abuse*, *30*, 107–131.

Reid, J. A., Baglivio, M. T., Piquero, A. R., Greenwald, M. A., & Epps, N. (2017). Human trafficking of minors and childhood adversity in Florida. *American Journal of Public Health*, *107*, 306–311.

Reid, J. A., & Fox, B. (2019). *Profiles of child sex traffickers: A forensic behavior analysis* [PowerPoint Presentation]. University of South Florida—St. Petersburg.

Reid, J. A., Huard, J., & Haskell, R. A. (2015). Family-facilitated juvenile sex trafficking. *Journal of Crime and Justice*, *38*, 361–376.

Reid, J. A., & Jones, S. (2011). Exploited vulnerability: Legal and psychological perspectives on child sex trafficking victims. *Victims & Offenders*, *6*, 207–231.

Reid, J. A., & Piquero, A. R. (2014). On the relationships between commercial sexual exploitation/prostitution, substance dependency, and delinquency in youthful offenders. *Child Maltreatment*, *19*, 247–260.

Reid, J. A., Richards, T. N., & Kulig, T. C. (2021). Human trafficking and intimate partner violence. In R. Geffner, J. W. White, L. K. Hamberger, A. Rosenbaum, V. Vaughan-Eden, & V. I. Vieth. (Eds.), *Handbook of interpersonal violence across the lifespan: A project of the national partnership to end interpersonal violence across the lifespan (NPEIV)*. New York, NY: Springer Nature.

Roe-Sepowitz, D. (2019). A six-year analysis of sex traffickers of minors: Exploring characteristics and sex trafficking patterns. *Journal of Human Behavior in the Social Environment*, *29*, 608–629.

Roberson, L. N. (2017). She leads a lonely life: When sex trafficking and drug addiction collied. *Wake Forest Law Review*, *52*, 359–377.
Rothman, E. F., Bazzi, A. R., & Bair-Merritt, M. (2015) "I'll do whatever as long as you keep telling me that I'm important": A case study illustrating the link between adolescent dating violence and sex trafficking victimization. *Journal of Applied Research on Children: Informing Policy for Children at Risk*, *6*, 1–21.
Rothman, E. F., Preis, S. R., Bright, K., Paruk, J., Bair-Merritt, M., & Farrell, A. (2020). A longitudinal evaluation of a survivor-mentor program for child survivors of sex trafficking in the United States. *Child Abuse & Neglect.* Advance online publication. doi: 10.1016/j.chiabu.2019.104083
Salt, J., & Stein, J. (1997). Migration as a business: The case of trafficking. *International Migration*, *35*, 467–494.
Sanchez, R., & Stark, S. W. (2014). The hard truth about human trafficking. *Nursing Management*, *45*(1), 18–23.
Sapiro, B., Johnson, L., Postmus, J. L., & Simmel, C. (2016). Supporting youth involved in domestic minor sex trafficking: Divergent perspectives on youth agency. *Child Abuse & Neglect*, *58*, 99–110.
Savage, C., & Williams, T. (2018, April 7). U.S. seizes Backpage.com, a site accused of enabling prostitution. *The New York Times*. Retrieved from www.nytimes.com/2018/04/07/us/politics/backpage-prostitution-classified.html
Savona, E., Giommoni, L., & Mancuso, M. (2014). Human trafficking for sexual exploitation in Italy. In B. Leclerc & R. Wortley (Eds.), *Cognition and crime: Offender decision making and script analysis* (pp. 140–163). New York, NY: Routledge.
Serie, C. M. B., Krumeich, A., van Dijke, A., de Ruiter, E., Terpstra, L., & de Ruiter, C. (2018). Sex traffickers' views: A qualitative study into their perceptions of the victim-offender relationship. *Journal of Human Trafficking*, *4*, 169–184.
Shandro, J., Chisolm-Straker, M., Duber, H. C., Findlay, S. L., Munoz, J., Schmitz, G., … Wingkun, N. (2016). Human trafficking: A guide to identification and approach for the emergency physician. *Annals of Emergency Medicine*, *68*, 501–508.
Shelley, L. (2003). Trafficking in women: The business model approach. *Brown Journal of World Affairs*, *10*, 119–131.
Smith, M. J., & Clarke, R. V. (2012). Situational crime prevention: Classifying techniques using "good enough" theory. In B. C. Welsh & D. P. Farrington (Eds.), *The Oxford handbook of crime prevention* (pp. 291–315). New York, NY: Oxford University Press.
Sprang, G., & Cole, J. (2018). Familiar sex trafficking of minors: Trafficking conditions, clinical presentation, and system involvement. *Journal of Family Violence*, *33*, 185–195.
Sukach, T., Gonzalez, N., & Pickens, J. C. (2018). Experiences of female sex trafficking survivors: A phenomenological analysis. *The Qualitative Report*, *23*, 1422–1440.
Swaner, R., Labriola, M., Rempel, M., Walker, A., & Spadafore, J. (2016). *Youth involvement in the sex trade: A national study*. New York, NY: Center for Court Innovation.
Troshynski, E. I., & Blank, J. K. (2017). Interviews with human traffickers: Perceptions of sex and violence (online only chapter). In E. C. Heil & A. J. Nichols (Eds.), *Broadening the scope of human trafficking research: A reader* (2nd ed.). Durham, NC: Carolina Academic Press.

Tyldum, G., & Brunovskis, A. (2005). Describing the unobserved: Methodological challenges in empirical studies on human trafficking. *International Migration, 43*, 17–34.

U.S. Department of Health and Human Services. (2017, November 21). *Fact sheet: Human trafficking.* Washington, DC: Office on Trafficking in Persons. Retrieved from www.acf.hhs.gov/sites/default/files/otip/fact_sheet_human_trafficking_fy18.pdf

U.S. Department of Justice. (2017, January 6). Key legislation. Retrieved from www.justice.gov/humantrafficking/key-legislation

Varma, S., Gillespie, S., McCracken, C., & Greenbaum, V. J. (2015). Characteristics of child commercial sexual exploitation and sex trafficking victims presenting for medical care in the United States. *Child Abuse & Neglect, 44*, 98–105.

Victims of Trafficking and Violence Protection Act of 2000, Pub. L. 106–386, 114 Stat. 1464, codified as amended at 22 U.S.C. §§ 7101–7110 (2000).

Weisburd, D., Eck, J. E., Braga, A. A., Telep, C. W., Cave, B., Bowers, K., … Yang, S.-M. (2016). *Place matters: Criminology for the twenty-first century.* New York, NY: Cambridge University Press.

Weitzer, R. (2010a). The movement to criminalize sex work in the United States. *Journal of Law and Society, 37*, 61–84.

Weitzer, R. (Ed.). (2010b). *Sex for sale: Prostitution, pornography, and the sex industry* (2nd ed.). New York, NY: Routledge.

Wheaton, E. M., Schauer, E. J., & Galli, T. V. (2010). Economics of human trafficking. *International Migration, 48*, 114–141.

Williams, L. M., & Frederick, M. E. (2009). *Pathways into and out of commercial sexual victimization of children: Understanding and responding to sexually exploited teens.* Lowell, MA: University of Massachusetts Lowell.

Williams, P. (1997). Trafficking in women and children: A market perspective. *Transnational Organized Crime, 3*, 145–170.

Williamson, C., & Prior, M. (2009). Domestic minor sex trafficking: A network of underground players in the Midwest. *Journal of Child & Adolescent Trauma, 2*, 46–61.

Wilson, J. M., & Dalton, E. (2008). Human trafficking in the heartland: Variation in law enforcement awareness and responses. *Journal of Contemporary Criminal Justice, 24*, 296–313.

Zimmerman, C., Hossain, M., Yun, K., Gajdadziev, V., Guzun, N., Tchomarova, M., … Watts, C. (2008). The health of trafficked women: A survey of women entering posttrafficking services in Europe. *American Journal of Public Health, 98*, 55–59.

Zimmerman, C., Yun, K., Shvab, I., Watts, C., Trappolin, L., Treppete, M., … Regan, L. (2003). *The health risks and consequences of trafficking in women and adolescents. Findings from a European study.* London, England: London School of Hygiene & Tropical Medicine.

# Index

*Note*: Page numbers in *italic* indicate figures and in **bold** indicate tables, end of chapter notes are indicated by a letter n between page number and note number.